Globalization, Institutions and Socio-Economic Performance

Ertuğrul Yıldırım / Hamza Çeştepe (eds.)

Globalization, Institutions and Socio-Economic Performance

Macro and Micro Perspectives

PETER LANG

Bibliographic Information published by the Deutsche Nationalbibliothek
The Deutsche Nationalbibliothek lists this publication in the Deutsche Nationalbibliografie; detailed bibliographic data is available online at http://dnb.d-nb.de.

Library of Congress Cataloging-in-Publication Data
A CIP catalog record for this book has been applied for at the Library of Congress.

ISBN 978-3-631-76852-5 (Print)
E-ISBN 978-3-631-76860-0 (E-PDF)
E-ISBN 978-3-631-76861-7 (EPUB)
E-ISBN 978-3-631-76862-4 (MOBI)
DOI 10.3726/b14702

Peter Lang – Berlin · Bern · Bruxelles · New York ·
Oxford · Warszawa · Wien

This publication has been peer reviewed.

www.peterlang.com

Foreword

Many of the issues in the complicated world order are closely related to each other. Cause and effect relations interconnect economic, social, political, technological and cultural events. An excellent solution to the matter in hand most probably needs synthesis approach. Since one-sided approaches to current problems of our life may neglect the critical sides of the reality, this book is edited in a multidisciplinary manner by focusing on the core concepts of globalization, institutions, and socio-economic performance.

Globalization, which is one of the most controversial concepts in the world in the last 20-30 years, has different dimensions such as economic, social and cultural. However, the economic dimension of globalization is more prominent than the others. Globalization can be briefly defined as the integration of the country's economies into the world, and there are also different opinions on the effects of globalization on economies, which are not consensus on starting date, definition, and periods.

On the other hand, one of the most important indicators of the change in the welfare level of a country is economic growth performance. Some studies show different conclusions about the effects of globalization on growth. While some studies argue that globalization positively affects growth, some studies have suggested that globalization has a negative impact on the growth performance of countries.

In economic growth literature, formerly, classical factors such as labor, capital, and technology have been expressed as sources of growth. However, in recent times, factors such as geography, openness, and institutions have been put forward by various economists as sources of growth. In this context, openness is considered as a demonstration of globalization, and it is stated that institutions expressing the whole rules, regulations, and policies in a society will affect economic growth by activating various investments. Also, institutions are becoming economically crucial by affecting transaction costs, uncertainties and risks.

It is a fact that edited books have some disadvantages as well as advantages. We have experienced similar difficulties in this book. However, with the dedication and diligent work of our writers and the synergy created by our collaborative work, we have prepared the book in the shortest period possible. In this context, we would like to thank our authors for their contributions. Our colleagues Ferdi Kesikoğlu, Aykut Şarkgüneşi and Şenay Saraç encouraged us and were beneficial with their recommendation. We would also like to thank the colleagues. We could not neglect to thank Esra Bahşi and Susanne Hoeves from Peter Lang Academic Publishers, who facilitated the preparation of the book for publication. Last, we thank our families for their patience and sympathy during our intensive work program.

We would like to be beneficial to those who are interested in the topics mentioned in the book and those who work on these issues.

Assoc.Prof.Dr. Ertuğrul Yıldırım
Prof.Dr. Hamza Çeştepe
01/04/2018, Zonguldak Bülent Ecevit University-Turkey

Contents

Part II Institutions and Socio-economic Performance

About the Authors

Dr. Ertuğrul Yıldırım graduated from Karaelmas University, Faculty of Economics and Administrative Sciences, Department of Economics. He graduated from Social Sciences Institute of the same university with a master's degree in economics. Yıldırım acquired a PhD degree in economics, Erciyes University, Turkey. He acquired Associate Professor degree in international economics from Inter-University Council of Turkey. His research interests are international political economy, energy economics, globalization, regionalization, international trade, and economic growth. He is working as associate professor at Zonguldak Bulent Ecevit University.

Prof. Dr. Hamza Çeştepe is a full professor of economics. He received a BA and a PhD in economics from Istanbul University. He is currently a professor at Bulent Ecevit University, Faculty of Economics and Administrative Sciences, Department of Economics. He teaches undergraduate and graduate courses in international economics. He is also Head of Department of Economics. His research interests include international trade and finance, world economy, and economic integration.

Neslihan Ursavaş is a research assistant at the Economics Department at Bulent Ecevit University. She graduated from Akdeniz University in 2010. And then she graduated with a master's degree in economics from Bülent Ecevit University in 2015. She has been doing a doctorate at Bulent Ecevit University. Her research interests include energy economics, institutional economics, and globalization.

Prof. Dr. Famil Şamiloğlu: In 1997, he was appointed as Assist. Assoc. Dr. at the Faculty of Economics and Administrative Sciences, Department of Business at Niğde University; and he received his title of Associate Professor in 2005 and his title of Professor in 2010. He has published nearly 50 articles in the field of finance, his scientific papers have been published in nearly 40 national and international congresses, and has published five books. He was awarded by MUFAD magazine, which is a member of the Association of Accounting and Finance Teaching Members, because of being one of the four academicians who published the most articles in last ten years, in 2009. Prof. Famil Şamiloğlu is still working and serving as the Dean of Muğla Sıtkı Koçman University, Faculty of Economics and Administrative Sciences.

Dr. Haşim Bağcı: In 2008, he graduated from Dokuz Eylül University's business program. Then he completed his master's program in 2013. His thesis was a compareative study of the performance of commercial banks and participation banks using the Topsis method. In 2017, he completed his PhD program. His dissertation examined the relationship among financial development, oil prices, and oil consumption. Haşim BAĞCI, who is a doctor in the field of finance, has about 10 articles, 30 proceedings, 2 book chapters, and 46 citations. He has worked on all areas of finance like financial performance, financial literacy, financial development and behavioral finance.

Yunus Emre Kahraman graduated from the Social Sciences Institute, Faculty of Economics and Administrative Sciences, from Anadolu University in 2012. He graduated with a master's degree in business administration, Graduate of Social Sciences Institute, from Muğla Sıtkı Koçman University in 2015. Since 2016, he has been pursuing his PhD in accounting and finance in the Social Sciences Institute at Muğla Sıktı Koçman University. Yunus Emre Kahraman, up to now, has published five articles in the field of finance and attended 20 national and international congresses.

Dr. Yusuf Esmer graduated from Dokuz Eylul University, Faculty of Economics and Administrative Sciences, Department of Business Administration in 2008. In 2011, he graduated from Süleyman Demirel University, Social Sciences Institute, with a master's degree in business administration. In 2009–2011, he worked as a service assistant at T.C. Ziraat Bank Inc. Since 2011, In 2011–2018 he worked as a lecturer at Sinop University Tourism and Hotel Management Program. Since 2018, he has been working as Assistant Professor Doctor in Department of Management Information Management Systems at Bayburt University. He obtained his doctorate in business administration from Mehmet Akif Ersoy University, Institute of Social Sciences, in 2017. He speaks English and Greek at the intermediate level. He continues to work in business administration, management-organization, organizational behavior, banking, and finance. He is married and has one child. E-mail: yesmer@bayburt.edu.tr

Öznur Yavan is a member of the Faculty of Economics and Administrative Sciences at Bülent Ecevit University. She did her master's and PhD degrees in the business field. She worked in a secretarial position at the International Journal of Management, Economics, and Business in between 2006–2014. She has been performing editorship of the aforementioned journal in the field of management and organization. Her area of interests intensely includes management, organizational behavior, organization psychology, and strategic management. She teaches business science, human resource management, and behavioral sciences.

Dr. Asuman Koç Yurtkur is serving as a lecturer in the Department of Economics at Bulent Ecevit University. She graduated from Gazi University in 2002. In 2005, she completed her master's from Bulent Ecevit University. She received her PhD from İstanbul University in 2012. Since 2013, she has taught economics, monetary theory and politics, economic policy, and microeconomics at Bulent Ecevit University. At the same time, she has also published various articles and papers on various economic issues, especially macroeconomics, energy economics, and economics schools.

Esmeray Alacadağlı is the head of the Public Administration Department at Bayburt University's Faculty of Economics and Administrative Sciences since 2016. In 2106, she received the "The Institutional Performance Support Award" from Bayburt University. She has a master's degree ın the field of public administration from the Public Administration Institute for Turkey and the Middle East. She received a PhD in the field of environment and urbanization from Ankara University, Turkey in 2004. Her main research fields are the environment, health, public administration, urbanization, total quality management, migration, industrialization, and reorganization.

Yasemin Mamur Işıkçı is a Assoc. Professor at Giresun University Faculty of Economics and Administrative Sciences, Political Sciences and Public Administration Department. Her research interests are child rights policy, social rights, public policy analysis, public administration restructuring, rural development and woman rights policies.

Erol Işıkçı graduated from System Engineering programme in 1997 and was awarded his PhD degree in Business Administration in 2013. He works in the Ministry of National Defense. His research interests are strategy, management, public, administration, total quality management, large-scale organizational change, foreign trade.

Seda Canpolat Bıcakcı is a research assistant at Ankara University, Faculty of Political Sciences. She graduated from Ankara University, Faculty of Political Sciences, Public Finance Department, in 2005, and received her master's degree in public finance (public economics) from Ankara University, Institute of Social Sciences in 2009. She continues her research as a PhD candidate in the same program. Her research interests are state budget, fiscal sociology, and political economy.

Assoc. Prof. Dr. Alper Aytekin is working as a lecturer in Bartın University, Management Information Systems Department (2008–2018). He received a bachelor's degree in forest industry engineering and business administration. He did his PhD in the field of forest industry. His second doctorate continues work on numerical methods in the field of business administration. He is a computer programmer. He knows programming languages such as Basic, Pascal, Delphi, Visual Basic, C, C ++, C #, Java, and Android mobile programming. In addition, he is also working on Management Information Systems, Knowledge Management, Data Base Management. Currently, he is in charge of the department chair in the Department of Management Information Systems.

Dr. Mehmet Pekkaya acquired bachelor's degree both in physics, Bogaziçi University, Turkey, Educational Faculty (1990–1995), and in business administration, Anadolu University, Turkey, Business Faculty (2005–2009). He received his master's (2000–2002) and Ph.D. degrees (2006–2011) in business administration, Bülent Ecevit University, Turkey, Graduate School of Social Sciences. He acquired Associate Professor degree from Inter-University Council of Turkey in September 2015 on numerical decision methods/statistics-operation research. Academic positions held by him are in BEU, Business Administration Department as an instructor (2000–2011), assistant professor (2011–2015) and associate professor (2015–...). His research interests are multi-criteria decision-making, statistical analysis, time series methods, and portfolio optimization.

Dr. Fatma Sönmez Çakır is working as a lecturer in Bartın University, Management Information Systems Department (2009–2018). Her areas of expertise are multi-criteria decision-making, numerical decision techniques, artificial neural networks, and expert systems. She completed her master's and doctoral studies in the field of Numerical Methods of Business Administration. In January 2018, she graduated from Gebze Technical University's PhD program with the model named "Financial Time Series Estimation with Model Hybridization" and won the doctor title.

Dr. Yusuf Bilgin has been working in the Department of Tourism and Business Administration at the Faculty of Economics and Administrative Sciences at Bartın University since 2016. He graduated from Akçakoca School of Tourism and Hotel Management at Abant İzzet Baysal University in 2009. He completed his master's degree in the Department of Tourism Management in 2011 and a doctoral degree in the Department of Business Administration in 2015 from Düzce University, Institute of Social Sciences. He worked as a research assistant at Akçakoca School of Tourism and Hotel Management between 2009 and 2015. He is a member of the Association of Marketing and Marketing Research. His research interests include service marketing, marketing strategies, and positioning.

Dr. Ayhan Karakas is an assistant professor at Bartın University. He graduated from Gazi University, Department of Tourism Management. He has a doctorate in business administration from Dicle University. He is Deputy Director at Bartın University, Institute of Social Sciences, for the period 2015-2018. In 2015, he was Head of Department of Tourism Management, Faculty of Economics and Administrative Sciences, Bartın University. His research areas are tourism management and organizational behavior.

Dr. Ilkut Elif Kandil Goker is an assistant professor at the Department of Accounting-Finance, Faculty of Economics and Business Administration, Kirikkale University. She wrote her MA and PhD theses on finance. She was awarded a scholarship from The Scientific and Technological Research Council of Turkey. She has been working in Kirikkale University from 2006 to the present. She lectures on the following disciplines: Financial Management, Financial Statement Analysis, International Finance. She is currently working on risk-taking behavior of banks.

Hüsnü Bilir is an assistant professor at Aksaray University. He graduated with an MA in economic theory from Gazi University in 2011. Then he received his PhD in economics from Gazi University in 2017. He has also been working at Aksaray University since 2011. He has taught Applications in Economics II, Globalisation and Economic Crises and Philosophy of Sport and Olympism at Aksaray University. His research interests include the history of economic thought, economic sociology, heterodox economics, economic methodology, and neuroeconomics.

Assoc. Dr. Öznur Bozkurt received a doctoral degree in management and organization at Sakarya University in 2009. She investigated the relationship between internal entrepreneurship and innovation in his doctoral thesis. In 2010, she started as an assistant professor in the Düzce University School of Tourism and Hotel Management. She lectured in entrepreneurship, management, and human resources management. She has been a manager in the same school for three years. She left her manager role in 2014 and started at Düzce University Faculty of Business Administration. In 2017, she got a title of associate professor in the field of management and strategy. She is currently working at Düzce University Faculty of Business Administration. She lectures in management and organization, human resource management and entrepreneurship, and has many national and international publications in the same field. She conducts projects in the field of entrepreneurship (TUBITAK and BAP, by other name scientific research project).

Lecturer Irfan Yurt graduated from The School of Tourism and Hotel Management at Erciyes University in Nevsehir. Yurt completed her master's at Duzce University, Department of Tourism and Hotel Management in 2012. He worked as a clerk in the Credit and Dormitory Institution between 2009 and 2016. In 2016, he started to work at Karabük University Safranbolu Vocational High School as Lecturer. In 2017, he started his PhD education in Karabük University, Institute of Social Sciences Business Administration, and it continues. He is still working as a lecturer at Karabük University Safranbolu Vocational High School. His academic fields are food and beverage management, marketing, organizational behavior, and business management.

Assistant professor Sağbetullah Meriç completed primary, secondary, and high school education in Ahlat. He graduated from the Düzce University Akçakoca Tourism Management and Hotel Management School in 2006. He started his graduate education in Düzce University, Social Sciences Institute, Tourism and Hotel Management Department in 2011. He completed his master's degree in 2013 and started as a lecturer in the Faculty of Tourism and Hotel Management at Van Yüzüncü Yıl University. In 2014 he started his PhD at Atatürk University, Institute of Social Sciences, Tourism and Hotel Management. In 2017 he completed his PhD, after which he started to work as Assistant Professor in the same institution. His academic fields are tourism economics, travel management, business administration, entrepreneurship, innovation, and organizational behavior.

Işık Çiçek is an assistant professor in the field of management science, and an expert in human resource management, organizational behavior, and organization theory. He has specialized in fit methodology in organizations, group level organizational variables, department performance, evaluating the efficiency of training. He received his BS, MA, and PhD degrees from Istanbul Technical University. He has gained academic experience as a research and teaching assistant in the Department of Management Engineering in İstanbul Technical University, a research and teaching assistant and lecturer in the faculty of Economics and Administrative Science in Okan University, and an assistant professor in the Department of Management Engineering. He has worked as an assistant professor in the Department of Management Engineering at Alanya Alaaddin Keykubat University since 2015. He is involved in teaching courses related to his specialized areas. He is also vice-principal of Institute of Science and Technology. He has supervised eight graduate thesis.

Lec. Muhammet Yüksel graduated from Uludag University, Faculty of Economics and Administrative Sciences, Department of Business Administration in 2010. In 2015, he graduated from Ondokuz Mayıs University Social Sciences Institute with a master's degree in Business Administration. In 2011–2015, he worked as an officer at Turkish Ministry of Interior. Since 2015, he has been working as a lecturer at Ondokuz Mayıs University. He is still doing doctorate at Giresun University Institute of Social Sciences, in Business Administration program. He speaks English at the intermediate level. He continues to work in business administration, management-organization, organizational behavior, effective communication and good speaking. He is married and has two children. E-mail: muhammet.yuksel@omu.edu.tr

Dr. Gizem Mukiyen Avcı was born in İzmir in 1986. She graduated from Dokuz Eylul University in 2009. She got master's degree from Bulent Ecevit University on "The Effect of Working Women on Patterns of Household Expenditures in Turkey" in 2011. She got her PHD. degree in the same university in 2018 on "Role of Institutions on Export Led Growth: Dynamic Panel Data Analysis".

Dr. Şenay Saraç is Dr. Lecturer at Faculty of Economics and Administrative Sciences at Zonguldak Bülent Ecevit University. She was affiliated with Bulent Ecevit University as a research assistant for the period between 2001 and 2011 and as a lecturer since 2011. She got her master's degree in economics at Zonguldak Karaelmas University, the former name of Bülent Ecevit University. She got her PhD degree from Zonguldak Karaelmas University on "Economic Determinants of Innovation". She has various studies and publications in the fields of macroeconomy and technology-innovation particularly.

Aykut Yağlıkara is a research associate at the Economics Department at Bulent Ecevit University. He graduated from Middle East Technical University Northern Cyprus Campus in 2010. Since then, he has been enrolled in the integrated PhD program at the Department of Economics at Bulent Ecevit University in 2012 and continues his PhD His research interests include development economics, energy economics, and institutional economics.

Dr. Osman Bayraktar has been a lecturer at Istanbul Ticaret University since 2013. He is Head of the Department of Human Resources. He completed his MA and PhD at Istanbul University. He has been lecturing on Management and Human Resources Management. The up-to-date improvements in the field of management thinking and human resources are the areas he focuses on academically. He is emphasizing interdisciplinary associations in his articles.

Gülsüm Şeyma Koca is a research assistant at the Department of Health Management at Hacettepe University. She graduated with an MSc in Health Management from Hacettepe University in 2016, and since then she has been attending the PhD programme at the same department. Her research interests include health economics, health communication, organizational behavior. She knows English well.

Gülnur İlgün is a research assistant at the Department of Health Management at Hacettepe University. She graduated with an MSc in health management from Hacettepe University in 2014, and since then she has been attending the PhD programme at the same department. Her research interests include biostatistics, health economics, epidemiology, and performance management. She knows English well.

Seda Sönmez is a research assistant at the Department of Health Management at the Kırıkkale University. She graduated with an MSc in Health Management from Hacettepe University in 2014, and since then she has been attending the PhD programme at the same department. Her research interests include cost accounting, health financing, cost of illness, budget impact analysis, and value-based health. She knows English and German well.

Canan Atac is a HR Professional who has been working for more than 29 years in different sectors like automotive, machine production, pharmaceutical warehouse and textile. She is EFQM Licensed Advisor certified by KALDER since 2006. While she performs her recent duty as HR Group Manager in Durmazlar Holding, she also volunteers privileged organisations to make positive contributions on university students' HR knowledge particularly in terms of HR's future with Industry 4.0. She has PhD on PDR and still works on her academic progress.

Introduction

Globalization is a long-standing phenomenon which has been attracting the considerable attention of academicians, businessmen, politicians, bureaucrats, students, and other actors of societies by its causes and consequences in social, economic, cultural, and organizational order. In a theoretical sense, globalization may give an opportunity to counties, firms, and individuals for improving their well-being levels by a substantial increase in trade and financial services, the opportunity of social and cultural contacts, a global solution to political problems. Globalization leads to change traditional institutions and implementation in countries. Therefore, the effects of globalization in countries may be different from each other; the effect of globalization should be separately analyzed. This edited book evaluates the effect of globalization in the case of Turkey. Furthermore, since the effects of globalization on macro and micro level may change, this book contains analyses in sectoral level.

Globalization, however, has affected lots of countries in the world, and it could not give symmetric effect on their welfare. While some countries have difficulty in taking advantages of globalization, some fortunate countries such as Singapore, China, and South Korea benefit from globalization by increasing trade, foreign direct investment, other financial flows, human capital, technology level, and economic growth as well. Why have countries been affected asymmetrically by globalization? The answer to the question may be institutional differences among the countries. If the answer given by institutional economists is right, there should be a strong relationship between institutional quality and economic performance indicators in the globalized world. This edited book explores relationships between innovative institutions and socio-economic performance as well.

The book consists of two parts: (i) Globalization and Its Effects, (ii) Institution and Socio-Economic Performance. Nine articles in the first part concentrate on the definition of globalization, approaches to globalization, effects of globalization and various issues related to globalization such as global business ethics, carbon tax, public administration reforms, state spending, exports, tourism and foreign direct investment.

Neslihan Ursavaş and Ertuğrul Yıldırım prepared the first chapter titled "Globalization and the Impact of Globalization on Institutions: A Conceptual Approach". Ursavaş and Yıldırım, firstly, emphasize the definition of globalization and then handle the approaches to globalization in three categories: (i) hyper-globalization approach, (ii) skeptic approach to globalization, and (iii) transformist approach. Lastly, the authors discuss the effect of globalization on nation-states and institutions. The chapter's conclusion is that the changing force of globalization takes countries by storm and if the countries want to benefit from the opportunities of globalization they should improve pro-market institutions.

Famil Şamiloğlu, Haşim Bağcı, and Yunus Emre Kahraman concentrate on financial globalization in the second chapter. After describing the term of globalization, the authors urge the forms of financial globalization. According to the authors, inward foreign direct investment gives plenty of benefits to the countries. The liberalization of derivatives markets, however, leads to problems. Especially the countries having weak capital markets suffer from movement of hot money. So the authors assert that financial crises in the past are linked to financial globalization. Lastly, Şamiloğlu et al. state that financial globalization causes unequal and less fair world practice.

In the third chapter, Öznur Yavan focuses on the issue of "Global Ethics" which is a relatively new one. The author exhaustively explains the terms of ethics, global ethics, and global business ethics. Yavan urges that the global economic, political, cultural, and environmental problems require shared ethical values and standards. To create and implement global ethics norms, however, is a controversial issue. The author represents a rare application example of global ethics. Yavan concludes that many aspects of global ethics should be improved to resolve people's problems and to protect their interests.

In the fourth chapter, Asuman Koç Yurtkur tries to analyze the effect of carbon tax on environmental pollution, which is one of the global problems. Increasing environmental pollution arising from industrial revolution leads to global warming and climate change all around the world. The author tests whether a global carbon tax application reverses carbon-based environmental degradation or not. Since all countries in the world do not implement carbon tax application, 24 European countries are included in the econometric analyses. The employed model involves carbon tax, carbon dioxide emissions, and gross domestic product per capita variables. Dumitrescu and Hurlin approach to Granger causality analysis is followed. The author finds that there is a one-way causal nexus from carbon tax to carbon dioxide emissions. So, she concludes that if carbon tax application is globally implemented, the world may cope with great dangers such as global warming and climate change.

Esmeray Alacadağlı, Yasemin Mamur Işıkçı, and Erol Işıkçı investigate the effect of globalization on public administration. The authors emphasize that strategic management application, which is firstly implemented by the private sector is used in public sector in the more globalized competitive world. Applying strategic public management, which allows more transparent, democratic, and less future uncertainty, the public administration aims to cope with environmental changes, competition, financial crises, and other changing situations. After Alacadğlı et al. review some strategic planning applications in Turkey, they introduce their analyses, which is based on an interview in the Ministry of Health and Bayburt University. According to interview findings, there are some problems in the public strategic management culture arising from bureaucracy in public administration, traditions of resistance to change, omnipresent working groups and rule-lines. Since the problems of public strategic management applications lead to low institutional performance, the authors recommend further reform effort in Turkish public administration.

Seda Canpolat Bıçakçı studies on the effect of globalization on state spending in Turkey. Following O'Connor classification, the author, firstly, reviews the government expenditure budget including the 2000s. She finds that the most significant effect of globalization is in the finance sector in the economy and the interest payments in the budget. Furthermore, the rising budget expenditures replaced the declining interest payments share in the central budget, which is a consequence of fiscal discipline policy imposed by the institutions of globalization, and this revealed that the state's transferring mechanism of sources to the private sector has changed.

Alper Aytekin, Mehmet Pekkaya, and Fatma Sönmez Çakır focus on exports, which is one of the main pillars of the globalization process. Specifically, they analyze the determining factors of export performance of Turkey furniture industry. After presenting situation analyses of furniture industry both in Turkey and the world, authors review the related literature. In the empirical section, a survey analysis filled out by 182 furniture firms is introduced. According to survey results, furniture firms wanting more export should pay more attention to "complaints from the producers", "fast adaptation to demand", "not worrying about the new competition", "determination of sales price by competitors", "new market research", "developing different strategies for different products", "R&D Activities", "pioneer in new product", "eco-friendly product development", "quality personnel management", "export desire and support", and "having export motivation".

Yusuf Bilgin and Ayhan Karakaş employ on tourism sector which has increasing importance with the globalization process. The authors survey to examine the impact of market orientation on customer performance and financial performance in five-star hotels in Turkey. Three hundred and fifty five staff with the participation of at least 13 and at most 19 staff from hotel businesses were filled out the questionnaire. As a result of the analyses, Bilgin and Karakaş conclude that in the hotels, only the customer orientation of the market orientation components significantly affected the customer performance. In this direction, authors propose that business managers should focus on long-term outcomes rather than short-term outcomes when assessing the financial outputs of actions targeting market orientation.

İlkut Elif Kandil Göker touches on the outward foreign direct investment of Turkish banking sector. Using data envelopment analyses, she aims to investigate the effectiveness of foreign subsidiaries of Turkish commercial banks. According to reached results in the study, although none of the subsidiaries banks' has the efficiency score of 1, Halkbank Belgrade, JSC İşbank Georgia, JSC İşbank, Ziraat ASC Azerbaijan, Ziraat Moscow, and Ziraat Uzbekistan are relatively more efficient than the other banks from 2012 to 2016.

The second part of the book consists of nine articles. Hüsnü Bilir reviews Veblen's pioneering approach to institutional economics in the first chapter of the second part. He aims to underline the role of habit and instinct in the process of formation of institutions and to demonstrate the evolutionary perspective in Veblen's integrated analysis with anthropological, sociological, and economic aspects. As a result, the author underlines that while institutional and cultural structure determines man's action and behaviors, individual's decisions and actions may change the institutional setting.

Öznur Bozkurt, İrfan Yurt, and Sağbetullah Meriç analyze the effect of organizational culture on the performance of civil servants in public institutions in Turkey. The authors specifically test the cultural values that exist in public institutions and how those values reflect on employees' performance. To measure the organizational culture, they make Denison's Organizational Culture Survey, a questionnaire of 36 questions. One hundred and forty staff working at Düzce Governorship filled out the survey. As a result of the correlation analysis, the authors reach that the organizational culture and employee performance are strongly related to each other.

Işık Çiçek investigates the level and content of organizational socialization process, which is a synchronization course of individual's value, norm, and belief with that of the organization, depending on the degree of tenure starting from organization entry term. She conducts a survey to test the hypothesis that "the content of organizational socialization experienced by employees will be different regarding organizational tenure for employees". Four hundred and seventeen participants from 15 companies are included in the questionnaire. The author finds that the hypothesis is supported, except for the language dimension of organizational socialization.

Yusuf Esmer and Muhammet Yüksel study on the Akhism, which is an ancient organization founded in the 13th century in Anatolia. The Organization of

Akhism has paved the way for entrepreneurs who are sensitive to moral values such as integrity, honesty, altruism, fraternity, sharing, kindness, cooperation, generosity, and solidarity, as well as economic entrepreneurship. The authors aim to examine the connection between entrepreneurship and the Organization of Akhism. As a result, they find that there is a very close relationship between the Organization of Akhism and entrepreneurship, which adopts human-focused, liberal and halal gains. Furthermore, Esmer and Yüksel assert that the Organization of Akhism attaches more importance to social entrepreneurship than economic entrepreneurship, and goes even further and leads the development of the concept of "moral entrepreneurship" by raising "moral entrepreneurs".

Hamza Çeştepe and Gizem Mukiyen Avcı examine the relationships among globalization, institutional quality, and foreign direct investment using panel data techniques in the example of 48 developing countries. They, firstly, review foreign direct investment theories such as the Neoclassical Trade Theory, the Internationalization Theory, and the OLI Theory. The findings of the empirical analysis show that the improvement on the country's globalization and institutional quality levels have an increasing effect on foreign direct investment. So they conclude that it is crucial to enhance the institutional quality levels to ensure the necessary capital entry, particularly in the developing countries.

Şenay Saraç and Aykut Yağlıkara analyze the relationships between economic freedom which is an essential pillar of institutional structure and innovation that is one of the substantial sources of economic growth. By employing on panel data techniques, they reach that as the institutional structure in countries gets stronger, economic freedoms will get better, and as the R&D expenditures increase, the number of patents will increase. So Saraç and Yağlıkara conclude that increased economic liberalization increases economic freedom while reinforcing the innovation processes of countries.

Şenay Saraç concentrates on Technopark which is a kind of institution aiming to support technological progress in Turkey. She urges the concepts of Technopark and its effects on entrepreneurs, universities, and regions. The author reviews the history of technoparks both in the world and Turkey. Lastly, Saraç analyses the activities of firms in technoparks. As a result, she highlights notable findings concerning the development and current status of the technoparks in Turkey.

Osman Bayraktar and Canan Ataç handle both the theoretical background and the working environment that Industry 4.0 will emerge in industrial enterprises and the possible effects of this environment on the human resources processes. They aim to clarify the state of opinion, expectation, and preparedness about how the Industrial transformation will affect the processes of human resources. Using interview techniques, they find that (i) the work structure will become technologically more complicated, (ii) the demand for high-qualified staff will increase, (iii) it will be difficult to find and retain these qualities, (iv) some of the low-quality staff will lose their jobs.

Gülsüm Şeyma Koca, Gülnur İlgün, and Seda Sönmez study on the sustainable development issue. The concept of sustainable development can be examined by various indicators such as the increase in real incomes per capita of countries, improvement in health and nutritional status, educational achievements, access to resources, and increase in fundamental freedoms. The authors concentrate on the relationship between sustainable development and health in the sample of 84 countries. Using canonical correlation method, they find that a meaningful and strong relationship exists between sustainable development and health.

Assoc.Prof.Dr. Ertuğrul Yildirim
Prof.Dr. Hamza Çeştepe
Zonguldak Bülent Ecevit University

Part I Globalization and its Effects

Neslihan Ursavaş and Ertuğrul Yıldırım

Globalization and the Impact of Globalization on Institutions: A Conceptual Approach[1]

Abstract: While the concept of globalization represented a very long historical process, it began to become a popular concept in the late twentieth century. Given the work to explain globalization, from the development of the concept to its effect, there is no common result in many areas. It can be said, however, that globalization has not only an economic but also a social, cultural, technological, and political influence. In this paper, firstly the concept of globalization is tried to define, and the development of globalization is explained. After that, the implications of this concept on nation-states and institutions are discussed, with the approaches taken by advocates of globalization (hyper-globalizationists) and anti-globalizationists (skeptics).

Keywords: Globalization, Hyper-Globalization, Skepticism, Transformism, Nation-State, Institutions

Introduction

Although the phenomenon of globalization has frequently been discussed since the 1980s, the emergence of the word has been taken to a much earlier date. Some studies argue that globalization has spread in individual waves, but there is no consensus on the starting and ending dates. According to Mittelman (2000), there are three possibilities when the globalization model emerges. It may be argued that globalization belongs to the origins of civilization and is at least five thousand years old. When people first got in contact with other people through conquest, trade, and migration, the world began to shrink. Urbanization is seen as an integral part of the intensification process of communication and economic relations. Religion is another important aspect of this view. A different perspective that develops the theory of world systems is that globalization emerged in Western Europe during the development of the capitalism in the sixteenth century. Accordingly, the decisive changes between capital and labor, accompanied by high technological innovations, have caused capitalism to encompass the whole world. Thus, it is a new form of economy and social relations whose

1 This chapter is derived from the PhD thesis of Neslihan Ursavaş, Zonguldak Bülent Ecevit University, Social Science Institution.

main feature is the composition of competitive markets oriented to profit maximization, wage labor, and private ownership of the large instruments of production. A third interpretation is that capitalism is self-changing. The 1970s has become an important turning point in Western countries, beginning with a deep recession, and this decline has had significant consequences in many developing countries. By the end of the 1970s, socialist countries had experienced deep economic problems, and the Bretton Woods system collapsed. So the new strategies have become more flexible than the old Fordist industries, and a capital and technology-intensive production has accelerated. This tendency along with technological progress has resulted in the weakening of union power, reducing social expenditure and liberalization.

Regarding the development of globalization, Waters (2001) has taken a different view apart from the historical process. Accordingly, it advocates that the development of globalization must be examined through the transformation of economy, politics, and culture, which are the three regions of social life. It is argued that each of these areas consists of three types of variations, which are material, symbolic, and power, and each of them organizes social relations at a particular time. These three processes in all aspects of life support globalization. In this process, economies tend towards marketization – that is people are freer in the market economy. Policies tend to be liberalized and democratized – this provides deconcentration of power. Moreover, culture tends towards universalization. The primary source of transformation between these periods is the crisis and breaks experienced.

In the literature, there is much debate about what globalization means. Some studies have argued that globalization is synonymous with modernization, internalization, liberalization while some have defined it as the expansion of capitalism all over the world. In fact, globalization is associated with many things – economy, culture, politics, technology, media, social life. Therefore, this relationship network leads to difficulties in defining the concept and analyzing its effects. In this paper, firstly it has been argued about the different definitions of globalization, and then three basic globalization theses have been discussed. Finally, the impact of globalization on nation-states and institutions has been discussed regarding globalization thesis and opposing views.

Definition of Globalization

It is difficult to make a compromised definition of the concept of globalization due to its state as an ongoing fact at the present time with a rather long history. In addition to this, the existence of the sympathizers and the opponents of globalization adds an ideological dimension to the concept. When the studies about the concept are investigated, some of them deal with only the economic aspects, some focus on the political and the cultural changes created by globalization, while some focus on the historical development of the concept. In addition to this, each definition arises in parallel with a specific ideological perspective.

According to Robertson (1992, p.8), globalization as a concept means both compressions of the world and concentration of the consciousness of the whole world. Nowadays, the procedures and the actions that the concept of globalization refers to have been in progress for several centuries with interruptions, but the focus of the argument of globalization occurred in a relatively closer time. As long as this argument is closely linked with the nature of modernity, globalization refers to the recent developments quite explicitly. Nowadays, globalization and the concerns about globalization cannot be considered only as a part of the result of the project of the modern west. In the progressively globalizing world, civilization, social, ethnical, regional, and even individual consciousness increase.

According to Giddens (1990, p.64), globalization can be described as the concentration of the global social relations which connects the local events to events occurring kilometers away in a manner to be shaped by them, and this is a dialectical process. Economic globalization is just one aspect of globalization. According to Giddens (1990, pp.70–71), the main centers of the world's economy are the capitalist states. The domestic economy and the external economy of these states contain several forms of arrangement of economic activities. Nation-state system is the second dimension of globalization. These two dimensions depend on each other in many aspects. If the nation-states are the most important actors within the global political order, the corporations can be the agencies dominating the world's economy.

Friedman (2000, p.27) defines the system of globalization as a system that progressively turns into a system built around integration and networks from a system that is built from division and walls. According to this, the idea behind globalization is the free market economy. The more the market forces are allowed to be superior, the more the economy is receptive to free trade and competition, and the more it will be productive and developed. Globalization means the expansion of the free market capitalism almost all around the world. Therefore, globalization has its own economic set of rules. Removing the prohibitive rules which surround the economy, globalization makes it more competitive and attractive for foreign investments.

According to Stiglitz (2006, p.4), globalization contains lots of things: the international flow of thoughts and information, sharing of the cultures, global civil society, and global environmental movement. In addition to this, the economic globalization dimension which requires the close economic integration of the world countries through the increasing of the flow of the goods, services, funds, and labor is critical. The most prominent hope of globalization is to increase living standards all over the world. Globalization has the potential of providing a great deal of benefit, both to the ones in the developed world and the ones in the ever-developing world. However, proofs show that people fail to live this potential, but the problem here is not about globalization, but its way of management. However, politics shapes globalization, economy encourages globalization by decreasing the costs of transportation and communication. The rules of the globalization game are shaped by the industrial countries to develop their own interests. Along with not leaving any set of rules that might increase the welfare of the ones who live in the poorest countries of the world, no fair set of rules has been created.

Scholte (2014, p.112) makes a definition of globalization which is different from the definitions in the literature and defines it as the growth of the supranational relations between people and defends the fact that internationalism and globalization are different from each other. According to this, while the international relations are relations between territories, global relations are supraterritory relations. In short, globalization, internationalization, liberalization, universalization, and modernization are not the same. Therefore, the phenomenon of globalization should be evaluated in the light of deterritorialisation of the social life. Nevertheless, Held et al. (1999, p.89) define globalization as an activity between continents, territories, and a set of procedures which creates a flow and networks through the use of interaction and authority, evaluated in terms of its scale, intensity, and effects, and embodies the transformation of social relations and operations on the spatial organization. Therefore, the distinction of globalization from spatially more limited procedures such as localization, nationalization, territorialization, and internationalization will cause a deficiency in the comprehension of globalization.

Approaches to Globalization

Nowadays, in the present literature about globalization, there are various approaches to globalization. However, the theoretical approaches that are suggested take shape basically around the modern world system and liberal discipline. Modern world system theoreticians see the capitalistic system as responsible for the modern transformations (Giddens 2014, p.83). A world economy and capitalistic system act in unison. Since the world economies lack the connective feature of a political structure or a homogenous culture, the thing that holds them together is the effectiveness of division of labor, and this effectiveness is the function of an ever-growing fortune provided by the capitalistic system. During the pre-modern period, trade and capitalism could not be carried out to produce wealth and to transform the society because the market could not escape from the political control (Gilpin 2015, p.93). The world economies built until the modern ages either drifted apart or turned into world empires with the help of the military units. It became the modern world system that historically managed to survive for a long time. On the other hand, the capitalist system exists as long as it prioritizes the endless accumulation of capital. Here, the endless accumulation means that it is a continuous and endless process in which people and companies accumulate capital in order to collect more capital. If it is said that a system prioritizes this endless accumulation, it means the ones that act in accordance with other motivations are somehow punished, and structural mechanisms are disappearing on the social stage; suitable motivations are rewarded, and if successful, they flourish (Wallerstein 2015, pp.57–58).

The globalist perspective, which is connected to liberal philosophy, supports that the market economy, competition, free trade, and the expansion of western democracy are essential receptive tendencies. Capitalism is seen as a moral favor that encourages the economic growth and effectiveness and generally causes global welfare achievements. Globalization sympathizers often see globalization as the continuation of modernization and the logic of improvement and an inevitable part of the human evolution. Basically, the idea of the technological improvements being the driving force lies under this opinion (Murray 2006, p.12).

The globalist approach conceptualizes globalization as an important determinant and restriction under the act of the government which is independent from the definition. The mobility of the capital, companies, and technology causes governments to embrace – if they want to benefit from these global assets – liberal or more market-oriented strategies. In fact, the emergence of globalization decreased the possibility of the national industrial development or more generally playing an activist role in the economy. There are basically three reasons for this. Firstly, the globalists, the multinational manufacturing, and companies waiting for liberal strategies due to the reliability they give in order to carry the production of the countries that look for higher reliability rates to another country (Cortell 2006, p.6). Therefore, the governments should embrace the free market when they need to compete for the investments provided by the multinational companies. Therefore, the global economy owns more structures than the international economy, it takes shape at a supra-national level, and it consists of companies and other institutions which are active in an international field. The activities of these companies are prepared based on a global market, global manufacturing, and global services. Moreover, the major part of the economic activities occurs within their own global structures, outside the market. Consequently, the emergence of a global market is waiting for the production of common rules that forbids intervention of the nation-state (Garrett 1998, pp.792–793).

Secondly, it is under consideration that the states are becoming less critical and skilled regions on the construction of economic policy. While on one side, the globalists perceive that the end of the state is meaningful and essential in the international system, on the other side, some globalists support the idea that the state is not dead, but its role has changed. Even though the functions of the state from a structural perspective are central, in terms of the increase of the effects and the results of the political tools, they gradually become permanent. This transformation takes shape as a result of the state's effort to make itself attractive for the global companies through liberating and making itself restrictive. Even though there are conflicts on the dimension of the change caused by globalization, generally it is supported as the reform or the reconstruction of the power, functions, and authority of the national states (Cortell 2006, p. 7).

A third argument focuses on the effectiveness of the interfering strategies on a global economy. It is supported that in case the enterprises make a confederacy with the ones in other countries and thus sharing the benefits with themselves, the interfering strategies are pointless. Such confederacy, make such capitalizing difficult for the interventionist state for its own country. Consequently, it is under consideration that multinational industrialization causes the industrial policy to drift apart from the industrial development strategies (Cerny 1995, pp.6–11; Cortell 2006, p.8).

The theory of globalization is explained primarily by the liberal philosophy and the modern world theory; however, there are three more globalization approaches that take place in the literature quite a lot. These are hyper-globalization, skepticism, and transformism. The approaches to globalization is summarized in Tab. 1.

The Approach of Hyper-Globalization

According to the approach of hyper-globalization, globalization is an unprecedented new period in human history. In this age, political, economic, and cultural relations depend on each other so much so that the existence of nation-state becomes unimportant (Zengingönül 2004, p.16). In fact, it is supported that the

Tab. 1: Three Thesis of Globalization. Source: Adapted from "Geographies of Globalization" by Murray, Warwick E., 2006, Routledge, London-New York.

	Hyper-globalists	**Skeptics**	**Transformists**
What is it?	Global age	Increase of territorialization	Unprecedented interdependence
Basic characteristics	Global civilization based on global capitalism and governance	Regionalism, under the leadership of the core, made the world a lot more interdependent than it was in the late 19th century	Intensive globalization, intensity, and rapidity
Driving processes	Technology, capitalism, and creativity	Nation-state and the market	Modern powers that come together
Differentiation models	Disappearance of welfare differences in time when the market is equalized	Reinforcement of the environmental structure which causes global inequality	Including new networks which are more complicated than the old forms
Conceptualization of globalization	Limitless world and perfect market	Territorialisation, internationalization, and deficient market	Deviation which scales the interaction once again
Nation-State	Eroded	Stronger	Transformed forms of governance
Historical Process	Global civilization based on new supra-national choices and interclass groups	Conflicts of neo-imperialism and civilization through new blocks and the actions of neoliberal agenda	Uncertainty depends on the construction and the movement of the nation states and the civil society.
Core Position	Victory of capitalism and the markets being above the nation states	Powerful governments create the agenda of globalization to maintain their dominant position	Transformation of governance in all scales and new power networks.

traditional nation-states have become unnatural or even impossible units in the global economy. In this argument, the world's economy functions with a single cross-border global market through supra-national manufacturing, trade, and finance networks. Therefore, the forms of governance emerging over the nation states become crucial. The difference of the ideologies in this group is emphasized with its formation of a part of the school of both liberalists and some neo-Marxists. The liberals perceive the erosion of the regulatory power of the state as a positive factor implying the victory of capitalism over socialism. The radicals, on the other hand, claim that global capitalism is victorious, but they perceive it as repressive and reactionary. Both perspectives show that the economic powers are dominant, an integrated global economy actually exits, and that the government is stuck between local, regional, and supra-national governance agencies. The thesis of hyper-globalization claims that the new supra-national class confederacy is improved and this has created a new global choice that requires an ideological commitment to liberalism and consumerism. Some perceive this as the proof of not just liberal consumerism, but also liberal democracy and the first real global civilization that eases the expansion of new global forms of governance. The radical hyper-globalists also accept the existence of the global market civilization. The neoliberal hyper-globalists that repeat the neoclassical trade theory, while they create the losers, claim that the rise of the global free market uplifts everybody in the long term and eventually it will create a wealthy and modern homogenous society. Nevertheless, the radical-globalists support that the new inequality forms might be permanent (Murray 2006, pp.34–38).

According to the hyper-globalists, tendencies living in a global economy show a union within regions and between regions which deepens visibly. For example, global financial union causes an economic crisis which occurs in a region to expand quickly. Apart from the financial union, the activities of multinational companies unify national economies through production networks. Therefore, under these circumstances, national economies cannot continue to operate as elements that create wealth. On the other hand, since the territorialization of the economic activities does not occur against globalization, the improvement of territorialization did not separate the world into different blocks. On the contrary, regionalism became a mechanism which national economies might strategically contact with global markets, and thus, it encouraged globalization by easing it (Held and McGrew 2014, pp.35–36).

Skepticism

Skepticism questions the existence of globalization and provides a contrast for the claims about globalization being deterministic. According to this, the world's economy does not depend on each other more than it did in the past. It supports that during the period of gold standard, the world was more integrated than it is today. If the hyper-global thesis is real, then labor, investment, and trade flow need to be unlimited and free. However, this claim is far from real, and the labor remains still. In addition to this, international economy is an economy worth preserving. Supporting free trade instead of returning to general protectionism means that it will depend on the provisions of the present world economy with all its inequalities and injustices. The present system has been created only for the benefit of the wealthy countries, and it is not possible for it to be a system that can be supported regarding society and environment (Hirst and Thompson 2007, p.9).

According to the skeptics, national governments continue to be the central actors in building and inspecting the global economy. For the skeptics, while territorialization is against globalization, for others, it is considered as a progenitor for globalization. The national capitalist governments, mainly G8, are the leading designers of the new global economy. This group which consists of core countries insists on the free market in poor countries and claims that, within the context of inevitable globalization, it is necessary for survival. However, at the same time, these countries which support free market are the most protective countries. Therefore, the skeptics perceive globalization as an agenda or a project which wishes to increase the open land opportunities for the emergence of capital from developed capitalistic economies. This agenda appeared as a result of the reconstruction of the global economic order which creates the liberalization agenda which is controlled by the USA after World War II. It has been designed substantially for the interests of the dominating powers of the period. Therefore, the skeptics question the rise of a global civilization or a new global civil society. It rather increases the deepening of inequality, blocks of civilization, and new colonial tensions between ethnic groups. The statement of the global culture becoming homogenous is seen as a part of the domination project of the West, which was initiated during the period of colonialism. The primary result of the skeptic thesis is that the state's power suffers from erosion legend is not real (Murray 2006, pp.35–36).

Skepticism is suspicious about the views on establishing an equal and fair world system. Multilateral attempts with the purpose of removing the global inequalities by controlling the power of the global markets will fail because the weak ones do not have the sufficient means to threaten the power and wealth of powerful actors. Besides, a new world order will not be any more peaceful and fair than the unfair system of today. This problem will remain as a problem with no efficient solution in the international field. The problem of global inequality can efficiently be solved only within the borders of nation-states. Although the international cooperation between the states is auxiliary for correcting the adverse effects of globalization, the successful removal of inequalities will be possible only through the means of the national welfare regime and the execution of a determined national welfare programme. In this context, skepticism supports that the only reliable structure for removing the negative results of an unequal international economy is national governance (Held and McGrew 2014, p.45).

Transformism

Transformism states that the nature of globalization is not predetermined and it does not follow a particular evolution path. Instead, it is the result of human activities and particular political choices. The political results of this opinion are reformists; it has a role in opposition, regulation of citizens, and nation-states. So democratizing global institutions, promoting local affirmation
and universal education may lead to alternative and progressive globalization. Therefore, globalization might have positive and negative results depending on how it is built. Thus, the primary duty is to change the nature of globalization through human action, but not to destroy it (Murray 2006, p.13,352).

Transformism supports that globalization is real and the society is deeply reconstructed. This change, contrary to the claim of hyper-globalism which supports that globalization is an entirely new condition, comes from historical transitions. Transformists claim that globalization depends on condition, regarding historical and geographical, human action does it, and therefore it does not have a predetermined result. The role of nation-states has changed even if it is not definitely eroded. Since dual concepts such as international-local, domestic-external, and global-local have collapsed, new policy answers are required (Dicken 2003, pp.8–9). In this context, the rise of events about both domestic and international topics is mentioned. Even though there are explicit settlements about the periods of change in the past, modern globalization is no less different than the past. In the economic field, for example trade, it is seen that financial and productive organizations exceed their national limits and thus the fate of distant groups is connected to each other as qualitatively different from the past. Cultural exchange is much more extensive. National policy is managed not only by national governments but also by supra-national and international institutions (Sassen 2000, pp.373–374). The formation of supra-national social movements which are based on new identities that connect sub-national groups to each other beyond borders strains the government. In this context, today's domination is seen as an obstacle defined less territorially for diplomacy characterized by complex supra-national networks. Economic, cultural, and political governance expands from nation-states to both high and sub-geographic scales at the same time. According to transformism, a disorder of the global capitalistic system has increased. However, as the hyper-globalists claim, the disorder and division on earth are not stable forever. It is in the form of new hierarchies which penetrate each part and region of the world in particular spaces measured by referring to old divisions such as First and Third world, regardless of where they are located in the world system (Murray 2006, pp.38–39).

There are essential debate sources in the discussion between three globalization theses. The hyper-globalists and the skeptics conceptualize globalization as a so-called last state. The view generally supports that there is a global market that fulfills the provisions of perfect competition, excellent integration, and factor market equation. The skeptics test the proofs of globalization by comparing empirical tendencies according to this ideal type. On the other hand, the transformists perceive globalization as a more conditional and open-ended historical process, and this type of changes cannot be reflected in empirical data completely. Moreover, the transformists, unlike hyper-globalists support that the process of globalization is a quite differentiated process where it plays the role of neither cultural nor economical determinant (Held et al. 1999, p.11).

The second field of conflict is causality. What is important here is whether the process has one or more causative or not. While many studies on globalization degrade this fact to expansionist and sometimes imperial tendencies of capitalism, Ohmae (1995, p.28) claims that knowledge and technology are the motivations within this period. Besides, it is supported that in the globalization process many factors within the fields of culture, politics, economy, and technology are efficient accelerators. Moreover, some studies claim that globalization is about modernization. Another point of discussion is about whether globalization is a new thing or not. Some support that globalization comes from the late 1970s until today, some support it is a process experienced since the beginning of the twentieth century, and some support that it has begun with the migrations of the primitive men. Defining the historical process of globalization is complex and challenging as much as defining globalization. Another point of contention is about the effects of globalization. There are basically two opinions on this. First one is supporting that globalization has caused the end of the welfare state by dissolving the power of the nation-state and the application of neoliberal policies across the world. The second one is a deterministic argument, and it supports that the power of the nation-state adapts and transforms as a response to the obligations of globalization (Murray 2006, pp.39–41).

The Effect of Globalization on Nation-States and Institutions

In the literature of globalization, two primary arguments which form the core of the thesis of globalization are discussed. First one is that the pressure of globalization causes developed capitalistic nation-states to apply a common neoliberal programme. Especially, states are forced to lower the taxes on companies and investors, especially the welfare expenses of those taxes and liberate the economies in order to lower the costs. The most crucial element here is that competition is necessary for capital. The changes and improvements in the late twentieth century on transportation, telecommunication, and other technologies improved the knowledge of the companies worldwide on profitable economic opportunities to a large extent and increased the rapidity and activity that can follow these opportunities. Therefore, the mobility of the international capital has increased. With the collapse of the Bretton Woods system and liberalization of trade with GATT, the capital flow has become easier. Moreover, these elements increased the tendency of capital to transfer from one country to another due to more profitable opportunities. Therefore, states should compete more severely (aggressively) to attract and protect the capital investments within their own borders. Moreover, in order to achieve their goals, they need to apply neoliberal reforms. If the states do not apply these reforms, then they will face with rising rates of interest, lower economic growth, higher unemployment, and other economic problems. The precise effect here will be the states slowly designating their place in the international game according to the capital and managing their economies with similar policies and institutions. In this opinion, the states are becoming more vulnerable to the effects of the business world and their capacity to manage their economy through regulatory policies decreases after World War II. The possible results of this argument for the national political institution are strict (Campbell 2004, pp.125–126). Globalization has caused a decrease in state's authorized institutions on regulating the economy and a decline in the domination of the state due to instability. According to this, despite the fact that institutional state capacities are not mandatory, it is placed in the fields which are reconstructed and partially located outside the state (Sassen 1996, p.8).

The second argument of the theory of globalization is that globalization has changed national economies. Companies also develop gradually spreading institutional structures and strategies just like states. Companies have developed more decentralist organizational forms that exceed the national limits. Companies do this in order to respond more efficiently and flexibly to the volatile and unpredictable demands of a market that gradually becomes more global. All of this is important for institutional analysis because of two reasons. The theoreticians of globalization create a world where economic globalization becomes homogeneous between national politics, economic institutions, and countries. Moreover, the attribute of being an essential determinant of the eco-political power of these institutions gradually decreases. Moreover, the reason for this is globalization's prevention of these institutions and emptying them (Campbell 2004, pp.126–127).

Investment, industry, information technology, and individual consumerism factors which Ohmae (1995) defines as "four I rule" claimed to be destroying the central role of the nation-state. Investment is no longer geographically limited. No matter which part of the world an investor lives, if there is an opportunity for investment anywhere, that is where the money goes. The only thing that matters for investment is that the opportunity is qualified. Industry tends to be more global now. In the past, companies required to make agreements with host states to have access to the local market and to provide sources. However, now, the strategies of international companies are not shaped by states, and the companies go where there are attractive opportunities. The subventions financed by the state have become highly unimportant in relation to deciding on investing old fashioned tax reductions in order to invest in a particular place. The principal reason for this global movement of investment and the industry is the developments in the information technology. Using information technology, now an enterprise can operate in various parts of the world without establishing a facility thoroughly. Lastly, individual consumerism tends to be global, and consumers always want to buy the top-quality product for the lowest price. For consumers, where the product comes from is not important. Consequently, the fact that these four elements exceeding the national limits make the central role of the nation-state unimportant (Ohmae 1995, pp.3–4). Once the markets were under the dominion of the states, yet today states are under the dominion of the market in many important matters. The decreasing authority of the states shows itself in the growth of the expansion of authority to other institutions and organizations along with the local and regional agencies and the asymmetry between the major states that have a structural power and the weaker states (Strange 2014, p.156).

In contrast, the skepticism which contradicts the opinion of the nation-state is perishing, questions whether there is an absolute global economy like the theoreticians of globalization present or not; because there is a difference between a global economy and a substantially internationalized economy. For the first one, since the economic results are entirely determined by the world market forces and the decisions of supra-national companies, there is no need for national policies. However, for the second one, the national policies remain valid. In fact, these policies are necessary to protect commercial companies. A world economy where there is a high and increasing level of international trade and investment is not a globalized economy. Therefore, in such economy, nation states and the international regimes supported by them play the fundamental role in providing the governance of economy (Hirst and Thompson 2007, p.220).

Rodrik (2009, pp.201–202), who uses globalization as the meaning of increase of commercial and financial integration, supports that globalization creates both opportunity and difficulty for a combined economy. On the one hand, global expansion of the markets, according to the comparative advantages theory, provides more welfare by means of division of labor and specialization. Since this opportunity makes access to the technology and cheap capital goods in the world markets possible, it is particularly more important for developing countries. However, on the other hand, globalization removes the nation-states's superiority to establish regulatory institutions which also provide redistribution. The most significant problem with globalization here is, while the markets try to globalize, the institutions that are supposed to be supporting them remain pretty much national. The fact that the fire which has been established within national framework remaining limited restricts the economic union and this prevents the productivity. On the other hand, the manufacturers' and investors' wish to globalize weakens the institutional ground of national economies.

Conclusion

Globalization has a long history and is not only an economic sense but a phenomenon that affects people and countries in social, cultural, and politic areas. Especially with change and development of technology, globalization has spread more rapidly. This expansion has made the countries economically and politically more dependent on each other and has led the people to have a similar lifestyle and shared culture. The fact that the concept is useful in so many different areas makes globalization both difficult to identify and analyze its impact and consequences. In particular, the analysis of globalization around two fundamental views reveals opposite approaches. The globalist view that emerged on the axis of liberal philosophy argues that globalization is a whole new era and advocates that the rise of the global free market ultimately creates a homogeneous modern society while globalization creates its losses. On the other hand, there is an approach which argues that globalization does not homogenize the countries, but that the inequalities between the countries further deepen. Skeptics, which is another view, question the phenomenon of globalization, its impact, and consequences. According to the skeptics, globalization is a project for which developed countries are in favor of themselves. At the same time, the skeptical view also questions approaches related to the establishment of a more equal and fair world system. The problem of global inequality can only be efficiently resolved within the boundaries of nation-states. Another approach, the transformist view, argues that globalization is real and society is deeply restructured. One of the main discussions in the literature about globalization is whether it has destroyed nation-states and institutions. The globalist view argues that a global system of the world has eliminated the necessity of the nation-state. In this context, states must determine their international presence on the basis of global capital and manage economies with similar policies and institutions. On the other side, however, skeptics argue that globalization is not a global system as the globalist approach claims, and in such a system, the existence of a nation-state has a central role to protect the interests of itself. In fact, the phenomenon of globalization creates opportunities for countries but also leads to difficulties. On the one hand business circles want to be more integrated with the global system, but on the other hand, institutions that need to support markets are national. So there is a need to reform institutions in a way that will respond to the desire for the globalization of markets.

Bibliography

Campbell, John L.:*Institutional change and globalization*. Princeton University Press: New Jersey. 2004.

Cerny, Philip: "Globalization and the changing logic of collective action". *International Organization* 49(4), 1995, pp.595–625.

Cortell, Andrew P.: *Mediating globalization: Domestic institutions and industrial policies in the United States and Britain*. State University of New York Press: Albany. 2006.

Dicken, Peter: *Global shift: Mapping the changing contours of the world economy*. Sage Publications: London. 2003.

Friedman, Thomas L.: *The lexus and the olive tree*. Farrar, Straus Giraux: New York. 2000.

Garrett, Geoffrey: "Global markets and national politics: Collusion course or virtuous circle". *International Organization* 52(4), 1998, pp.787–824.

Giddens, Anthony: *The consequences of modernity*. Polity Press: Stanford, CA. 1990.

Giddens, Anthony: "Modernliğin küreselleşmesi". In: David Held / Anthony McGrew (eds.): *Küresel dönüşümler büyük küreselleşme tartışması*. (Trans.: M. C. Çelebi). Phoenix Yayınevi: Ankara. 2014, pp.81–87.

Gilpin, Robert: *Uluslararası ilişkilerin ekonomi politiği*. M. Duran / S. Oktay, M. K. Ceyhan / G. Polat (Trans.). Kripto Yayınevi: Ankara. 2015.

Held, David, A. G. McGrew, D. Goldblatt ve J. Perraton: *Global transformations: Politics, economics and culture*. Polity Press: Cambridge. 1999.

Held, David / Anthony McGrew (2014); *"Büyük Küreselleşme Tartışması", Küresel Dönüşümler: Büyük Küreselleşme Tartışması*, (Trans.: A. S. Mercan / E. Sarıot), Phoenix Yayınevi, Ankara, s.7–70.

Hirst, Paul / Grahame Thompson: *Küreselleşme sorgulanıyor*. (Trans.: Ç. Erdem / E. Yücel). Dost Kitabevi: Ankara. 2007.

Mittelman, James H.: *The globalization syndrome: Transformation and resistance*. Princeton University Press: New Jersey. 2000.

Murray, Warwick E.: *Geographies of globalization*. Routledge: London-New York. 2006.

Ohmae, Kenichi: *End of the nation state: The rise of regional economies*. Harper Collins Publishers: London. 1995.

Robertson, Roland: *Globalization; social theory and global culture*. Sage Publication: London. 1992.

Rodrik, Dani: *Tek ekonomi çok reçete*. (Trans.: N. Domaniç). Efil Yayınevi: Ankara. 2009.

Sassen, Saskia: "*Losing control? Sovereignty in an age of globalization*". Columbia University Press: New York. 1996.

Sassen, Saskia: "Territory and territoriality in the global economy". *International Sociology* 15(2), 2000, pp.372–393.

Scholte, Jan Art: "Küreselleşmede küresel olan ne?". In: David Held / Anthony McGrew (eds.): *Küresel dönüşümler: Büyük küreselleşme tartışması*. (Trans.: M. C. Çelebi). Phoenix Yayınevi: Ankara. 2014, pp.107–115.

Stiglitz, Joseph E.: *Making globalization work*. W. W. Norton & Company: New York. 2006.

Strange, Susan: "Devletlerin azalan otoritesi". In: David Held / Anthony McGrew (eds.): *Küresel dönüşümler: Büyük küreselleşme tartışması*. (Trans.: C. Boyraz). Phoenix yayınevi: Ankara. 2014, pp.155–163.

Wallerstein, Immanuel: "The modern world system as a capitalist world economy". In: Frank J. Lechner / John Boli (eds.): *The globalization reader*. Wiley Blackwell Publishing: UK. 2015, pp.56–62.

Waters, Malcolm: *Globalization*. Routledge: London. 2001.

Zengingönül, Oğul: *Küreselleşme: Yoksulluk, gelişmişlik ve işgücü piyasaları ekseninde*. Adres Yayınları: Ankara. 2004.

Famil Şamiloğlu, Haşim Bağcı and Yunus Emre Kahraman

Financial Globalization[1]

Abstract: The term globalization is fundamentally described as the integration of the world economy. Globalization has several types. In this study, however, within the framework of financial globalization, economic effects of financial globalization, causes of financial globalization and effects of financial crisis on financial globalization were theoretically described. Financial globalization is the capital's maintenance of movement in the world banking and finance market as a result of crossing the local border by gaining an international quality and the transfer of capital to safer regions against the negative conditions countries face, such as crisis and war.

Keywords: Globalization, Financial Globalization, International Movement of Capital

Introduction

The term globalization began to be used in the 1980s and has continued to develop until today. However, there are many positive and negative opinions about the effects and consequences of the concept of globalization. There is no clear idea about the definitions of these ideas and discussions about what is the concept of globalization continue (Kuruoğlu 2004, p. 2).

There are different views on the concept of globalization in the literature and about its use. One of these views is that Marshall McLuhan (1962) is the first person to use globalization. In McLuhan's book *Gutenberg Galaxy* written in 1962, it is expressed that the concept of global village has emerged with the change of the world. Also in this book, McLuhan brings the concept of globalization to the forefront, determining that some part of the world would turn into a global village with the use of technology. In the second view, McLuhan's concept of globalization was supported, and the concept was updated along with the upgrades made by Zbigniew Brezinski in the 1980s. Anthony Giddens, who owns the third opinion, has supported the spread of this concept at the beginning of the 1990s. According to Giddens, globalization is a situation that happens in any country of the world and directly affects other countries or social relations are concentrated on the world scale (Elçin 2012, pp. 2–3).

1 The draft of this study was presented at the International Congress on Management Economics and Business in Zonguldak on 7–9 September 2017.

The concept of globalization takes place in many disciplines. It has many different definitions in many branches such as sociology, anthropology, literature, language science, and economics. It is a more correct approach to analyze globalization in economic science in the context of the study. Dunning (1993) defines globalization as companies carrying their productions to the international dimension and the increase in world production changes the structure of international resources. According to Rodrik (1997), globalization is influencing societies to change traditional practices in the integration process of goods, services, and capital markets.

Globalization is the network that affects the world economically, financially, politically, socially, and culturally, and makes this interaction through technological connection and connects the world's distances through people, institutions, and markets.

These are liberty in trade of goods and services between countries, liberty in international capital mobility, freedom in labor transfer, legal regulations to increase competition, and producing and using technology and different types of employment (Elçin 2012, p. 5).

The first element that comes to mind in terms of the international capital mobility that globalization has emerged is the transfer of funds between countries. These fund transfers take place in different ways. These are direct foreign capital investments, portfolio investments, and other investments. Foreign direct investment refers to investing directly in the foreign country, together with the external sources of the investor and as a result of which the investment is partly or wholly owned by the investor. Portfolio investments are investments in capital market instruments such as stocks and bonds, taking on the risks that saving owners may face in order to obtain capital gains, dividends, and interest. Other investments are all financial transactions except these investments. Such investments include short- and long-term capital movements in the money market (Karahan and Ipek 2013, pp. 300–301).

Globalization is multidimensional because it affects many sciences as it is expressed in definitions. Generally speaking, globalization is classified as economic, cultural, and political (Modelski 2008, p. 75–80).

The concept of financial globalization, which forms the main theme of the work, is one of the types of economic globalization. Financial globalization is affecting the whole world. Because international capital markets are interdependent and are frequently directed, technology allows capital flows to flow in very high volumes among economies in a very short time (Went 2001, pp. 80–81). Thus, financial globalization is defined as the free movement of capital in all world markets, the evaluation of earnings opportunities, and the movement of safer markets as opposed to adverse conditions. This movement is realized as an international capital movement in the form of foreign direct investments, portfolio investments, and other investments (Öztürk 2007, p. 251).

Globalization

Many developments such as technology, transportation, etc., have brought the countries of the world closer together. This is the technological development that brings proximity and reduces distances to a minimum. It can be said that the single most important factor affecting globalization is not technology, but the most important factor is developments in the field of technology. The costs of transportation and communication have been reduced by technological advances, and local boundaries have now been lifted through the pervading use of electronic commerce. Ordering books from abroad and internationally made online shopping are examples of these developments. Consumer culture also has examples of globalization. For example, companies such as Coca-Cola, McDonald's, and Burger King have branches in many parts of the world, and people can consume these brands even if they are their own local products (Aktan and Şen 1999, p. 19).

In the financial markets, the flow of hot money used in the oil trade between countries is one of the causes of globalization. Crisis or political events occurring anywhere in the world as a result of globalization can affect many countries. Globalization can create a butterfly effect on all the events in the world. The precautions should be taken by considering that a small negativity would cause great and unpredictable results in the future (Bozkurt 2006).

While globalization is useful for some countries, it is risky for some countries. The increasing international capital mobility with globalization ensures the rapid growth of world trade. In addition, globalization increases competition. Globalization requires redefining the concepts used in the markets such as risk, discipline, stability, control, etc. Since globalization has brought these concepts to an international dimension, banking transactions have become more complex. Globalization also has social, economic, financial, cultural, and political risks. Because every country does not benefit from globalization in the same way. The reasons for this are unstable and weak economic policies, fragile and vulnerable economies, unstable exchange rates, and an increase in international capital movements. In addition, the crisis affects many countries at the same time in the globalizing world. For these reasons, while globalization is an opportunity for well-managed countries, it can be a risk factor for poor governance (Erçel 2000, pp. 3–7).

Technology is at the top of the factors that accelerate the globalization process. Because, as technology develops and technological innovations increase, communication and transportation costs are reduced. Thus, it became easier access to many world markets. For example, while public announcement had lasted for months with the technological infrastructure of a product, now this time has been shortened with technological tools. This creates the potential to sell products on the global market. In this way, both institutions and individuals have reached the opportunity to earn more quickly and similarly, consumers can meet their needs in a short time. Another important factor accelerating the globalization process is political events. Great events such as the collapse of the Berlin Wall and the dissolution of the Soviet Union have accelerated globalization. Because of the collapse of the Berlin Wall, trade has increased in Germany and Germany has made progress. Many countries established as a result of the disintegration of the Soviet Union have brought vitality to the European market, and the single-headed system in Europe has come to an end. All these developments have allowed the countries to open up to the outside world by increasing the privatization movements in the countries (Aktan and Şen 1999, p. 16).

Many innovations have been made in the world to expand globalization. Banks, insurance, and logistics companies have implemented a renewal strategy in their business plans to keep pace with emerging technological systems. Cheap and easy transportation is provided to the market with this new system, the development of production techniques has also increased globalization, and through the new production techniques, more efficient and effective products have been made. One of the innovations that accelerated the process of globalization is the World Trade Organization (WTO). Thanks to this organization, competition and efficiency increased in trade and markets have become more transparent and reliable. Because, the markets have become self-controllable and have auto control mechanisms. States have encouraged companies to open up to the world by placing limits on their national policies (Elçin 2012, pp. 10–11).

Since the 1980s when globalization emerged, foreign capital has begun to attract the attention of countries. Moreover, they have attempted to attract foreign capital to the country instead of controlling foreign capital. Among the countries that are leading this area are China and Singapore. The countries have begun to compete for the foreign capital to turn to the countries. The technology of the foreign direct capital of the country is thought to be beneficial to many areas such as growth, tax revenues, employment, financing, export, etc. For these reasons, it is stated that the most important part of development is direct foreign capital investments. It is expressed that direct foreign capital affects the employment and also positively affects technological infrastructure, product development, production efficiency, and labor potential and increases the country's income situation, tax revenues, and the potential for foreign exchange creation. Countries need to apply some policies in order to attract foreign investments. These are applications such as competition, privatization and taxation policies, incentive measures, effective administrative procedures to reduce bureaucratic procedures, appropriate labor and employment policy, economic and political stability, and membership in the world trade system. It is determined by factor hardware, wage potential, efficiency, and technological structure whether or not countries are strong in terms of competition. Countries with high competitiveness dominate the market. As a result, it turns out that globalization is unfair and unscrupulous. Since globalization makes a positive contribution in every sense for the strongest countries, the weakest countries make it even weaker. Globalization increases the income inequality cliff. The most fundamental reason for this is inadequate policies, politicians, and institutions in undeveloped countries. Developing countries with globalization approach rich countries, but the biggest problem in front of these countries is inflation. In order to eliminate this problem, countries raise the interest rates and facilitate the entry of hot money (Sabir 2002; Hirst and Thompson 1999, p. 95; Temel 2001 Aklan 2002; Uras 2006; Stiglitz 2002, p. 34). All these indicators imply that globalization is very important for world countries in terms of economic direction.

Economic Globalization

It is a fact extending from past to present that economic transactions take place on an international scale. However, it is understood that all of the applications made in the past are superficial, including the concept of globalization. Because, the technology that developed with globalization has led the world to become an information society. The information society has directly influenced the economies of countries in every field including trade by crossing national boundaries and establishing international links between countries. On this account, global economic integration has been established (UNCTAD 1993, p. 113).

Economic globalization has very important consequences for the countries. These are the disappearance of the rules of capital mobility, the dominance of monetary exchanges on the real economy, the advancement of information and communication technologies along with new technological developments, and the redesign of companies (Gallino 2007, p. 28). In the context of these results, there are different definitions in the literature regarding the globalization of the economy. According to Acar (2004), with the reduction of inter-country economic barriers, economic globalization is an economic integration that enables the flow of goods, services, labor, and capital, which may be subject to commercial transactions, in order to become more active and easier. Prakash (2001) defines economic globalization as the integration of the processes used to achieve commercial flow without regard to border demarcation of multinational companies. According to Kleinert (2004), the globalization of the economy is the process of increasing economic integration after the unification of many local economies. Giddens (2000) noted that there are some negative aspects besides the positive aspects of economic globalization. For example, it has been emphasized that economic globalization affects underdeveloped countries in the negative direction, monopolies the economies, and forms a range-dependent structure. Economic globalization cannot be expressed directly as good or bad because globalization is a complex phenomenon in itself. However, no country in the world has survived globalization. Keeping up with globalization is a necessity for the development of national economies. In addition, globalization is a risk factor for some country groups. Developed countries are hampering the transfer of developing countries to their own countries by imposing restrictions on the flow of commodities. Countries have used short-term capital mobility to find a solution to this situation, but this solution has dragged the country's economy into an unstable structure. They have also provided foreign direct investment with customization practices as another solution. This leads the developing countries to lose their qualified workforce and becomes poor in the long run (Stiglitz 2009, p. 288).

The concept of economic globalization is itself divided into three. These concepts are the globalization of trade, globalization of investment and production, and financial globalization (O'loughlin et al. 2004, pp. 156–257).

Globalization of Trade

The first type of economic globalization is the globalization of trade. The concept of commercial globalization is internationalization, development, and increase of trade. The degree of globalization of countries in terms of trade is the ratio of import and export totals (foreign trade) to Gross National Product (GNP). These are the reasons for the increase in the global dimension of trade: reduction of customs restrictions, reduction of logistical costs, increment in outsourcing, the similarity of social consumption and pleasure, global marketing activities, development of the trade system with the establishment of the WTO, innovations in banking system and foreign trade finance, increment in the number of domestic and foreign tourists resulting from the increase in tourism, increment in technological competition with technological innovations, and getting production international dimension by dividing it into production processes (Dorman 2000, p. 46; Özel 2012, p. 23).

The most important development that ensures the globalization of trade is the establishment of the WTO. Until the WTO's founding, the Customs Tariffs and Trade General Agreement (GATT) rules were in force to accelerate globalization. The GATT is not an institution or organization. The GATT is a trade agreement signed in Geneva in 1947 that removes the obstacles and limitations in international trade. This agreement was delegated with the establishment of the WTO in 1995 (Eraltuğ 2012, pp. 87–88).

Globalization of Investment and Production

The globalization of investments and production is pointing to foreign direct investments. Foreign direct investment is either the establishment of a company in other countries by moving the production facilities established in the country where it operates in the international dimension or the purchase of a production facility in those countries. The globalization of production is the spreading of the productions of goods and services by other means such as fixed capital investments and freight production. With the globalization of production, multinational companies have shown great growth. Because globalization has reduced production costs and with it profits of multinational corporations have also increased significantly. This increase has continued, and the position and prospects of multinational companies in the world economy have increased, and even it caused some underdeveloped countries to be left behind economically (Ekin 1997, pp. 34–35; Balkanlı 2002, p. 16; Çaşkurlu 2010, p. 51).

Fiscal Globalization

The concept of fiscal globalization is also called financial globalization, and this concept is one of the important parts of the process that accelerates globalization. The freedom that emerges with financial globalization is one of the important factors that also provides globalization of production. Financial liberalization policies are classified as internal and external financial liberalization. Internal financial liberalization is the practice of reducing and eliminating all restrictions on transactions where the local currency is used. There is freedom in determining real and nominal interest rates in internal financial liberalization, and it also reveals foreign capital support in the banking sector. External financial liberalization gives freedom to both established domestic and foreign investors and non-established foreign investors. External financial liberalization allows all transactions such as domestic and foreign market borrowing and investment, domestic and foreign capital transfers and provides liberalization of financial transactions (Keyder 1996, p. 265; Chussudovsky 1999, pp. 76–77).

Detailed information on financial globalization is included in the next section.

Financial Globalization

The main issue in financial globalization is the free capital movement. Liberalization of capital mobility increased steadily in the 1970s, and financial liberalization has both accelerated globalization and become part of globalization. The reasons why financial globalization began to gain momentum in the 1970s are: avoiding the risk of uncertainty caused by fluctuations in interest rates and exchange rates following the 1972 Bretton Woods system, oil revenues of countries exporting oil being too high, reduction in banking costs of developments in information technology, entering of banking sector in process of structuring, operating of foreign banks in different countries, and its contribution to the growth of banking sector by increasing competition (Karabulut and Solak 2012, p. 1082; Özel 2012, p. 25). As a result of these reasons, together with the accelerating globalization, futures and options contracts have begun to be used, and the transaction volume has increased considerably.

1994–1995 Mexican Crisis

As a result of the erroneous policy implemented by Mexico, the crisis was encountered in 1994–1995. This policy aims to reduce inflation and reduce government debt by giving primary budget surpluses. Throughout this policy, the exchange rate was used as a nominal anchor. Mexico's current account deficit has begun to increase, and the value of local money has increased because consumer price increases have fallen from 159% to 7%. In 1994 the volume of money increased, but the current account deficit reached 8% of GNP. It was understood that Mexico was not able to step through this exchange rate policy that it had implemented during this crisis because the current deficit has risen considerably. For this reason, the Mexican crisis has been resolved by changing the exchange rate policy because it is thought that the Peso is the local currency. In the framework of a new program implemented in 1995, the crisis was overcome, and stability was restored. The main objective of this program is to overcome the crisis by destroying Mexico's local currency, Peso, which is Mexico devaluation. The region most affected by this crisis is South America. Since 1996, the market has turned to normal flow all over the world (State Planning Organization 2000, pp. 37–38).

1997–1998 Global Financial Crisis

This crisis emerged in 1997 from Thailand's local currency and spread to other Southeast Asian countries. However, this crisis affected not only Asia but all world markets. Similar to the Mexican crisis, Thailand's current account deficit has increased considerably, and Asian countries such as Korea, Indonesia, Philippines, and Malaysia have also been directly affected by this crisis, resulting in a significant increase in current account deficits. The main reason for this is the increase in the value of the local currency of these countries. As a solution, the devaluation was made, and capital outflows from the country were realized. However, this crisis has spread to the banking sector due to the fact that Asian markets are not transparent. These countries partially mitigated the damage they had suffered by the International Monetary Fund (IMF). The Asian crisis has sprung up to other countries in the world by the investors. Investors have caused this crisis to become global affected by the capital outflows of these countries and the devaluation policy they implemented. Russia has started to give the current account deficit due to the fall in the price of oil and natural gas, which is the most important export revenue and it declared a moratorium, unable to pay the state debts. After this moratorium, Brazil has also been dragged into crisis and capital outflows from the country. Supported by the IMF and signing a stand-by agreement in 1998, it was able to reduce the effects of the crisis. It also minimized the risk of repetition of the crisis with the new policy applied, but the local currency was significantly depreciated. The most fundamental destiny of this crisis is the IMF, and the IMF has brought the international market back to its former state. The points that this crisis should take from the perspective of the whole world are the need to have a well-supervised, transparent banking system, the consequences of high current account deficits and budget deficits, wrong and incorrectly chosen exchange rate policies, economic instability, and the consequences of investor behavior (State Planning Organization 2000, p. 40).

Systemic Crisis Caused by Derivatives Market

Another consequence of globalization is the spread of a crisis that has taken place in any region all over the world. This is called systemic risk and contagion effect. The most common of these spreads are the derivative markets. Because the trading volume of derivative instruments has reached quite high figures worldwide. Crises originating from derivative markets are spreading to all the markets with the feature of infectious, creating destructive effects on the markets. Companies such as Procter & Gamble, Metallgesellschaft, Barings Futures, Sumitomo Bank, and Orange County are examples of large spin-offs as a result of derivatives trading (State Planning Organization 2000, p. 41).

The G-7 countries, which are the United States, France, Italy, Germany, Japan, Canada, and the United Kingdom, have approved the action plan to be taken when the crises are encountered, and in the plan (Bulut and Bahişov 2009, p. 29):

- By helping banks and financial institutions, their destruction will be reduced, and no end will be allowed.
- The markets will be kept alive by providing credit flows in the markets and increasing credibility.
- The funds will be transferred to the bank from the investors.
- The system which guaranteed the deposit will be replayed.
- Mortgage will move again.

With the application of these materials, it is aimed that the markets should be prepared against the crisis.

In Turkey, developments have been made in the banking sector related to financial globalization. Turkish banks have opened branches in foreign countries through purchasing, and they have established these branches especially in the centers of Europe. With the Secondary Banking Directive of 1993, Turkey has begun to take advantage of it. When the content of this right was examined, Turkish banks had the right to a license called Single License and were able to branch offices in all countries within the boundaries of the European Union.

Instead of Conclusion: Critiques of Globalization

With the concept of globalization, many social, economic, and political, negative and positive, events have been linked, and many approaches to globalization have been derived by stating that globalization is a concept that has both the cause and the ability to solve these problems. As the emergence of this concept, the Soviet Union's disintegration in the 1980s was mentioned. From this process, the system called global capitalism has begun. The greatest criticism of this system is the Marxist thinkers. Marxist scientists are seeking answers to questions about this concept such as reasons for the world becoming the only market if capitalism has caused emergency of globalization, why globalization only wants richer wealth and why globalization wants the state to shrink. Some of these questions have proved to be a reality with the events that occur in the coming. It has been found that globalization enriches wealthy countries, while poor countries are poor, and cause injustice in the distribution of income among countries. There are also thinkers against this criticism of globalization that has increased the income of the countries constantly by opening the countries outwards compared to the old. According to another criticism, it is stated that globalization is the empire of capitalism. Thus it is the idea that globalization is only the center and that it has fed its subsidiary units and supporting peripheral units in order to strengthen the center. It is expressed that globalization does not exhibit a pro-just and equality-oriented attitude and prefers to expand an imperialist attitude. In addition, another criticism of globalization emphasized that the poverty of globalization is mainly seen in women and children, and thus the concept of feminism of poverty has been revealed. With this concept, it has been seen that the most women and children have been impoverished in the framework of harmonization to globalization and therefore anti-globalization demonstrations were made (Yayman 1999, p. 62; Leba 2001, p. 1; Nakiboğlu 2004, p. 42; Şahin 2005, p. 128; Kaya 2009, p. 1; Aydın 2014, p. 1).

Bibliography

Acar, Mustafa: "Küreselleşme mi küreselleştirme mi". *Piyasa Dergisi* 12(Güz), 2004, pp. 2–7.

Adanur Aklan, Nejla: "Dış borçlanma gelişmekte olan ülkeler için etkin bir finansman yöntemi midir?". 2002, retrieved 01.11.2017, from http://www.foreigntrade.gov.tr/ead/DTDERGI/temmuz2002/disborclanma.htm.

Aktan, Can C. / Şen, Hüseyin: "*Globalleşme Ekonomik Kriz ve Türkiye*". Tosyöv Yayınları: Ankara. 1999.

Aydın, Durmuş: "Küreselleşme ve yoksulluk". *İnsani ve Sosyal Araştırmalar Merkezi*. 2014, retrieved 01.11.2017, from http://www.ihhakademi.com/kuresellesme-veyoksulluk/.

Balkanlı, Ali O.: "Küresel ekonominin belirleyici faktörleri üzerine". *Uludağ Üniversitesi İktisadi ve İdari Bilimler Fakültesi Dergisi* 21(1), 2002, pp. 13–26.

Bozkurt, Veysel: "Küreselleşme kavram gelişim ve yaklaşımlar". 2006, retrieved 01.11.2017, from http://www.isguc.org/vbozkurt1.htm.

Bulut, Cihan / Bahişov, Namık M.: "Finansal küreselleşme ve ekonomik etkileri". *Stratejik Araştırmalar Dergisi* 13, 2009, pp. 27–29.

Chussudovsky, Michel: "*Yoksulluğun Küreselleşmesi*". (Trans.: Neşenur Domaniç). Çiviyazıları Yayınevi: İstanbul. 1999.

Çaşkurlu, Sibel: "Küreselleşen işgücü krizi ve küresel eşitsizlik". *Ekonomik Yaklaşım Dergisi* 21(77), 2010, pp. 49–100.

Dorman, Peter: "Actually existing globalization" In: Preet S. Aulakh & Michael G. Schechter (Eds.): *Rethinking globalization*. Palgrave Publishing: New York. 2000. p. 46.

Dunning, John H.: "*The Globalization of Business: The Challenge of The 1990s*". Cengage Learning Emea: United Kingdom. 1993.

Ekin, Nusret: "*Küreselleşme ve Gümrük Birliği*". İstanbul Ticaret Odası Yayın No:1997–47, İstanbul, 1997.

Elçin, A. Bora: "*Küreselleşmenin Tarihçesi*". Merit Denetim-Danışmanlık-Yeminli Mali Müşavirlik, 2012.

Eraltuğ Kökkılınç, Ayşegül: "Uluslararası ticaret antlaşmalarının sosyal hükümleri". *Türkiye Barolar Birliği Dergisi* 99, 2012, pp. 81–124.

Erçel, Gazi: "*Küreselleşme ve Uluslararası Finansal Gelişmeler*". İstanbul: 17. Asya Bankalar Birliği Genel Kurulu, 2000.

Gallino, Luciano: "*Küreselleşme ve Eşitsizlik*". (Trans.: Durdu Kundakçı). Dost Yayınevi: Ankara. 2007.

Giddens, Anthony: "Üçüncü Yol Politikaları" In: Murat Yalçıntan (Ed.): *Üçüncü Yol Arayışları ve Türkiye*. Büke Yayınları: İstanbul. 2000.

Hirst, Paul / Thompson, Grahame: "*Küreselleşme Sorgulanıyor*". (Trans.: Elif Yücel / Çağla Erdem). Dost Kitabevi: Ankara. 1999.

Karabulut, Recep / Solak, Bilal: "Finansal sistemin küreselleşme serüveni". *Turgut Özal Uluslararası Ekonomi ve Siyaset Kongresi* (Küresel Değişim ve Demokratikleşme), Malatya, 19-20 April 2012, p. 1082.

Karahan, Özcan / İpek, Evren: "Türkiye'ye yönelik yabancı sermaye akımlarının hacim ve kompozisyonundaki gelişmeler". *Yönetim ve Ekonomi Araştırmaları Dergisi* 21, 2013, pp. 299–316.

Kaya, Mehmet: "Küreselleşme yaklaşımları". *Dicle Üniversitesi Ziya Gökalp Eğitim Fakültesi Dergisi* 13, 2009, pp. 1–16.

Keyder, Nur: *Para Teori-Politika-Uygulama*. Nobel Yayıncılık: Ankara. 1996.

Kleinert, Förn: *The Role of Multinational Entergrises In Globalization*, Springer Publishing: Berlin. 2004.

Kuruoğlu, Huriye: "Reflections of cultural globalization in tv programmes in Kyrgyzstan". *UNISCI Discussion Papers* 4, 2004.

Leba, Reyhan: "Küreselleşmenin öteki yüzü: yoksulluk". *Mevzuat Dergisi* 4(43), 2001, p. 11.

Mcluhan, Marshall: "*Gutenberg Galaxy*". Toronto University Publishing: Canada. 1962.

Modelski, George: "Küreselleşme". In: David Held / Anthony Mcgrew (Eds.): *Küresel Dönüşümler*. Phoenix Yayınevi: Ankara. 2008. pp. 75–80.

Nakiboğlu, Cüneyd: "*Neoliberal Küreselleşme Sürecinde Yoksulluk ve Yoksullukla Mücadele*". Ankara University Social Sciences Institute Master Thesis: Ankara. 2004.

O'loughlin, John / Staeheli, Lynn / Greenberg, Edward: "Economic globalization, political changes and social outcomes", In: John O'loughlin / Lynn Staeheli / Edward Greenberg (Eds.): *Globalization and its outcomes*. The Guilford Press: New York. 2004. pp. 156–257.

Özel, Hasan A.: "Küreselleşme sürecinde ticari ve finansal açıklığın ekonomik büyüme üzerine etkisi: Türkiye örneği". *Yönetim Bilimleri Dergisi* 10(19), 2012, pp. 1–30.

Öztürk, Nurettin: "Finansal küreselleşme ve küresel sermaye akımları". In: Oğuz Kaymakçı (Ed.): *Küreselleşme Üzerine Notlar*. Nobel Yayıncılık: Ankara. 2007. pp. 251–288.

Prakash, Aseem: "The East Asian crisis and the globalization discourse". Review of International Political Economy 8(1) Spring, 2001, pp. 119–146.

Rodrik, Dani: "Trade, social insurance and the limits to globalization". *NBER Working Paper Series: 5905*. National Bureau of Economic Research, Cambridge. 1997.

Sabır, Hasan: "Doğrudan yabancı sermaye yatırımlarını gelişmekte olan ülkelere yönlendirici politikalar". 2002, retrieved 01.11.2017, from http://www.dtm.gov.tr/ead/DTDERGI/Ekim2002/sabir.htm.

Stiglitz, Joseph E.: "*Küreselleşme Büyük Hayal Kırıklığı*". (Trans.: Arzu Taşçıoğlu). Plan B Yayınevi: İstanbul. 2002.

Stiglitz, Joseph E.: "Küreselleşen dünyada kalkınma politikaları" In Fikret Şenses(Eds.): *Neoliberal Küreselleşme ve Kalkınma.*. İletişim Yayınları İstanbul. 2009, pp. 281–306.

Şahin, Mehmet: "Küreselleşme kaynaklı yoksulluk ve yolsuzluk". *Muhasebe ve Finans Dergisi* 25, 2005, pp. 124–134.

Temel, Serdal: "Globalleşme sürecinin gelişmekte olan ülkelerde işgücü istihdamı üzerindeki etkileri". 2001, retrieved 01.11.2017, from http://www.universite-toplum.org/text.php3?id=34.

UNCTAD: "World investment report: Transnational Corporations and Integrated International Production", *United Nations Conference on Trade and Development*, New York, 1993.

Undersecretariat of State Planning Organization: *Sekizinci Beş Yıllık Kalkınma Planı-Küreselleşme Özel İhtisas Komisyonu Raporu*. T.C. Başbakanlık Devlet Planlama Teşkilatı Müsteşarlığı: Ankara. 2000. pp. 37–41.

Uras, Güngör: "Tayland sıcak para girişini engelledi". 2006, retrieved 01.11.2017, from http://www.milliyet.com/2006/12/20/yazar/uras.html.

Went, Robert: "*Küreselleşme: Neoliberal İddialar, Radikal Yanıtlar*". (Trans.: Emrah Dinç). Yazın Yayıncılık: İstanbul. 2001.

Yayman, Hüseyin: "Küreselleşme tartışmalarının Türkiye özeline yansımaları". Sayıştay Dergisi 34, 1999, pp. 59–76.

Öznur Yavan

Global Formulation of Business Ethics

Abstract: Businesses are purpose-built corporations. Communities continue their existence by their own social benefits. The ethics concept is based upon the protection of common interest. In this context, ethics is a social and economic topic. Whether global ethics or global business ethics, the concept of ethics aims to maintain the universal interest in an equal, fair and rational way. In that sense, ethics is a social issue depending on the economic values. The discussions on the global ethics are as much significant as the sustainability of universal values. In the global environment where there is a butterfly effect, or a minute change can create a major impact in the far end of the world, business leaders committed to the world's future need to make the global ethical issues crystal clear.

Communities are consistently evolving in an impetuous process of globalization, whose value and pace are constantly increasing. In an economic and social sense, the global ethical values must be created towards a global universe. With the contextual codes and traditions in different cultures, establishing an egalitarian, impartial and reasonable universal order can be unsustainable. The international economic and social relations should be maintained in the supra-cultural milieu of interests. In the present study, the aim is to investigate the practical possibility of global ethics or global business ethics, the potential actions for a global ethical environment, the global value of business ethics, the interested parties of global business ethics, the compliance monitoring of global business ethics with the ethical values, application examples, and the critical views against global business ethics formulation.

Keywords: Globalization, Global Business Ethics, Management

JEL Codes: M10, M14, M16.

Background

There has also appeared a popular issue throughout the past two decades: Global Ethics. It has been a source of inspiration for a number of initiatives, such as the Journal of Global Ethics, an office in the United Nations, the International Global Ethics Association, charities, academic centers, a few graduate programs, e-library (45,000 subscribers), etc. However, it is apparent that the Hegel's dialectics or thesis-antithesis-synthesis theory is valid in global ethics: a new paradigm was proposed in order to discover the contradictory arguments made in this field. There is limited focus on its scope and content that global ethics would be found valid and reasonable by the world population. A practical success has been made on this subject despite the fact that the concept totally lacks a theoretical basis (Drydyk 2014, p. 16).

The ethical values are historically and socially the product of the dynamic processes (Karababa *et al.* 2006, p. 102). As a set of principles and values, ethics are guiding human relations and are the determinant of people's attitudinal, behavioral and decision making processes that they are underlying the operations and relationships of production. Production is a social process in which people necessarily and not optionally make engagements. At the end of this, physical assets are produced as well as ideas, ethics, and beliefs. In this framework, the economic and hence institutional structure in any society are designed and shaped by the ideologies developed on the basis of production sharing (Karababa *et al.* 2006, p. 20).

Globalization has bonded world's corporations, communities and organizations from all over the world, more than before, and the barriers between these entities have become clearer and more transparent, which enhances and accelerates the interactive process between the interested parties (Akçay and Bağcan 2016, p. 170). The world's globalization is persistently increasing (Shoham, 1999:24), and questioning the reason of a universal strategy has intensely attracted academic topics either in theory or practice for a couple of decades (Griffith et al. 2000, p. 303).

Economic crises may cause social tensions and hence give birth to social conflicts (Küng 1997, p.18). About 'New Global Economic Ethic Manifesto' launched during a business ethics symposium at UN Headquarters on 6 October 2009, Professor Küng declared his views such below (Hemphill and Lillevik 2011, p. 215):

> *"The call for an ethical framework for the global financial markets and global economics has loudly been heard from many sides worldwide since the beginning of the current crisis… This new Declaration on a Global Economic Ethic reminds all stakeholders in global businesses of their individual responsibilities for humanizing the functioning of the global economy: Globalization needs a Global Ethic"*

From the 1990s on, business ethics has become prominent as well as corporate governance and social responsibility along with the global spread of capitalism (Tayşir and Pazarcık 2013, p. 295)

Organizations are seen as the sustenances of society and the dynamics of social development. Any social events for or against the public interest are very related to the activities of organized democratic institutions in consequence of their being element of oppression (Karababa *et al.* 2006, p. 97). International business corporations are leading world population, and their huge power from globalization is one of its contributing factors. Until quite recently, multinational companies whose concentration was just business and trade are now too active within the international political system, and even do not hesitate to give bribes or abuse media power in lobbying (Dalpour 2012, p. 274–275).

Business ethics is one of the oldest concepts in organization and management (Tayşir and Pazarcık 2013, p. 295). Desai and Rittenburg (1997) suggest that the topic of global ethics was first seen as a popular issue among researchers in the discipline of international management (Yeşil 2011, p. 184).

The manifesto of 'Toward Global Ethics' is one of the concrete outcomes from the Parliament of the World's Religions held in 1993 (George 1996, p. 359). The discussions must involve religions, yet with the concern of its depth that might make the process complex, it should be enough to profess the ethical issues shallowly (Falk 1999, p. 69).

Global Ethics

Ethics is an activity of thinking while an ethic is a set of guiding values for human behavior (Dover 2005, p. 26). From a different angle, morality philosophically differs rights from wrongs, yet ethics practically develops, justifies and applies the universal moral values (Issitt, 2016).

Homo sapiens would become human only and only in a society. This development will require acquiring respect and dignity through the application of the established values and manners which provides safety for traveling man in this life (Stückelberger *et al.* 2016, p. 46)

A remarkable product of the Universalist thought, the Universal Declaration of Human Rights of 1946 was, by chance or just with good intent, not created, unfortunately, in the wake of the Second World War, which influenced more or less all over the world though it was mostly experienced in Europe. This manifesto offers a color-, gender-, class-blind protection for and by all. Indeed, the Declaration was a sign for globalization or more accurately, intercultural interaction before it. Maybe, globalization was either an effect of interconnection or a motive for ruling relations that ethics is a requirement for a global community or a strategic diffusive way of a fair and trustworthy order. We consider that it is useful for strategy developers to determine if the primary goal of global ethics is just protection or motivation for freedom and welfare. If the latter was precluded, the process would become authoritarian in disfavor of freedom (Issitt 2016).

A global consensus on our individual attitudes and behaviors is transformed into binding rules on international agreements and irrevocable provisions on interpersonal contracts. Otherwise, the global order would be collapsed, and if there is no limitation on global actions, cross-border interactions will be interrupted (Loye 1999, pp. 221–222). The ethical formulation should be maintained through the participation of virtually all the parties so as to smoothly abide by and enforce the produced rules. Global ethics is an interdisciplinary initiative not specific to a culture or religion, and the number of researches on globalization popped up in the 1990s (Issitt 2016).

Associated with the religious traditions, the ethical standards were tried to be compiled by World Parliament of Religions in the assembly of Chicago in Fall 1993, and the "Declaration Toward a Global Ethic" was released under the four foundations: solidarity, equal rights, tolerance and nonviolence (Muck 1997, p. 215). To be human, the Global Ethic was determined as guiding or inspiring standards not only for worshippers but also for nonbelievers (Liu 2001)

Stückelberger *et al.* (2016, p.33) suggest the major concepts of global ethics, such as essentialist, convergence and contractual theories. The first includes the fact that the ethical order is essentially derived from the *natural* order and hence universal. The second theory states that the ethical principles are or should be *common* for any contextual values. The third one accepts that the ethical rules only have power on people only with their prior *consent.*

Global ethic is a joint point for believers and nonbelievers, and even if it was historically and theoretically based on religions and philosophies, it is in effect bunching by binding not just followers but also disengaged people with morality and ethics at a minimum standard (Küng 1999, p. 5).

The Ethical Concept

In this study, Tepe (1998) stated that businesses are naturally the profit-maximizing corporations, and asked the questions of "which one is of first priority for businesses: the profitability by any means or the condition of employees" and "Can the profit be protected together with humanity or ethics?" Tepe declared his view such as "instead of business ethics, mentioning the ethical problems of businesses will be more appropriate because ethics is just a single informative discipline." (Karababa *et al.* 2006, p. 98).

The immaterial problems that people face and seemingly insoluble can be caused by the material actions and the concrete matters, like ethics. Global ethics aims to investigate their causes not only the physical ones but also the spiritual-oriented psychological factors contributing to our response. The globally connected and dependent people must seek ways to reconcile with one another and fight against the bad persons or wrong actions, or they will have to suffer from any damages and losses from wars, calamities, and deceits (Drydyk

2014, p. 18). The global ethical issues are ranging from the moral use of military options to the ethical use of environmental resources to the ethical practice of business and trade (Issitt 2016). In the study that Moellendorf and Widdows conducted in 2014 ten years after the first publication of Journal of Global Ethics, the questions of war, disagreement and violence, poverty and development, economic fairness, bioethics and health justice, and environmental and climate justice are dealt with, and the researchers of ethics are now seeking a real, actual justice in detail (Moellendorf and Widdows 2014, p. 319).

The investigation in pursuit of a ruling worldview, religious, philosophical, or utilitarian, or human rights-based can generally be made or into a particular domain such as environment, development, war, and peace, etc. Based on its including global ethical values concerning unity and diversity and cross-border obligations, etc., can be classified under global ethics. Between the general and the applied ethics, there are specific ways of inquiry into the universal values such as global justice and human rights (Dover 2005, pp. 27–28).

Global ethics is related to universal values and/or common responsibilities throughout the world. The end of ethical development is a set of extensive ethical values as guidance to one having to contact with the world. One can evaluate a behavior whether it is ethical or not by measuring the reasons for and against different proposals. Another inquiry method is trying to answer certain ethical problems (Drydyk 2014, p. 17–18).

We need to go beyond our limitations, or otherwise, our creativity will be killed by our narcissist thoughts. That's why we have to get to the bottom of ethics, the classical virtues for being a human including Confucius thoughts (Cheng 2013, pp. 91–92). The ethical development process requires benchmarking our values to other cultures or vice versa (e.g., UNESCO Universal Ethics Project).

There are four topics to address (Dover 2005, pp. 28–29):

1. Who is the addressee: person, group, state or business?
2. How is the content: thick or thin?
    a) The complete or global ethic or just its limited part
    b) Values plus worldviews?
    c) Which is more important: universal or transnational responsibility?
3. Which one is a global ethic: Applicable to all, widely agreed, or universally shared?
4. What kind of justification: reasoning by others' views, responding by agreed principles, and producing from shared traditions?

For the economic institutions such as businesses, governments, international organizations, the Global Economic Ethic Manifesto helps them recognize how to act legally, ethically and equally in their economic activities. It is established on the foundations: *shortly,* humanity, honesty, and tolerance, mutual esteem and partnership, non-violence and respect for life, justice. Gaining the moral dimension to transnational business and also a board of directors and executive managers, this framework may compensate for the critiques to globalization as a capitalist movement (Hemphill and Lillevik 2011, pp. 213–214). Manifesting itself in almost every field, the standards of the International Organization for Standardization (ISO) or other global standard-setting organizations are the products of substantial labors and money spent on the incorporation of ISO 9001 to particular sectors and the legitimization of the enterprises' transactions through licensing their meeting the standards (Gueorguiev and Sakakushev 2016, p. 971).

The interest in global ethics inclines to disperse into various narrower areas of study, and the discussions on this topic have declined for a decade, and this will go on maybe for another decade. The specialization of ethicists creates new sub-categories such as "the ethics and economics in remittances, the possibilities of adaptation technologies in climate change, or the ethics and governance of intellectual property," and with this, a specialist for global ethics is seemingly obliged to go out of existence (Moellendorf and Widdows 2014, p. 324).

Contributing Factors of Global Ethics (1970–2020)

Global ethical development is in association with a number of such factors as geopolitical and economic trends; economically, culturally, socially, and politically transformed lifestyles with technological advances; national and international tensions; ideological, reformative impact on religions; populist propaganda techniques; supra-national bodies; increasing academic researches; civic participation (Stückelberger *et al.* 2016, p. 28).

Culture is multidimensional structure and homogeneity in one society differing from another (Grifith *et al.* 2000, p. 304). In a literature review on management that about 70% of the articles included the discussions over the cultural role. These articles revealed that culture is significant to understand the organizational behavior and management (Miller and Sharda 1997, p. 19).

One of the most important sources of global ethic is the cultural tradition based on the concept that humans are vulnerable and show the ethical response in order to mitigate what he or she suffers when applicable and get secured from harmful actions. The inspirations for a global ethic may be classified as cultures, experiences, biographies, spiritual aspects (Küng 1997, p. 20).

The social researches for global ethics were associated with globalization in political and economic systems, and the prioritization of contextual ethics with the ideological protectionism (Stuckelberger *et al.* 2016, p. 28).

The ethical issues cannot be dealt with apart from the socio-economic factors. Two aspects of ethics are the reactive and proactive direction. By a conservationist approach, ethics criticize new fashions and innovations, the economic and political pressure of transformation or legitimize them. The second is a way that ethics proactively act like a strategist to affect and transform the society, maybe as a counter-attack strategy, give support for new economic orders and new universalist morality, and end partisanship (Stuckelberger *et al.* 2016, p. 28).

Globalization and Ethics

The myriad cultures and cultural differences have been melted in a pot by means of globalization through the processes of interaction, integration, and homogenization. Furthermore, the contemporary digital innovations accelerate the interconnection of different parts of the world, also with the support of the rising international business and trade. Expectedly, the studies on global ethics burst out with this globalization story (Issitt 2016).

In the 1970s, the economic shocks hit the capitalist system, and the production style was modified from mass to flexible model. This new approach aims to root up all ongoing value judgments. Such disengagement corresponds to the terms of “the New World Order”, “restructuring” and “globalization” (Karababa *et al.* 2006, p. 22). Despite all critiques, ethics maintains its impact as a phenomenon. Capitalism expresses itself on an ethical basis within the prevalent thought methodology, in the process of NWO or globalization under the name of restructuring (Karababa *et al.* 2006, p. 101).

During globalization, ethics plays a crucial, indispensable role (Küng, 1997, p. 17). Globalization is defined as a jointedness process in which a variety of socio-economic structures are interwoven and quasi-fused rather than being simply interdependent, which is one of the most significant factors that now affect business and management (Yeşil 2011, pp. 181–182).

Like public goods in a community, there are globally common goods such as atmosphere, oceans, land, etc. We can define the world as a global city, and it should have a supra-national administration, or otherwise, the unfair distribution of resources now occurs as well as negative externalities to the future (Engel 2004, p. 41).

Even though we might acclaim that among the globalization objectives the most naïve is the global welfare and sustainable wealth, this phenomenon can aggravate and accelerate the spread of economic and financial crisis. This is one of the reasons for global ethical values in international commerce and cooperation (Küng, *et al.* 2009, p. 3).

Defined as human home of cultural contexts, the global community is a new reality in the new century, and global ethics should govern the boundary game, the contextual interaction of the parties with the characteristics of relationship, processing, and meaning (Chen 2015, p. 75).

We as humans have our linguistic, cultural, legal or political identities crossing the state lines and some way turn our national identity to the global one subject to the recent developments (Drydyk 2014, p. 21). Today some daily activities we perform to meet our physical, cultural, social needs can be the channels to be simply connected to the world, such as feeding, listening, watching, dressing, entertaining, etc. By this means, the cultures interact, the characters meld, and the contours fade (Dalpour 2012, p. 273). Hypothetically, if one coughs on the other end of the world, another feels ill on the other end. This situation must be a lesson to the global business leaders that they yearly congregate to discuss the future of the world (Howard 2010, p. 515).

Is Global Ethics Possible?

World politics and world economy requires the world ethic, the most popular topic like global ethic by globalization (Küng 1997, p. 18). The business world and many international organizations make efforts towards creating global business ethics and in line with this purpose, release a variety of reports and declarations. The acceptance of and correspondence to these initiatives in the international context may offer evidence for its possibility. In business, the views that a number of fundamental principles in ethics are accepted worldwide and followed have become prevalent, and the signals of its possibility have been already noticed (Yeşil 2011, p. 186).

Why have not ethics been moved in parallel with globalization? What reasons can be for the disability of contextual values to transform into the global standards? Instead of ethics, a specific ethic is preferable that there is consensus on the most fundamental moral principles, and it is not to stipulate the manner of how to morally respond to specific actions and situations (Gebhardt 2000, p. 506).

In ethics, values mean the inclined fundamentals for individuals towards high concepts such as peace and justice while virtues refer to the ethical standards for individual actions such as modesty and honesty. The fundamental values constitute the ethical framework with a holistic, long-term approach, yet they can shift towards the course of events in the life. On the other hand, the core virtues are seen in all systems, but their applications can be specifically different (Stückelberger *et al.*,2016, p. 11).

We should – or really could – be inclusive to others' moral values in consequence of global ethics. This may provide the harmonization of the contexts from various cultures. But how so? The question is actually how global ethics can be achieved with the global effectiveness (Drydyk 2014, p. 22). Can one definitely acclaim the immediate incompatibility among contextual ethics or otherwise? Then, we should look into the historical or philosophical background of cultures, religions, traditions, and ethics (Küng 1999, p. 16).

Upon the moral decision on what is right or good, a consensus is among the goals of ethical discussions. However, it is not extremely possible as the diverse values are naturally effective. As for global ethics, this outcome is inevitable because it is like to sail through the oceans with a great variety of special species of creatures. The question might arise that one ethic can be formulated on a global scale or a set of common values can be universally adopted by all. Nevertheless, we cannot overlook the possibility of skepticism from the particular relativities, which discourages us to go ahead of the present situation and beyond the ready templates (Dover 2005, p. 28).

In effect, those who do favor of global ethics are all humans, and they have the distinctive backgrounds such as from religions, ideologies or personal stories. If one or a group of people stipulate the adoption of their own thoughts and beliefs by others in order to agree on what is right or wrong, it will be an unjust obstacle to close or collapse the bridge to connect two opposite sides. Whereas, one can have to do – or learn to – translate or transmit his or her views into their words, and vice versa. Highlighting the differences should not mean and cause the presupposition of disagreement between, for example, Christians, Jews, and Muslims or a capitalist, liberalist, or socialist (Dover 2004, p. 16). For the universal consensus in future, some exciting international developments are not unavailable even if it is not effective to the desired extent, such as the Earth Charter which is an arguably complex manifestation and a new phenomenon of getting a large consensus despite not being universal, or this is the best accepted by the majority till the more best agreed (Dover 2004, pp. 25–27).

In 2000, the international quasi-NGO, the Earth Council agreed and released the declaration of the Earth Charter which is guidance referred by individuals and institutions in their actions. This is also applied for educational purpose to foster children's attainment of moral values, including the respect for earth and the diverse lives, caring for socialization and empathy, building democratic governance, and security for the inheritance of our world to the offspring (Dover 2005, pp. 38–39).

Global Business Ethics

Business Ethics

As an academic concept, business or corporate ethics is relatively new, although this has existed throughout the whole history as a phenomenon, and it was first used after the 1970s in the U.S. in the Western world. Business ethics concerns explicitly about the assessment of ethical nature of business conduct since business relations are essentially related to human welfare and well-being. While ethics is about the knowledge of human affairs as a whole, business ethics, by and large, examines social relations with the thought that public domain (apart from family and state) is of the people's economic relations (Yardımlı 2014).

Human emotion is formed by such actions as experience and expression, usage and avoidance in general. One is spontaneously interactive with others in socialization even if with a smiley face to show affection. For organizations, differentiation in the environment by shaping the climate with its characteristics is supportively used to manage the staff's perceptions (Parke and Seo 2017, p. 336). As time goes by, the managers whose decisions are influencing our lives are also getting more influenced in their policies and procedures by ethical issues that are reflecting our thoughts and feelings of what is right or wrong (Sroka and Lőrinczy 2015, p. 157).

What relationship is there between ethics, politics, and economy? According to Aristotle, these three seemingly different fields are actually interwoven in nature. Ethics is a fundamental way of human development so that politics and economy can merge into one another (Cheng 2013, p. 95). Actually, their point of exit and arrival is the same as people's well-being, and ethics might be regarded as the cement in societal building and the mortar between politics and economy.

Understanding ethics and business ethics has a key role in making global business ethics clear and definite in mind (Yeşil 2011, p. 182). The word ethics is originated from '*ethos*' in Greek, meaning one's fundamental orientation toward life (Sroka and Lörinczy 2015, p. 157). However, business ethics refers to the ethical issues regarding businesses and their operations (Yeşil 2011, p. 182).

Due to the hugeness of global businesses, states have less negotiating power against them as well as their rivals, and these big firms create big problems for small enterprises through cartelization. They have focused on more lucrative businesses and leave the remaining portion. The local companies have to compete with these giants under the unfair and unequal circumstances. Furthermore, they make no know-how transfer including new techs to the developing countries, exploit their resources and gain more benefits for the developed products.

They also have very excessive economic power and so can lead the nations' policies to their own interests (Yeşil 2011, pp. 183–183).

It can be acclaimed that every decision is guided by the desire for profit maximization and also have political and social, and ultimately ethical dimensions (Küng 1997, p. 18). Loye (1999, p. 231) extracted from Küng's views on the common ethical points in global business that can be on the same religious ground, in a nutshell:

- Must of global ethic in globalization
- Universal human rights
- No violence, and high respect for living
- Solidarity and egalitarianism
- Tolerable and truthful lifestyle
- Equal opportunities and gender partnership

Business ethics is interchangeable to corporate social responsibility (CSR), a currently popular concept in business operations (Sroka and Lőrinczy 2015, p. 157).

Global Value of Business Ethics

Especially in the twentieth century, the concept of ethics had greater significance and higher value. Many problems that the industrial revolution brought about had an effect on this result. Furthermore, a number of outstanding problems that have been recently undergone all over the globe, such as the environmental problems, unemployment, corporate scandals, population growth, and inequality in the distribution of income, have drawn attention to the importance of ethics (Yeşil 2011, p. 183). We may add to these drawbacks the Western scandals of Enron and WorldCom – if the executives had acted in the ethical way, they would not have harmed the credibility of their corporations (Çelikdemir and Tukel 2015, p. 531).

Without a world or global ethic, the new world order would obviously turn to be anarchy with the unpunished crime organizations, the all ravaged environment, and the genocide of human race. For prevention of this catastrophe, we immediately need no ethics as a system but just an ethic as a set of shared moral values and so the ethic globalization (Küng 1999, p. 16; Falk 1999, p. 69).

We see a misunderstanding or disagreement on the term of ethics. On the contrary of Professor Küng, Cheng (2013, p. 91) suggests that ethics is a necessity for common goals so as to have or get respect, fairness, justice, trust, wisdom, etc.. These virtues counted are included in the definition of an ethic, not ethics. Accordingly, we conclude that it is a must to deal with the incomprehensibility issue in the ethics concept before anything else.

As Küng self-confidently advocates his arguments about bearing global ethics, it seems so simple to achieve the success in the theoretical and practical establishment. Is it really so? Professor Küng naively expects a religious revival for the universal values from the followers of major religions in the world, maybe though not their homogenization (Falk 1999, pp. 72–73). May religious intimidation have pressure over people in this materialist world?

We have recently seen many serious problems in the environment as well as human rights with globalization. Unfortunately, politicians are rather unaware of the global issues at least as much as the business leaders who are persistently keeping in pursuit of their desire for profit maximization. However, despite the fact that sustainability and equality in the future seems just a dream, the capitalist world seriously made some encouraging moves in the right direction in 1990s such as the "Declaration Toward a Global Ethic" of the Parliament of the World's Religions in Chicago in 1993, the "Universal Declaration of Human Responsibilities" submitted to the UN by the InterAction Council of political leaders in 1997, the reports by the UN Commission on Global Governance and the World Commission on Culture and Development in 1995, the agenda at the World Economic Forum in Davos and the UNESCO Universal Ethics Project. These were the footsteps of the transformations from "market fundamentalism" to "responsible globality" (Falk 1999, p. 72–73; Küng 1999, p. 16). From 1990s on, business ethics has become prominent as well as corporate governance and social responsibility along with the global spread of capitalism (Tayşir and Pazarcık 2013, p. 295).

This Declaration invites all stakeholders in global business and trade to remember their personal responsibilities for the humanization of economic activities and business operations. There is even no requirement of an ethical system to do right things but the common values basic for all are enough to commit oneself to abide by the fundamental moral values and if any, convict oneself for wrongdoing (Küng 2009, p. 21).

Views on the Requirement of Global Business Ethics

Can ethics be varied among individuals, organizations, or professions? Is it possible to view wrongdoing as a right thing? Alternatively, one can consider something right or wrong but does it mean that another person will also accept or reject it just as one does? Are ethical issues subjective that may change by which community, organization, or profession one belongs to? (Domino *et al.* 2015, p. 453).

How can people be protected from unethical behaviors in the commercial relations with people of other countries? That a global ethic cannot be established and adopted by all requires most states to put into force their own legislation to save their citizens' business rights. When considering the essence of the issue, there is no distinction between one global ethic and two national ethics as we as humans have the instinct and intent of protection almost in common. Unfortunately, the countries fail to cooperate to establish global business ethics even though their laws are only valid in their own territory (O'Brien 2009, p. 103).

Whereas, the human history is full of all bloody actions including wars, massacres, enslavement that are going on yet in pursuit of resources, assets, ideologies, and judgments to obtain from, protect against and dominate over others. The mass movements such as intercontinental wars, trade ways, and religious diffusions have been conveyors of currents of thought and cultures. People had to find solutions to overcome moral depressions due to social crises caused by wars, a conglomeration of wealth into the same hands, pompous lifestyle and depravedness, and correspondingly intolerable living conditions (Karababa *et al.* 2006, pp. 20–21). Ethic relations and ethical behaviors are eroding day by day under the pressure of exploitation and wars (Karababa *et al.* 2006, p. 94).

Consider the global financial markets of drugs. The illegal drug dealers are using the legal ways across the legal states to convey their "goods" or the items under the same name. Well, why would not the politicians seriously combine their efforts to obstruct this illegal course of action simply with the establishment of global ethical system? We think, as an example, the Latin world where the proportion of Christians or even Catholics is very high, but drug use is also highly common in there. What obstacles have stopped the religious leaders to declare and enforce the universal ethical values grounded into their religions? Money laundering is a "serious" crime in the world, yet how many individuals or organizations are seriously punished or even charged with these atrocious crimes? Should we suspect that those whom people pin their hopes upon for a greater and better future have dirty relations with the illegal abusers? Could they possibly share a common handicap to gain a cooperation and collaboration in overcoming this global issue? Whereas, believers or nonbelievers support the ethics philosophically (Küng 2001, p. 98).

Also, on the one hand the protectionist, nationalist, and fundamentalist political ideologies give priority to the context of social and cultural identities against global ethics, and on the other hand "freer" people with internet and digital technologies share their views of freedom and justice on social media such as Facebook, Google, Twitter, etc. Why could not such views democratically contribute to the authoritarian politics? We consider that the global ethics cannot be without the global governance – equivalent to public governance, which is shortly defined as the democratic process of civil participation (Stückelberger *et al.* 2016, p. 9). The mercantilist and hence economically protectionist approach that time-travels from the "Middle Ages" – ironically or maybe not coincidentally with an implicit message to a restrictive and conservative combination of politics and religion, is common among nations in this "open" international business, trade and finance.

Nevertheless, the present economic crises have become more severe to easily and rapidly prevail up to the remotest place throughout the world (Cheng 2013, p. 92). We may fall down the barriers and open to the goods and benefits from outside but even if there is no ethical question, a "normal" crisis in an economy can turn to be abnormally more effective globally. This can be a risk, but global ethics is not a wide-open door to any action or attack, rather it is to set a limitation not just outside but also inside businessmen with religion or any other belief by means of raising awareness on global ethical issues. And correspondingly, competition should be fair, innovation useful, and ambition beneficial for all in the framework of ethical principles actualized (Vadastreanu *et al.* 2015, p. 1070).

Caux Round Table

The means of communication allow global exchange of information, yet the crucial point is who characterizes this information environment with regards to physical-technology and its content though (Karababa *et al.* 2006, p. 90). Taking the lead of global ethical development, politicians should internationally collaborate with business managers, legal professionals, and academic professors in order to maintain the cooperation for and make the achievement of producing shared and desired "good" or ethic (O'Brien 2009, p. 104).

As a success factor, leadership is indispensable in any social developments. Two fields of ethics and business are overlapping, and some questions need to be solved through the leadership of one or a few pioneering men taking the initiative. A leading organization in this issue, "The Caux Round Table" has already become prominent. This association was founded by Frederik Phillips (head of Phillips Electronics) and Olivier Giscard d'Estaing (deputy head of INSEAD) in 1986. Business leaders from Europe, Japan, and the United States convene for the Round Table meeting. This has a belief that business world plays a key role in developing the economic and social conditions in a community. Therefore, it has focused on the social responsibilities of corporates globally and set the global standards to evaluate the individual ethical behaviors. These are based on two fundamental principles: The first is living and working together for a shared benefit to offer the provision of common development and growth. The other is general basic principles ranging from overall principles, including the protection of environment to more specific ones such as the promotion of multilateral trade in the world (Yeşil 2011, p. 191).

From the French Revolution until today, the parties of wars have changed from the princes, nations, and ideologies, respectively (Küng 1999, p. 5). Buller's ethical model is related to four interconnected areas of ethics: individual, business, social, and global ethics. Individual ethics refers to the ethical values and principles of a specific person while business ethics include those of all formal organizations and institutions. Despite its interconnection, the way and style of this relationship are not much clear but complex. Individual ethics is affected by social and business ethics though the latter is rather influenced by social ethics and the ethics of organizational members. Social ethics is also affected by the history, traditions and at the same time institutions and individuals of the society. Social and business ethics affect global ethics. Furthermore, global ethics is under the impact of international organizations, religions, ideologies, global entities, media, academics, and scientific associations (Yeşil 2011, p. 187).

Ethics Formulation

Socialization is an internalization process of the guiding values and culture of the community within which one lives in either his or her interpersonal relations or behavior and decision-making processes. In other words, shortly it is one's interaction with the community. Naturally, this process is directly influenced by all the social, economic, political, and cultural factors that are contributing to shaping the community (Karababa *et al.* 2006, p. 25).

Human development is possible if he or she persistently make attempts in that way not alone but just together with others in the community. Towards being good, the specific values are set and adopted by all to follow in their personal development. The goals of values include understanding the significance of ethical life (Stückelberger *et al.* 2016, p. 47,49).

An interactive life in community is natural just like our basic biological needs, and also this is not caused by economic requirements but otherwise economy may be the result of this human nature. This forces to erase any differences among humans such as gender, race, etc. And even, the Golden Rule of reciprocity was developed to form common values on the fundamental principle of acting just like our expectations from others. As religions and philosophical disciplines might have been derived from this commonality need, the establishment of universal values dates back to the earliest human history, explicitly, as well as ethics (Stückelberger *et al.* 2016, p. 25).

One cannot eradicate the human distinctions and also extremely kill all, however she can terminate any negative effects of the diversity by means of socialization and ethics. This inference can of course or should be extended to the global ethics, and naturally business ethics.

Nevertheless, such attributes as geography, nationality, belief, gender, etc., are so differential that the contextual values are to some extent conflicting due to the global and technological transformations (Stückelberger *et al.* 2016, p. 25).

Globalization is today leading to the ethical crisis as well as ecological and economic crises. The need for integrated ethics into the communities and at least as much as it is, the prioritization for the closer one out of the ethical forms rather than the others can be identified as the factors of ethical crisis. The utilitarian ethics, for example, gives priority to being 'homo economicus' that extremely keeps in pursuit of their own self-interests while the fundamental ethics spurs 'homo sapiens' to be good for all (Cheng 2013, p. 92).

Should science engage in the formulation of global ethics at least philosophically? This idea is very hard to embrace not only for a large number of nonbelievers in science and religion, which makes a success of the new attempt 'skeptical'. We should keep in our mind Darwin's case of his overlooked attempt (Loye 1999, p. 231).

Ethics forms within the natural interactions of the production function, which is social like religions or languages. The ethical values transmit from one society to another through inter-community relations, gain validity in the latter as they are internalized and establish into its culture in time (Karababa *et al.* 2006, p. 17–18).

As scientific revolution targeted at the supernatural beasts, capitalism also attacked the prophecies for afterlife like Heaven and created the cravings for this life. Accordingly, ethical and moral codes would not have to follow religions and beliefs, and humans would make their own norms and value judgments to bring themselves to a blissful future. People's goals for existence have been happiness, health, information, self-development, and welfare and safety for all since then (Karababa *et al.* 2006, p. 22).

Who is the Addressee of Global Ethics?

Is it significant to differentiate the ethical values by the identity of addressee? Can an ethic be taken as essential by all, including persons, states, companies, leaders, officials, etc? Ain't their responsibilities and expectations different from each other, which influence their own decisions and behaviors? Individuals have personal emotions but states have democratic rules, or international commitments or corporations have shareholders' interests, which might be in conflict with the public interests (Dover 2005, p. 29).

To create an ethical organization or more precisely company in business ethics, the ethical standards such as the Global Economic Ethic Declaration need to be embedded into the strategic plan of HR Management and the ethical performances of the staff should be monitored. The articulation of specific values and the awareness of ethical applications are the requirements to establish an ethical environment within the firm structure. In practice, many firms have much trouble in performing the standards and accomplishing the result. Not just the approval of ethical charters to apply to universal ethical values is enough, but also a systematic, dynamic control process should be maintained with the involvement of stakeholders and the coherence of the personal attitudes and actions with organizational acceptances as business ethical values. This approach requires the prespecification of the internal and external incentives individually from bottom to top level in the hierarchy and the generosity of the distribution of rewards and the seriousness of the infliction of punishments (Hemphill and Lillevik 2011, p. 223).

Currently, the cultural prevalences throughout the world are interestingly getting reactions from the destination points. This apparently single-direction flow-in has so far been perceived by regional peoples as cultural hegemony, and the conservative approach has developed with the effort of re-challenging to the seemingly destructive attacks by the Western consumerism. As a slogan called out 'McWorld', the modern living style consists of wearing American products, such as Nike, Adidas, etc., having fast food such as McDonald's, spreading the violent images globally, or reversely using Dalai Lama symbol in Apple Electronics. Some resist for external cultural contexts to ooze into their own homes, or maybe just in speech while the proponents of liberalism give support for transportation of not only goods but also values. People may not welcome the cultural clashes, but the social mobility will bring about the interaction and expansion of people's worldviews as a source of global development including economic rising. The introverted attitudes are popular against popular culture, and this nationalist movement is considered ethical (Schweiker 2007).

A global ethic is not necessarily adopted by all and a large territorial, and organizational approval is appropriate to define value as an ethic (Dover, 2005, p. 32). A CSR model for consolidated ethical activities with four "institutional drivers": from the national business orders to its environment, the organization and a member in it (Hemphill and Lillevik 2011, p. 222).

How can you react to someone's move toward you, even he or she is located at a remote place far away from you (Dover 2005, p. 27)?

Effectuation or Practicality of Global Ethics

Now the reputation of being socially responsible and correspondingly, ethically aware is crucially important in their business of American and European companies and coherently, academies. Hence, the organizations or corporations adapt and apply the charters or codes of conduct including ethical values and norms while business ethics programs take place in the curriculum of graduate schools yet (Sroka and Lörinczy 2015, pp. 156–157). Practicing an ethic is far more effective than attempting to develop it consistently (Howse and Nicolaidis 2016, p. 262). In order to establish universal ethics, it is necessary to investigate and analyze social goals, social norms, ethical standards, and cultural values that belong to all the countries with the international business operations (Yeşil 2011, p. 185).

Macro-, meta-, meso-, and micro-level researches can largely contribute to developing ethical values with the recognition of a variety of contextual values by culture, tradition, region, and belief and their global transformation in time. One of the global projects, the World Values Survey, WVS, help social researchers compare the current and dynamic values sectorally and temporally. Global Value, as another example, is very largely funded project by EU within the scope of measuring and monitoring global business outcomes on sustainable development. It guides trans-national corporations to design and establish a framework and toolkit for the reasonable assessment and effective management (Stückelberger *et al.* 2016, p. 30).

The need for GBE formulation has led to various researches conducted by academic faculty, business groups, and international organizations. In this context, there are three out of many strategies reported, such as, the principles established by the international agreements and contracts (NAFTA, Global Warming Treaty, OECDAnti Bribery Treaty, Infant Formula Agreement), the rules of global business (Caux Round Table's Principles for Business, The Global Sullivan Principles, the United Nations Global Compact with Business) and individual voluntary initiatives of business managers. In addition, the academicians perform several studies in the scientific context for setting GBE principles and standards. Furthermore, there are also the ones produced by the ecclesiastics of major religions (Küng 1997). O'Brien (2009, p. 104) indicated that GBE is inevitable for global corporate and in forming GBE there are three considerable strategies. The first strategy is to find the parallel ethical standards between different cultures and use them to set GBE standards. For the meeting on common ground, the second one is to find the common ethical standards accepted within the varied cultures and assess them in the GBE framework. Another one is to discover the best creative practices worldwide that can be accepted by all, and apply these cases for the purpose (Yeşil 2011, pp. 186–187).

A leader organization should be assigned to identify the common global ethical principles and do planning, organizing, directing, coordinating, and auditing. This corporation can be either one of the current institutions, corporations or groups or above them (Yeşil 2011, p. 200).

The underlying approach of the Universal Declaration of Human Rights adopted by United Nations that protects any nationality, creed, race, gender, class, or political affiliation promotes one global community having core ethical values valid for any person or people interdependent in the world (Issitt 2016). That all humans who give and take support for this universalist approach is raising hopes for the establishment of generally accepted ethical standards.

For the reflections of global ethics, we should pay attention to common international movements on global ideologies, religions, human rights, environmental issues. If the world's peoples share some values and ideas in freedom of speech and democratic rights, we can definitely manage the challenges in cultivating the global ethics. Once there is a consensus made on global ethics, or better as the number of agreements is increasing, business and social ethics got influenced by these positive moves in the meaning of closing any gaps (Yeşil 2011, p. 188).

Is the global business ethics targeting just at prevention against big companies mostly located in the West in order not to exploit the resources of wretched people in the East? Is it for the sake of human rights or sustainable life? Issitt (2016) points out that global ethics have been transformed into the legislative instruments, the activist movements, and the great-value works. That is, this transformation is from mind to hand, from the abstract to concrete world, like 'creation'. Global ethics is being generated as a phenomenon by philosophers and applied as a practice by politicians. We consider that this process requires high sensitivity to involve all people ranging from the ones having high IQ to those with high EQ and blend both their thoughts and feelings because ethics is either of mind or heart or either of cognition or emotion.

Between the Western to the Eastern world, we cannot escape from the table, disengage from others, even if it seems to be the easiest way, in consideration that we are dependent on each other because the natural resources necessary for energy generation mostly exist in the East and the economic and military power in the West. It should also be kept in mind that we, unfortunately, inherit from our history hostilities and revenge especially between both. Under these circumstances, there have been highly heated debates on globalization and for the last two decades on global ethics, which are fed by activists, academicians, and policymakers from different parts of the world. Nevertheless, is there any hope for seeing the happy end? Or is the situation enduring that show must go on and it never ends? Do we not have to catch the hunt or is it the end product just keeping in touch with one another on a reasonable platform? On no account, people should not stop seeking ways to discuss the issues and develop the values in ethics, ranging from the liberals in the North West to the fanatics in the North East, to the natives in the South of the World (Drydyk 2014, p. 21).

Considerations to Take Steps in Global Business Ethics

There is a strong relationship between contextual or local and global ethics, and we cannot neglect this interdependency in establishing global ethical values and standards. If we aim to help global ethics diffuse the local tribes, communities or any groups, we should take into consideration the individual cultures, beliefs, political, and economic contexts that interact with global acquisitions. For instance, the environmental problems have recently been the most remarkable issues in the international arena. Correspondingly, an African belief that all realities are continuum and harming the nature is immoral would implicitly contribute to developing a global ethical standard against the environmental 'crimes'. With this, global and contextual ethics are like two poles of a magnet. Nonetheless, the protectionism of local sections and the domination of global framework will, in time, harm this negotiable process (Stückelberger *et al.* 2016, p. 27).

Globalization might not be welcomed by locally settled inhabitants mostly because of the negative perception against its exploitative part, however from this view; it should not be inferred that the single solution is taking down shuttles against business. Instead, with rising international dialogues the most important alternative is to establish the business ethical values, rules and standards even valid for all over the world by supporting with legal instruments.

The global business ethical process should contain the universal rules and principles taking place in the multinational agreements legally binding corporations, such as (Yeşil, 2011, pp. 192–193):

- United Nations Universal Declaration on Human Rights (UDHR, 1948)
- European Convention on Human Rights (ECHR, 1950)
- Helsinki Final Act (1975)
- OECD Guidelines for Multinational Enterprises (1976)

- ILO Tripartite Declaration of Principles concerning Multinational Enterprises and Social Policy (MNE Declaration) (1997)
- UN Code of Conduct on Transnational Corporations (1972)

The first two are of human rights binding governments and indirectly corporations. Helsinki Act encompasses the measures of environmental protection as well. All the agreements have several basic points, such below (Yeşil 2011, pp. 193–194):

- Working Conditions and Employment Policies
- Health and Social Security Standards
- Protection of Clients' Rights
- Environmental Protection
- Political Dues
- Fundamental Human Rights and Freedoms

All these rules restrict the operations of multinational enterprises and identify the guidelines on what actions they should take in many areas of activity. In addition to that list, such agreements as (Yeşil 2011, p. 194):

- NAFTA
- Global Warming Treaty
- OECD Anti Bribery Treaty
- Infant Formula Agreement

Stückelberger's six models of Global Ethics are presented in the Tab. 1 (Stückelberger et al. 2016, pp. 32–33).

Discussions over absolute concepts – Domination Model (DM)
DM *plus* exclusion of others' values – Confrontation Model (CM)
Amalgamation of diversity – Syncretisation Model (opposite of CM)
Combination of global with contextual values – Contextualisation Model (ConM) (e.g., justice with gender justice)
Strengthening interior entity against exterior domination – Regionalization Model (from the 1990s), Asian (from Malaysia), European (against Islam), African (mainly Pan-African) Values
Concretization of global values at local site– Glocalisation Model (another form of ConM)

Global ethics is expected to be more specific than ethics, or if not the nuances between two concepts would be indistinguishable. Global concepts are more practical than philosophical arguments in accordance with the objectives of

Tab. 1: Six Models of Global Ethics Source: (Stückelberger *et al.* 2016, p. 32)

Model	Description	Examples
1 **Domination**	'We have the truth' one model is valid for all	Some religious ethics
2 **Confrontation**	'You or me': Clash of Civilisations	Fundamentalism
3 **Syncretisation**	'All are the same': Forget the differences	Mystic ethics, new age
4 **Contextualisation**	'Global values adapted to my context'	Islamic Banking in my country
5 **Regonalisation**	'We have the same values in our region'	'Asian Values' 'African Culture'
6 **Glocalisation**	'Think global, act local'	Global Climate Justice, local energy saving

globalization. For this purpose, the points and cases in global actions are focused on more than the areas and comments in ethical discussions. Furthermore, without cross-border relations, the global ethical discussion cannot go beyond its nature of social matters. The harmless to living organisms including humans should be added into the global ethical discussion not alone but with international cooperation. This equal consideration can become untied because of disagreements on the harms suffered, and therefore the concept of "perceived harm" is produced to undermine the stipulation of harmless that in effect gain ethical aspects into global issues (Drydyk 2014, p. 20).

Application Examples

To exemplify the application of global business ethics, the "Statement of Ethics" is a good one out of Walmart's a couple of global policies and provides single guidance to its business partners at the varied locations. However, the local market conditions might be changeable, and correspondingly the ethical policies need to be separately developed by each local unit from the central charter or the peripheral sub-policies. The Company just need to know all the specific strategies, and that's it! If a policy or an action was seen by an individual working at the site as unethical, he or she would communicate to the higher officer, the Legal Department or the Global Ethics unit (Walmart, 3).

In addition, the firm has established an uninterrupted hotline called Global Ethics Helpline specific for the partners from all over the world, linguistically supported by most of the local dialects. With a very sensitive approach, this service is outsourced and the callers' information is kept secret unless any legal requirements. To protect and respect the associate's privacy, the service provider gives just the content of a complaint or an offer to Global Ethics and the record is traced merely with a case number and he or she will be given feedback at a certain time upon his or her will (Walmart, 8).

A number of international companies such as Kellogg, Coca-Cola, Colgate, Pepsi, Rolls-Royce, etc., have identified their own business ethics and hearken to these in their global operations. For instance, Kellogg has formulated the ethical principles and shares these rules with their stakeholders on their website, www.kelloggcompany.com . This firm would like their employees to understand these ethical standards and act in this framework. Moreover, it is asking for their clients to be having high ethical standards. Also, on the websites of Colgate (www.colgate.com) and Rolls-Royce (www.rolls-royce.com), their global business ethical principles were released and shared with the global community. Hundreds of companies that are operating in the international area communicate their global business ethics to their stakeholders on their websites (Yeşil 2011, p. 190).

Monitoring the Compliance with the Ethical Values

Culture affects the effectiveness of organizing the inter- and intra-cultural relationships with global business partners. It is crucial to standardize the process of motivation and evaluation as regards to these bonds on a global scale. A multidimensional cultural framework relates theoretical distinctions to the dimensions of individuality, power distance, and avoidance from ambiguity. These three dimensions in culture are theoretically associated with the behavioral perspective of relationship development (Grifitth *et al.* 2000, p. 304).

Program standardization, to a great extent, differs from process standardization for relationship development with its particular strategies in managing the relationship. The latter is to build the universal principles for specific relationships like trust, commitment, satisfaction, etc. (Griffith et al. 2000, p. 304).

The strategy of standardization might be ineffective in the process due to different levels of intense cultural relationships so that the corporations should make sensitive measurements in considering the potential setbacks in advancing the relationship with international business partners having a different cultural identity (Griffith *et al.* 2000, p. 304).

A possible way of monitoring the employees' compliance with global ethical values is a social cognitive theory that is based on the fact that one formulates his or her own spiritual and motivational sources in accordance with value judgments (Domino *et al.* 2015, pp. 454–455).

In this theory, human behaviors are the results of the repetitive self-assessments to alter the individual code of conduct if any, in accordance with environmental changes and of course ethical atmosphere. A difference of personal ethics and ethical climate, even in an organization, is supposed to be closed subject to continuous evaluations, potential regulations, and lacking reprehensions. For instance, a manager will try to fix the gap through adaptation to the ethical climate of a company, possibly exploitative order against labor rights (Domino *et al.* 2015, pp. 455–456).

Critical Views on Global Ethics Formulation

The criticism of global ethics may hover around which rights will be protected. If we accept the majority votes for a right to shield, we may leave out a few exploitative or oppressive actions. A moral belief that has been ruled out in the ethical system could be "majorly" violated. In practice, the contemporary approach to global ethics cannot be effective in being universal though global organizations like the UN has gone for shared well-being (Issitt 2016).

As a "victory" for global capitalism, globalization has led to the inequality worldwide and the destruction of regional contexts for cultural homogeneity as well as the exploitation of underdeveloped countries, environmental pollution, and rendering any resources and relations commodity for sale. If so, most people may not typically consider a theological and ethical value in globalization (Sezgül 2009, p. 507).

Due to the nature of morality and accordingly ethics, some philosophers propose that a universal ethics is impractical that their basic source is derived from a specific culture and history. As an example, Islam's stance against iconography is considered a moral belief and so should be ethical. An artistic depiction of the Prophet Muhammad is perceived as an unjust attack on Islam and Muslims, whereas, in an ethical system this can be regarded as free and moral. According to the consequentialist, those icons are unethical. As such, many moral beliefs like religion and/or culture are so unique that they cannot be generalized (Issitt 2016).

It is a fact that the share of income distribution, the level of development, and the rights to legal remedies of the engineers in the developed countries is much better than those of the engineers of our country. The first ones prefer the conformity with to the contradiction against the political order. Under these circumstances, the engineers are to formulate the ethical principles for the purpose of securing his or her own position and defending the established order. As the great majority of engineers in Turkey have their economic interests conflicting with the order, they act in an inconsistent way with the state's ideology. This situation is another indicator of the impossibility of convergence in the context of the single ethical code. The moral judgments of one culture are not affirmed with those of another (Karababa *et al.* 2006, p. 89).

Our Remarks

Globalization is continuously increasing and getting more valuable day by day. Developing some standard strategies is required to establish the order and rules in accordance with the shifts and transformations caused by globalization. In this sense, one of the most important criteria is the concept of ethics to enhance and maintain this necessary order. In international affairs, the universal ethical values and standards that have the power of legal sanction over all the nations in the world should be formulated rather than the contextual rules and procedures variable for the national cultures. The reason is why lack of the standardization of the ethical values underlies the international crises experienced, particularly the global economic crisis. The global ethical values should be picked out as the ethics in question here, which is supra-cultural and includes all nations and the international systems. On the other hand, these considered values must be a power to enhance and accelerate the globalization process.

The most valuable topics on contributing to and maintaining the globalization hover over economics. In consideration that the global community area encompasses the area of economic affairs, we can infer that global ethics fundamentally aim at social relations. Thus, the basic issue and starting point for global ethics is the performance of the ethical values in industrial and business sectors. All stakeholders in global business should concentrate on how they can more humanize the economic mechanism since it is obvious that the underlying factors of social conflicts and threats are the economic developments and crises. The ethics concept is so global that it cannot differ from the fields of economy and business.

There will commonly become a supra-national consensus when the practicality of the formulated standards of global business ethics is dealt with, and the suffered crises can swiftly be overcome the most appropriately. Among all world nations, necessary measures will be taken on such issues as trust, justice, equality, fairness, accountability, international mutual respect, non-discrimination. As long as global business ethical values are identified and practiced, their defects will be recognized, and they will be persistently developed, and hence the hoped environment of trust and order will probably be established in the social and economic life, even if to some extent. The august leaders and businesses of tomorrow will have to consider and make decisions in a decentralized way, and besides the future will belong to those of who can adopt the supra-cultural, reasonable beliefs, attitudes, behaviors and value judgments for all nations and act in this way.

Bibliography

Akçay, Deniz / Sarp Bağcan: "Intercultural Communication and Crisis Management: Ikea Case Study". *Global Media Journal TR Edition* 7(13), 2016, pp. 169–187

Çelikdemir, Deniz Zaptçıoğlu / Irem Tukel: "Incorporating Ethics into Strategic Management with regards to Generation Y's view of Ethics". *Procedia - Social and Behavioral Sciences* 207, 2015, pp. 528–535.

Chen, Guo-Ming: "Theorizing Global Community as Cultural Home in the New Century". *International Journal of Intercultural Relations* 46, 2015, pp. 73–81.

Cheng, Chung-Ying: "Moral Reflection on Global Crisis: Learning Harmony and Ethics as a Solution". *Procedia - Social and Behavioral Sciences* 77, 2013, pp. 90–101.

Dalpour, Shahrokh W.: "Interpreting Global Earth". *International Journal of Economics and Finance Studies* (4)2, 2012, pp. 267–275.

Desai, Ashay B. / Terri Rittenburg: "Global Ethics: An Integrative Framework For MNEs", Journal of Business Ethics, (16)8, 1997, pp. 791–800.

Domino, Madeline Ann / Stephen C. Wingreen / James E. Blanton: "Social Cognitive Theory: The Antecedents and Effects of Ethical Climate Fit on Organizational Attitudes of Corporate Accounting Professionals—A Reflection of Client Narcissism and Fraud Attitude Risk". *Journal of Bussiness Ethics* 131, 2015, pp. 453–467.

Dover, Nigel: "The Earth Charter and Global Ethics". *Worldviews* 8(1), 2004, pp. 15–28.

Dover, Nigel: "The Nature and Scope of Global Ethics and the Relevance of the Earth Charter". *Journal of Global Ethics* (1)1, 2005, pp. 25–43.

Drydyk, Jay: "Foundational Issues: How Must Global Ethics be Global?". *Journal of Global Ethics*, (10)1, 2014, pp. 16–25.

Engel, J. Ronald: "A Convenant Model of Global Ethics". *Worldviews* 8(1), 2004, pp. 29–46.

Falk, Richard: "Hans Küng's Crusade: Framing a Global Ethic". *International Journal of Politics, Culture and Society* (13)1, 1999, pp. 63–81.

Gebhardt, Giinther: "Towards a Global Ethic". *The Ecumenical Review* 52(4), 2000, pp. 503–510.

George, William P: "Looking for a Global Ethic? Try International Law". *The Journal of Religion* 76(3), 1996, pp. 359–382.

Griffith, David A. / Michael Y. Hu / John K. Ryans Jr.: "Process Standardization across Intra- and Inter-Cultural Relationships". *Journal of International Business Studies* (31)2, 2000, pp. 303–324.

Gueorguiev, Tzvetelin Kirilov / Borisov Sakakushev, "Current Advances in the Standardization of Management Systems", Journal of Thermal Engineering 2(6), 2016, pp. 971-977.

Hemphill, Thomas A. / Waheeda Lillevik: "The Global Economic Ethic Manifesto: Implementing a Moral Values Foundation in the Multinational Enterprise". *Journal of Business Ethics* 101, 2011, pp. 213–230.

Howard, Anthony: "A new global ethic", *Journal of Management Development* 29(5), 2010, pp. 506–517.

Howse, Robert / Nicolaidis Kalypso: "Toward a Global Ethics of Trade Governance: Subsidiarity Writ Large". *Law and Contemporary Problems* 79, 2016, pp. 259–283.

Issitt, Micah: "Global Ethics", Salem Press Encyclopedia, Research Starters, 2016, http://eds.b.ebscohost.com/eds/detail/detail?vid=1&sid=2d97a25d-3409-49fe-a17c-86c39d19ac6c%40sessionmgr104&bdata=Jmxhbmc9dHI mc2l0ZT1lZHMtbGl2ZQ%3d%3d#AN=101071976&db=ers, (Access date 26.07.2017).

Karababa, İhsan, "Küreselleşme Etik Kodlar ve Örgütler", Elektrik Mühendisleri Odası Yayınları: Ankara. 2006.

Küng, Hans / Klaus M. Leisinger / Josef Wieland: "*Manifesto Global Economic Ethic Consequences and Challenges for Global Businesses*". Published by the Global Economic Foundation, Germany, 2009, pp. 1–14.

Küng, Hans: "A Global Ethic in an Age of Globalization". *Business Ethics Quarterly* 7(3), 1997, pp. 17–32.

Küng, Hans: "A Global Ethic in World Politics: The Middle Way Between "Real Politics" and "Ideal Politics"". *International Journal of Politics, Culture and Society* (13) 1, 1999, pp. 5–19.

Küng, Hans: "A New Global Economic Ethic: Now's the Time", 2009, pp. 19–21, http://www.weltethos.org/1-pdf/40-literatur/eng/Yale_Divinity_School_Journal.Pdf, (Access date 19.07.2017).

Küng, Hans: "Basic Trust as the Foundation of a Global Ethic". *International Review of Psychiatry* 13, 2001, pp. 94–100.

Liu, Lihua: "How We Chinese Should Relate to The Global Ethic". *Journal of Ecumenical Studies* (38)2/3, 2001, pp. 379–382.

Loye, David: "Can Science Help Construct a New Global Ethic? The Development and Implication of Moral Transformation Theory". *Zygon* (34)2, 1999, pp. 221–235.

Miller, George A. / Bam Dev Sharda: "Cultural and Organizatinal Structure: A Multinational Comparison". *International Review of Modern Sociology* (27)1, 1997, pp. 19–39.

Moellendorf, Darrel / Heather Widdows: "Global Ethics: A Short Reflection on Then and Now". *Journal of Global Ethics* (10)3, 2014, pp. 319–325.

Muck, Terry C.: "A Global Ethic Update". *Buddhist-Christian Studies* 17(1997), 1997, pp. 215–217.

O'Brien, Roderick: "Global Ethics: Beyond Local Leadership". *Journal of International Business Ethics* (2)1, 2009, pp. 102–106.

Parke, Michael R. / Myeong-Gu Seo: "The Role of Affect Climate in Organizational Effectiveness". *Academy of Management Review* (42)2, 2017, pp. 334–360.

Schweiker, William: "Whiter Global Ethics? Moral Consciousness and Global Cultural Flows". *Journal of Ecumenical Studies* (42)3, 2007, pp.425–439.

Sezgül, İbrahim: "Küreselleşme, Neo-Liberalizm ve Etik". *TÜBAV Bilim Dergisi* (2)4, 2009, pp. 504–509.

Shoham, Aviv: "Bounded Rationality, Examination Planning, Standardization of International Strategy, and Export Performance: A Structural Model". *Journal of International Marketing* (7)2, 1999, pp. 24–50.

Sroka, Włodzimierz / Marketa Lőrinczy: "The Perception of Ethics in Business: Analysis of Research Results". *Procedia Economics and Finance* 34, 2015, pp. 156–163.

Stückelberger, Christoph / Walter Fust / Obiora Ike: *"Global Ethics for Leadership - Values and Virtues for Life"*. The Globalethics.net: Ceneva. 2016.

Tayşir, Eyüp Ergün / Yener Pazarcık: "Business Ethics, Social Responsibility and Corporate Governance: Does the Strategic Management Field Really Care about These Concepts?". *Procedia - Social and Behavioral Sciences* 99, 2013, pp. 294–303.

Tepe, Harun, "Bir Felsefe Dalı Olarak Etik", Doğu Batı Düşünce Dergisi (1)4, 1998, pp. 11-27.

Vadastreanu, Adela Mariana / Dorin Maier / Andreea Maier: "Is the Success Possible in Compliance with Ethics and Deontology in Business?". *Procedia Economics and Finance* 26, 2015, pp. 1068–1073.

Walmart, Gobal Statement of Ethics, https://www.walmartethics.com/Landing.aspx., 2017, pp. 1–37, (Access date 17.07.2017).

Yardımlı, Aziz: Küreselleşme ve İş Etiği, TEİD Etik ve İtibar Derneği, http://www.teid.org/kuresellesme-ve-is-etigi/, 2014, (Access date 07.08.2017).

Yeşil, Salih: "Küresel İş Etiği Üzerine Alternatif Stratejiler, Eleştiriler ve Değerlendirmeler". *Elektronik Sosyal Bilimler Dergisi* (10)35, 2011, pp. 180–201.

Asuman Koç Yurtkur

Economic Analysis of Carbon Tax: Panel Causality Test

Abstract: Environmental pollution has become one of the most important problems that need to be carefully considered in terms of the rapidly developing and growing economies with globalization. The increase in carbon dioxide emissions brought by the growth processes has made the suggestion of global dimension solutions necessary. The carbon tax is at the forefront of the proposed solutions. It is the objective of studying the economic efficiency of carbon tax, which is a consumption tax on carbon dioxide emissions. In this framework, the causality relationship between carbon tax, carbon emissions and economic growth is being investigated by panel data analysis for 24 European countries. Findings indicate the existence of a one-way causality relationship between carbon tax and carbon emissions. In addition, a one-way causality relationship is found towards the growth of carbon tax.

Keywords: Carbon Tax, Economic Growth, Panel Causality Analysis

Introduction

The rapid increase in production activities, which started with the industrial revolution, has made energy consumption, which has become a global dimension due to excessive capacity utilization, as one of the most important issues to be included in the agenda. This process, involving issues such as global warming and climate change that need to be addressed on a global scale, has required a focus on the relationship between economic growth and environmental issues. For the first time, the relationship between growth and environmental pollution is discussed in the reports of Roma Club[1]. The process, which started with these

1 The Rome Club was founded in 1968. The aim of the club is to investigate the long-term causes and consequences of the increase in resource consumption in parallel with the increase in population in the world and the increase in environmental pollution due to the increase in consumption. Meadows et al. (1972) argue that the global system will collapse in the middle of the twenty-first century if uncontrolled growth continues with scarce resources, which are the result of the debate that they are beginning with the book "The Borders of the Growth". Thus, the Roma Club has been regarded as a constitution advocating that growth rates should be slowed (Bruvoll and Medin 2003, p. 28). The report provides a basis for the relationship between economic growth and

reports, led to a growing debate and work based on the relationship between environment and growth.

The Worldwatch Institute (2000) indicates that natural, air, soil and water pollution sooner or later will reach its natural capacity. For this reason, it is argued that some environmentalists grow up and consumption should be reduced. However, critics of Roma Club say that the relationship between growth and pollution is not at a certain rate to limit the growth model. Nevertheless, technological change and the discovery of new sources lead to the linkage of environmental problems to economic growth (Bruvoll and Medin 2003, p. 28) and thus the link between environment and growth becomes increasingly important.

Energy, in terms of countries, is an important resource that they use in their growth processes. Energy use, on the other hand, causes carbon emissions to rise and these gases, which are released, bring about the problem of global climate change. It is stated that carbon emission is the main factor that causes climate change. Countries need more energy for more production on the way of development, increasing the usage rate of fossil fuel (coal, oil, natural gas, etc.). The harm caused by carbon dioxide gases, which are the result of the use of fossil fuels, is also increasing parallel to the use rate. Therefore, the necessity of taking various measures in order to limit the consumption of fossil fuels is among the outstanding topics. In this context, some measures have been put in place to reduce the harm that fossil fuels have on the environment. Many legal and economic instruments such as regulation of regulations, fees, taxes and trade in pollution rights are among these. Environmental taxation is one of the economic instruments used in this sense. In this respect, the relationship between carbon tax, economic growth and carbon emissions in this study is studied economically with empirical results.

The Use of Energy and Climate Change Prevention: Carbon Tax

At the beginning of the 21st century, the main issues that human beings must struggle with are climate change and the precautions to be taken to prevent it. The main source of this basic concern is the use of energy. The fact that economies are generally dependent on energy consumption for economic growth, and therefore on fossil fuel use, makes it difficult to combat this problem. Activities such as promoting clean energy use and increasing renewable energy sources play an important role in preventing global climate change and at the same time

---

environmental policies. It is also pointed out that rapid economic growth will destroy the ecological balance.

meeting the energy needs of the world. European Union politics play an important role in ensuring this energy transfer (EEA 2017, p. 20).

The global climate is rapidly changing, posing increasingly serious risks for human health, economy and ecosystem. It is expressed in the EEA 2017 report that the effects of sea, storms, floods and drought rising in certain regions are more evident. It is stated that the most important factor in this situation is the use of fossil fuels. It is understood that most of the greenhouse gases emitted by the use of energy on a global scale come from carbon emissions from human activities such as heating, industry, transport and electricity use. It is reported that for Europe in 2015 the largest share of greenhouse gases is owned by energy processes and is 78% (EEA 2017, p. 20).

The Kyoto protocol is an environmental protocol with international relevance to ensure fighting on global warming and climate change. The protocol, which was signed in 1997 and entered into force in 2005, covers 160 countries. The aim of this protocol is to "ensure that the concentration of greenhouse gases in the atmosphere is balanced at levels that do not cause dangers." The protocol is a protocol aimed at reducing greenhouse gases and emission levels in countries with OECD member countries and transition economies and aiming to change global warming policies in these countries (Flavin and Dunn 1998). The protocol contains a subclass of gas such as carbon dioxide gas (CO2), methane gas (CH4), nitrogen oxide gas (N2O), sulfur hexafluoride (SF6), perfluorocarbons (PFCs) and hydrofluorocarbons (HC-FC) (Pehlivan and Demisbas 2008).

The Paris Treaty, which is a new agreement on the global scale after the 1997 Kyoto Protocol, is the first time for a global agreement and legally binding agreement. According to this agreement, 195 countries are obliged to reduce emissions in order to avoid climate change. However, under this reduction obligation, developed countries are expected to undertake more reduction commitments and to make absolute reductions while developing countries are expected to make a reduction compared to existing capacities in accordance with the principle of "common but differentiated liability". For the post-2050 period, the developed countries are expected to be in a position to provide zero emission (www.mfa.gov.tr).

The existence and the seriousness of ecological hazards such as environmental pollution and global warming have brought carbon taxation into the scope of environmental taxes that are applied within the framework of green tax reform. The existence of carbon taxation has become a subject that has been advocated by economic circles and international organizations since the early 1990s (EEA 1996; OECD 1996). Emission based taxation has significant advantages because it is a market-based tax. The direct effect of taxation is to increase the costs of fossil fuel use which cause carbon emissions through the price mechanism. After the determination of tax rates, the cost increase on emission-intensive goods will lead to price increases as it will result in low profit rates. Therefore, market forces will pursue a cost-effective way to reduce emissions. The return of taxation from the financial system under the name of carbon taxation has an indirect effect by changing investment and consumption patterns and empowering effects (Baranzini et al. 2000, pp: 395–396).

The carbon tax is defined as a consumption tax solely from carbon-containing fuels (Zhang 2004, p. 508). In addition, a carbon tax is also defined as a tax per unit of emission and fossil fuels (Al-Abdullah 1999, p. 5). The difficulty in determining the amount of carbon emissions leads to the definition of carbon tax that can be taken in two ways. Accordingly, this tax can be taken as the carbon tax for each ton of carbon emissions left in the air, or as a carbon tax per unit of energy (Baranzini et al., 2000).

Friedman et al. (2012) state that a carbon tax on carbon dioxide emissions could be a strong policy in the face of market failures, such as externalities. Wu et al. (2006) state that the calculation and monitoring of the carbon content of fossil fuels are easy, and thus the tax burden can be distributed to all areas. It is stated that the distribution effect of the tax will help to protect the environment (Pehlivan and Demirbaş 2007) because increasing costs are expected to encourage the passage of clean technologies (Green 2008). In this respect, it is stated that carbon taxation is less costly than the carbon independence system (Parry 1997). If the income from the carbon tax can offset other taxes, it is expected that carbon tax will be effective in enhancing economic efficiency.

The carbon tax supports the internalization of economic externalities caused by greenhouse gas emissions, which is the problem of global warming caused by fossil fuel users. In addition, a carbon tax is classified under the Pigouvian tax approach, which advocates the internalization of negative externalities through the price mechanism and is described as the "polluter pays" principle adopted in the Rio Declaration on Environment and Development in 1992 (Kovancılar 2001). The tradition of Pigouvian taxation serves the purpose of reaching the social optimum (Baumol 1972). In this context, it can be said that carbon tax is the social welfare-enhancing effect and therefore this tax rate should be equal to the environmental costs.

The problem of environmental pollution becoming a global problem is an issue on the agenda since the 1970s. With the existence of joint initiatives such as the Kyoto Protocol to solve the problem at the global level, some regulations of the European Community have been the subject for the first time to produce common policies. There have been some developments in this struggle since the

1990s, and the years of carbon taxation began in the 2000s when environmental problems began to increase rapidly. It was first implemented in 1990 in Finland to slow down the rate of energy consumption and to reduce the harmful effects caused by this situation. Then Norway provided the mitigating effects of carbon tax and carbon dioxide emissions within the framework of tax reform in the period 1991–1992. In the same period, the Netherlands and Denmark also applied carbon tax. Therefore, the importance given by the European countries to this taxation activity to increase the environmental sensitivity emerges. For this reason, the scope of work is limited to European countries.

At this point, the healing effects of carbon tax on the environment need to be examined. The positive effects of carbon taxation on the environment are attributed to various factors (Baranzini et al. 2000, pp. 406–407):

- Carbon tax incomes should be used in order to achieve sustainable development and to prevent global climate change. Some of the revenues obtained for this purpose can be used to subsidize renewable energy sources or be used to support renewable energy investments and research and development activities that do not lead to energy saving and CO2 emission reduction.
- Carbon taxes should tax the products that are at the top of the energy chain. In this case, both the cost of administering the vaccine is reduced and the ability of the market to respond to price changes increases.
- The tax must be indexed to inflation in order for the effect on the costs to be permanent.
- In order to be able to realize the discounts foreseen in the emission amount, the tax rates must be adjustable considering the emission amount.

The relationship between environmental pollution and per capita national income is theoretically based on the Environmental Kuznets Curve (EKC) hypothesis. Based on the EKC hypothesis, Grossman and Krueger (1991, 1995) first established this relationship between environmental pollution and income level. With this study, the relationship between economic growth and income inequality has been transformed into income and environmental pollution. According to the EKC hypothesis, environmental pollution increases during the first years of growth, while pollution decreases in the later stages of growth (Dinda 2004, p. 433). Agras and Chapman (1999) also show that income is the most important indicator of environmental quality. The acceptance of growth as a prerequisite for increasing the quality of the environment has enabled the creation of literature that tries to establish the relationship between economic growth and environmental factors. The studies on carbon taxation within these tax rates also provide an increasingly widespread literature.

Literature Review

A limited number of studies have been conducted in the literature on the effect of environmental (carbon) tax on carbon dioxide emissions and economic growth. Different findings were encountered in these studies. In some studies it has been determined that carbon taxation has reduced the environmental pollution (Bruvoll and Medin 2003; Dökmen 2012; Bayar and Şaşmaz 2016) and in some studies carbon tax has not had a significant effect on environmental pollution (Hotunluoğlu and Tekeli 2007; Friedman et al. 2012). There are studies in the literature that investigate the causality relationship between carbon emissions and economic growth (Gülmez 2015; Bayramoğlu and Yurtkur 2016).

Bruvoll and Medin (2003) investigated the impact of environmental pollution on eight factors in 1980–1996 in Norway using variables such as economic growth, population, comparative production quantities and changes in energy use. According to the findings of the study using the decomposition method, the economic growth causes a significant increase in the amount of emissions. It has been found that the increase in population and energy use also causes an increase in carbon emissions.

In the study by Dökmen (2012), the relationship between the panel VAR method and the 1996–2010 data for 29 European countries and environmental taxation and economic growth was examined. The findings of the study are that statistical and positive effects have been achieved in the face of a shock in the environmental tax. Thus, it is theoretically and empirically put forward that environmental tax increases economic growth.

Bayar and Şaşmaz (2016) examine the causality relationship between carbon tax, economic growth and carbon emissions for the period of 1996–2011 for 5 European countries. The result of the study suggests that there is a one-way causality relation to carbon dioxide emissions from economic growth.

Gülmez (2015), in the study of the relationship between air pollution and economic growth in terms of 24 OECD countries, found that economic growth increases the long-term air pollution. According to the results of the causality test, it is seen that there is not any causality relation from the air pollution to the economic growth while the one-way causality relation from the economic growth to the air pollution is detected.

Bayramoglu and Yurtkur (2016) are investigating the relationship between carbon emissions and economic growth in Turkey. Using the linear and nonlinear cointegration techniques, the study for the 1960–2010 period found a nonlinear positive relationship between economic growth and carbon emissions for the long term.

Tekin and Şaşmaz (2016) examined the effect of environmental taxes on environmental pollution in 25 EU countries in 1995–2012 period. As a result of the study, it has been determined that total environmental taxes and transportation taxes have no effect on environmental pollution and energy taxes have a negative effect on environmental pollution.

Lin and Li (2011) examined the effect of carbon tax on per capita CO2 emissions using the dynamic panel regression method in five European countries which applied carbon tax in the period 1981–2008. As a result of the study, it was found that (i) carbon tax had a negative effect on per capita emissions in Finland and Norway, (ii) carbon tax had a positive effect on per capita CO2 emissions, (iii) no statistically significant relationship had been established in Denmark, Sweden, and the Netherlands. In some countries, it has been stated that carbon tax has a low impact on CO2 emissions because of the application of certain tax exemptions on certain energy-intensive industries.

Hotunoglu and Tekeli (2007) investigate the emission reduction effect of carbon taxation with data from 18 European countries. According to the results of the regression analysis made with 1995–2003 period data, it turns out that carbon tax is not effective enough to reduce carbon emissions. Friedman et al. (2012) state that local effects of regional or national policy changes on carbon emissions need to be examined. They have reached the conclusion that the additional tax increase will be less effective in the regional study using the Markal model.

Data Set

In this study, using the Dumitrescu and Hurlin (2012) causality test, the interaction between carbon tax, economic growth and carbon emissions in 24 European countries during 1995–2013 was analyzed. The number of European countries in employment is limited to the countries where common denominator can be reached (Austria, Belgium, Bulgaria, Czech Republic, Denmark, Ireland, Greece, Spain, France, Italy, Cyprus, Lithuania, Luxembourg, Malta, Netherlands, Norway, Poland, Portugal, Romania, Slovakia, Finland, Sweden, Switzerland, United Kingdom).

The data used for the study were obtained from Eurostat and the World Bank. Energy taxes issued by Eurostat are used as carbon tax (TAX). Carbon emissions (CO2) are metric tonnes per capita. Economic growth (GDP) is represented by using real GDP variable. The names of the variables, their symbols, and the sources from which they are retrieved are shown in Tab. 1.

E-views and Gauss codes were used for the empirical analysis of the study.

Tab. 1: Variables, Symbols and Data Sources Used in Work

Variables	Symbols	Sources
Carbon Tax	TAX	Eurostat
CO2 Emissions	CO2	World Bank Indicator
GDP (per capita)	GDP	World Bank Indicator

Methodology

In the study, the time dimension of the data set (T = 18) and the cross-section dimension (N = 24) were formed. Where the time dimension is smaller than the cross-section size (T <N), the cross-sectional dependence between the variables is controlled by Pesaran (2004) CD LM test. CIPS (Cross-Sectional Augmented), ISP (Im, Shin and Pesaran (2003)) and CADF (Cross-Sectionally Augmented Dickey-Fuller) tests developed by Pesaran (2007) were used as unit root test. Finally, the causality relation between variables was analyzed by Dumitrescu and Hurlin (2012) causality test.

This section describes the tests used in the analysis. Cross-sectional dependency test, panel unit root test and Dumitrescu and Hurlin (2012) causality test are theoretically considered.

Cross-Sectional Dependence Test

Panel data analysis leads to advantages such as causality testing, more flexible movements than time series analysis, and more effective observation with shorter time periods (Bozoklu and Yılancı 2013, p. 175). With panel data analysis, it is possible to reveal the causality relation more effectively by using more observations. As a matter of fact, Dumitrescu and Hurlin (2012) emphasize that it is highly probable that an economic situation in a country is valid in terms of other countries in terms of a valid causality relationship. In other words, a shock in a country is likely to affect other countries as well.

The most important problem that can be encountered when using panel data analysis when forecasts are done is the cross-sectional dependence problem. Therefore, firstly it is necessary to test the cross-sectional dependence. Breusch and Pagan (1980), Pesaran (2004) state that the results are considerably affected when the cross-sectional dependence is not taken into consideration. Cross-sectional dependence test results should be decided on the next stage tests. In order to obtain effective estimation results, it is necessary to apply unit root tests that take cross-sectional dependence into account (Nazlıoğlu, 2010: 104).

If the cross-sectional dependence is determined in the series, second generation methods should be used.

Studies on cross-sectional dependence first started with the CDLM test by Breusch and Pagan (1980). Afterwards, Pesaran (2004) tested Cross-Section Dependence (CD) and Pesaran et al. (2008) LM test (LMadj) cross-sectional dependence tests have emerged. The existence of cross-sectional dependence is significant when the time dimension is greater than the cross-section size (T> N); Breusch / Pagan (1980) CD LM1 test, when the time dimension is equal to the cross-section size (T = N); with Pesaran (2004) CD LM2 test, when the time dimension is smaller than the cross-section size (T < N); Pesaran (2004) CD LM test is controlled. CD LM Test:

$$CDLM = \sqrt{\frac{2T}{N(N-1)}}\left(\sum_{i=j}^{N-1}\sum_{j=i+1}^{N}\hat{\rho}_{ij}\right) \sim N(0.1)$$

is determined by the equation, the test statistic to be obtained here is asymptotically standard normal distribution (Pesaran 2004). Test hypotheses:

H0: There is no cross-sectional dependence.
H1: Cross-sectional dependence.

When the probability value of the test is less than 0.05, the H0 hypothesis is rejected at the level of 5% significance. Moreover, the cross-sectional dependence between the panellular units (Pesaran 2004). The LM test statistic is as follows (Pesaran et al. 2008):

$$LM_{adj} = \sqrt{\frac{2}{N(N-1)}\sum_{i=j}^{N-1}\sum_{j=i+1}^{N}\frac{(T-k)\hat{\rho}_{ij}^{2}-\mu_{Tij}}{v_{Tij}}}$$

In this study, the presence of cross-sectional dependence in variables, using Gaussian codes; the existence of cross-sectional dependence in the equation was checked using Eviews codes.

Panel Unit Root Test

In order to avoid conflicting test results with misleading test results or misleading analysis results, it is necessary to examine whether the serial process is stable over time or not. The panel unit root tests are divided into two groups according to whether the cross sections are independent of each other or not. First-generation tests assume that there is no correlation between the units. Fisher ADF (Maddala and Wu 1999), Breitung (2001), Hadri (2000); Fisher type test (Choi, 2001), Levin, Lin and Chu (2002), and Im, Pesaran and Shin (IPS, 2003) are the best known of first-generation tests (Tatoğlu 2013, p. 199).

Second-generation tests assume that there is a correlation between the panel unit root tests and the series of units, that is, cross-sectional dependence. In the second-generation tests, the assumption that all series have a common autocorrelation coefficient is made flexible, allowing each unit to have its own autocorrelation coefficient instead of a common autocorrelation coefficient, and is valued in terms of p units. In these tests, the basic hypothesis "no unit is stable" is tested against the alternative hypothesis that "at least one of the units is stationary" (Tatoglu 2013, p. 212).

Since the cross-sectional dependence of the countries forming the study panel was determined, the stability of the series was tested with CADF from the second generation unit root tests and the stability of the equation with CIPS.

In CADF test, the error term for all series and each series being specific to its environment, it is assumed that it consists of two parts. The form of the equation in this case is as follows:

$$Y_{it} = \beta_i Y_{i,t-1} + u_t$$

and

$$u_{it} = \lambda_i f_t + \varepsilon_{it}$$

In this equation, *ft*; represent an unobservable common item, it is always assumed to be stationary. ε_{it} is a sequence-specific element, which is independent and identical. In this model, it is assumed that the cross-sectional dependence is due to the presence of the unobserved common element. Test hypotheses are as follows:

H_0:bi=o Unit root has.
H_1:bi<0 Unit root has not.

In this test, CADF statistics are calculated for each country first. These calculated values are compared with the table values calculated by Monte Carlo simulation

Tab. 2: Cross-Sectional Dependence Test Results

Tests	Test Statistics	Prob. Value
LM (Breusch and Pagan, 1980)	2335.390	0.00
LM adj. (Pesaran vd., 2008)	86.63194	0.00
LM CD (Pesaran, 2004)	27.73736	0.00

by Pesaran (2006). When the calculated CADF statistic is less than the table critical value, H_0 is rejected. That is, it is decided that there is no unit root in this country's data and that the shocks are temporary.

In order to be able to decide the unit root existence in the whole panel, the CIPS statistic is calculated by the following formula, taking the arithmetic mean of the CADF statistics for each country. Pesaran (2007) obtains the CIPS statistic by taking a simple arithmetic average of each series as follows:

$$CIPS = \frac{\sum_{t=1}^{N} CADF_t}{N}$$

Calculated CADF and CIPS values are compared with Pesaran (2007) table values. If the calculated CIPS value is less than the table value, Ho is rejected. In this case, it is decided that for all the countries that make up the panel, the relevant unit root is not and that the shocks are temporary. Table values and calculated statistics are given in Tab. 3.

Dumitrescu and Hurlin Causality Test

Causality analysis was originally developed by Granger (1969). This analysis helps to examine whether variables outside the relevant variable provide useful information when estimating the future value of a variable (Bozoklu and Yılancı 2013, p. 174). As a heterogeneous version of the Granger (1969) causality test, the Dumitrescu and Hurlin (2012) panel causality test appeared. This test considers both heterogeneity and cross-sectional dependence (Dumitrescu and Hurlin 2012, p. 1450). The panel causality test of Dumitrescu and Hurlin (2012) takes into account the cross-sectional dependence between panel-constituting countries, whether the time dimension (T) is greater than the cross-section size (N) or less, and also produces effective results in unbalanced panel data sets (Bayar and Şaşmaz, 2016: 37). Dumitrescu and Hurlin (2012), within the framework of their simulations, $Z_{N,T}^{HNC}$ test statistic revealed that this statistic is very strong not only in the panels with only a small number of units but also in the case of incorrectly determining the length of the lag (Bozoklu and Yılancı 2013, p. 177). Dumitrescu and Hurlin (2012) calculate three different statistical values in the panel causality test. When the null hypothesis is rejected according to these statistical values, it is stated that causality relation exists between variables. The statistical values are calculated according to the following formulas (Dumitrescu and Hurlin 2012, pp. 1453–1454):

Tab. 3: CADF and CIPS Panel Unit Root Test Results

		Constant		Constant +Trend		Constant		Constant +Trend		Constant		Constant +Trend
		CO2		CO2		GDP		GDP		TAX		TAX
Country	p	CADF Statistics	P	CADF Statistics	p	CADF Statistics	p	CADF Statistics	P	CADF Statistics	p	CADF Statistics
Austria	1	−1.8378	3	−3.9204	2	−1.0712	2	−1.3142	2	−0.8556	4	−2.8934
Begium	3	-0.0001	2	-6.2457	2	−1.6057	2	−2.2453	4	-6.5947	4	−0.7600
Bulgaria	1	−0.9923	1	−1.8933	1	−2.9769	3	−1.4778	2	−0.8474	4	−3.4629
Cybrus	1	−2.0849	1	−1.7113	2	−1.0385	2	−1.3259	1	−1.7279	1	−1.9587
Czech Rep.	1	−1.8716	1	−3.4827	2	−1.8142	2	−1.1456	4	−3.7145	4	1.5528
Denmark	1	−4.0011	1	−4.0125	1	−2.6532	2	−2.7789	1	−1.4479	4	−1.7587
Finland	3	−3.9292	1	−0.8557	1	−1.6590	2	−2.1821	2	−3.2797	4	−1.7287
France	1	−0.1379	1	−1.8489	1	−2.0563	2	−3.0760	1	0.0800	1	−0.7457
Greece	1	−3.3490	1	−2.3092	1	−2.0414	1	−1.9455	3	−2.5186	3	−2.2170
İreland	1	−1.4397	1	−2.5718	3	−0.4227	2	−1.1378	1	−2.4593	4	−1.8004
İtaly	1	−4.1573	1	−4.2102	5	0.0000	1	−1.0386	1	−1.6750	3	−1.3862
Lithuania	1	−1.8079	1	−2.0114	1	−4.9378	1	−4.7607	4	−3.3583	1	−2.0167
Luxembourg	1	1.3616	1	−4.4545	2	−4.0418	2	−4.1930	4	−2.5932	4	−0.5521
Malta	1	−1.9782	1	−3.0983	1	0.3435	1	0.6860	1	−2.5602	1	2.4502
Netherlands	1	−2.8798	1	−2.4047	1	−1.6881	2	−2.1271	1	−0.6861	2	−1.7302
Norway	4	−1.7591	4	2.8142	2	−2.4145	1	−2.7873	2	−2.2974	1	−2.2210
Poland	1	−2.0824	1	0.6766	1	−2.5440	1	−1.3963	4	−2.2727	2	−1.4972
Portugal	1	−1.8862	1	−1.8632	1	−1.8394	2	−1.6042	1	−2.8721	1	−2.8702
Romania	1	−2.1829	1	−1.6270	1	−3.1704	1	−2.7936	4	−2.1558	4	−1.2803
Slovakia	1	−1.8211	1	−1.2134	1	−3.8480	2	−1.3211	1	−.17736	1	−0.3937
Spain	1	−3.5368	1	−2.6691	2	−2.1695	2	−2.2518	1	−2.7001	1	−2.5241
Sweden	1	−2.9039	1	−3.5099	1	−2.5100	2	−2.9086	1	−0.0567	3	1.4636
Switzerland	1	−1.5816	1	−6.1128	2	−4.0115	2	−3.1383	1	−2.0782	1	−1.7492
United Kingdom	1	−0.4150	1	−1.5063	3	−2.8530	3	−1.8490	1	−2.3443	1	−2.6522
CIPS İstatistiği		−2.0832		−2.5017		−2.2379		−2.1452		−2.1996		−1.5680

Note: Refers to the optimal lag length. 1% significance critical value for CADF = -4.35 (Constant); -4.97 (Constant + Trend) (Pesaran 2007, pp: 275–276), 1% critical value for CIPS = -2.32 (Constant); -2.83 (Constant + trend) (Pesaran 2007, pp: 280–281).

$$W_{N,T}^{Hnc} = \frac{1}{N}\sum_{i=1}^{N} W_{i,T}$$

$$Z_{N,T}^{Hnc} = \sqrt{\frac{N}{2K}}\left(W_{N,T}^{Hnc} - K\right)\xrightarrow[N,T\to\infty]{d} N(0.1)$$

$$Z_{N}^{Hnc} = \frac{\sqrt{N}\left(W_{N,T}^{Hnc} - N^{-1}\sum_{i=1}^{N} E(W_{i,T})\right)}{\sqrt{N^{-1}\sum_{i=1}^{N} Var(W_{i,T})}}\xrightarrow[N,T\to\infty]{d} N(0,1)$$

The Dumitrescu and Hurlin (2012) panel causality test does not consider whether there is a cointegrating relationship between variables. This situation has no significance and the test is working whether or not there is a cointegrating relation.

Empirical Findings

The cross-sectional dependence, panel unit root and causality test results obtained as a result of the analysis are tabulated below.

Cross-Sectional Dependence Test Results

Cross-sectional dependence is important in selecting the unit root test to be used. In the study, Pesaran (2004) CD LM test was used because the time dimension of the data set used was T = 18 and the section size was N = 24. Since the probability value is smaller than 5% according to the findings, the null hypothesis that there is no cross-sectional dependence is rejected. Therefore, there is cross-sectional dependence in the equation used. Growth, tax or carbon emissions shocks from one country are also affecting others. Because of the existence of cross-sectional dependence in the equation, panel unit root tests are used which take cross-sectional dependence into consideration. Tab. 2 shows the cross-sectional dependence test results.

Panel Unit Root Results

In the time series unit root test, tests that consider both the time dimension and the cross-section size are considered more powerful than the ones that only consider the time dimension. The inclusion of the cross-sectional dimension increases the variability (Im et al. 1997, 2003; Levin et al. 2002). Tab. 3 shows the CADF and CIPS panel unit root test results.

Tab. 4: Causality Test Results

Ho hypothesis	W-Stat.	Zbar-Stat.	Prob.Value
GDP ↛ CO2	6.60373	7.00621	2.E-12
CO2 ↛ GDP	2.39842	-0.00264	0.9979
TAX ↛ CO2	**4.09057**	**2.81762**	**0.0048**
CO2 ↛ TAX	2.79277	0.65462	0.5127
TAX ↛ GDP	5.09585	4.71182	2.E-06
GDP ↛ TAX	**3.95193**	**2.73908**	**0.0062**

Calculated CIPS statistic values are smaller than the table critical value (both constant and constant and trend) and Ho is rejected. In this case, the series are stable at level values. Any growth, tax or emission shock that may occur for the countries concerned is immediately losing its effect.

Dumitrescu and Hurlin (2012) Test Results

The causality relationship between carbon tax, carbon dioxide emissions and economic growth was analyzed using the causality test developed by Dumitrescu and Hurlin (2012), and the results are given in Tab. 4. According to the results of causality test, it is determined that there is a significant relation between carbon tax and carbon dioxide, while economic growth affects carbon tax. The null hypothesis that carbon tax is not the cause of carbon emissions is rejected. The null hypothesis that economic growth is not the root cause of carbon taxation has been rejected.

A one-way causality relationship from carbon tax to carbon emission has been established to confirm the relationship of purchasing the pollution right. The increase in the tax increases the carbon emissions. On the other hand, there is a one-way causality relation from growth to carbon data. A relationship has been found that indicates that the income will increase as the economic growth increases. According to the results, it is necessary to study the carbon tax so that the right to pollution can be used for purposes other than purchasing and generating income. Policies should be developed to serve the purpose of less harm to the environment while achieving economic growth with the use of carbon taxation to really serve its own purposes.

Conclusion

The industrial revolution, and the rapid globalization process that followed it, led to an increase in production in the world while causing negative effects on the environment on the other hand. Environmental taxes, especially taxes on energy, are at the forefront of the measures taken in this area. The countries that emphasize the necessity of tax measures in the fight against these negative consequences that have been taking place in the environment have been European countries. In this direction, it is important to establish the relationship between the taxes used in European countries and economic growth.

This study examines the interaction between carbon tax, CO2 emissions and economic growth in 1995–2013 using the causality test developed by Dumitrescu and Hurlin (2012) for 24 European countries. As a result of the study, it was determined that there is a one-way causality between carbon tax and CO2 emissions, from carbon tax to CO2 emissions. At the same time, it has been determined that there is a one-way causality to growing carbon tax. In the light of these findings, the necessity of the existence of environmental sensitivity is revealed while carrying out production activities, and carbon tax application may be an efficient stimulant. In this context, it is important to develop and implement global policies that will minimize the harm to the environment.

Bibliography

Agras, Jean / Chapman, Duane: "A dynamic approach to the Environmental Kuznets Curve hypothesis". *Ecological Economics* 28(2), 1999, pp. 267–277.

Al-Abdullah, Anwar Y.: "The Carbon-tax debate". *Applied Energy* 64(1), 1999, pp. 3–13.

Baranzini, Andrea / Goldemberg, Jose / Speck, Stefan: "A future for carbon taxes". *Ecological Economics* 32(3), 2000, pp. 395–412.

Baumol, William J.: "On taxation and the control of externalities". *The American Economic Review* 62(3), 1972, pp. 307–322.

Bayramoğlu, Arzu Tay / Yurtkur, Asuman Koç: "Carbon Emission and Economic Growth Relationship in Turkey: Nonlinear Cointegration Analysis". *Abant Izzet Baysal University Journal of Social Sciences Institute* 16(4), 2016, pp. 31–45.

Bozoklu, Şeref / Yılancı, Veli: "Causality Relation Between Financial Development and Economic Growth: Analysis for Emerging Economies", *Dokuz Eylul University Faculty of Economics and Administrative Sciences Journal* 28(2), 2013, pp. 161–187.

Breitung, Jörg: "The local power of some unit root tests for panel data", *In:* Badi H. Baltagi / Thomas B. Fomby / R. Carter Hill (Eds.): *Nonstationary Panels, Panel Cointegration, and Dynamic Panels (Advances in Econometrics Volume 15)*. Emerald Group Publishing Limited:UK. 2001. pp. 161–177.

Breusch, Trevor Stanley / Pagan, Adrian Rodney: "The Lagrange multiplier test and its applications to model specification in econometrics". *The Review of Economic Studies* 47(1), 1980, pp. 239–253.

Bruvoll, Annegrete / Medin, Hege: "Factors behind the environmental Kuznets curve. A decomposition of the changes in air pollution". *Environmental and Resource Economics* 24(1), 2003, pp. 27–48.

Choi, In: "Unit root tests for panel data". *Journal of international money and Finance* 20(2), 2001, pp. 249–272.

Dinda, Soumyananda: "Environmental Kuznets curve hypothesis: a survey". *Ecological Economics* 49(4), 2004, pp. 431–455.

Dumitrescu, Elena-Ivona / Hurlin, Christophe: "Testing for Granger non-causality in heterogeneous panels". *Economic Modelling* 29(4), 2012, pp. 1450–1460.

Dökmen, Gökhan: "Environmental tax and economic growth: a panel VAR analysis". *Erciyes Üniversitesi İktisadi ve İdari Bilimler Fakültesi Dergisi* 40, 2012, pp. 43–65.

European Environment Agency (EEA): "Shaping the Future of Energy in Europe: Clean, Smart and Renewable", EEA Report No 11, 2017.

European Environment Agency (EEA): *Environmental Taxes Implementation and Environmental Effectiveness, Publications Office of the European Union,* 1996.

Eurostat: Energy taxes, 2016. http://ec.europa.eu/eurostat/data/database (08.08.2017).

Flavin, Christopher / Dunn, Seth: "Climate of opportunity: renewable energy after Kyoto". *Power Economics* 2(9), 1998, pp. 41–43.

Friedman, David / Klein, Yehuda / Sun: "Guodong. Environmental and economic impacts of a carbon tax: An application of the Long Island MARKAL model". *Middle States Geographer* 44, 2012, pp. 18–26.

Granger, Clive WJ: "Investigating causal relations by econometric models and cross-spectral methods". *Econometrica: Journal of the Econometric Society* 37, 1969, 424–438.

Green, Richard: "Carbon tax or carbon permits: The impact on generators' risks". *The Energy Journal*, 2008, pp. 67–89.

Grossman, Gene M. / Krueger, Alan B.: "Environmental impacts of a North American free trade agreement". *National Bureau of Economic Research*, 1991, No: 3914, pp.1-57.

Grossman, Gene M. / Krueger, Alan B.: "Economic growth and the environment". *The Quarterly Journal of Economics* 110(2), 1995, pp. 353–377.

Gülmez, Ahmet: "Economic Growth and Air Pollution in OECD Countries: Panel Data Analysis". *Kastamonu University FEAS Journal* 9, 2015, pp. 18–30.

Hadri, Kaddour.: "Testing for stationarity in heterogeneous panel data". *The Econometrics Journal* 3(2), 2000, pp. 148–161.

Hotunluoglu, Hakan / Tekeli, Recep.: "Economic Analysis and Effects of Carbon Vaccine: Does Carbon Vaccine Have an Emission Reducing Effect?". *Sosyoekonomi* 6(6), 2007, pp: 255-620.

Im, Kyung So / Pesaran, M. Hashem / Shin, Yongcheol.: "*Testing for Unit Roots in Heterogenous Panelso*". DAE, Working Paper 9526, University of Cambridge, 1997.

Im, Kyung So / Pesaran, M. Hashem / Shin, Yongcheol.: "Testing for unit roots in heterogeneous panels". *Journal of Econometrics* 115(1), 2003, pp. 53–74.

Kovancılar, Birol.: "Carbon Tax and Activity in the Solution of Global Warming Problem". *Management and Economics: Celal Bayar University Journal of Economics and Administrative Sciences* 8(2), 2001, pp. 7–20.

Levin, Andrew / Lin, Chien-Fu / Chu, Chia-Shang James.: "Unit root tests in panel data: asymptotic and finite-sample properties". *Journal of Econometrics* 108(1), 2002, pp. 1–24.

Lin, Boqiang / Li, Xuehui.: "The effect of carbon tax on per capita CO 2 emissions". *Energy Policy* 39(9), 2011, pp. 5137–5146.

Maddala, Gangadharrao S. / Wu, Shaowen.: "A comparative study of unit root tests with panel data and a new simple test". *Oxford Bulletin of Economics and Statistics* (61), 1999, pp. 631–652.

Meadows, Donella H. / Meadows D.L. / Randers, J. / Behrens, W.W.: "*The limits to growth: a report for the culb of rome's project on the predicament of mankind*". Universe Book: New York. 1972.

MFA: Paris Treaty, retrieved from http://www.mfa.gov.tr/paris-anlasmasi.tr.mfa (5.08.2017).

Nazlıoğlu, Şaban.: "The effects of macroeconomic policies on the agricultural sector: A comparison for developed and developing countries". Unpublished Doctorate Thesis, *Erciyes University Social Sciences Institute, Kayseri*, 2010.

OECD: *Implementation Strategies for Environmental Taxes*. OECD: Paris. 1996.

Parry, Ian WH.: "Environmental taxes and quotas in the presence of distorting taxes in factor markets". *Resource and Energy Economics* 19(3), 1997, pp. 203–220.

Pehlivan, O. / Demirbaş, A.: "Energy economy, energy policy, and energy/carbon taxes of Turkey". *Energy Sources, Part B: Economics, Planning, and Policy* 3(1), 2007, pp. 26–40.

Pesaran, M. Hashem: "General diagnostic tests for cross section dependence in panels". University of Cambridge, Faculty of Economics, Cambridge Working Papers in Economics No. 0435, 2004.

Pesaran, M. Hashem: "Estimation and inference in large heterogeneous panels with a multifactor error structure". *Econometrica* 74(4), 2006, pp. 967–1012.

Pesaran, M. Hashem: "A simple panel unit root test in the presence of cross-section dependence". *Journal of Applied Econometrics* 22(2), 2007, pp. 265–312.

Pesaran, M. Hashem / Ullah, Aman / Yamagata, Takashi: "A bias-adjusted LM test of error cross-section independence". *The Econometrics Journal* 11(1), 2008, pp. 105–127.

Tatoglu, Ferda Yerdelen: *Advanced panel data analysis: Stata applied.* Beta: İstanbul. 2013.

Tekin, Ahmet / Şaşmaz, Mahmut Ünsal: "The Impact of Environmental Taxes on the Ecological Risk Reduction in the Globalization Process: The European Union Case". *Management and Economics: Journal of Celal Bayar University Faculty of Economics and Administrative Sciences* 23(1), 2016, pp. 1–17.

World Bank: CO_2 emissions (metric tons per capita), 2016a, retrieved from http://data.worldbank.org/indicator/EN.ATM.CO2E.PC (07.08.20017).

World Bank: GDP per capita growth (annual %), 2016b. retrieved from http://data.worldbank.org/indicator/NY.GDP.PCAP.KD.ZG (07.08.2017).

Worldwatch Institute: *State of the World 2000.* W.W. Norton & Company: New Yor. 2000.

WU, Kai / Nagurney, a. / Liu, Z. / Stranlund, J.K.: "Modeling generator power plant portfolios and pollution taxes in electric power supply chain networks: A transportation network equilibrium transformation". *Transportation Research Part D: Transport and Environment* 11(3), 2006, pp. 171–190.

Zhang, ZhongXiang / Baranzini, Andrea: "What do we know about carbon taxes? An inquiry into their impacts on competitiveness and distribution of income". *Energy policy* 32(4), 2004, pp. 507–518.

Esmeray Alacadağlı, Yasemin Mamur Işıkçı and Erol Işıkçı

Globalization, Reform in Public Administration and Strategic Management Practices in Turkey

Abstract: Economic, political and technological developments that accelerated together with the last quarter of the 20th century have also accelerated the process of economic integration throughout the world. This process, defined as globalization, has changed the nature of many inhabitant human interaction and has deeply affected public administration. With the globalization process leading to serious changes in the public service and public administration understanding, in parallel with this new understanding, restructuring and reforming studies in public administration started. New management techniques such as strategic planning and strategic management, which have become more prevalent in the private sector, have been put into practice in the process of transformation. In the United States, the Government Performance and Result Act, adopted in 1993, envisages the preparation of a strategic plan by all public institutions.

After the 2000s, reforms in public administration have been intensified to provide both globalization and EU candidacy. The "Financial and Public Sector Adjustment Loan Agreement" signed with the World Bank in 2001 foresees the implementation of strategic planning in the public sector to support the medium-term reform programs of the financial sector and public administration. A number of studies have been conducted in this framework under the leadership of the State Planning Organization in that period. In this context, restructuring studies have been initiated in public institutions under the leadership of the World Bank. In 2003, Law No. 5018 on Public Financial Management and Control was issued, and strategic planning became mandatory for public institutions.

With this study, in a period of 14 years, it has been tried to show the extent to which the transformation required by strategic management and restructuring in public administrations in Turkey is based on the strategic planning and management practices put into practice as a postmodern management technique in parallel with globalization and new public administration approach. For this purpose, a literature review was conducted, and the strategic plans and applications of two universities and two public institutions were examined. The results show that the new management approach based on results-based and performance-based implementation of public reforms and the implementation of the strategic management technique to achieve this have not yet been fully internalized.

Keywords: Strategy, Strategic Planning, Strategic Management, Culture, Culture of Strategic Management

Introduction

The process of integration of the global economy actually began with the European colonial period five centuries ago. However, this process has gained momentum in today's world, based on the rapid developments in information technology, the widespread use of the Internet, the removal of trade barriers, and the increasing political and economic strength of multinational corporations (Ellwood, 2001). In this process of globalization, the traditional boundaries separating individuals and societies are gradually lagging behind. The nature of many human, economic, political, social, cultural, environmental and technological interactions in the field and the way in which time and space are perceived and the way of thinking change (Kunitz 2000, p.90 ; Lee 2000, p.22).

The multifaceted dynamics of change emerging from globalization have affected all the countries of the world and have caused radical changes and transformations in the socio-economic and cultural structures of societies. In this framework, there is a multifaceted change in the world economy, health, and all cultural areas surrounding it. This change process has also changed the forms of production, the qualities of the products produced, and the way of doing business, while differentiating the demands of the service areas, based on ever-increasing knowledge (Özata and Sevinç 2010, p.16). With these changes and transformations that have different discourses on them, from the industrial society to the information society, from Fordist production to flexible production, from the nation-states world to the globalized world, from the modernist world to the postmodernist thought are evolved (Tekeli 2012, p.624).

On the other hand, the phenomenon of globalization and increased competition has also led to the need for a faster and more radical reform program for organizations in the public, private or other sectors. The philosophical subdivision of these reforms is the "New Management Approach". This understanding is based on the principles of economy, efficiency and efficiency (Tutum 2012, p.478). It is the "New Management Approach" that constitutes the philosophical substructure of these reforms. With this understanding emerging to respond to developments that include principles and values that can be applied to all organizations, the differences in public or private organizations and their management approach are largely decreased. Organizations that are unable to meet the needs of today's rapid change with structures that have been useful and effective in the past have inevitably had to go through restructuring in an increasingly competitive environment based on ever-increasing and varied demands. For this reason, the public or private sector is questioning all organizations, organization, manner, and understanding of service; they aimed at strategies and methods to ensure that their aims, structures, technologies and human dimensions they use are constantly monitored and improved. In this context, public or private organizations have planned a long-term vision by aiming to reach their goals and targets, and have tried to design more flexible structures that set strategies, implement them and meet the constant change to realize this vision (Özer 2008, p.22). Because the new world order formed in the globalizing world and its universal values imposes the adoption and application of the new management concept. With the reform studies carried out in parallel with these imperatives, new structures have been created "based on the post-modern premises on which the philosophy of management of the information age is based, away from traditional and modern management approaches" (Saran, 2001: 39). The "New Public Management Approach", which started its first applications in the USA, UK, Canada, Australia and New Zealand, has gradually expanded its domain to other countries. This model, which was called differently in the form of the Government Re-discovery in America, the Reform of the Institutions for Future Steps in England, and the Vision 2000 in Canada, has been put into practice without much deviation from its basic elements (Kutlu 2012, pp.73–74).

With the "January 24th Decisions" in our country, the liberalization of the economy has been put on the button for privatization and autonomy. After this date, the World Bank has begun the process of making the Turkish economy and public administration part of the global system with loans provided for structured or sectoral adaptation. Turkish Public Administration has been transformed into "Structural Transformation Programs" aimed at restructuring the public sector under the supervision of the World Bank and under the "New Public Management Approach" using new management techniques.

In this transformation, many approaches and techniques such as Governance, Strategic Management, Total Quality Management, Change Management, Performance Evaluation and Measurement, Synergic Management, Learning Organizations are the techniques that emerge in the climate of general change and indirectly and directly reflected to public administration systems (Saran 2001, p.39) and many of these techniques have also been used in our country.

From these new perspectives, management techniques such as strategic management, total quality management, and governance are widely discussed and used in recent years, which are more intense in public administration practices. Strategic Management, one of the new management techniques that has been accepted and increasingly accepted all over the world since the beginning of the 1990s, has been applied to all kinds of organizations in the public sector and the third sector. While redesigning public administration and economy in Turkey, the legal infrastructure was created and used predominantly in 2003.

Aim and Method

The purpose of this study is to determine the extent to which the transformation required by the strategic management in Turkey can be achieved/revealed in the light of a strategic management culture of existing administrative and human capacities in public administrations in line with the strategic management approach.

The data and information needed in the study were obtained using literature review and qualitative analysis methods. The literature review provided information on the conceptual framework of strategic management and management culture, strategic management process, steps, implementation in public, legal basis. Strategic plans and annual reports of four universities, two universities, and two public institutions, have been examined to provide data on the implementation in the public sector. This analysis is based on the parameters (mission vision definitions, the establishment of the strategic management team, current situation analysis, participation, etc.) that will reveal the basic elements that constitute strategic management and the extent to which the stages provide. In addition, two institutions, one of which is a university and one of which is a public institution, were interviewed with the persons involved in the preparation and implementation of the strategic plan. Based on these negotiations, it was tried to verify the information obtained by examining the reports and plans of the implementation examples with the assumption that "implementation of the current political and administrative culture and strategic management in Turkish Public Administration is not so easy".

Strategy, Strategic Planning and Strategic Management

The strategy is a military term used for the first time in the military field. This term with etymological root in Ancient Greek is defined as "the art and art of using a combination of political, economic, psychological and military forces to support a nation or a nation of nations in support of the policy adopted in peace and war" in TDK Dictionary. As an antiquarian military art, Strategy is to direct all resources, mostly the soldiers, to reach a goal (Shafritz et al. 2016, p.326). This concept, which is widely used in the military field, has started to be used in management field over time. The necessity of having a long-term vision for keeping up with this change and creating the necessary strategies to implement it in all organizations that want to keep their assets in the face of changing management approach and methods parallel to the globalizing world has increased the importance of strategic management in all institutions and organizations (Özer 2008, p.22). In this context, Strategic Management, which is based on the concept of Strategy, is confronted as a process related to the management of jobs that will make it possible to live long-term rather than daily and ordinary jobs and to give it a competitive edge.

In terms of conceptual content, it is one of the universal principles of planning management and strategic planning is a function of strategic management. In this context; "The development of strategic management and strategic planning can be considered as identical developments. In other words, strategic planning can be regarded as a managerial activity within and within the concept of strategic management" (Tortop et al. 2016, p.226). Determining the path to be followed in the management process, the strategy, is a task that must be done by the management and this is a step of strategic planning with the evolved definition of the planning of the stage. Strategic planning is aimed not to be adversely affected by current uncertainties in the present world, but to influence the direction of change. With strategic planning, a tool of strategic management understanding, the future can be affected and the future can be directed; difficulties can be avoided (Steiner 1979, p.12).

"Strategic management is a management technique that sets out what an organization is doing, why it is, and what goals it wants to reach in the future" (Bryson 1988, p.5). In management science, the strategy is used in the sense of an organization's means to achieve its goal, and it shows how to use the resources in the most effective and efficient way in the face of changing environmental conditions. Strategic Management is defined by W. Barry (1986), who works in the field of management and informatics, as "the goals that an organization wants to achieve in the future and the analysis of the process that shows how this goal is attained" is one of the most important areas of research and application in management science today. In fact, strategic management is a management methodology that emerges after evolution, depending on the scientific, technological and economic developments of management thinking. Strategic management, which is the modern application of the ancient art of military service in business and public administration; the conscious choice of policies, the development of skills, and the organization's environment to be interpreted by managers to focus their organization's activities on achieving predetermined goals (Shafritz et al. 2016, p.327).

Elements, Features and Stages of Strategic Management

In general, it is observed that all strategic management activities involve steps that are required by the planning approach of the organization, the purpose of existence and the future where it wants to be. In this context, it can be said that strategic management is built on four basic elements as "Vision, Mission, Strategy, and Activity". The mission is the cause of an organization and distinguishes it from other similar organizations. The vision symbolizes the future of the organization and reveals what it wants to do in the long run. An organization vision; a management philosophy that will guide the whole organization, an effective image to be possessed in the future, and future predictions. Vision is a picture of the future that the organization wants to achieve. The strategy is a general plan showing how and in what way the future will be achieved, and the action or action defines the steps to be followed in the framework of the identified strategies. These four concepts are of great importance in strategic management.

The most important feature of strategic management is that the organization can analyze both its own situation and the outside of the organization. It is not possible for an organization that does not recognize its own internal structure, systems and processes to achieve success. In this respect, cultural dimension is an important factor in providing the needs of strategic management. This is because the ability to respond quickly and effectively to the present day depends on the cultural characteristics of the society in question, especially on administrative culture. The habits, management sense, and culture involved in this can be either an engine or a brake to provide change. Culture is "In the broadest sense, the sum, learned and shared values, beliefs, behavior patterns and symbols" (Koçel 2005, p.30), and organizational culture is common values that hold together the individuals of the organization. Because of the phenomenon of globalization nowadays, organizations have to increase their competitiveness so that they can compete both nationally and internationally. Increasing competitiveness depends on employees being able to integrate themselves into the organization, and to be able to easily struggle for the organization. This kind of behavior is only concerned with an organizational environment in which a participatory culture is dominant, allowing for initiative use. In this sense, strategic management is a management technique based on teamwork and advocating that the objectives of the organization can be attained with the participation of all stakeholders and it helps "strategic thinking".

Strategic management, on the other hand, requires the analysis of the environment outside the organization (the market structure, the power of competitors, the desires and expectations of customers, the power of suppliers, etc.). The next step is to determine the vision and mission of the organization. In the next step, strategy and action plans are prepared in line with the determined mission and vision. With all these steps, strategic management helps to determine and solve the problems in the organization in the most efficient way. The aim of strategic management is to increase the future performance of the organization, increase profitability and productivity.

When Strategic Management and its undergoing development process is in scope, change, change adaptation and management of change are emerging concepts in the realization of strategic management. In this sense, the ability of organizations to manage their environment is a critical success factor in the case of change adaptation and competition. It is possible to see that internal and external environment analyses are frequently used in today's organizations. In this context, SWOT analysis and similar approaches clearly and concisely describe the main factors and impacting factors affecting the situation in the organization.

The processes related to strategic management and the processes that need to be done consist of five steps. In the first stage, the strategists who will direct and determine the functions and functions of the strategies should be defined so the strategic management process will be carried out with the analysis of "What?" and "Why?" questions to explain why strategic management has to be implemented. SWOT analysis is needed to analyze this situation in the framework. Then, by applying strategic management, it should be revealed where it is desired to be reached; vision and mission statements should be prepared. In the third stage, strategies for how to achieve the desired goal should be identified. At this stage, it is important to make strategic choices by using competition and portfolio analysis. The next step is to determine the application and transfer the tasks. Finally, the applied plan must be reviewed and, if necessary, some changes to the plan must be made.

Strategic Management in Public Administration and Turkish Public Administration

Today, all organizations that are established for different purposes in different sectors, despite their differences in purpose and sector, gives more importance to strategic thinking, strategic planning and decision-making due to global competitiveness. In the face of increasing information, communication and increasing competition based on globalization, management understanding has changed and structuring and steps that can manage this change have been taken.

The use of concepts related to strategic management in the private sector started after World War II. Strategic management is said to have taken its present shape through a process that started with planning. Strategic management has been passed after the stages of "budget and financial control, long-term planning, commercial strategic planning, joint strategic planning and strategic management". Operational efficiency in the 1950s, strategic planning in the 1960s, and market position in the 1970s came to the forefront in order to provide competitive advantage. (Özgür 2004, p.218).

The economic, social, political and technological developments that have begun to take place since the late 1970s have affected not only the private sector but also the public sphere. From these years, traditional public management understanding has begun to be questioned, and it has been expressed that new management understanding and techniques should be applied in public administration. The impact of democratization, liberalization, and smuggling has also changed people's expectations for public services. Strategic management is a management style that is implemented in the public sector in order to respond to these changing expectations and is essentially a management style, such as TQM, that is tried to be implemented in the public sector after successful applications in the private sector (Parlak and Sobacı 2012, p.322). In this framework, strategic management, which is known only in the private sector in the early 1980s, has applied to organizations in all sectors such as multinational corporations, holding companies, public, private and third sectors.

Beyond responding to changes that occur, organizations can become more active in managing changes in their environment with strategic management, which allows them to control and be prepared for change. With this feature, strategic management is an important means of reducing the ambiguity of both the private and the public future, restoring itself against such changes and being able to survive and succeed in the long run. It is also possible to avoid threats from environmental changes and to make maximum use of opportunities through analysis (SWOT) to evaluate internal and external situations used in strategic management. "Strategic management is, therefore, an important tool for public administration to minimize its future uncertainty and to reposition itself against such changes and to enable public organizations to succeed and survive in the long run" (Parlak and Sobacı 2012, p.332). It is also possible to understand the transformation that led to the commencement of strategic management practices with the public administration in the public sector in the context of "compliance with the environment, competition, financial crises and rising demands for transparency and democratization" (Özgür 2004, p.231–233).

When we look at the transition process to strategic planning and strategic management in Turkish public administration, it is seen that the first applications for planning started after World War I and adopted the concept of government-assisted development and the basic investments made by the state in the framework of the principles determined by the İzmir Economics Congress. In the following period, Stateism became dominant in public policies, and the first national scale plan, the First Five-Year Industry Plan, was implemented in 1933 (Ergun 2004, p.74). In the framework of the planned development concept adopted in the 1960s and beyond, organizational arrangements for the new system were created, and the State Planning Organization was established and placed at the center of this system. As a consequence of this legislation, development plans have been a guide for the private sector, for the public sector to develop and activate the market economy. With this planning approach, the arbitrary movements of public institutions were prevented and behavior according to the decisions taken for development and the principles set was ensured, and the openness, responsibility and supervision conditions required in the democratic administration were also tried to be fulfilled.

In Turkey, reform efforts in public administration have been intensified, especially in the 2000s, in order to ensure the necessity of globalization and EU candidacy. In policy documents and legislative harmonization studies, strategic planning, participation, transparency, and accountability are the basic concepts on which reform is based. It is foreseen that the strategic planning of the financial sector and public administration in order to support medium-term reform programs in the Public Finance and Public Sector Adjustment Loan Agreement signed with the World Bank in 2001 is envisaged. The action, which is expected to be implemented in this framework and is defined as a step in the reform of the public sector, is a realization of strategic plans in order to strengthen the policy-making capacity in public institutions (Yılmaz 2002, p.76). Especially after the loan agreements based on the realization of these forecasts, taking part in the Turkish National Program for the Adoption of the EU Acquis, Long-Term Strategy and Eighth Five-Year Development Plans, total quality management, financial control, performance audit as well as strategic management have become mandatory for public institutions.

Legal arrangements have been made to ensure that both the new world order that emerged after globalization and the needs of the determined policies of the commitments given to the country.

At the end of 2003, Law No. 5018 on Public Financial Management and Control (PFMC) was put into force. With this legal arrangement, it is imperative to make strategic plans for public institutions with the aim of ensuring effectiveness, efficiency, and transparency in management, increasing the accuracy and appropriateness of plans and institutional capacity, putting the plans on a budget basis. In accordance with the decisions of the High Planning Council numbered 2003/14 and 2004/37, pilot applications were launched in 2004, and strategic planning and performance budgeting studies were started in the public sector in Turkey.

Authorities and responsibilities related to the execution of strategic planning activities in the level of public administration in the level of organization are defined in the PFMC numbered 5018. By law, the Ministry of Finance is authorized to determine the appropriateness of the budgets of the public administrations to the performance indicators specified in the strategic plans and to determine the activities to be carried out by the administrations in this framework and other matters related to the performance-based budgeting (PFMCL 2003, Article 1). According to the law, public administrations have to base their budgets, program and project-based resource allocations on their strategic plans, annual goals and targets, performance indicators for public services to be offered at the desired level and quality. The same Court of Accounts has been tasked with determining whether public resources are used effectively, economically and efficiently in the context of an external audit, measuring the results of activities and evaluating them in terms of performance (PFMCL 2003, p.68). In 2003, a "Regulation on Procedures and Principles Regarding Strategic Planning in Public Administrations" was issued and a transitional period for this implementation process was set up in order to regulate the application of the strategic plan that was created with the legal basis. The period defined for the transition to strategic management to public administrations by law and the designated transition program was completed by the end of 2010.

Rules and procedures have been defined in order to prepare and implement the five-year strategic plans of the public institutions with participatory methods and to implement monitoring and performance audits with the PFMC and the Implementing Regulation and the communiqués and circulars issued in this respect. In this context, all public institutions and organizations should establish their mission and vision for the future, determine their goals and objectives in a measurable manner, measure their performances in accordance with predetermined indicators and monitor and evaluate this process. Based on the determined activities and projects, the resource requirement is costed and the institutional budget making the plan is created. In this context, an action step that needs to be done is the performance program which constitutes the annual application slices of strategic plans prepared for five years. Within the framework of accountability responsibilities, the Executive Committee and the authorizing officers of the Agency have organized annually on the basis of performance programs (PFMCL 2003, Article 41). Public institutions have to explain their objectives, realization situation and the causes of deviations in the activity reports. Activity reports have to be prepared based on the results of monitoring and evaluation of strategic plans.

Control/Audit is the last and most important phase of strategic management. Internal audit is an independent, objective assurance and consulting activity aimed at evaluating and guiding the management of resources in accordance with the principles of efficiency, efficiency, and efficiency in order to add value to and enhance the public administrations' work (PFMCL 2003, p.63). External audit, by the Court of Auditors, which is expected to be realized in two ways: regularity audit consisting of financial and compliance audit and performance audit. Performance audit, complementary to the strategic management process; to determine whether public resources are used effectively, economically and efficiently, to measure the results of activities and to evaluate them in terms of performance (PFMCL 2003, p.68).

According to the Law and Implementing Regulation, public administrations allocate budgets, programs and project-based resources so that public services can be offered at the desired level and quality; based on their strategic plans, annual goals and objectives and performance indicators and to carry out the process in accordance with the steps defined here, to monitor, monitor and report on the events. The period of transition defined as the "Regulation on the Procedures and Principles for Strategic Planning in Public Administrations" was completed at the end of 2010 and the public administrations are now obliged to fulfill all the requirements in full in the strategic planning process in which the legal ground was established in 2003.

Findings of Strategic Management Application Examples

Strategic management practice in the Turkish Public Administration, in which the legal infrastructure was established in 2003 and pilot applications were initiated in 2004; two for the qualitative analysis, are examined thoroughly by four examples: two for the university and two for the ministry. By examining the establishment laws, mission, vision, goals and targets, strategic plans and annual reports of the selected samples, it has been tried to determine the extent to which these applications meet the provisions of PFMC and Implementation Regulation. In addition, four institutions were interviewed with eight people in each institution, one of whom was in the process of preparing/implementing the strategic plan. The strategic plans and annual reports of the two universities and the two public institutions, which are examined to provide data on the implementation in public, as well as the requirements regarding the strategic planning and management processes; based on the "planning, implementation, supervision" processes, the following findings were obtained:

Ministry of Health

The Ministry of Health Strategic Plan has set four Strategic Goals and 32 Goals to achieve this goal with a Final Goal as "Equitably protecting and improving the health level of our people". The Mission set in Plan is "Protecting individual and community health at the highest level with a human-centered approach, providing timely, appropriate and effective solutions to health problems", and the Vision is "Turkey is a country in which a healthy lifestyle is adopted and everyone has the right to health." When the definitions are examined, it is found that the conceptual content of the mission and the vision is comprehended and the definitions providing the legal requirements are observed. Although it is not considered to be measurable in the first place, it is also determined in the following sections that the present situation regarding each target and the target to be reached in 2017 are embodied.

A comprehensive structure (consisting of the Supreme Council for Strategy Development, the Strategic Planning Executive Committee, the Strategic Planning Working Groups and the Strategic Planning Coordination Unit) and a team have been established to provide the requirements for Strategic Management in the Ministry of Health (MoH). The MoH prepared the 2013–2017 Strategic Plan with WHO-supported work (WHO European Region showed this work as an example for other countries). Training was provided for the preparation of the "Strategic Plan" and the "Information and Policy Dialogue Meetings" were held with the stakeholders. The MoH provided with surveys and face-to-face interviews opinions and recommendations of the people it serves and stakeholders. In this context, 44 representatives from outside stakeholders, 110 from internal stakeholders were interviewed by MoH. At the same time, the Ministry conducted a questionnaire application too (including those in the central and provincial offices, governorships, municipalities, universities and the relevant public and 4,042 persons representing internal and external stakeholders from institutions and organizations). The SWOT Analysis made by the Ministry in the survey conducted was also evaluated. In the examinations made, it was seen that the activities and responsibilities to be carried out by the Ministry of Health in line with the aims and targets were determined, and everything had to be done in terms of planning.

In the examination of the Ministry's annual reports for 2014 and 2016, it was determined that there be only 14 targets in 32 goals determined under the four main objectives set under the heading "Performance Information" but there were no evaluations related to deviations and improvements in 2014. Besides, in the 2016 Annual Report, despite the sentence 'We are monitoring the strategic plan through performance indicators'; there is no evaluation regarding realization rates, deviations, and improvements. In the 2016 Annual Report Under the heading of audit, it is mentioned that as the web-based Strategic Plan Monitoring and Evaluation application started to be developed for the monitoring and evaluation of the Strategic Plan/plans, it is said that the practice continues to work for the introduction of activity entry, sub-activity entry and institution identification modules and the addition of new modules.

Ministry of Environment and Urbanization

The 2013–2017 Strategic Plan is the first Strategic Plan of the Ministry of Environment and Urbanism since the Ministry of Environment was organized in the form of Ministry of Environment and Forestry in 2003 during the restructuring process, the last regulations made in 2011 and the issued Decree No. 644 and the Ministry of Environment and Urbanization were structured. Strategic plan studies in the Ministry restructured in 2011 were carried out with the participation of all the units in the company and all related institutions and organizations in accordance with the legislation in this subject, and they were put into practice as of January 2013. Under the four main objectives (Planning and Transformation, Environment, Building and Professional Services, Institutional Capacity Development), 42 targets and 216 indicators were determined.

In the process of implementation of the 2013–2017 Strategic Plan, the updating of the strategic plan with the change of the Ministry priorities was initiated and the number of targets was reduced to 26 and the number of targets was reduced to 141, in order to make the targets more measurable and the indicators easy to be perceived. Strategic goals and targets and development plans are embodied with the necessary budgets related to the established goals and the targets that need to be available as years. However, there is not a chart of responsibilities that shows which unit is responsible for which objective and which units of audit trails are to be made, and there are also problems in terms of vision and mission definition. In 2014, four main objectives were identified under the umbrella, 42 targets and 216 indicators were identified under the general directorates, and the deviations and reasons were assessed (196 indicators were evaluated). In the year 2016, the same approach was followed by the performance and deviations of 132 performance indicators related to the ministry's projects and activities in terms of the performance results of the Ministry units.

Bayburt University

The strategic plan of University, which covers 2014–2018, has identified 15 objectives under five objectives. Mission; "To improve the social, cultural and economic conditions of the people of the region and country through quality education, research and service programs, to work for the benefit of the society and to train the individuals who can take responsibility". Shortly it is aimed to be one of the world-renowned universities in education, research, and service in the plan. When the definitions made by the university are evaluated, it is observed that both the conceptual content and the legislation are appropriate for defining missions. However, it has been seen that the determined vision is not appropriate in terms of conceptual and content (it is not very compatible with the vision concept), and it is seen as a slogan to be repeated and difficult to adopt (the vision was revised during the preparation of this study). Although the targets were not considered measurable in the first place, the plan was made measurable by the current situation and targets table.

Two committees (Strategic Planning Committee and Strategic Planning Sub-Committee) were established in Bayburt University in order to ensure the strategic planning and execution requirements. Members of both commissions consist of staff working in academic and administrative units. Attention was paid to the issue of participation in the preparation of the plan, and the views and ideas of all academic and administrative personnel were consulted. Plan Preparation Commission Members are informed about SWOT analysis, determination of strengths and weaknesses, determination of goals, targets, and strategies in the planning process. An implementation plan was prepared by the Strategic Planning Board of the Rector of the Presidency, and the process of preparing the plan was carried out accordingly. When the strategic plan prepared by the university is examined, it is observed that from the current situation analysis, the views and suggestions of the stakeholders are taken, and the SWOT Analysis is established in accordance with the requirements of this regulation. However, although the activities to be carried out and the budget for this are defined by a table, it is not determined who is responsible for which activity.

When the university's annual reports for 2014 and 2016 are examined, the aims and objectives of the University within the scope of the Strategic Plan were listed under a heading, but the facts and deviations there were not mentioned in the 2014 Annual Report. Besides only the activities and projects have been carried out in 2014. The reason for not making an assessment of the achievements of the objectives and targets under the heading "Performance Information" of the Report; It is based on the provision of "public administrations can include as many activities and projects as they prepare their first performance programs". A similar situation exists in the 2016 Annual Report. In the 2016 report, there are strategic goals and objectives under a heading, but no informational report on the achievements has been included. In this context, in this activity report, only the reasons for deviations stemming from budget targets and actions are included. Bayburt University's 2016 Annual Report also contains no reviews of the Strategic Plan, realization rates, deviations, and improvements.

Giresun University

Giresun University has a Strategic Plan for 2010–2014. In that Strategic Plan, 51 targets have been identified under 12 strategic goals. The University started with the preparation of the Strategic Plan covering the years 2015–2019 with an Internal Circular issued in 2012 in accordance with PFMC numbered 5018 and the "Regulation on Procedures and Principles on Strategic Planning in Public Administrations". In accordance with the legislation, the university formed a team consisting of academical administrative staff under the presidency of a rector, and a draft of the Strategic Plan (SP) of Giresun University prepared by participant method and stakeholder opinions was completed on January 2014 sent to the Ministry of Development for evaluation. As stated in the 2015–2019 Strategic Plan, it has been seen that the mission, vision, values and principles determined in a participatory process are appropriate for the requirements of the legislative requirements. (This evaluation is also valid for the previous strategic plan.)

In the 2015–2019 SP, 31 goals were identified under five objectives, and the targets were made concrete with the specified performance indicators. In addition, a cost table covering the years 2015–2019 has been prepared for each of the objectives and targets. As in the previous examples, the assessments in the 2014 Annual Activity Report were made for 2010–2014 SP. At Giresun University, the evaluations in the 2014 Annual Report were made according to the 2010–2014 SP, and it was seen that only 51 out of the 12 strategic objectives identified in this study were related to the budget for the four. In the 2016 Annual Report, only two objectives were assigned to the four budget targets. In both activity reports, there are no evaluations regarding monitoring of the strategic plan, realization rates, deviations and improvements

Strategic Management Interview Results

In the qualitative analysis to determine the status of implementation and adoption, the Ministry of Health and the University of Bayburt have a total of eight (8) persons, who are in the process of preparing and implementing the SP (those in commissions or at positions in the decision) have been interviewed. In that interview, five questions were asked in order to measure the information infrastructure on the bases of the work done and to show how the approaches to the participatory applications and the implementation process were followed.

In the process of SP preparation and implementation, the answers to the question about "What are the mission, vision, purpose, and objectives of the institution" were checked. It is found that participants' answers are in close to the definition in SP 85% only about the mission. Despite their involvement in the process of preparation and implementation of the "part of the problem" that relates to the "purpose, objectives and vision", adequate answers have not been given. It was observed that the administrators had very limited information about these concepts (38% were able to get a partial answer about the vision and goals) and the employees had no information at all.

The question of "whether or not the process of preparation and implementation is sufficiently participatory" is answered by the participants. Three out of four respondents said 'not enough' and stated that the participants also saw this as a meeting to be attended at the moment and that they did not participate in anything afterward. Two persons who are in the implementing position of the plan and administrative duties stated that they had knowledge of correspondence from the plan preparation, but they did not know what was done. Other employees also stated that they did not have news and information about this topic.

The answers from the practitioners and preparers to the questions on "how the activities related to the strategic goals related to the different units in the institution are coordinated and monitored" are "We cannot do enough coordination in this subject, we can not monitor, we are trying to evaluate the information from the units". These answers reveal that the identified goals are largely on paper and that they cannot be passed on to define all responsibilities for implementation.

The questions are asked about SP which is put into practice in public administration after 2003, to find out "whether a new management mentality has been settled and or it has produced a specific management culture". It has been questioned in the form of "What do you mean by the culture of strategic management, new management understanding?" and found out that the annual administrative activity report could not go beyond the stage of preparation in the reconstructed format in accordance with this plan.

Two individuals in the administrative position participating in the planning process, responded questions about "Whether it is more effective and efficient in using resources through strategic planning and management practices" and "whether performance improvement can be achieved individually and institutionally" as "improved performance and productivity partially" while the executive or six employees in the working position responded "things have not changed much before".

Results and Conclusion

One of the concept couples that will best define today's world is "globalization and change". Globalization; as the multinational corporations, such as powerful and new actors, entered the political scene; we have changed the nature of the interaction between people and societies in economic, political, social, cultural, environmental and technological areas. This change affects not only such areas but also affects public institutions that provide public services and makes it difficult to change. Under the pressure of this change, the public administrations regulated the basic structures and processes, and they put new management techniques into practice. The ability to manage change, adaptation and change has come to the forefront; Strategic management is aimed at managing long-term rather than day-to-day work and managing the business so that it can gain competitive advantage. The public administration, which has lost the monopoly of technological developments and has had to open the competition, is based on strategic management practices and principles of transparency and accountability; and has to answer questions of what, why, why and why you are doing that?

Globalization and the rapid spread of new management techniques such as strategic governance, governance, good governance, total quality management, which are increasingly applied in all sectors are largely promoted by international organizations such as the Organization for Economic Cooperation and Development (OECD), the International Monetary Fund (IMF) and the World Bank (WB). Particularly with the structural adjustment programs implemented under the initiative of the World Bank, many countries have adopted reorganization policies and have begun to be implemented.

As mentioned earlier, the strategic management model is being implemented in a wide range of countries, from governments in many countries, such as the US, UK, Sweden, and Australia, to local governments, higher education institutions to public health institutions. In Turkey, strategic management practices were laid in 2001 under the structural adjustment program signed with the WB. Strategic planning and performance-based budgeting studies were initiated in eight pilot organizations selected in Turkey under the High Planning Council decisions after the PFMC numbered 5018, which was put into force in 2003. The legislator has introduced a 10-year transition period, taking into account the difficulties in implementing this technique, which has been practiced in the west for at least ten years. After this period, which ended in 2010, public administrations are now obliged to carry out the process by fully fulfilling the requirements related to strategic management. In this context, both central and local governments have been intensively involved in making strategic plans.

On the other hand, besides the literature review, findings and interviews on the following examples of public practice suggest that the strategic plan and the management mentality are not well understood by the rulers.

Considering the application examples in general, it has been observed that the activities in the "Planning" phase in relation to the four-phase Strategic Management (SM) were made in accordance with the legislation and requirements in this respect. By setting up teams according to the legislation, the current situation, threats, and opportunities have been identified so that the stages in the planning process have been achieved through participatory methods, with some delays. Problems with SM implementation are generally starts at the "Implementation and Control" phase in defining the economic resources and responsibilities to achieve the determined targets. When we examine SP's, it is found that objectives and activities have been determined, but the resources and responsibilities for them have not been clearly defined. On the other hand, the interviews revealed that managers and planners view the long-term planning with the strategic plan as well as the reporting to monitor annual events as a legal requirement. In this context, those who implement the plan do not know how to provide resource management and performance criteria in this process and cannot give clear answers on how these criteria are determined. It is stated that SP's priorities are determined in accordance with the instructions given to the senior management, even though participatory methods are used as written in the process. The scale of success expected from the strategic management and the validity of the service to be provided and fewer complaints from the service areas. Findings in all these application examples show us that strategic management practices are not enough aware of the basic assumptions such as efficiency, productivity, shifting of resources from strategic priority areas, and is not given enough importance.

On the other hand, bureaucracy in public administration, traditions of resistance to change, omnipresent working groups and rule-lines are also hampering the transition to new participatory and flexible approaches such as strategic management. Based on the current political and administrative culture; problems such as the inability of the democracy to institutionalize, the lack of development of the active citizenship consciousness, the failure to create an organized society structure, the failure of the administrative participation principle to be fully violated, the lack of full administrative transparency and the proper operation of public opinion control also negatively affect the implementation of strategic management in Turkish Public Administration. Strategic management practice based on efficiency, efficiency and performance, which comes to our mind as a result of change-transformation in the world rather than need and as a result of globalization, has been put into practice with the influence of international actors such as World Bank. However, the strategic plan implementation process, which started pilot applications at the end of 2003 and ended the transition period in 2010, has not been carried out in accordance with the principles and steps that this model is based on.

As a result, the literature survey, the examples of the applications examined and the impressions obtained from the interviews show us that the Strategic Management culture has not been formed yet despite the fourteen years, the implementation including plan makers has been done only to fulfill the legislative requirements, and the activities are not fully internalized in line with this management concept. It is not right to think of strategic management as a magical tool to solve all problems, and as a model to achieve absolute success. It is also not right to expect that this model has succeeded in an area and that it will succeed in other areas.

In our country is the obvious problems that require reorganizing of public administration and there is low performance of many institutions. It is a matter that has been revealed in many studies in which some public services are either never seen or conducted under the standard. All this points to the need for restructuring of the public administration. The creation of solutions to overcome the problem is only possible if the source is not imposed by external constraints or fashion trends but by identifying real needs.

On the other hand, if a model is to fulfill some of the basic issues while some of others cannot be achieved, then it should not be expected to reach the target with that method. We believe that the success of strategic management in public administration can only be achieved through practices that will provide public benefits, taking into account the priorities of the country and implementing institutions and the current management culture in this management process. It should not be forgotten that all these goals can be achieved by the managers who can change, embrace and grasp the Strategic Management approach and by those employees who make it into institutional culture. This is the only way to manage the transformation process imposed by globalization.

Bibliography

Barry, B.W.: Strategic Planning Workbook for Public and Nonprofit Organizations. Amherst Wilder Foundation: St. Paul. 1986.

Bryson, John M.: Strategic Planning for Public and Nonprofit Organizations. San Jossey-Bass: Francisco. 1988.

Bayburt University: *2014-2016 Administrative Activity Reports*, Bayburt University Publications: Bayburt. 2017.

Bayburt University: *2014-2018 Strategic Plan*, Bayburt University Publications: Bayburt. 2014.

Giresun University: *2014-2019 Strategic Plan*, Giresun University Publications: Giresun. 2014.

Giresun University: *2014-2016 Performance Program*, Giresun University Publications: Giresun. 2016.

Ellwood, W.: *The No-Nonsense Guide to Globalization*, New Internationalist Publications: Toronto. 2001.

Ergun, T.: *Kamu Yönetimi-Kuram, Siyasa, Uygulama [Public Administration-Theory, Politics, Practice]*, TODAİE Yayını: Ankara. No:322. 2004.

Koçel T.: *İşletme Yöneticiliği [Business Management]*, Beta Yayınları, İstanbul. 2005.

Kunitz, S. J.: "Globalization, States and The Health of Indigenous Peoples", *American Journal of Public Health* 90(10), 2000, pp.1531–1539.

Kutlu Ö.: *Karşılaştırmalı Kamu Yönetimi[Comparative Public Administration]*, Çizgi Kitabevi, Konya. 2012.

Lee, K.: "The Impact of Globalization on Public Health: Implications for The UK Faculty of Public Health Medicine", *Journal of Public Health Medicine* 22(3), 2000, pp.253–262.

Ministry of Environment and Urbanization: *2015-2017 Strategic Plan*, Ministry Publications: Ankara. 2017.

Ministry of Environment and Urbanization: *2016-2014 Administrative Activity Report*, Ministry Publications: Ankara. 2015.

Ministry of Health: *2013-2017 Strategic Plan*, Ministry Publications: Ankara. 2012.

Ministry of Health: *2014 Annual Report*, Ministry Publications: Ankara. 2015.

Ministry of Health: 2016 Annual Report, Ministry Publications: Ankara. 2017.

Parlak B. / Sobacı Z.: *Kamu Yönetimi. [Public Administration]*, MKM Yayıncılık: Bursa. 2012.

Özata M. / Sevinç İ.: *Türk Kamu Yönetimlerinde Bilgi Sistemleri ve E-Dönüşüm [Information Systems and E-Transformation in Turkish Public Administration]*. Eğitim Akademi Yayınları: Konya. 2010.

Özgür H.: Kamu Örgütlerinde Stratejik Yönetim [Strategic Management in Public Organizations] in *Çağdaş Kamu Yönetimi-II:Konular Kuramlar*

Kavramlar [Contemporary Public Administration-II: Conceptual Theories Concepts], (Eds. M. Acar / H. Özgür), Nobel Publishing: Ankara. 2004.

PFMCL, Public Financial Management and Control Law No.5018, 2003.

Saran U. (2001). Küresel Değişim Dinamiklerinin Kamu Yönetimi Alanındaki Etkileri [The Effects of Global Change Dynamics on Public Administration], *Türk İdare Dergisi [Journal of Turkish Administration]*, Year: 73, Number: 433:41-49.

Steiner G.A: Stratecig Planning, Free Press Paperbacks. Simon & Schuster: USA. 1979.

Tekeli İ.: "Yönetim Kavramı Yanısıra Yönetişim Kavramının Gelişmesinin Nedenleri Üzerine [The Concept of Management and the Reasons for the Development of the Concept of Governance]", in *Türkiye'de Kamu Yönetimi [Public Administration in Turkey]*. (Eds: B. Aykaç / Ş. Durgun / H. Yayman). Nobel Publishing: Ankara. 2012.

Tortop N. / İspir E.G. / Aykaç B. / Yayman H. / Özer. M.A.: *Yönetim Bilimi [Management Science]*, Nobel Publishing: Ankara. 2016.

Shafritz J. M. / Russell E.W. / Borick C.P.: *Introducing Public Administration*. New York: Published by Routledge. 2016.

Tutum C.:"Kamu Yönetiminde Yeniden Yapılanma"[Restructuring in Public Administration], in Türkiye'de Kamu Yönetimi *[Public Administration in Turkey]*. (Eds: B. Aykaç / Ş. Durgun / H. Yayman). Nobel Yayınevi: Ankara. 2012.

Yılmaz, K.: Kamu Kuruluşları İçin Stratejik Planlama Uygulaması[Strategic Planning Practice for Public Organizations], *Sayıştay Dergisi*, Ankara, 2002, pp.50-86.

Seda Canpolat Bıcakcı

Globalization and State Spending in Turkey

Abstract: The 2000s in Turkey witnessed a series of breakthroughs which emerged as a consequence of global transformation the world economy has faced after 1970. These breakthroughs specifically in public financial system occurring as a result of neoliberal globalization affected the role and functioning of the state. One of the important indicators of the state's role in the economy is the amount and structure of state spending. This study aims to analyze the effects of neoliberal globalization to the post-2000s' state spending structure in Turkey by enlarging the framework of James O'Connor's theory: "the fiscal crisis of the state". In this regard, relying on the categories of O'Connor's theory, concepts of "global accumulation" and "global legitimization" are developed to discuss the transforming role of the state in an analytical and conceptual framework and the contradictory characteristics of the concepts are emphasized.

Keywords: Government Expenditures, Neoliberalism, Turkey, James O'Connor, Fiscal Crisis of the State

Introduction

Globalization is a big transformational process and a fact that affects every sphere of society and economy, particularly policy-making process. It has been discussed in the frame of 'nation-state' under the extremely wide and growing literature. In this regard, basically two approaches can be mentioned: *globalists* make the most of the literature (Savran 2008) with the concept of "one world"; *skeptics* use the concepts of "internationalization" and "regionalization" instead of the term "globalization". The former claims that there is an erosion of state sovereignty, autonomy, and legitimacy, thus the nation-state is declining. The latter disclaims the notion of "declining nation-state" and sees the process as a stage of new imperialism (Held and McGrew 2000, p. 38). In both approaches, the *state* is the main actor of this transformational process. Apart from these arguments, this study focuses on the effects of this transformational process on the changing role of the state in Turkey after 2000.

In this last big transformation, world has faced after the 1970s, neoliberal globalization and financialization were responsible for the economic crises and the shift in economic policies. Since then, the rapid progress in financialization and accompanying neoliberal economic policies that took shape with the institutions of globalization and with deregulation, liberalization and privatization policies dominated by them caused a series of financial crises all over the world, especially in developing countries.

Turkey, as a developing country, has started to experience transformational effects that come with neoliberal globalization from the 1980s onwards. Bahçe and Köse (2014) divided the three decades of neoliberalism in Turkey into three phases; preparatory neoliberalism between 1980 and 1989, the chaotic neoliberalism between 1990 and 2001, and the mature neoliberalism from 2002 onwards. Until the 1990s, in the preparatory neoliberalism period, the infrastructure of financialization had been built by implementing neoliberal economic policies (Koç 2015, p. 124). In the aftermath of integration into the global economy and financial liberalization in 1989, the chaotic neoliberalism period began. International capital flows had an important role in economic growth in this period. However, they frequently caused boom and collapse cycles between 1990 and 2001 and created a crisis-growth-crisis cycle. During this period, huge public deficit, high-interest rates, and chronic inflation were the main characteristics of the economy.

In the episode of mature neoliberalism, it came forward as a solution suggestion to the crisis that the state's corporate support should be increased for the markets and the structural transformations should be put in a legal frame. As most of all other developing countries under the IMF stabilization programs, Turkey also implemented the precautions such as devaluation of the local currency, de-unionization, postponing of external debts, finding new debt sources and along with these reducing state intervention. One of the most significant developments of this period was the founding of independent regulatory agencies (IRA hereafter) to reduce the state intervention. These agencies are out of the traditional administrative structure and autonomous. They are restructuring the market relations in accordance with the system necessities by the regulations in the relevant fields that are suitable for their laws. Different global institutions specifically OECD, by using the sanction power of IMF, dictated the fast founding of these agencies as a local scale of global bureaucracy in developing countries and became successful (Temelli, web).

In the leadership and domination of global institutions, it has been anticipated to make a rearrangement in public fiscal administration to provide the public services efficiently; in time, with high quality and with optimal costs. Providing fiscal discipline and fiscal sustainability was the main priority of the suggested regulations. The implementations suggested ensuring the fiscal discipline were mainly for the budget process. In one hand, in accordance with the "transparency principal" the announcement of the accounts about the activities of all the institutions those are in or out of the budget was suggested. On the other hand, people in charge and on duty of obtaining and using the public resources were held responsible for reporting to the essential units for the efficient use and misuse of the resources. Although these suggestions were implemented in Turkey, it might be told that the principals founding these suggestions were reflected to the budget process formalistically, but they were not in reality. This situation points to one of the state's basic contradictions with its angle studied in this work. The suggestions were shown as if they had been reflected to the budget process in line with the concealing role of the state. This means that the state is trying to cloud its basic functions with a complex budget structure. This contradiction is debated in accordance with a basic study and a seminal work by James O'Connor (1973) which has a remarkable place in public finance literature and founds the construction of this study.

As it was built before the aforementioned transformational process has begun, "The Fiscal Crisis of the State" (FCS hereafter) — work of O'Connor (1973) does not include a globalization category. However, its analytical framework is functional and useful because it approaches to the state and state spending in a different way as being against the mainstream economics and traditional Marxism. We apply the categories of this theory to Turkey's expenditure budget with some adjustments in order to investigate the effects of globalization on the Turkish state's conflicting roles. We attempt to internalize globalization category affecting the functions of the state in the analytical framework of FCS. However, we should mention that this is not a theoretical attempt of adding a category to the FCS, but a restricted analytical assessment. In this regard, we evaluate the basic categories of FCS in a global context which we conceptualize as "global capital accumulation" and "global legitimization". The first section presents the basic categories of FCS; the second section interprets Turkey's central government budget expenditures in the analytical framework of FCS, with a tentative classification considering some structural adjustments for Turkey's economy; the third section discusses the transformation of state functions with the concepts of "global capital accumulation" and "global legitimization". In this context, particularly, "fiscal discipline" is dealt as a reflection of the state's global capital accumulation function and "independent regulatory agencies" is dealt as the reflection of global legitimization function of the state in Turkey.

Functions of the State and State Spending in FCS

Like in the work of O'Connor (1973)[1], this study accepts as a premise that the state has two contradictory functions, which are *accumulation* and *legitimization*.

---

1 The state tries to legitimize the system by aiding the groups harmed by capital accumulation. In order to both provide and maintain social harmony, the state encounters

In O'Connor's view, on the one hand, the state must try to provide the conditions of capital accumulation (accumulation function), on the other hand, it must try to maintain social harmony (legitimization function). While fulfilling these contradictory functions, the state makes more and more spending that tends to outweigh the revenues and leads to a "structural gap". Thus, the FCS arises from the conflicting roles of the state.

O'Connor (1973) claims that the national accounts cloud class relations. To reveal the political, economic forces behind the budget decisions, each budget item should be examined in detail[2]. In this regard, he divides the state spending into two categories consistent with the two basic functions of the state. Budget expenditures serving accumulation of capital are categorized as *social capital* called as "accumulation expenditures" in this study. Social capital consists of social investment and social consumption. The expenditures required for social harmony are categorized as *social expense* called as "legitimization expenditures"[3]. This categorization is anticipated to be helping us understand the

---

difficulties in clouding its main function as being the accumulation function. The reason for this is that the contradicting process is shaped by the power relations in private economy.

2 According to O'Connor (1973), due to the dual and contradictory characteristics of the capitalist state, almost all state units are included in the accumulation and legitimation functions. Almost all of the expenditures also have this duality. For example, while providing equipment for developing the technical abilities of the labor power and some educational expenditures made for teachers form accumulation expenditures, other expenditures such as campus security can be seen as legitimization expenditure. And highways, from the point of providing transportation from and to work, can be categorized as social consumption which is a sub category of accumulation expenditures. Highways also serve the commercial transportation and from this point of view, can be evaluated as social investment. On the other hand, the state also needs the highways, so highways can be counted in the legitimization category. Despite the complex character of state expenditures, the political-economic reasons that the budget decisions serve to and the basic purpose of each budget item can be determined by examining each item thoroughly (Canpolat Bıcakcı 2017, pp. 1089–1090).

3 Social capital consists of direct and indirect expenditures required by the profitable private accumulation those expand the surplus value. Social investments contain all kinds of state activities increasing the productivity such as road services, industrial parks and human capital activities. The social consumption contains the state activities decreasing the reproduction costs of the labor. Educational expenditures, social security system and unemployment insurance are some examples of this category (O'Connor 1973, pp. 6–7).

state's changing role in Turkey after 2000, under a different conceptual framework on government budget and in line with globalization process.

O'Connor (1973) asserts that the state in a capitalist economy cannot be independent, but it has to pretend as if it is. The global transformational process did not change this reality over the time but affected the relative weight of the functions of the state which can be particularly seen in state spending. Budget discipline, particularly in mature neoliberalism, replaced the structural gap of the Keynesian post-war period. Increasing legitimization expenditures is replaced by the regulations of IRAs.

Analyzing the State Spending in Turkey

In mature neoliberalism period, the most important transformation was in public finance in Turkey. A new budget system was introduced with the law no. 5018. Through this law amendment, a budget structure was tried to be built within the frame of the principals such as "fiscal transparency" in public service providing and "accountability", "efficiency" and "productivity" in the usage of resources. In this regard, the responsibilities of the officials having a role at expenditure making stages were redesigned, extra-budgetary funds were started to be shown in the central government budget, a new coding system was introduced named as "analytical budget classification," and budget items were classified up to level four.

When the state budget is examined thoroughly, it can be seen that the principles were not attended enough despite these important steps. The quantitative weight of "unclassified" expenditure items does not allow examining the items having a significant share in the budget. In the functional classification of central government budget, the roughly 91.82% of "social security and aid" item is unclassified. From this point, economic classification gives more detailed data than the functional classification. In the context of this study, the first level of expenditures and only the central government budget is taken into consideration.

Decomposition of Central Government Budget Expenditures

The first level codes of economic classification presented at Tab. 1, are divided into two categories in Tab. 2. In consistence with the aforementioned categories that O'Connor (1973) defines, 'compensation of employees,' 'social security contributions' and 'lending' items are included in legitimization expenditures. The items of 'goods and services purchases,' 'current transfers,' 'capital expenditures,' and 'capital transfers' fit to the category of accumulation expenditures. Interest is dealt with differently from the work of O'Connor (1973), considering the global

Tab. 1: Economic Classification of Budget Expenditures

Economic Classification of Budget Expenditures
Compensation of Employees
Social Security Contributions
Goods and Services Purchases
Interest
Current Transfers
Capital Expenditures
Capital Transfers
Lending

Tab. 2: Classification of Budget Expenditures in Turkey Based on FCS

CAPITALIST STATE	
LEGITIMIZATION EXPENDITURES	**ACCUMULATION EXPENDITURES**
Compensation of Employees	Goods and Services Purchases
Social Security Contributions	Interest
Lending	Current Transfers
	Capital Expenditures
	Capital Transfers

transformational process, the effects of this process to Turkey's economy and the structural differences of Turkey as a developing country.

Interest is considered as legitimization expenditure in O'Connor (1973) because he regards all administrative operations as related to social harmony. In the post-war period, primary sources of US government debt and interest payments were mainly military and social expenditures in the great depression (Miller 1986, p. 245). Because of this reason, Miller (1986) regards 'net interest paid' as a social expense in his critical analysis of FCS. In Turkey, as the government debt is shaped due to the needs of private economy (Canpolat Bıcakcı 2017, p. 1097) and interest payments are related to the segments of society those have enough wealth that enables them to lend to the government (Özuğurlu 2005, p. 82), the interest item is considered as accumulation expenditure, but analyzed separately.

Empirical Analysis

In mature neoliberalism episode, macroeconomic stabilization goal was carried out as first priority with the reforms on public finance administration. After

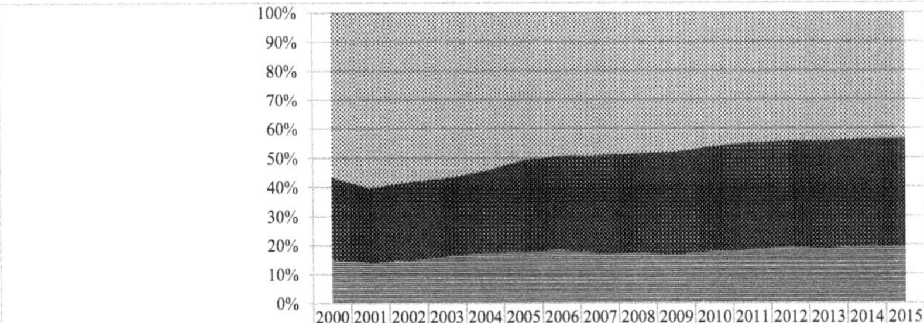

	2000	2001	2002	2003	2004	2005	2006	2007	2008	2009	2010	2011	2012	2013	2014	2015
Accumulation exp. (include interest)	78.9	81.2	80.0	77.7	75.7	74.2	72.7	73.9	73.6	74.3	72.1	70.9	69.4	70.2	68.8	68.9
Accumulation exp.	39.1	34.0	36.8	36.3	38.6	45.6	46.9	50.0	51.3	54.5	55.7	57.5	56.0	57.9	57.7	58.4
Legitimization exp.	21.1	18.8	20.0	22.3	24.3	25.8	27.3	26.1	26.4	25.7	27.9	29.1	30.6	29.8	31.2	31.1

Fig. 1: Central Budget Shares of Categories, 2000–2015. Source: The Ministry of Finance Directorate General of Public Accounts (MFDGPA), Public Accounts Bulletin. Access: 10.12.2017.

executing the IMF stabilization program in 1994, Turkey started to apply a rule-based fiscal policy based on the criteria specified by IMF. After the 2001 crisis, the tightly applied non-interest surplus goal was shown as the basic element of Turkey's macroeconomic programs and became a rule at the programs supported by IMF (BSB 2007). Within the frame of this goal, to provide the fiscal discipline after 2001 crisis, the steps taken to minimize the internal debt stock significantly limited the increase in the interest payments. The institutions of globalization set the primary goals, and the effects of globalization arouse as some significant changes in the budget expenditure composition, significantly as a decline in interest as seen in fig. 1 and fig. 2.

Fig. 1 indicates that there is a general tendency for the two categories to rise when interest is not included. State spending for accumulation function has a significantly high share in central budget. It seems that the state in Turkey functions explicitly for capital accumulation and there seems to be no essential need to cloud this for social harmony. However, further analysis is needed to verify this statement[4]. This study's aim is to observe the general tendency of the

4 According to the analysis based on functional classification presented by Canpolat Bıcakcı (2017), the two functions of the state are converging over the time period. The analysis starts in 2006, and decomposes the expenditures to the third level. Despite being started in 2000, our analysis based on economic classification, decomposes the

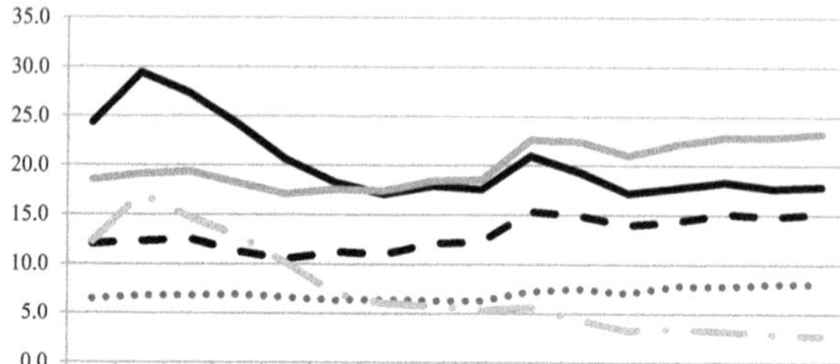

	2000	2001	2002	2003	2004	2005	2006	2007	2008	2009	2010	2011	2012	2013	2014	2015
Legitimization exp.	6.5	6.8	6.8	6.9	6.6	6.4	6.4	6.3	6.3	7.2	7.5	7.0	7.8	7.8	8.0	8.1
Accumulation exp.	12.1	12.3	12.5	11.3	10.5	11.2	11.0	12.1	12.3	15.3	14.9	13.9	14.3	15.1	14.8	15.2
Accumulation exp. (include interest)	24.3	29.4	27.3	24.1	20.6	18.3	17.1	17.9	17.6	20.9	19.3	17.2	17.7	18.3	17.7	17.9
Total (primary) exp.	18.6	19.1	19.4	18.2	17.1	17.6	17.4	18.4	18.6	22.6	22.4	21.0	22.1	22.9	22.8	23.2
Interest	12.3	17.1	14.8	12.9	10.1	7.0	6.1	5.8	5.3	5.6	4.4	3.3	3.4	3.2	2.9	2.7

Fig. 2: GDP Shares of Categories, 2000–2015. Source: MFDGPA, Public Accounts Bulletin. Access: 10.12.2017.

functions of the state and the effects of globalization on state spending. We see that the main effect is on the interest item.

Chaotic neoliberalism episode was characterized by extremely high-interest payments which are a form of transferring public funds to the private sector. With the growing financialization, rising share of interest payments indicated that the state uses borrowing not only for eliminating public sector deficits but also as a transfer mechanism of funds to the capitalist class via state budget. As we see from the starting year of 2000 in fig. 2, the share of interest in GDP is increasing in 2001, just like in the chaotic neoliberalism's debt crisis, then starts to decline over the time. This represents the significant shift in state's role of accumulation. The state changes the way of serving capital mostly in the form of other political power instruments such as regulating the markets, public-private partnerships, and changing the composition of budget expenditures.

first level expenditures because of the consistency concerns. Data is available only for the first level for the period of 2000–2005. In a fourth level decomposition, the results will probably change but general tendency of rising expenditures by two categories will remain same. In a further analysis current transfers consist of social transfers that need to be classified as social expense and the item of goods and services purchases should be examined in fourth level.

According to the categorization which is firstly presented by Canpolat Bıcakcı (2017) in the framework of FCS and functional classification, declining share of interest (26% to 10%) is replaced by the rising shares of general public services (3.76%), public order and safety (1.77%), social security and aid (5.07%), economic affairs (2.64%) and education (4.69%) in central government budget between 2006 and 2015. It seems like the share of legitimization expenditures is rising relatively faster. However, Canpolat Bıcakcı (2017) also notes that roughly 91.82% of social security and aid item is unclassified. This situation restricts the analyses substantially. Moreover, the effects of the transformation cannot be observed on spending in all aspects directly and explicitly. For instance, the declining share of health can be interpreted as a decline in accumulation function. On the other hand, it can be seen as an effect of marketization on health services.

In economic classification, declining share of interest is mainly replaced by personnel expenditures and social security contributions and current transfers. The composition of expenditures presented in fig. 3 indicates that the most significant increase is in the current transfers' share. The increase in accumulation expenditures is mainly a result of rapid increase of current transfers. In a further analysis, this item should be examined in detail to distinguish the shares of categories precisely. Even if the share of interest is declining, the shares of other expenditures in the budget and total expenditures in GDP are rising. This means that the significant shift in state's functions is a result of neoliberal globalization. In chaotic neoliberalism, the main transfer mechanism was the interest. In mature neoliberalism, the state has transformed into a regulatory actor.

Evaluating the Results

The analysis on state spending revealed that the state is transforming dramatically. The global transformation's most significant effect is on interest payments. This much decrease of the interest means that the state provides the transfer of the sources to the capitalist class in different ways. In chaotic neoliberalism, the main transfer mechanism was the interest payments. In mature neoliberalism, the state has transformed into a regulatory actor. The transfers to capitalist class became possible by increasing public-private partnerships and privatization. In accordance with the goal of reducing the state's share in the economy, it was necessary to leave the public production in areas such as education and health to the operation of market mechanism. The reason for this can be interpreted as creating new valuation areas for the capital depending on the tendency of rate of profit to fall. In O'Connor's terms, the fulfillment of the production of services by the public economy, such as education and health which are in social

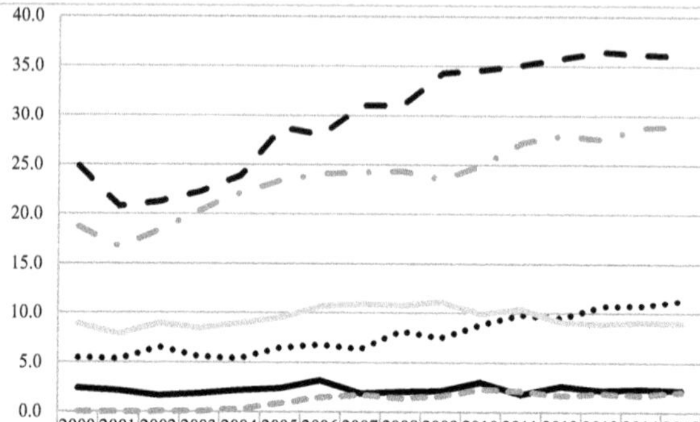

	2000	2001	2002	2003	2004	2005	2006	2007	2008	2009	2010	2011	2012	2013	2014	2015
Personnel Expenditures and Social Security Contributions Paid by the State	18.7	16.7	18.4	20.4	22.1	23.4	24.1	24.2	24.3	23.5	24.9	27.3	28.0	27.6	28.8	28.9
Lending	2.4	2.1	1.6	1.8	2.2	2.4	3.2	1.9	2.0	2.1	3.0	1.8	2.6	2.2	2.4	2.2
Capital Expenditures	5.5	5.3	6.5	5.6	5.4	6.5	6.8	6.4	8.2	7.5	8.8	9.8	9.5	10.7	10.7	11.3
Capital Transfers	0.0	0.0	0.0	0.1	0.3	0.9	1.5	1.7	1.4	1.6	2.3	2.1	1.7	1.9	1.7	2.1
Purchase of Goods and Services	8.8	7.8	8.9	8.4	8.9	9.5	10.7	10.9	10.8	11.1	9.9	10.4	9.1	8.9	9.1	9.0
Current Transfers	24.8	20.8	21.2	22.3	23.9	28.7	28.0	31.0	31.0	34.3	34.6	35.1	35.8	36.4	36.2	36.1

Fig. 3: Central Budget Shares of Expenditures, Economic Classification, 2000–2015. Source: MFDGPA, Public Accounts Bulletin. Access: 10.12.2017.

consumption category, is relatively increasing the profitability of the capital as it increases the labor productivity and socializes the reproduction costs of labor. However, as the economic crises deepen depending on the tendency of rate of profit to fall, the capital looks for new valuation fields to expand. At this point, it comes up for the public productions such as education, health and many more fields to be left to market mechanism meaning to be privatized (Özuğurlu 2005, pp. 78–79).

After the integration to the global markets process — chaotic neoliberalism period, with the structural adjustments and the 'successfully' implemented fiscal rule policy, budget deficits were decreased, non-interest surplus, the cost coverage ratio of public revenues and expenses were increased and due to this, public debt burden decreased since the mid-2000s. In this reorganization process, the transfers from the public sector to the private sector through interest payments yielded to incentives for private sector borrowing; the finance sector was strengthened. While Turkey was stabilizing its finance sector, the global crisis emerged in 2007. In a capitalist system, during crisis periods, the role of the state becomes more significant because the conditions threatening the sustainability of capital accumulation are eliminated by the state. The previous sections' figures indicate that the total expenditures are rising rapidly during the crisis periods. The crisis periods emphasizing the accumulation function of the state and the structure of public expenditures changing in accordance with this function require the income distribution to be rearranged according to the capital accumulation conditions.

Over the time period the state has grown, so has the spending as O'Connor (1973) argues[5]. However, neoliberal globalization transformed the expenditure composition, as significantly seen in interest item. When it is included in accumulation category, it seems that the role of the state in providing the conditions of capital accumulation is declining over the time period. When we exclude it, we see that non-interest accumulation expenditures are rising relatively faster than legitimization expenditures. These results are not consistent with O'Connor's view because of the missing globalization category. O'Connor (2009), however, gives some key points to add this category into the analysis[6]. In the context of this study, globalization is tried to be internalized and considered as a process, not as a category that has to be included in a theoretical analysis. Further analysis should include globalization as a theoretical category. Next section discusses the transforming accumulation and legitimization functions in a global context.

Global Capital Accumulation versus Global Legitimization

As O'Connor (2009) stated, for the FCS to explain the 'globalization age', the categories of neoliberalism, financialization, and globalization should be added to the theory. O'Connor (2009), while explaining why *Fiscal Crisis* failed to anticipate the revolutionary changes of globalization age, he also notes that his work included neoliberalism but with a less proper explanation:

---

5 In the process causing the fiscal crisis of the state, the determinative role of power relations in the private economy and the role of the state have a central importance. O'Connor (1973) divides the capitalist economy into three sectors as the *competitive sector*, the *monopoly sector*, and the *state sector*. The monopoly and competitive sectors together, constructs private economy. The monopoly sector exhibits the causality at the basic thesis of FCS from the angle of its relation to the state sector. The causality between the state sector and the monopoly sector is reciprocal. O'Connor (1973) defines the basic thesis of the theory on the grounds of this causality; *the growth of total production and the monopoly sector cause the state to grow; as the state grows the monopoly sector grows* (Canpolat Bıcakcı 2017, p. 1087).

6 "[... It's the monopoly sector, of course, that's being globalized (in the form of foreign direct investment, outsourcing, downsizing, joint ventures across borders, mergers and acquisitions across borders, the establishment of a single world market price for many commodities, etc.)]." (O'Connor 2009, p. xxii)

> "[… On the other hand, the pillars of neoliberalism — privatization, liberalization of foreign exchange markets and investments, and deregulation — are all consistent with the analysis in FCS, although as noted above a proper explanation of neoliberalism would have required a more global theory than the one I provided in FCS]." (O'Connor 2009, p. xxii)

Developing a more global theory based on FCS by adding the missing categories requires an advanced theoretical work. However, evaluations made by only taking into consideration the effects of the categories can also be highly explanatory. In this section, the functions of the state are debated as considering the effects of globalization to internalize the globalization category.

Results of the study revealed that the state both provided global legitimization and served global accumulation in mature neoliberalism period. Also, contradictions and dual structure of these functions and globalization's effects on state spending are revealed. One of the dualities is emerged in terms of IRAs. These agencies were first founded in the USA; then in several European countries and the 1980s, they were transferred to the developing countries as a part of deregulation process. They structured the connection between especially the local, the country, and neoliberal accumulation regime. The sector containing most intensely these agencies is the finance sector and creating an autonomous structure for this sector was the first priority for the neoliberal accumulation regime (Temelli, web). From this standpoint, it might be stressed that these agencies were founded with the aim of serving to global accumulation. On the other hand, it might be stated that as a strict practitioner of neoliberal policies, the state is trying to legitimize the domestic system against global institutions. In Turkey, these agencies also function as a legitimizing instrument against capitalist class damaged by the instabilities in the chaotic period in accordance with their demands. Hence, duality reveals in regards to the functions. However, in terms of Turkey, it seems that global legitimization is in the foreground.

In terms of global accumulation, the most significant effect on state spending is observed in the interest payments. This exhibits the importance of fiscal discipline and fiscal sustainability goals. As a means of macroeconomic stabilization, it is obvious that these goals serve the accumulation function. After the 2007 global crisis, the neoliberal accumulation regime was started to be questioned. Especially the global institutions' undertaking of the burden of bankrupting giant finance corporations, exhibits that the intervention of the state to the private sector increases contradicting the statements of neoliberalism. O'Connor (1973)'s prediction about the relationship between monopoly sector and the state is also observed on a global scale. The state recreated the conditions of global financial accumulation in accordance with the needs and demands of the monopoly sector. In Turkey, the effects of the global crisis emerged in the real sector and intervention of the state was required as in the global context.

Conclusion

This study investigated the effects of globalization on state spending in Turkey. For this investigation, the analytical framework of FCS was used, and the missing category of globalization is tried to be internalized. In this context, the items of central government budget based on economic classification were decomposed and categorized as accumulation and legitimization expenditures. The composition and development of these categories were represented from 2000 to 2015 which corresponds to the end of chaotic neoliberalism and episode of mature neoliberalism. According to the results of the decomposition, the most significant effect of globalization which should not be dealt without the categories of neoliberalism and financialization is in the finance sector in the economy and the interest payments in the budget. The rising budget expenditures replaced the declining interest payments share in the central budget which is a consequence of fiscal discipline policy imposed by the institutions of globalization, and this revealed that the state's transferring mechanism of sources to the private sector has changed.

The implementations like public-private partnerships, privatization, and regulations built the dimension of this mechanism that cannot be reflected directly to the budget. Regulations were implemented through the IRAs during the mature neoliberalism. To conclude, it might be told that while the global accumulation function overrides in fiscal discipline policy whose effects can be observed in the budget, the global legitimization function overrides in terms of IRAs whose effects should also be traced out of the budget. However, although the IRAs were founded with legitimization concerns, when the duality between the functions is taken into consideration, it can be stated that they were structured to serve global capital accumulation function in the background. When the globalization function is internalized, the importance of the basic analytical construction of FCS comes forward.

Bibliography

Bahçe, Serdal / Köse, Ahmet Haşim: "The Effects of the New Welfare System on the Inter- and Intra-Class Distribution of Income in Turkey." Paper Presented at *Global Labour University Conference*. Berlin. 2014.

Bağımsız Sosyal Bilimciler (BSB): *IMF Gözetiminde On Uzun Yıl: 1998–2008, Farklı Hükümetler, Tek Siyaset*. Yordam Kitap: İstanbul. 2007.

Canpolat Bıcakcı, Seda: "Bütçe Kategorizasyonu Gölgesinde Devletin İşlevleri: Bir Kategorizasyon Denemesi." *Ankara Üniversitesi SBF Dergisi* 72 (4), 2017, pp. 1081–1106.

Held, David / McGrew, Anthony: "The Great Globalization Debate : An Introduction." In: Held, David / Mcgrew, Anthony (Ed.): *The Global Transformations Reader*. Polity Press: Cambridge. 2000, pp. 1–50.

Koç, Celil A.: "Küresel Kapitalizmin Finansallaşmasına Türkiye Ekonomisinin Eklemlenme Süreci." In: Mıhcı, Hakan (Ed.): *Finansallaşma, Devlet ve Politik İktisat*. NotaBene: Ankara. 2015, pp. 115–146.

Miller, John A.: "The Fiscal Crisis of the State Reconsidered: Two Views of the State and the Accumulation of Capital in the Postwar Economy." *Review of Radical Political Economics* 18 (1–2), 1986, pp. 236–260.

O'Connor, James: *The Fiscal Crisis of the State*. St. Martin Press: New York 1973.

O'Connor, James: *The Fiscal Crisis of the State: With a New Introduction by the Author*. 4th ed. Transaction Publishers: New Brunswick and London. 2009.

Özuğurlu, Yasemin: "Kamu Harcamalarının Bölüşüm İlişkileri Üzerine Etkisi: Türkiye Açısından Bir Değerlendirme." *Ekonomik Yaklaşım* 16 (55), 2005, pp. 69–88.

Savran, Sungur: *Kod Adı Küreselleşme: 21. Yüzyılda Emperyalizm*. Yordam Kitap: İstanbul. 2008.

Temelli, Sezai: Neoliberal Düzenin Düzenleyicileri: Bağımsız Düzenleyici Kurullar, retrieved 28.12.2017, from https://www.karasaban.net/neoliberal-duzenin-duzenleyicileri-bagimsiz-duzenleyici-kurullarsezai-temelli/.

Alper Aytekin, Mehmet Pekkaya and Fatma Sönmez Çakır

Determining Factors of Export Performance in Furniture Industry: An Application on Turkey[1]

Abstract: The furniture industry is expected to grow very fast worldwide, with turnover-based growth (2.7%) and also it is an essential aspect of the analysis of issuer determinants, because of 20% increase targeted in exporting of Turkey's furniture industry for 2017. The study aims to determine the items and the factors affecting the export performance in the furniture industry and to present the findings to the academicians, the managers, and decision-makers in the related industry. In this sense, 182 firms, majority of them are from İnegöl, Turkey, have an important place in exporting of Turkey's furniture industry, and make up the research sample of the questionnaire. Literature-based 63 items are measured via 7-point Likert scale. The factor scores of items' eighth dimensions based on related literature and confirmed via factor analysis are calculated. The items and dimensions that have a potential effect on firm export performance are examined comparatively for non-exporting /exporting firms, and the relations between dimensions are evaluated.

Keywords: Furniture industry, Determiners of export performance, Factor analysis

Introduction

A country that wishes to grow in the area of industrialization should have strategies such as "to export products" or "to ensure that goods are produced domestically". In fact, these two strategies complement each other (Subaşat 2004). There are great similarities between these two strategies. Reducing the balance-of-payments deficit, industrialization, economic growth, and ensuring a high level of employment are the primary objectives of both strategies. The main difference between the strategies is that all efforts in the import substitution industrialization strategy aim at restricting imports, while in the outward-looking industrialization strategy, all efforts are directed towards increasing exports (Ay 2007; Yapar 2009).

1 This study is based on Alper Aytekin's (Mehmet Pekkaya as advisor) ongoing doctoral thesis study, recorded in the program of Business Administration, Bulent Ecevit University.

The year 2016 can be evaluated as a year in which world trade shrank due to the decline in oil and commodity prices as well as the increase in the USD. According to the first ten months data of World Trade Organization, world trade declined by 4% on a dollar basis and decreased by 15.8 trillion dollars. However, the intensity of this decrease has begun to slow down in recent months. The contraction in world trade in the first six months was observed at 5.5%. With the recovery in oil and commodity prices, global trade is expected to reach around $ 16 trillion at the end of 2016 and increase again in 2017. On a country basis, US exports fell 4.6% in the first ten months, while imports fell 4%. In the same period, exports and imports of the EU declined by 1.2% and 0.7%, respectively, while exports by Russia decreased by 21.9% and imports by 2.7%. According to the data of first 11 months, China's exports decreased by 7.4%, imports by 6.2% (Alsan 2017).

The furniture industry is an important foreign trade area in the world. Furniture consumption is foreseen to grow by 2.7% globally in 2017. Although Asia and the Pacific continue to be the fastest growing regions, it is noteworthy that in 2016, China's exports of furniture declined and Vietnam became the fastest growing country. Over the last five years, US furniture imports have increased from $23 billion to $32 billion, becoming the main source of growth in this industry. In 2016, Turkey exported furniture to more than 170 countries through 204 customs points. Despite the difficulties in 2016, the total export volume was $2.5 billion and projected to $3 billion as an increase of 20% in 2017 is targeted (MOBSAD 2017). The total export volume projection of furniture industry for 2023 is $10 billion (MOBSAD 2016) which means annually more than 21.9% compound increase in average for the following seven years when the annual growth ratio of 5% is acceptable as for Turkey. According to the IMF, the expected growth rate is 5.1% for 2017 and 3.5% for 2018 (AA 2017). For this reason, these growth ratios of export in furniture industry are very high for Turkey.

Furniture has begun to be accepted as a demonstration of welfare level over time as well as being a product used in every field of daily life. In this context, improvements in income levels and living conditions have become the most decisive factors in the development of the furniture industry. When all these are taken into account, in the classification of furniture, the usage areas and the characteristics of the user are of great importance. For example, users in the high-income group are choosing furniture in the direction of personal liking to transform their daily life more comfortable, whereas those in the middle-income group prefer functional, high-strength furniture for more extended use.

In the export dimension, furniture manufacturers in Turkey need to be able to measure the power of Turkey in foreign markets. To be successful in world trade in terms of export is possible by following a competitive policy at the global level. From here, it is possible to increase the foreign trade ability of a country by determining the factors affecting export performance.

The aim of the study is to determine the factors affecting the export performance in the furniture industry and to present the obtained findings to the academicians, the managers, and decision-makers in the related industry. Accordingly, the 63 items and eight main dimensions/factors, affecting export performance are determined as a result of the extensive literature review. The items and dimensions obtained from the related literature were surveyed on 182 firms operating in the furniture industry, especially the exporting firms, the attitudes that firms followed/adopted about the items were measured in terms of the 7 points Likert scale. For each identified dimension/factor with their items are confirmed by reliability and one-dimensional exploratory factor analysis. The items and dimensions that have a potential effect on firm export performance are examined comparatively for non-exporting and exporting firms, and also the relations between dimensions are evaluated.

Since this study concentrates on the determinants of export performance of specifically furniture industry which are exporters in Turkey in general, our study according to related literature studies can be accepted as original.

The study consists of four parts. In the following second chapter, the determinants of furniture exports and the review of the literature are discussed by referring to the situation of the furniture industry in the world and Turkey. The third section contains the findings of field research and analysis. The final section consists of an evaluation of findings and recommendations.

Furniture Exports Determiners

Furniture is defined as all functional, aesthetically pleasing items, usually made of wood, in order to safely and comfortably meet the fundamental social and cultural needs of daily living such as working, sitting, resting, eating, storing (Sakarya and Doğan 2014).

Furniture is highly functional products because they are useful to provide for people's needs. Furniture is produced either for inside or outside places, using the building production items such as fiberboard, flakeboard, plywood, melamine coated chipboard, or some of them together. Besides wood-based by-products, they can be used with natural or artificial materials such as metal, marble, plastic, and glass.

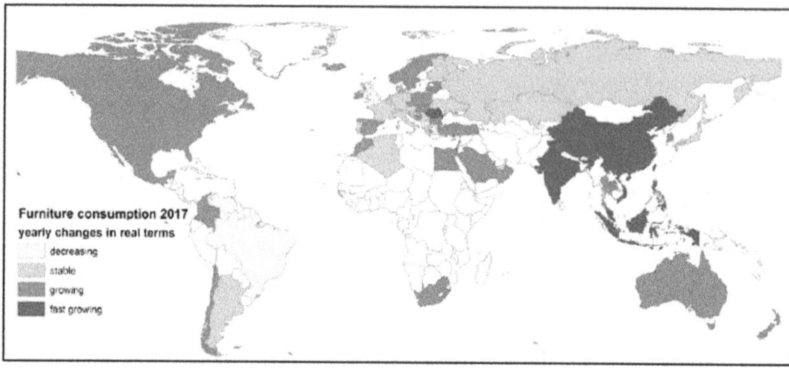

Fig. 1: Change in Furniture Consumption in 2017 Compared to Previous Years. Source: CSIL processing of United Nations, Eurostat, and national data.

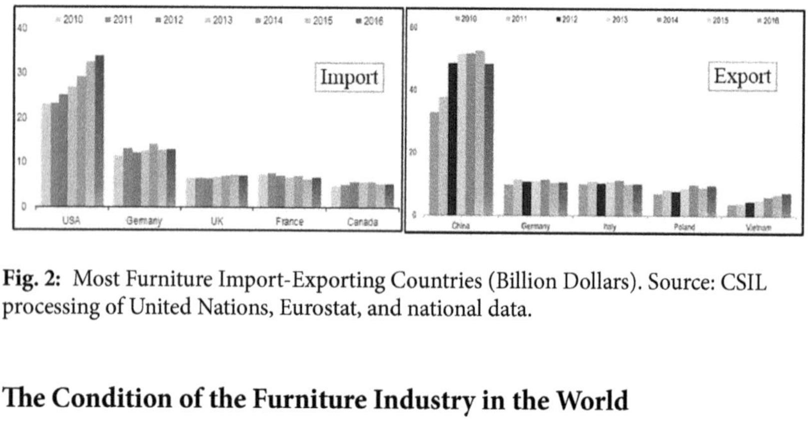

Fig. 2: Most Furniture Import-Exporting Countries (Billion Dollars). Source: CSIL processing of United Nations, Eurostat, and national data.

The Condition of the Furniture Industry in the World

While furniture consumption is growing in the United States, Saudi Arabia, Turkey, Egypt and Australia, this growth is much more in China and India. In addition, in Russia, the situation is stable compared to previous years, while it shows a decrease in Brazil (Fig. 1) (CSIL, 2017).

The countries with the highest imports of furniture in the world are the United States, Germany, the United Kingdom, France and Canada, while the top exporting countries are China, Germany, Italy, Poland, and Vietnam. It should be underlined that Vietnam has made considerable progress in recent years. The furniture exports and imports of these countries for the last seven years are given in Fig. 2 (CSIL 2017).

Turkey is in the 15th rank in furniture exports in 2016 (TradeMap 2017). In the same year, Turkey exported furniture to more than 170 countries through

Tab. 1: Number of Firms and Employees by City.
Source: Çanakçı, 2016.

City	Firm Number	Employee Number
Istanbul	6 458	35 633
Ankara	5 361	30 062
Izmir	2 379	14 142
Bursa	2 130	16 096
Kayseri	740	20 280
Other	12 278	42 000
Total	29 346	158 213
Retail Sales	32 382	100 000
Grand Total	61 728	258 213

204 customs points. The total export volume was $2.6 billion in 2016, despite a very serious difficulty such as the coup attempt, the aircraft crisis with Russia; in 2017, and an increase of 20% is targeted.

Condition of Furniture Industry in Turkey

In Turkey, the furniture industry is a sector, which is managed by traditional methods, often a family business, small-scale, workshop-type enterprises. In Turkey, especially in the last 20 years, the number of small and medium-sized enterprises, as well as small-scale enterprises, is rapidly increasing.

According to TURKSTAT and MOSDER, there are a total of 61728 firms in Turkey, 29346 of which are producers and 32382 of which are retailers. It can be said that the number of people working in the furniture industry is around 258213 and this number may be about 500000 together with the sub-industry. The number of firms and employees according to cities is given in the Tab. 1(Çanakçı 2016).

The furniture industry in Turkey is densely located close to the market and raw materials. These include Bursa, Kayseri, Ankara, Istanbul, and Izmir (Tab. 1). Besides, furniture production is also high in such cities as Adana, Bolu, Eskişehir, Antalya, Antalya, Sakarya, Burdur, Balıkesir, Zonguldak, and Trabzon. In other words, furniture production in Turkey concentrates mainly in industrial areas, especially in the north-west regions and partly in the middle regions.

Literature Survey on Factors Affecting Furniture Exports

A literature search was conducted to determine factors in the study. The main factors affecting exports have been identified and classified in previous studies.

The used factors in all studies at the end of the evaluations can be summarized as in Tab. 2 under three main groups (Beleska-Spasova 2014). At the end of the literature survey, researchers studying factors affecting export performance have been found to concentrate on similar factors. These factors can be grouped among themselves as internal factors, external factors, and others. Domestic factors consist of sub-headings such as management features, export strategy, and expertise, firm characteristics; external factors also consist of internal and external market characteristics, competition situation and sales policies. Customer satisfaction, new technologies and expertise areas are gathered under the heading of other factors.

A Survey on Factor Determinants Affecting Exports in Turkey

The aim of the survey is to determine the items and factors affecting the export performance of the furniture industry in Turkey. Therefore, the questionnaire conducted in the second quarter of 2017 for 182 furniture industry firms, the majority of them are basic furniture industry exporters of Turkey, the majority of them operate in İnegöl. The measured attitude and strategies of these furniture industry firms in terms of items, according to the managers of them via questionnaire, are the source of obtaining data which are used in the analysis of this study.

Material and Method

In the questionnaire prepared to be used in the analysis of the study, opinions about the characteristics, attitudes, and strategies of the firms were collected by a total of 95 questions, 63 items of which are in 7 points Likert scale, and 32 of which consist of mostly open-ended ratio scaled and some nominal scaled for characteristics of firms. The 7 points Likert scale is used to succeed the more sensitive data measurement, the structure of data more prone to the normal distribution characteristics (Pekkaya and Akıllı 2013), and parametric analysis. The interval scale is used 1 to 7, four refer to indecision and seven refer to agree strongly.

As the random process is not conducted in sampling, the evaluations obtained from the analysis represent the properties and the attitudes of the 182 firms. Based on the literature research, it is decided to examine all the influential variables in determining the exporting of the furniture industry. Accordingly the attitudes/trends of the firms in terms of 63 items and eight factors/dimensions listed below are measured, in order to determine the effective items/factors in exporting.

Tab. 2: Factors Affecting Exports

	Content	Research
Internal Factors	**I1) Management features and perceptions:** export commitment and support, international experience, international orientation, export motivation, perception of export advantages, age, education	Aaby and Slater, 1989; Cavusgil and Zou, 1994; Cavusgil, 1984; Ibeh and Wheeler, 2005; Katsikeas et al., 2000; Lages and Montgomery, 2004; Zou and Stan, 1998.
	I2) Organization skills - advanced technology and product/service quality	Chetty and Hamilton, 1993; Madsen 1989; Rodriguez and Rodriguez, 2005; Contractor et al., 2007; Haahti et al., 2005; Yeoh, 2004.
	I3) Organizational skills - export strategy: general export strategy, export planning, export organization, market expansion, service strategy, risk-taking, control, process	Aaby and Slater, 1989; Ibeh and Wheeler, 2005; Zou and Stan, 1998; Shoham, 1999; Contractor et al., 2007; Haahti et al., 2005.
	I4) Organization skills - marketing mix: product strategy, price strategy, promotion strategy, distribution strategy	Cavusgil and Zou 1994; Lages and Montgomery, 2004; Madsen, 1989; Shoham, 1999; Brouthers and Nakos, 2005; Morgan et al., 2004; Zou et al., 1998; O'Cass and Julian, 2003; Brouthers and Xu, 2002.
	I5) knowledge-based factors - export expertise: International experience	Brouthers and Nakos, 2005; Brouthers and Xu, 2002; Contractor et al., 2007; O'Cass and Julian, 2003.
	I6) Knowledge-based factors - export knowledge: Market research, customer information, market information, competitor information, supply chain channel information	Hart and Tzokas, 1999; Ling-yee, 2004; Morgan et al., 2004; Richey and Myers, 2001; Solberg, 2002.
	I7) Relational factors - business and institutional relationships: Distribution channel relationship, customer relationship, supplier relationship, Relationship between partners, membership in registered and unregistered commercial networks, relations with state and other institutions	Cadogan et al., 2009; Ibeh and Wheeler, 2005; Styles and Ambler, 2000; Styles et al., 2008; Zou and Stan, 1998.
	I8) Firm characteristics: Company size, internationalization grade, firm age, industry/product type, organizational culture, financial resources, ownership structure	Balabanis and Katsikea, 2003; Brouthers and Nakos, 2005; Brouthers and Xu, 2002; Contractor et al., 2007; Haahti et al., 2005; Shoham, 1999.

(*continued on next page*)

Tab. 2: (continued)

	Content	Research
External Factors	**E1) Characteristics of the export market:** Legal and political, cultural similarity, market competitiveness, Eco-friendly, economic similarity, channel accessibility, customer exposure	Balabanis and Katsikea, 2003; Brouthers and Xu, 2002; O'Cass and Julian, 2003; Lages and Montgomery, 2004; Cadogan et al., 2009; Cadogan et al., 2012.
	E2) Characteristics of domestic market: Domestic market conditions, export assistance, Eco-friendly	Lages and Montgomery, 2004; Gençtürk and Kotabe, 2001; Alvarez, 2004; Francis and Collins-Dodd, 2004; Robertson and Chetty, 2000.
	E3) Sales-related: Export intensity (increase), export sales efficiency, export sales growth, export growth compared to competitors, export sales investment return, export sales volume, export sales volume compared to competitors	Gençtürk and Kotabe (2001); Lages and Lages (2004); Balabanis and Katsikea (2003); Brouthers and Xu (2002); Shoham (1999).
	E4) Market related: exports market share, export market share compared to competitors, export market share growth, export market share growth compared to competitors, market solidarity, market diversification, rate of entry to new markets, rate of entry to new markets compared to competitors	Brouthers and Xu (2002); Lages and Lages (2004); Lages and Montgomery (2004). Morgan et al. (2004); Richey and Myers (2001); Shoham (1999).
	E5) Other: The level of export performance by competitor, general export performance, general export performance compared to competitors, strategic export performance	Balabanis and Katsikea (2003); Brouthers and Xu (2002); Gençtürk and Kotabe (2001); Lages and Lages (2004); Lages and Montgomery (2004); O'Cass and Julian (2003); Styles (1998).
Other Factors	Achievement of targets about the response to competition pressure, awareness and image formation in offshore countries, contribution of exports to firm growth and firm contribution to management quality, customer satisfaction, new technology/expertise, product/service quality compared to competitors, quality of customer relations compared to competitors, quality of distributor relations, quality of distributor relations compared to competitors, reputation of firm compared to competitors	Gençtürk and Kotabe (2001); Morgan et al. (2004); Myers (1999); Prasad, Ramamurthy, and Naidu (2001).

1. Factor: Research and development activities
2. Factor: Customer Satisfaction
3. Factor: Environmental and Economic Factors
4. Factor: Management Style and Format
5. Factor: Competition Status
6. Factor: Brand-Advertisement-Packaging
7. Factor: Personnel Status
8. Factor: Export Structure

The listed items, evaluated in the following tables are selected according to conducted factor analyses for each dimension, separately. The scores of selected 50 items among 63 items are the arithmetic means of the items' attitude scores attributed by firms, and factor scores of these eight factors/dimension are the means of the items' scores of the factor's own members.

As shown in Tab. 3, the KMO statistics which is above 0.60 indicates the sampling adequacy or suitability of the data of items for the factor analysis. The p-values obtained from the Bartlett test are statistically significant at 0.05 level (p-value: 0.000 <0.05), so it is decided that the correlation matrix between the variables not be a unit matrix, the variables/items in the same dimension are

Tab. 3: Reliability Analysis and Goodness-of-fit Indicators of Factor Analysis for Dimensions

Dimensions / Factors	No of Items	Cronbach's Alpha	Variance Explained	Kaiser-Meyer-Olkin Statistics	P value of Bartlett's Test of Sphericity
F1 Brand-Advertisement-Packaging	8	.803	.890	.844	.000
F2 Customer Satisfaction	7	.892	.854	.883	.000
F3 Competition Status	7	.869	.787	.799	.000
F4 Export Structure	7	.905	.721	.871	.000
F5 Environmental and Economic Factors	7	.934	.709	.890	.000
F6 Management Style and Format	6	.896	.702	.912	.000
F7 R&D Activities	5	.804	.691	.920	.000
F8 Personnel Status	3	.899	.654	.873	.000
All data	50	.924			

significantly correlated with each other and factor analysis could be conducted (Akbulut et al. 2014, p.81). For the total variance explained, a higher value than 0.60 is accepted as fair. These three statistics can be accepted as goodness-of-fit test indicators for factor analysis.

To determine the subjects to be included in the content of the factors, the items are grouped by way of literature; then, the items with low communality and creating a new dimension have been removed from the model. Namely, the item's statistics of communality and factor loads, and being identified in only main factor are the selecting determinants of the items for each factor. In addition to these criteria, it can be decided that the factors supported by the goodness of fit indicators are the most appropriate representation of the components and the valid model. Analyzes have been made by examining the exporting and non-exporting furniture firms, in terms of these factors.

After selecting the 50 items for eight factors model, the calculated goodness-of-fit test indicators of these factors with their Cronbach's Alpha statistics of reliability analysis are reported in Tab. 3. It can be decided that the measurements of dimensions are very reliable according to Cronbach's Alpha statistics which have a minimum value of 0.804, which is much higher than 0.60. When the explained variances are examined, it is seen that the highest total variances explained are observed in the dimensions of "F1 Brand-Advertisement-Packaging" with 89%, followed by "F2 Customer Satisfaction" and "F3 Competition Situation". In other words, the measurement of these dimensions and the generated factor scores represent the dimension quite well. The lowest explained variance or representation among eight dimensions is 65% for the dimensions of F8, which is also sufficiently represented.

In the following sections, inferences have been made by using statistical methods and hypothesis tests in terms of measured dimensions and subjects.

The Differences of Exporting Firms in terms of Dimensions

In this section, the measured attitude scores, attributed according to managers of firms for each item of eight dimensions are reported comparatively with respect to the non-exporting and exporting firms. In this sense, it is examined whether exporting firms have different characteristics in terms of items and factors. If each sub-samples' volume is over 30, it is decided that that data series of subgroups are in normal distributions according to the central limit theorem, and the differentiation in attitudes between the exporting and non-exporting firms can be examined via independent samples t-tests. The normal distribution is examined by using Kolmogorov-Smirnov and Shapiro-Wilk tests for the subgroups below sample volume of 30. Moreover, none of these group's data has been observed to have statistically normal distribution at the 0.05 significance level, then the attitude differentiation between subgroup are examined by using Mann-Whitney U test. In this case, in the tables that p-values of the Mann-Whitney U test are given, decisions of the attitude differentiation are examined according to the Mann-Whitney U test, although there is no difference between the results of these tests. For some questions that are addressed exclusively to the exporting firms, the statistics/findings of the non-exporting firms are not reported on the tables in this section.

The highest total variances explained among eight dimensions is observed in the "F1 Brand-Advertisement-Packaging" dimension whose items' statistics are reported in Tab. 4. According to the items, it is seen that firms pay higher attention to "Q59 Giving Importance to Packaging" and "Q62 Not having a marketing problem". Despite the high importance given to these items, it can be decided that these issues not be effective on exports because according to the independent sample t-test, there is no statistically significant difference in the views of

Tab. 4: Evaluation of the Questions Related to the Brand-Advertisement-Packaging Factor

F1- Brand-Advertisement-Packaging	Non-exporting			Exporting			t-test p-value	Mann W. U test p-value
	n	Mean	Std. Dev.	n	Mean	Std. Dev.		
Q14 The Importance of Internet Sites in Promotion	47	5.13	2.15	133	6.05	1.33	.008	
Q15 Congress Fair Participation	47	4.64	2.10	135	6.04	1.41	.000	
Q33 Promotion of New Product in Short Time	41	5.78	1.25	133	6.08	1.21	.168	
Q55 Advertisement Promotion Activities	19	5.53	1.93	134	5.65	1.78	.780	.963
Q59 Giving Importance to Packaging	41	6.22	1.04	135	6.15	1.37	.759	
Q60 Being a Brand of Every Product				135	5.89	1.53		
Q61 Being a Recognized Brand				134	5.82	1.60		
Q62 Not Having a Marketing Problem	41	6.12	0.68	135	6.15	1.18	.859	
F1-Factor Items' Mean	47	5.38	1.28	135	5.97	1.09	.002	

Std. Dev.: Standard deviation. t-Test: Independent samples t-test; Mann W. U: Mann Whitney U test.

the firms for these items. In the study, it can be decided based on the t-test that "Q14 The Importance of Internet Sites for Promotion (p-value: 0.008<0.05)" and "Q15 Congress Fair Participation (p-value: 0.000<0.05)" are effective on exporting situation. The firms exporting furniture stated that they score higher at the Q14 and Q15 items with the value of 6.05 and 6.04, respectively, can be categorized as approve category than non-exporting firms which score is 5.13 to 4.64, respectively, can be categorized as partly approve category. The being in categories of 7 point Likert scales can be decided according to Cural et al. (2016, p.91) as partly disapprove category is between the scores of 2.72-3.57; undecided category between 3.58-4.43; partly approve category between 4.44 -5.29; approve category between 5.30-6.14.

When the standard deviations of the series that is an indicator of the homogeneity are examined, it can be observed that there are more homogeneity or agreement tendencies in the views of especially the item of Q62, and also Q33, Q59. In this sense, it can be said that the subgroups are relatively quite consensual in their approach to these items. It can be deduced from the statistics in the line of "F1 Factor Items' Mean" that the exporting furniture firms generally pay more attention to the "F1 Brand-Advertisement-Packaging" factor and this factor is accepted as effective in export performance.

In the dimensions of determining export performance, the dimension of "F2 Customer Satisfaction" is observed as having the second rank in total variances explained performance. According to the items in this dimension (Tab. 5), it is seen that firms give higher importance especially to "Q13 Compliance with Technical Requirements" and "Q12 On-time Delivery". Despite the high importance given to these items, it is decided that these dimensions not be effective items in exporting since statistically no significant difference at the level 0.05 is not observed between exporting and non-exporting firms. In this study, it can be decided based on the t-test that only "Q10 Complaint about the product (p-value: 0.001 <0.005)" is effective on exporting. Exporting firms declared they agreed for the item of Q10 with the level of 5.67, as non-exporting firms with the level of 4.49. Then it is decided that, exporting firms with being in approve category, attach higher importance to Q10 item than non-exporting firms with being in partly approve category which score is very close to undecided category according to t-test and category classifying in terms of Cural et al. (2016, p.91)'s 7 point Likert scales. For the "F2- Customer Satisfaction" factor items generally, it is decided that these items not be effective on export performance, according to the statistics reported on the line of "F2 Factor Items' Mean".

Statistics for the items of "F3 Competition Status" dimension are reported in Tab. 6. It can be said that firms give a higher priority to "Q9 Fast adaptation to

Tab. 5: Evaluation of the Questions about Customer Satisfaction

F2 - Customer Satisfaction	**Non-exporting**			**Exporting**			**t-test**	**Mann**
	n	**Mean**	**Std. Dev.**	**n**	**Mean**	**Std. Dev.**	**p-value**	**W. U test p-value**
Q10 Complaint for product	45	4.49	1.98	134	5.67	1.68	.001	
Q12 On-time Delivery	46	6.02	1.04	133	6.04	1.34	.942	
Q13 Compliance with Technical Requirements	46	6.20	1.22	134	6.16	1.33	.861	
Q23 Customer Expectation in New Product	46	5.72	1.28	133	6.01	1.44	.227	
Q40 Quality Based Satisfaction	44	5.91	1.01	134	6.09	1.35	.348	
Q41 Price Based Satisfaction	43	5.77	1.34	134	5.99	1.36	.360	
Q42 Design Based Satisfaction	45	5.87	1.25	131	6.17	1.28	.174	
Q45 Technical Team for Customer Satisfaction	22	5.36	1.87	134	5.61	1.70	.533	.723
Q47 Satisfying Warranty Period	42	5.81	1.33	134	6.19	1.10	.067	
F2- Factor Items' Mean	47	5.93	0.97	135	6.06	1.11	.458	

demand" and partly to Q11, Q19, Q21, and Q34. It can be concluded that Q9, Q11, Q16, Q21, and Q48 are effective on exporting when the perspective of the non-exporting/exporting firms are examined according to the independent samples t-test. In this case, it is observed that the exporting firms are more attentive for Q9, Q11, Q16, Q21, and Q48 and the exporting firms are clearly distinguished from the non-exporting firms with their approach to these items. The fact that the statistically significant difference at 0.10 level observed for the items of Q19 and Q22 among the nine items. For the items of Q9, Q11, Q16, Q21, and Q48, statistically significant difference observed at 0.05 level reflect the presence of the differentiating perspectives between non-exporting/ exporting performances for this dimension (there is no significant difference for Q34 and Q39). Accordingly, it can be interpreted that the "F3 Competition Status" dimension and the listed items as significant are strongly absorbed by exporting furniture firms. While Q16, Q22, Q39, and Q48 have a certain degree of heterogeneous attitudes, for the other items it can be seen that firms reflect a more like-minded attitude. It can be deduced from these statistics that the "F3 Competition Status" factor is effective on export performance in general.

Tab. 6: Assessment of Questions Related to Competition Status

F3 - Competition Status	Non-exporting			Exporting			t-test	Mann
	n	Mean	Std. Dev.	n	Mean	Std. Dev.	p-value	W. U test p-value
Q9 Fast adaptation to demand	47	5.64	1.42	133	6.13	1.29	.031	
Q11 Not worrying about the new competition	47	5.38	1.65	133	5.99	1.50	.021	
Q16 Determination of Sales Price by competitors	47	4.55	2.03	133	5.36	1.94	.016	
Q19 Taking the Quality Document Easily	46	5.54	1.66	135	5.97	1.42	.093	
Q21 New Market Research	46	5.59	1.45	134	6.03	1.26	.050	
Q22 Being Pioneer in Price Determination	45	5.13	1.67	135	5.68	1.68	.060	
Q34 Ensuring Price Advantage	26	5.62	1.27	132	5.66	1.60	.896	.391
Q39 Possessing Competitive Power in the industry	23	5.00	2.07	129	5.37	1.70	.351	.516
Q48 Developing Different Strategies for Different Products	23	5.04	1.89	134	5.99	1.29	.030	.019
F3- Factor Items' Mean	47	5.43	1.01	135	5.91	1.14	.011	

The items about the perspectives of the exporting firms are presented at Tab. 7, the response of non-exporting firms are not evaluated for these items, so perspectives of non-exporting are not presented in the table. Exporting firms expressed their own exporting strategies with 5.79 level can be categorized as approve category. They see themselves as leading /pioneering in exporting, having sufficient export strategy and organizations (Tab. 7) with high-level scores which can be categorized as approve category and very close to strongly approve category. According to the replies given by the participants on the exporting items in open-ended questions, a deduction has been reached that "if a firm does not have an export department of their own, or if this work is not carried out as a separate department from internal marketing, there is not much chance of success". Moreover, the requirements and the structure of each country may be different, and it is difficult to determine these differences as long as there is no right export strategy and practice.

Statistics for the items of "F5 Environmental and Economic Factors" dimension are reported in Tab. 8. When analyzing conducted according to the items,

Tab. 7: Evaluation of Questions Related to Export Structure of Firms

F4 Export Structure	n	Minimum	Maximum	Mean	Standard Deviation
Q5 Pioneering in Exporting	132	1	7	5.97	1.53
Q6 Having an Export Strategy	134	1	7	6.03	1.43
Q7 Having an Export Organization	132	1	7	5.96	1.37
Q8 Receiving Professional Support in the Export Strategy	134	1	7	5.61	1.84
Q35 Export Agreement Period	131	1	7	5.95	1.27
Q38 Making Export in the last 5 years	133	1	7	5.75	1.53
F4- Factor Items' Mean	135	1.29	7	5.79	1.22

Tab. 8: Assessment of Questions about Environmental and Economic Factors

F5 Environmental and Economic Factors	Non-exporting			Exporting			t test p value	Mann W. U test p value
	n	Mean	Std. Dev.	n	Mean	Std. Dev.		
Q29 Internal Market Shrinkage	39	5.00	1.72	133	5.69	1.72	.029	
Q30 Export to EU Countries	25	4.72	1.88	132	5.75	1.62	.005	.003
Q31 Distance to Market	24	4.62	2.39	134	5.16	2.10	.258	.381
Q32 Cultural Similarity with Market	22	5.59	1.97	133	5.76	1.61	.661	.937
Q43 Attention to Demographic Characteristics	22	5.27	1.61	134	5.76	1.57	.179	.107
Q44 Change in Exchange Rates	20	6.40	1.73	133	6.84	1.56	.245	.169
Q54 Effect of Interest Rates	19	5.68	1.57	135	5.89	1.52	.585	.584
F5- Factor Items' Mean	39	5.13	1.39	135	5.69	1.23	.016	

it is seen that firms pay higher attention to "Q44 Change in Exchange Rates" and "Q54 Effect of Interest Rates" than other items of the dimension. Despite the high importance given to these items, there is no statistically significant difference in terms of the Mann Whitney U test results at the 0.05 level (for non-exporting firms' data volume is below 30 and the normal distribution is not accepted), then, it is decided that that item is not an effective item in exporting. Nevertheless, the test results of t-test and Mann Whitney U are not conflicting, "Q29 Internal Market Shrinkage (p-value: 0.029 <0.05)" and "Q30 Export to EU

Tab. 9: Evaluation of Question on Management Style/Format of Exporting Firms

F6 Management Style and Format	n	Minimum	Maximum	Mean	Standard Deviation
Q1 Compliance with the export	135	1	7	5.74	1.63
Q2 Desire and Support for Exporting	134	1	7	5.94	1.46
Q3 Appreciating Export Opportunities	135	1	7	5.94	1.31
Q4 Having Export Motivation	134	1	7	6.02	1.31
F6 - Factor Items' Mean	135	1.83	7	5.95	1.14

Tab. 10: Evaluation of Questions Related to R&D Activities

F7 R&D Activities	Non-exporting			Exporting			t-test	Mann
	n	Mean	Std. Dev.	n	Mean	Std. Dev.	p-value	W. U test p-value
Q17 Pioneer in New Product	47	5.43	1.38	134	5.93	1.45	.038	
Q20 Eco-friendly	45	5.24	1.68	134	6.04	1.35	.006	
Q24 Innovative in ARGE	46	5.80	1.09	133	6.02	1.40	.338	
Q53 Having Detailed Information about the Market	20	5.55	1.70	135	5.93	1.42	.283	.448
Q63 Following Technology	42	6.14	0.93	134	6.27	1.15	.520	
F7- Factor Items' Mean	47	5.57	1.00	135	6.02	1.14	.016	

Countries (p-value: 0.005<0.05)" are decided as effective items on exporting. It can be observed in general that the dimension of "F5 Environmental and Economic Factors" is effective on export performance.

As it is observed in Tab. 9, the exporting firms stated that they attach high importance to the items of desiring/supporting to export, using/appreciating export opportunities and having export motivation. The paying attention to these items and their dimension by the firms can be categorized as approve category and very close to strongly approve category. It can be inferred that the firm manager's willingness/desire for exporting affect the motivation of the staff of furniture firms.

Statistics for the items of "F7 R&D activities" dimension are reported in Tab. 10. When it is examined according to the items' mean scores, it is observed that firms pay more attention to "Q63 Following Technology" than other items, but there is no statistically significant difference at 0.05 level between the exporting

Tab. 11: Assessment of Questions about Personnel Status

F8- Personnel Status	Non-exporting			Exporting			t-test p-value	Mann W. U test p-value
	n	Mean	Std. Dev.	n	Mean	Std. Dev.		
Q56 In-service training	40	5.68	1.31	135	5.85	1.48	.497	
Q57 Provision of Qualified Personnel	42	4.14	2.14	133	5.56	1.72	.000	
Q58 Employee Ambience Satisfaction	42	5.90	1.08	134	6.07	1.40	.432	
F7 - Factor Items' Mean	42	5.21	1.16	135	5.81	1.35	.010	

and non-exporting firms, and it is decided that this item not be an effective issue on exporting. However, according to the t-test, items of "Q17 Pioneer in New Product (p-value: 0.038 <0.05)" and "Q20 Eco-friendly (p-value: 0.006 <0.05)" are positively effective on exporting. It can also be inferred that the "F7 R&D activities" factor is influential on export performance in general.

Statistics for the items of "F8 Personnel Status" dimension are reported in Tab. 11. When items' mean scores are compared, it can be said that firms pay more attention to item of "Q58 Employee Ambience Satisfaction" than others, but there is no statistically significant difference according to t test (p-value: 0.432> 0.05) for exporting and non-exporting firms, or we can decide that this item has no effect on exporting. However, according to t-test, the item of "Q57 Provision of Qualified Personnel (p-value: 0.000 <0.05)" and also the factor of "F8- Personnel Status (p-value: 0.010> 0.05)" have a positive effect on exporting. However, it should also be noted that the answers to the item of Q57 are relatively heterogeneous which means the reply scores are relatively more differentiating from firm to firm than other item replies. The "F8 Personnel Status" factor is effective on exporting in general.

According to ranks of attitude means of non-exporting and exporting firms, the attitudes to the factors can be accepted in the same order, but the severities can be differentiating (Tab. 12). Factors of F1 and F7 can be accepted a little bit more important factors than others according to factor means /ranks, for both non-exporting and exporting firms. Factors of F1, F3, F5, F7, and F8 are paid more attention by the exporting firms than non-exporting ones. These dimensions can be thought as the determiners of the exporting performance for the furniture firms in Turkey. Since the ordering of the factors are quite similar in terms of non-exporting and exporting firms, we cannot get any significant conclusion in differentiating about the importance of the factors according to their

Tab. 12: Comparisons of Measured Factors in terms of Non-exporting /Exporting Firms

		F1	F2	F3	F4	F5	F6	F7	F8
Non-exporting Firms	Attitude Mean	5.38	5.93	5.43		5.13		5.57	5.21
	Rank	4	1	3		6		2	5
Exporting Firms	Attitude Mean	5.97	6.06	5.91	5.79	5.69	5.95	6.02	5.81
	Rank	3	1	4	5.5	6	3.5	2	5
p-value of t-test for examining mean difference		,002	.458	.011		.016		.016	.010

Rank numbers which are not integer, are used for fair rank comparisons of non-exporting and exporting firms.

Tab. 13: Relations between Dimensions for Non-Export Firms

	F1 Brand-Advertisement-Packaging	**F2 Customer Satisfaction**	**F3 Competition Situation**	**F5 Environmental and Economic Factors**	**F7 R&D activities**
F2 Customer Satisfaction	.696**	1			
F3 Competition Status	.810**	.795**	1		
F5 Environmental and Economic Factors	.423**	.469**	.527**	1	
F7 R&D Activities	.740**	.794**	.798**	.497**	1
F8 Personnel Status	.580**	.343*	.596**	.116	.521**

** Significance relationship at 0.01, * significance relationship at 0.05.

ranks. According to the Tab. 12, the importance degree of factors of F4 and F6 scored by the managers of exporting firms can be comparatively observed. As F6 can be accepted as more important than F3, but less important than F1; F4 can be accepted as more important than F5, but less important than F8 for exporting furniture firms.

Evaluation of Relations between Dimensions for Exporting/Non-exporting Firms

Taking the arithmetic means of the items identified in a factor, correlations between each factor scores for the exporting and non-exporting firms are

Tab. 14: Relations between Dimensions for Exporting Firms

	F1 Brand-Adv.-Pack.	F2 Cust. Satisf.	F3 Comp. Status	F4 Export Structure	F5 Envir. & Econ. F.	F6 Man. Style & Format	F7 R&D Activities
F2 Customer Satisfaction	.752**	1					
F3 Competition Status	.872**	.779**	1				
F4 Export Structure	.875**	.706**	.894**	1			
F5 Envir. and Econ. F.	.723**	.720**	.739**	.658**	1		
F6 Man. Style and Form.	.622**	.744**	.665**	.593**	.658**	1	
F7 R&D activities	.845**	.845**	.832**	.830**	.668**	.663**	1
F8 Personnel Status	.813**	.719**	.806**	.781**	.652**	.649**	.776**

** Significance relationship at 0.01.

examined separately in this section. Thus, for exporting and non-exporting firms, calculated correlations are compared and also evaluated.

Tab. 13 shows the Pearson correlation coefficients showing the levels of relations between the six factors according to the factor scores of their item scores attributed by the managers of non-exporting firms. As it can be seen from the table, for example, while "F1 Brand-Advertisement-Packaging" dimension is significant highly correlated with "F2 Customer Satisfaction", "F3 Competition Status" and "F7 R&D activities", significant moderately correlated with " F5 Environmental and Economic Factors" and "F8 Personnel Status". The factor of "F8 Personnel Status" has least correlation with the other dimensions, not statistically significant even at 0.05 level with F5, while the factor of "F3 Competition Situation" has the highest correlations with the other dimensions.

Tab. 14 shows Pearson correlation coefficients among the eight factors, produced according to the attitude of the managers of the exporting firms. As it can be seen from the statistics in the table, all the dimensions are statistically correlated with each other at 0.01 significance level. This can be interpreted as the fact that all eight dimensions measured of the exporting firms and supported each other in the positive direction. In other words, for example, the "F1 Brand-Advertisement-Packaging" dimension is correlated with some other dimensions at the very high level (F3, F4, F7, and F8) or high level (F2, F5, and F6). Since the relationship between these dimensions is not at this level for non-exporting firms, it can be interpreted that exporting furniture firms focus systematically on items of these mentioned eight factors, sustaining each other.

Conclusion and Evaluation

Exporting is very important for every country and its companies to increase the level of prosperity expand/increase competitive power, and economic performance of them. By exporting, firms increase their sales/profits, gain share from world markets, decrease dependency on internal markets, keep market fluctuations in balance, use inert capacity, increase competitive power, increase employment and help to decrease foreign trade deficit.

The furniture industry is an important economic sector that produces a value of annual average of $376 billion over the last five years. Socio-economically, it has a remarkable value in the topic of employment. The EU countries have been highly developed in terms of furniture production and trade compared to many parts of the world. Especially Germany and Italy are ahead of other European countries in terms of both productions, import, and consumption. China is leading the way in furniture production in the world and has been giving direction from various ways to the industry over the last five years. About one-quarter of the furniture produced all over the world is produced in China alone, followed by, respectively, USA (15%), Italy (8%), and Germany (7%). Turkey has a share of 1% in volume of the industry of the world and potentially tends to rise above this rate. When the export ratios of Turkey are examined, it is seen that China is the first with 35.3%, and, respectively, Germany (7.6%), Italy (6.8%), Poland (5.7%), USA (4.8%) and Mexico (3.9%) were followed China (TradeMap, 2017). Turkey's rank is 15th among exporting countries with a ratio of 1.3%. Despite all the negativities experienced in 2016, total export volume in the furniture industry was $2.6 billion. With the overcoming of the Russian crisis and the elimination of adverse consequences, an increase of growth about 20% is targeted in this industry where the overall growth of 5% can be accepted as well for the general growth of Turkey. It can also be considered that the furniture industry is a quite untouched area for Turkey, with a growth potential of 20% in the furniture industry. It is foreseen that with growth target, the furniture industry firms of Turkey aim to increase its exporting share of furniture industry by more than 2%. Thus, it can be evaluated as an important opportunity for increasing the performances of not only the furniture exporting firms but also exporting of Turkey, and then this condition may give an accelerant integration opportunity of Turkey to the world competitive environment.

Accordingly, the purpose of this study is to determine the items and the factors affecting the export performance in the furniture industry and to present the findings to the academicians, the managers, and decision-makers in the related industry. For this purpose, firstly, a comprehensive literature study was carried out and put together obtained different scales, and a created questionnaire applied to 182 firms of Turkish furniture industry. Export performance is generally defined as the output of the firm in international sales. Despite the several researches conducted to examine the determinants of export performance, there is no consensus on the determinants of export performance (Aaby and Slater 1989; Madsen 1989; Shoham 1999; Zou and Stan 1998). It is difficult to compare the conducted researches since different export performance indicators, and different measurements are used in the studies. In this study, more than 200 studies in the literature was searched, and common indicators are used in order to evaluate export performance.

The most important inferring of this research is to determine the items and the factors affecting the export performance in the furniture industry, so these findings are interpreted as exporting and non-exporting firms are diverging in their attitudes to these items/factors. However, the other quite important inferring of this research is to determine some items which are not diverging in terms of exporting/non-exporting firms' attitudes. When the analysis findings are evaluated as a whole, it is observed that non-exporting firms attach importance to some items as exporting firms do. However, the most important result to be deduced from this analysis is that, like exporting firms, non-exporting firms attach importance to certain items /factors which are interpreted as these items/ factors exist for furniture industry firms' surviving in general. In other words, exporting and non-exporting firms give almost same importance to some items, or there is no difference between the attitudes of them for these items, so it is interpreted that exporting and non-exporting firms are showing critical sensitivity to these items and decided that these items do not cause any divergence between exporting and non-exporting firms.

The "Brand-Advertisement-Packaging" dimension is observed to be at the first rank with 89% explained total variance, and it can be said that this dimension measurement is relatively better than others. Then, while the "Customer Satisfaction" and "Competition Situation" dimensions accounted well in the explained total variance, the lowest explained total variance is observed in the "Personnel Situation" dimension with 65%.

It is seen that furniture firms pay higher importance to the items of "giving importance to packaging" and "not having a marketing problem" in the dimension of "Brand-Advertisement-Packaging" in general. Despite the high importance given to these items, it is observed that there is no statistically significant difference between the views of the exporting and non-exporting firms. It is decided that exporting firms pay less attention to the items of "importance of internet sites for promotion" and "congress fair participation" and then these items are counted as effective in exporting.

It is observed that the exporting firms pay more attention to the item of "complaints from the producers" as well as non-exporting firms pay less attention to this item. On the other hand, it is decided that there is no significant difference detected between exporting and non-exporting firms to the approach of "Customer Satisfaction" dimension. While it is accepted that the promotion of product and brand is important for customer satisfaction dimension, it has been observed that exporting and non-exporting firms attach almost equal importance to related items and the dimension in general. Therefore, regardless of whether or not they are exporting, it can be said that the furniture industry firms give equal importance to customer satisfaction dimension. Especially, exporting firms are more concerned about product complaints by customers, then, the solving all problems related to the products are considered as an effective item in export performance.

When "Competition Situation" dimension is assessed, it can be concluded that exporting firms (compared to non-exporting firms) generally give more importance to this dimension and the most of its items. The items of "fast adaptation to demand", "not worrying about the new competition", "determination of sales price by competitors", "new market research", and "developing different strategies for different products" are given more importance by exporting firms than non-exporting firms; it can be decided that exporting /non-exporting firms' attitudes are distinctly distinguished to these items. The competitiveness dimension can be considered as quite important dimension in affecting export performance in this respect.

It is observed that exporting firms pay more attention to the "Environmental and Economic Factors" in general and in particular to the items of "internal market shrinkage" and "export to EU countries". Especially, the furniture firms which consider themselves narrowed in the domestic market can be better than others in exporting and concentrate mainly on the export to the EU countries.

It is understood that exporting firms generally give more attention to "R&D Activities". It is statistically determined that the items of "pioneer in new product" and "eco-friendly" are important in affecting export performance for this dimension.

It is observed that exporting firms give more importance to the "Personnel Status" dimension in general and in particular to the item of "quality personnel management". The personnel situation is also accepted as a dimension that affects the export performance.

The paying attention to the exporting performance factors by non-exporting/exporting firms can be accepted in the same way, but their priorities are differentiating. Some dimensions which are differentiated according to non-exporting/exporting firms, mentioned above, can be thought as the determiners of the exporting performance of the furniture firms in Turkey. Since the importance of the factors is quite similar according to non-exporting/exporting firms, we cannot get any conclusion about the importance of the factors related to their priorities. The importance degree of factors of "Export Structure" and "Management Style and Format" are comparatively evaluated among all the factors for only exporting firms, since these factors' items are addressed to exporting firms. The fact that any firm which has a special export-related unit, may urge its exporting performance via the items of "export desire and support", "appreciating export opportunities", and "having export motivation" according to the dimension of "Management Style and Format" which tendency is categorized as approving category and very close to strongly approve category. These results are consistent with the literature (Cavusgil and Zou 1994; Aaby and Slater 1989). The most important aspect of management has been determined as eagerness and enthusiasm.

When the relations among the factors are examined, it is seen that the factor correlations in the exporting firms are established upon the strongly positive relations in the positive direction. It is seen that exporting firms give quite importance to all factors as a whole, but it is revealed that non-exporting firms do not show interest in a similar sensitivity to the measurable factors. This finding allowed us to express another important conclusion of our work. It is interpreted for the exporting firms that all eight export factors which are the dimensions of the study are all interacting with each other systematically and sustaining each other. For non-exporting firms, the interaction of these factors and the mutual supporting are relatively weak than exporting firms have. Thus, all these findings and conclusions can be transmitted to the managers and the decision makers of firms operating in the furniture industry and even the academicians dealing with the export field.

Bibliography

AA, (Anadolu Agency): "IMF Türkiye'nin büyüme beklentisini yükseltti", retrieved 27.11.2017, from https://www.ntv.com.tr/ekonomi/imf-turkiyenin-buyume-beklentisini-yukseltti,YZpvFV7ipU-IxAsEX3_b0w.

Aaby Nils-Erik / Slater, Stanley F: "Management influences on export performance: A review of the empirical literature 1978–1988". *International Marketing Review* 6(4), 1989, pp. 7–23, retrieved 15.12.2017, from DOI 10.1108/EUM0000000001516.

Akbulut, Halim / Pekkaya, Mehmet / Aksakaloğlu, Hakan: "Meslek mensuplarının bakış açısıyla ticaret meslek liselerindeki muhasebe eğitimi: Bursa ili üzerine bir uygulama". *MUFAD Muhasebe ve Finansman Dergisi* 62, 2014, pp. 73–91.

Alsan, Murat: "Türkiye ve dünya ekonomisinde makro gelişmeler", *Bakış Dergisi* 5, 2017, pp. 1–34.

Alvarez, Roberto: "Sources of export success in small and medium-sized enterprises: The impact of public programs". *International Business Review* 13(3), 2004, pp. 383–400, retrieved 15.12.2017, from DOI 10.1016/j.ibusrev.2004.01.002.

Ay, Ahmet: *Türkiye'de Dış Ticaret ve Kur Politikaları Uygulamaları*, Çizgi Kitabevi: Konya, 2007.

Balabanis, George I. / Katsikea, Eva S: "Being an entrepreneurial exporter: Does it pay?". *International Business Review* 12(2), 2003, pp. 233–252.

Beleska-Spasova, Elena: "Determinants and measure of export performance-comprehensive literature review". *Journal of Contemporary Economic and Business Issues* 1, 2014, pp. 63–74.

Brouthers, Lance E. / Nakos, George: "The role of systematic international market selection on small firms' export performance". *Journal of Small Business Management* 43(4), 2005, pp. 363–381, retrieved 15.12.2017, from DOI 10.1111/j.1540-627X.2005.00142.x.

Brouthers, Lance E. / Xu, Kefeng: "Product stereotypes, strategy and performance satisfaction: The case of Chinese exporters". *Journal of International Business Studies* 33, 2002, pp. 657–677.

Cadogan, John W. / Kuivalainen, Olli / Sundqvist, Sanna: "Export market-oriented behavior and export performance: quadratic and moderating effects under differing degrees of market dynamism and internationalization". *Journal of International Marketing* 17(4), 2009, pp. 71–89, retrieved 15.12.2017, from DOI 10.1509/jimk.17.4.71.

Cadogan, John W., et al: "Strategic flexibilities and export performance: the moderating roles of export market-oriented behavior and the export environment". *European Journal of Marketing* 46(10), 2012, pp. 1418–1452, retrieved 15.12.2017, from DOI 10.1108/03090561211248107.

Çanakçı, Erdinç: *TR72 Mobilya Sektör Raporu*. Oran Kalkınma Ajansı: Kayseri. June 2016.

Cavusgil, Tamer S: "Differences among exporting firms based on their degree of internationalization". *Journal of Business Research* 12(2), 1984, pp. 195–208, retrieved 15.12.2017, from DOI 10.1016/0148-2963(84)90006-7.

Cavusgil, Tamer S. / Zou, Shoaming: "Marketing strategy-performance relationships: An investigation of the empirical link in export market ventures". *Journal of Marketing* 58(1), 1994, pp. 1–21.

Chetty, Sylvie K. / Hamilton, Robert T.: "Firm-level Determinants of Export Performance: A Meta-analysis". *International Marketing Review* 10(3), 1993, pp. 26–34.

Contractor, Farok J. / Kumar, Vikas / Kundu, Sumit K: "Nature of the relationship between international expansion and performance: The case of emerging market firms". *Journal of World Business* 42(4), 2007, pp. 401–417, retrieved 15.12.2017, from DOI 10.1016/j.jwb.2007.06.003.

CSIL: *World Furniture Outlook 2017-2018*, Centre For Industrial Studies, 2017, Italy.

Cural, Mehmet / Pekkaya, Mehmet / Dibek, Erdem: "Sağlık hizmetlerinden memnuniyet ile vergi tutum ve davranışları arasındaki ilişki". *Uluslararası Yönetim İktisat ve İşletme Dergisi* 12(27), 2016, 83–104.

Francis, June / Collins-Dodd, Colleen: "Impact of export promotion programs on firm competencies, strategies and performance – The case of Canadian high-tech SMEs". *International Marketing Review* 4(5), 2004, pp. 474–495, retrieved 15.12.2017, from DOI 10.1108/02651330410547153.

Gençtürk, Esra F. / Kotabe, Masaaki: "The effect of export assistance program usage on export performance: a contingency explanation". *Journal of International Marketing* 9, 2001, pp. 51–72, retrieved 15.12.2017, from DOI 10.1509/jimk.9.2.51.19886.

Haahti, Antti, et al: "Cooperative strategy, knowledge intensity and export performance of small and medium sized enterprises". *Journal of World Business* 40, 2005, pp. 124–138, retrieved 15.12.2017, from DOI 10.1016/j.jwb.2005.02.003.

Hart, Susan / Tzokas, Nikolas: "The Impact of Marketing Research Activity on SME Export Performance: Evidence from the UK". *Journal of Small Business Management* 37(2), 1999, pp. 63–76.

Ibeh, Kevin I. N. / Wheeler, Colin N: "A resource-centered interpretation of export performance". *International Entrepreneurship and Management Journal* 1, 2005, pp. 539–556.

Katsikeas, Constantine S. / Leonidou, Leonidas C. / Morgan, Neil A: "Firm-level export performance assessment: Review, evaluation and development". *Journal of the Academy of Marketing Science* 28(4), 2000, pp. 493–511.

Lages, Luis F. / Lages, Cristiana R: "The STEP scale: A measure of short-term export performance improvement". *Journal of International Marketing* 12(1), 2004, pp. 36–56, retrieved 15.12.2017, from DOI 10.1509/jimk.12.1.36.25647.

Lages, Luis F. / Montgomery, David B: "Export performance as an antecedent of export commitment and marketing strategy adaptation: Evidence from small and medium sized exporters". *European Journal of Marketing* 38(9/10), 2004, pp. 1186–1214, retrieved 15.12.2017, from DOI 10.1108/03090560410548933.

Ling-yee, Li: "An examination of the foreign market knowledge of exporting firms based in the People's Republic of China: its determinants and effect on export intensity". *Industrial Marketing Management* 33, 2004, pp. 561–572, retrieved 15.12.2017, from DOI 10.1016/j.indmarman.2004.01.001.

Lopez-Rodriguez, J. / Garcia-Rodriguez, R: "Technology and export behavior: A resource-based view approach". *International Business Review* 14, 2005, pp. 539–557, retrieved 15.12.2017, from DOI 10.1016/j.ibusrev.2005.07.002.

Madsen, Tage K: "Successful export marketing management: Some empirical evidence". *International Marketing Review* 6(4), 1989, pp. 41–57, retrieved 15.12.2017, from DOI 10.1108/EUM0000000001518.

MOBSAD, Declaration of deputy chairman of Furniture Industry Businessmen's Association of Turkey, retrieved 07.11.2016, from http://www.mobsad.com/mobilya-fuari-gercek-yerinde-gercek-zamaninda.

MOBSAD: Declaration of deputy chairman of Furniture Industry Businessmen's Association of Turkey, retrieved 27.11.2017, from http://www.haberturk.com/ekonomi/is-yasam/haber/1570941-abd-ye-yapilan-mobilya-ihracati-5-yilda-4-kat-artti.

Morgan, Neil A. / Kaleka, Anna / Kastikeas, Constantine S: "Antecedents of Export Venture Performance: A Theoretical Model and Empirical Assessment". *Journal of Marketing* 68(1), 2004, pp. 90–108.

Myers, Matthew B: "Incidents of gray market activity among US exporters: Occurrences, characteristics, and consequences". *Journal of International Business Studies* 30(1), 1999, pp. 105–126.

O'Cass, Aron / Craig, Julian: "Examining Firm and Environmental Influences on Export Marketing Mix Strategy and Export Performance of Australian Exporters". *European Journal of Marketing* 37(3/4), 2003, pp. 366–384, retrieved 15.12.2017, from DOI 10.1108/03090560310459005.

Pekkaya, Mehmet / Akıllı, Fatma: "Hava Yolu Hizmet Kalitesinin SERVPERF-SERVQUAL Ölçeği ile Değerlendirmesi ve İstatistiksel Analizi". *AİBÜ İİBF Ekonomik ve Sosyal Araştırmalar Dergisi* 9(1), 2013, pp. 75–96.

Prasad, V. Kanti / Ramamurthy, K. / Naidu, G. M: "The influence of Internet-marketing integration on marketing competencies and export performance". *Journal of International Marketing* 9, 2001, pp. 82–110.

Richey, R. Gleen / Myers, Matthwe B: "An investigation of market information use in export channel decisions". *International Journal of Physical Distribution & Logistics Management* 31(5), 2001, pp. 334–353, retrieved 15.12.2017, from DOI 10.1108/09600030110395157.

Robertson, Christopher / Chetty, Sylvie K: "A contingency-based approach to understanding export performance". *International Business Review* 9(2), 2000, pp. 211–235, retrieved 15.12.2017, from DOI 10.1016/S0969-5931(99)00037-2.

Sakarya, Sevil / Doğan Öykü: *Mobilya Sektör Raporu*, Orta Anadolu İhracatçı Birlikleri Genel Sekreterliği: Ankara, 2014.

Shoham, Aviv: "Export performance: A conceptualization and empirical assessment". *Journal of International Marketing* 6(3), 1999, pp. 59–81.

Solberg, Carl Arthur: "The perennial issue of adaptation or standardization of international marketing communication: organizational contingencies and performance". *Journal of International Marketing* 10(3), 2002, pp. 1–21, retrieved 15.12.2017, from DOI 10.1509/jimk.10.3.1.19546.

Styles, Chris: "Export performance measures in Australia and the UK". *Journal of International Marketing* 6(3), 1998, pp. 12–36.

Styles, Chris / Ambler, Tim: "The impact of relational variables on export performance: an empirical investigation in Australia and the UK". *Australian Journal of Management* 25(3), 2000, pp. 261–281.

Styles, Chris / Patterson, Paul G. / Ahmed, Farid: "A relational model of export performance". *Journal of International Business Studies* 39(5), 2008, pp. 880–900.

Subaşat, Turan: *Ticaret ve Kalkınma,* Nihal Mızrak Yıldırım (ed.): *Dünya Ekonomisinde Bütünleşme Hareketleri ve Türkiye: Sorunlar ve Çözüm Önerileri.* Siyasal Yayınevi: Ankara, 2004, pp. 181–228.

TradeMap: *Trade statistics for international business development*, retrieved 13.11.2017 from http://www.trademap.org/.

Yapar Saçık, Sinem: "Dış Ticaret Politikası ve Ekonomik Büyüme İlişkisi: Teorik Açıdan Bir İnceleme". *KMU İİBF Dergisi* 11(16), 2009, pp. 162–171.

Yeoh, Poh-Lin: "International learning: antecedents and performance implications among newly internationalizing companies in an exporting context". *International Marketing Review* 21(4/5), 2004, pp. 511–535, retrieved 15.12.2017, from DOI 10.1108/02651330410547171.

Zou, Shoaming / Stan, Simona: "The determinants of export performance: A review of the empirical literature between 1987 and 1997". *International Marketing Review* 15(5), 1998, pp. 333–356, retrieved 15.12.2017, from DOI 10.1108/02651339810236290.

Zou, Shoaming / Taylor, Charles R. / Osland, Gregory E: "The EXPERF scale: A cross-national generalized export performance measure". *Journal of International Marketing* 6(3), 1998, pp. 37–58.

Yusuf Bilgin and Ayhan Karakaş

Impact of Market Orientation on Customer Performance and Financial Performance: Findings from Five-Star Hotels

Abstract: The purpose of this study is to examine the impact of market orientation on customer performance and financial performance in hotel businesses. Moreover, the impact of market orientation and customer performance on financial performance will be analyzed in hotel businesses. The population of the study, in which the convenience sampling method was used, consisted of five-star hotels operating in Turkey. The research data were obtained through face-to-face surveys from the staff of the restaurant, front office and marketing departments of the hotels. The obtained data were analyzed using the Lisrel 8.7 packet program. As a result of the analysis, it was determined that the customer orientation from the market orientation components significantly influence the customer performance in the hotels. On the other hand, it was determined that competitor orientation and interfunctional coordination in hotels have no significant effect on customer performance. Moreover, market orientation in five-star hotels was found to have no significant effect on the financial performance of businesses. Findings, however, show that customer performance in hotels significantly affected financial performance at a high level.

Keywords: Market orientation, customer performance, financial performance, five-star hotels

Introduction

In the last two decades, competition among businesses operating in the tourism sector, one of the fastest growing sectors in the world, has become increasingly acute both locally and internationally. The main determinant of the competitive power of tourism businesses that wants to maintain their presence and profitability in an increasingly competitive environment is the customers who make up the source of business revenues. Today, a significant portion of tourism businesses are facing customers looking for new discoveries and experiences beyond traditional tourist activities. Tourism enterprises, which offer traditional touristic products, provide services to a mass of customers with high level of knowledge, demand, and expectancy getting harder every day by sharing experiences through information technology. In such an environment, it is vital for businesses to be able to respond to customer requests and expectations more quickly. When the effects of actions taken by other businesses operating in the sector on the customers are considered, efforts to provide customer satisfaction for tourism businesses are becoming more important. Furthermore, the performance of a business cannot be accurately assessed in terms of the quality of the products it offers and the quality of the relationship with its customers, regardless of the market conditions in which it operates. In this context, businesses need to focus on the activities of competitor businesses, which are guiding strategic decisions and applications, in addition to the customer-focused approach responding to ever-changing environmental conditions.

This also applies to hotel businesses that fulfill the function of meeting accommodation, nutrition and other needs of tourists during their travels. In addition to changing consumer demands and expectations, hotel businesses face difficulties in responding to the actions of their competitors. In fact, changing customer expectations deeply influence hotel businesses in a large spectrum from the way they operate, to the activities carried out as well as from social projects to the positioning of the hotel in the tourism market. In the lodging industry, the widespread emergence of environmentally friendly *green hotels* and *halal hotels* based on Islamic beliefs in recent years is a clear indication of the impact of competitors, and customer wishes and expectations on hotel operations. It is only possible with the implementation of market-oriented applications of all business units of hotels, for hotel businesses to position themselves in a competitive market and create customer value in terms of both the quality of the products offered and the price. In this sense, market orientation, a result of the modern marketing concept in hotel businesses, is defined as collecting information about customers' present and future needs and desires, sharing information obtained between departments, and creating a reaction to be given to the market (Kohli and Jaworski 1990). Therefore, the way of achieving this for hotel management is to provide critical information about customer requests and needs and parallel with this, to develop and present products and services. Services such as dry cleaning, hairdresser, transportation and recreational activities offered in addition to basic activities in most of today's hotel businesses can be considered as examples of market orientation in hotels. Because customers satisfied from the provided products are more likely to prefer the business in comparison to its competitors (Carev 2008; Ha and Jang 2010), customer retention is provided for businesses, and sales revenues get higher (Chow et al. 2007). In the literature, there are some studies that show the effect of market orientation on the financial performances of hotel enterprises (Sin et al. 2005; Dev et al. 2008; Wang et al. 2012; Zafar et al. 2016).

The purpose of this study is to examine the impact of market orientation on customer performance and financial performance in five-star hotels. In addition, in this study, reflections of market orientation and customer performance on financial performance will be analyzed. In this direction, first, the concept of market orientation and the components of market orientation were discussed. Next, the effect of each component of the market orientation on the customer and financial performance was examined, and research hypotheses were established. In the method section, the research population, sample, data collection tools and data analysis technique were explained. In the findings section, findings obtained from the analysis were presented. In the discussion and conclusion section, the findings were discussed within the framework of the results obtained from the literature, and the results of the study were explained. Finally, recommendations were given for researchers and practitioners.

Theoretical Framework

The concept of market orientation in businesses is a reflection of the modern marketing approach. It can be said that the focus of modern marketing is simply to maximize profits through customer satisfaction. In other words, profitability in modern marketing is the natural consequence of customer satisfaction (Kotler et al. 1999, p.4). But, it is not easy for businesses that are an open system constantly in contact with the environment to provide customer satisfaction. In this sense, market orientation is an important element in the integration of businesses with the environmental changes on which they operate. The first studies on direct market orientation in the literature have been carried out by Kohli and Jaworski (1990) and Narver and Slater (1990). First, Kohli and Jaworski (1990, p.6) defined market orientation as "[the organization-wide generation of market intelligence pertaining to current and future customer needs, dissemination of the intelligence across departments, and organization-wide responsiveness to it]." That is, according to Kohli and Jaworski (1990), the components of market orientation are intelligence generation, dissemination, and responsiveness. The findings of Kohli and Jaworski (1990), which emphasize market orientation as the sensitivity given to marketing intelligence by the whole organization, have contributed significantly to the transformation of market orientation into a functional structure (Pitt et al. 1996). Concurrently with them, Narver and Slater (1990, p.20) defined "[the market orientation as a business culture that most effectively and effectively creates superior value for customers]." According to Narver and Slater (1990), market orientation in businesses consists of three behavioral components and two decision criteria. Behavioral components that indicate market orientation in an enterprise are customer orientation, competitor orientation, and interfunctional coordination. Decision criteria are expressed as long-term focus and profitability.

In the ongoing process, Slater and Narver (1994) have shown that environmental variables have an impact on businesses' market orientation. In addition, Jaworski and Kohli (1993) found that market orientation in a business is influenced by organizational variables such as senior management attitude, interdepartmental conflict, centralization, and environmental variables such as market turbulence level, the intensity of competition and technological turbulence. Moreover, Kohli et al. (1993) proposed the MARKOR scale with 32 items to measure market orientation in businesses. Gray et al. (1998) proposed a new measurement model by combining the dimensions set by Narver and Slater (1990) and Jaworski and Kohli (1993) in measuring market orientation in businesses. In addition to that, Matsuno et al. (2000) proposed a measure of market orientation by revising the MARKOR scale. At this point, when the literature is examined, it is clearly seen that the research on market orientation is built on the foundations of Narver and Slater (1990) and Kohli and Jaworski (1990).

One of the most comprehensive research on the definition of market orientation has been undertaken by Lafferty and Hult (2001). They categorized the differences between researchers' approaches in definitions of market orientation. It can be said that this classification is very functional for practitioners and researchers working on market orientation. The first of these categories is market orientation as emphasized by Shapiro (1988) as a decision-making process based on effective information sharing and interdepartmental alignment, from the top management to staff of the business. The second is the market orientation that is expressed by Kohli and Jaworski (1990) as a whole of activities focused on market intelligence. The third is market orientation as a business culture based on superior customer satisfaction as expressed by Narver and Slater (1990). The fourth is a strategic perspective that reflects the customer focus of the strategic planning process put forward by Ruekert (1992), who is driven by the fact that the most critical element of market orientation in a business environment is the customer. The last one is the customer-focused perspective set forth by Deshpandé et al. (1993), which argues that inter-functional coordination is an important part of customer orientation, but that competitor orientation may conflict with customer orientation and therefore competitor orientation must be excluded from market orientation. These viewpoints agree that market orientation, in general terms, plays a decisive role in business performance, although they carry some differences in terms of key components of market orientation. After all, the point of difference in these viewpoints is to try to take into account the effects of other components in the reflections of market orientation on performance at the application level.

In this study, market orientation was examined in terms of customer orientation, competitor orientation, and inter-functional coordination put forth by Narver and Slater (1990). Customer orientation, the cornerstone of marketing philosophy, is constant monitoring of customer desires and needs, and a continuous effort to meet these desires and needs in order to offer superior value to customers in the target market (Narver and Slater 1990). In other words, customer orientation is to see the customer as part of the business and the highest authority in all decision-making processes (Civelek 2016). The success of products or actions that support product delivery (technical service, fast delivery, price, brand value, etc.) offered by a business can be measured by customer preferability and reactions. For an enterprise, the meaning of preferability is to maintain its existence and its profitability. This is only possible if the customer's secret and open requests and needs are known. Kohli and Jaworski (1990) stated that customers' desires and needs, as well as information about the factors that affect customers' desires and needs are of critical value in the effectiveness of market orientation. In a dynamic environment, understanding customers' desires and needs allow businesses to more clearly define their marketing actions and strategic goals (Pitt et al. 1996). For this reason, customer desires and needs should constantly be monitored, and products should be offered to satisfy them according to the information obtained. After all, when attention is paid to the development process of marketing understanding, non-repairable demolitions experienced by non-customer oriented businesses provide clear evidence of the importance of customer orientation for businesses.

Another aspect of market orientation is competitor orientation. Kohli and Jaworski (1990) listed competitors under external environmental factors that are important in obtaining the needed market intelligence and that affect customer needs and preferences. Marketing understanding is to provide customer satisfaction by meeting the needs and desires of the target markets of the businesses better than their competitors (Çakıcı and Eren 2005). In other words, the actions of competitors that offer similar products are determinative in the success of the products that a business offers. The most obvious element of the effect of the actions that the competitors have made is the regulations on prices. Customers are trying to maximize their benefits in the products they buy. Therefore, they will prefer a business offering products at a more suitable price for their desires and needs. In this respect, businesses should be informed about the actions that competitors have taken on the market, from the quality of the products they offer, to the price policies, and from the distribution channels to the decisions on promotional combinations. Narver and Slater (1990) defined competitor orientation as the business's understanding of the strengths and weaknesses in the short run, and talents and strategies in the long run, of the current and future potential competitors.

The other aspect of market orientation is inter-functional coordination. Interfunctional coordination is crucial in creating superior customer value from the production of a product to the presentation of after-sales services. Because, regardless of its level of critical knowledge about customers and competitors, a business needs to share and coordinate efforts to achieve actions that will turn that information into profitability (Deng and Dart 1994). Kohli and Jaworski (1990) stated that the market orientation is not solely the responsibility of the marketing department and that it is important that inter-functional coordination and sharing of market information among departments are important in meeting customer desires and needs. Slater and Narver (1994) stated that building value for customers requires much more than the marketing function, and defined inter-functional coordination as activities that provide coordinated use of business resources in order to create high value for customers.

Development of Research Hypotheses

Market orientation has been considered as an important variable affecting business performance since the first studies on market orientation (Kohli and Jaworski 1990; Narver and Slater 1990; Deshpande et al. 1993; Pitt et al. 1996; Egeren and O'Connor 1998). Findings from initial research in this area provide limited evidence of the impact of market orientation on business performance, while the findings of today's research clearly support the impact of market orientation on business performance. In this respect, the hypotheses to be tested particularly for hotel businesses were supported by the literature and explained as follows.

Since customers are the main source of cash flow in businesses, actions targeting them have a decisive role in operating profitability. Competitor orientation and inter-functional coordination as the other components of market orientation have the ultimate goal to create superior customer value. Therefore, customer orientation can be considered as the most important component of market orientation (Wrenn, 1997). After all, the marketing understanding is based on the principle that all the actions carried out in the businesses should be customer oriented. Esteban et al. (2002) defined customer orientation as to know what customers' desires and needs are prior to marketing actions. Shoham et al. (2005) stated that customer orientation reflects actions necessary to obtain information about customers and share it within the organization. Knowing what customers need and what they want will make it easier for businesses to meet those desires and needs by providing quality services. As businesses become more able to satisfy their customers' desires and needs by providing quality services, customers' satisfaction, loyalty and their tendency to bring potential customers to the business will increase (Kohli and Jaworski, 1990).

McCullough et al. (1986) found a positive relationship between market orientation and customer satisfaction in their research study. Ciric et al. (2014) stated that market orientation in hotel businesses positively influences customer satisfaction. Customer satisfaction, which is the clearest indication of customer orientation in practice, is often used in businesses to measure customer performance. In addition to this, criteria such as loyalty level, lifetime customer value, and willingness of customers to maintain business relations are used to measure customer performance (Ghanavati 2014; Sin et al. 2005). Financial performance is generally examined in terms of variables such as sales growth, profitability, market share, and return on investment (Pitt et al. 1996; Shoham et al. 2005). Agarwal et al. (2003) have found that market orientation in hotel businesses positively influence both non-financial performance, such as service quality and customer satisfaction, as well as financial performance such as occupancy rate, gross operating profit, and market share. Similarly, Grissemann et al. (2013) found that market orientation in hotels affects customer performance and financial performance. Sin et al. (2005) have found that customer orientation in hotel businesses is the dominant variable explaining financial performance. Çakıcı and Eren (2005) have found that four- and five-star hotels in Turkey have a positive relationship between market orientation and performance. The hypotheses formed in the direction of the obtained findings are as follows:

H1: Customer orientation has a significant effect on customer performance in five-star hotels.

H2: Customer orientation has a significant effect on financial performance in five-star hotels.

Product orientation or sales orientation in less competitive markets can offer more profitable opportunities for businesses than customer orientation (Gray et al. 1998). However, all businesses that want to reduce uncertainty about profitability in the future and reach a competitive position in the market should develop positive long-term relationships with customers (Crosby et al. 1990). However, winning a customer once does not mean keeping it for life. Because, in sectors other than sectors such as the defense industry where the level of competition is negligible, there are many businesses that aspire to what a business wants to accomplish and offer similar products and services. Therefore, in today's competitive conditions, an operator's success depends not only on the activities of the business but also on the incompetence or inability of the competitors. Pulendran et al. (2003) stated that directly obtained information about competitors is critical in responding to customer desires and needs faster than competitors or responding promptly to competitor actions. Market intelligence about competitors is important in terms of clarifying the strategic decisions of businesses in the success of marketing planning programs (Conant and White 1999). As mentioned before, the tourism sector is a competitive sector, and touristic activities are largely composed of activities that are held for pleasure (belief tourism and dark tourism can be excluded from this). Those with high levels of education, income, and knowledge will prefer businesses that offer them high quality, affordable, and authentic experiences during their touristic travels. In this case, tourism operators have to collect information to create customer satisfaction and meet customer desires and expectations better than their competitors in order to create a competitive advantage (Ciric et al. 2014).

If the services provided by competitor hotel businesses and the promotional actions carried out are more attractive to customers or if there are agreements made with businesses that act as intermediaries in the sector such as travel agencies and tour operators, these can directly impact the customer and financial performance of the business. Customers who are aware of the low-price policies and all-inclusive applications of hotel businesses offering similar products and services (which are very likely to be) may feel cheated and this may be negatively reflected in customer satisfaction and loyalty. It is necessary to reiterate that competitor knowledge is of critical importance in a competitive market. For example, at the peak season, knowing the occupancy rates of competing hotel businesses is decisive in the price policy of the business and can contribute to financial performance in a worthwhile manner. Hilman and Kaliappen (2014) have found that competitor orientation in the Malaysian hotel industry affects business performance positively. On the contrary, Ladipo et al. (2016) have found that competitor orientation did not affect financial performance in their research on small-scale hotel businesses. Sin et al. (2005) achieved similar results in their research on hotels in Hong Kong. The hypotheses formed in this direction are as follows:

H3: Competitor orientation has a significant effect on customer performance in hotels.

H4: Competitor orientation has a significant effect on financial performance in hotels.

The other determinant of market orientation in hotel businesses is the coordination between the functions of the business. Interfunctional coordination is the coordination of the use of business resources in creating superior customer value over the target customers (Narver and Slater 1990). The destructive risks that interfunctional incompatibilities or conflicts carry for businesses are obvious. This risk, by nature, is incomparably high for the service industry in which the production and consumption happen concurrently. Interfunctional coordination is important at the point of spreading critical customer and competitor knowledge within the organization and taking the necessary precautions (Kohli and Jaworski 1990). In all services offered in hotel businesses as a service industry, customer and staff interaction is determinative in the quality of service experience. Service experience is a fragile structure that requires maximum attention at each stage of the presentation, and it is not possible for the experience to be returned or changed. For example, a mismatch between the front desk and the food-and-beverage department may cause a customer to be served dinner outside of his or her request, or disharmony with housekeeping may cause the customer to encounter a dirty room at the end of the day. That is, coordination between the functions of hotel businesses is important at the point of providing customer satisfaction.

Raposo et al. (2010), in their study examining the market orientation of the largest hotel groups in Portugal, have concluded that the most important problems for businesses are that information gained by marketing professionals is not shared with other departments. Pulendran et al. (2003) found that connections and de-conflicts between departments positively influence market orientation. Similarly, Harris (2000) found that the level of interdepartmental connection affects market orientation positively, whereas formalization and centralization negatively affect market orientation. The hypotheses formed in this direction are as follows:

H5: Interfunctional coordination has a significant effect on customer performance in hotels.
H6: Interfunctional coordination has a significant effect on financial performance in hotels.

In addition to these hypotheses, the relationship between customer performance and financial performance in hotel businesses was examined. Customer performance is related to the level of customer satisfaction with hotels, loyalty, lifetime customer value, and business continuity. A strong relationship between hotels and its customers can help to ensure the continuity of its customers (Sin et al. 2006). In hotels, the likelihood of customers to re-choose the business increases as their level of satisfaction with the goods and services offered increases (Ranaweera and Prabhu 2003; Qin and Prybutok 2008). Customers' preferring the hotel again will increase their behavioral loyalty, and their tendency to recommend their preferred hotels to other people will increase their attitudinal loyalty (Carev 2008; Khan 2013). The financial return of behavioral loyalty of customers to the business can be easily understood. However, it is not possible to fully measure the financial results of customers' sharing their experience concerning the business and the recommendations they have made. Nevertheless, there is evidence in the literature about the effect of customer satisfaction and loyalty on financial performance in hotel businesses (Chand, 2010). Customers' sharing about the business will contribute to the awareness and brand value of the business, and the brand value will increase the sales potential of the business and its market share (Schulz and Omweri 2012). In addition to that, the tendency of customers who are satisfied with the goods and services offered to maintain business relations means financial revenue for the business throughout the lifetime of the customers. Continuity in customer relationships ensures profitability for businesses and accelerates the financial return of the marketing actions taken. Zhou et al. (2009) have found, in their study, that there is a significant relationship between market performances and financial performances of businesses.

Roxana et al. (2013) have found that customer orientated practices in hotel businesses have a significant effect in achieving sales targets. Sin et al. (2005) have found that there is a significant and positive relationship between market orientation, marketing performance, and financial performance in a hotel. Wang et al. (2012) found a high level of relationship between customer performance and financial performance in hotels. The hypothesis generated in this direction is as follows:

H7: Customer performance has a significant effect on financial performance in hotels.

Method

The purpose of this research study is to examine the impact of market orientation on customer performance and financial performance in the context of five-star hotels. Besides, in the study, the effect of customer performance on the financial performance of hotel businesses will be analyzed. In this respect, the research model proposed for testing research variables and hypotheses between variables is as shown in Fig. 1.

Population and Sample

The population of the study consisted of five-star hotels operating in Turkey. According to the data provided by the Ministry of Culture and Tourism of the

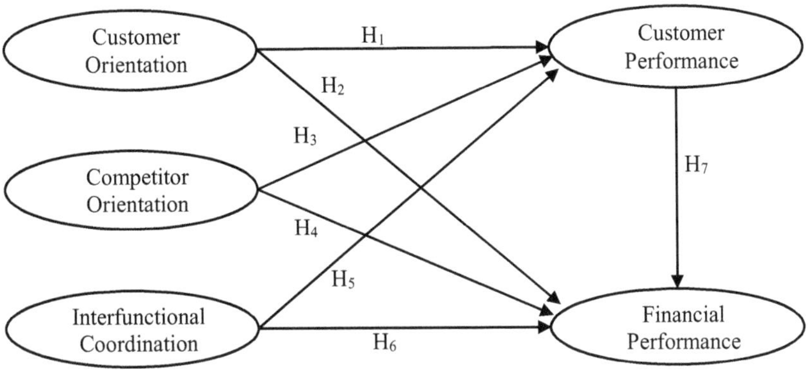

Fig. 1: Proposed Research Model

Republic of Turkey, there are 685 five-star hotels in Turkey with tourism operation certificates. Because of the geographical availability of the research population and the reluctance of hotel businesses to participate in the research, the convenience sampling technique was used in the research study.

Data Collection Instruments

Data of the study were obtained using the questionnaire technique. The research questionnaire consisted of three parts. In the first part, there were 15 expressions aimed at measuring the market orientation of hotel businesses. These expressions were taken from the research conducted by Narver and Slater (1990). In the literature, there are studies in which these expressions were used to measure the market orientation of hotels (Zhou et al. 2009; Tajeddini 2011). The measurement of market orientation in hotels was measured using a five-point Likert type scale (1=strongly disagree, 5=strongly agree). In the second part, there were four expressions about customer performance and four expressions about financial performance in hotel businesses. Expressions regarding the customer performance and financial performance of the hotel enterprises were created using the research conducted by Wang et al. (2012). The measurement of customer performance and financial performance in hotels was made using a scale of five (1=well below expectations, 3=as expected, 5=well above expectations). At the end of the scale, descriptive information about the hotels and the participants' gender, age, educational status, and departments was given. The descriptive information of the participants was measured using closed-ended questions.

Data Collection and Analysis

Following the creation of the data collection instrument, 25 hotel business administrators from the population were contacted by taking into account the geographical proximity and were informed about the study. Four of these hotel business administrators indicated that they could support collecting data from their businesses. In this respect, the research questionnaire was applied to those who work in marketing, front office, and food-and-beverage departments in these businesses. The reason for the preference of the personnel who worked at the specified departments in the data collection process is that these departments in the hotels are the departments that directly interact with the customers. In the hotels, the data obtained from 83 people working at these departments were subjected to a reliability analysis. As a result of the reliability analysis, the Cronbach Alpha value for all expressions on the scale was 0.90. This value indicates that the scale was very reliable (Kalaycı 2016, p.405). Following a preliminary test, the research data were obtained through the face-to-face surveys between April 01, 2017 and September 12, 2017, with staff from marketing, front office, and food-and-beverage departments of 20 five-star hotels. In this context, the research data were obtained from 355 staff with the participation of at least 13 and at most 19 staff from hotel businesses. Tab. 1 shows the hotels from which the research data were obtained.

The obtained data were analyzed using SPSS 18.0 and Lisrel 8.7 packet programs. In the analysis of the research data, Exploratory and Confirmatory Factor Analyzes were applied, respectively, and the proposed research model was tested using the Path Analysis.

Tab. 1: Hotel Businesses Participating in the Study

• Kervansaray Thermal-Convention Center & Spa	• Ankara Altinel Hotel & Convention Center	• Grannos Thermal Hotel & Convention Center
• Hotel Seyhan	• Margi Hotel	• Büyük Abant Hotel
• NG Sapanca Wellness & Convention	• Wyndham Grand Hotels and Resorts	• Anadolu Hotels Esenboğa Thermal
• Latanya Hotel-Ankara	• Byotell Hotel Istanbul	• Barida Hotels
• Azka Hotel	• Dinler Hotels Ürgüp	• Meyra Palace Hotel
• Adenya Resorts Hotels & Spa	• Presa Di Finica Hotel & Suites	• Utopia World De Luxe Hotel
• Salmakis Resort & Spa	• Taksim International Abant Palace Hotel	

Findings

Characteristics of Respondents and Hotels

In the course of the analysis of the research data, first, descriptive information about the hotel businesses and participants was examined. One hundred and sixty eight of the participants were female, and 187 were male. Of the participants, 277 were below age 35, and there were only 11 participants over 45 years of age. When the education levels of the participants were examined, it was seen that 98 had education at high school and below, 110 had associate education and 135 had an undergraduate education. Twelve of the participants had education at the graduate level. One hundred and twenty one of the participants worked in the marketing department, 120 at the front office department and 114 at the food-and-beverage department. When the descriptive statistics related to the hotels were examined, 13 of the hotels were privately owned hotel businesses, 4 were national chain hotels, and 3 were international chain hotels in terms of ownership. When the customer profiles of the hotels were examined, it was seen that seven hotels served the business customer type, five hotel businesses served the leisure customer type, and eight hotels served both of these customer segments. Tab. 2 provides information on the hotels and participants.

Exploratory Factor Analysis

In order to examine the effect of market orientation on customer performance and financial performance in hotel businesses, first, the construct validity of the data obtained was tested through the Exploratory Factor Analysis (EFA). In this context, Exploratory Factor Analysis (EFA) was applied to the data related to market orientation, customer performance, and financial performance included in the scale of the study. KMO and Barlett tests were performed to test the suitability of the obtained data for factor analysis. As a result of the analysis, for the data on market orientation, KMO was .926, and the $\chi 2$ value of the Barlett test was 2602.336 ($p<.000$). For the data on customer performance, KMO was .813, and the $\chi 2$ value of the Barlett test was 581.082 ($p<.000$); for the financial performance variable, KMO was .764, and the $\chi 2$ value of the Barlett test was 533.127 ($p<.000$). The resulting values indicate that the data obtained were suitable for factor analysis (Kalaycı 2016, p.322).

After understanding that the data set was suitable for factor analysis, EFA was applied to the expressions in the market orientation measurement model of the hotels. The market orientation in the hotel business has a structure with three factors. For this reason, in the exploratory factor analysis, the market orientation

Tab. 2: Information on Participants and Hotels

Respondents	N	%	Hotels	N	%
Gender			Hotel ownership		
Male	187	53.7	Private propriety	13	65
Female	168	47.3	National hotel chain	4	20
Ages (Years)			International hotel chain	3	15
Younger than 25	101	28.5	Customer type		
26-35	176	49.6	Business	7	35
36-45	67	18.9	Leisure	5	25
Older than 45	11	3.1	Both	8	40
Education level					
High school and below	98	27.6			
Associate degree	110	31.0			
Undergraduate	135	38.0			
Graduate	12	3.4			
Department					
Marketing	121	34.08			
Front office	120	33.80			
Food-and-beverage	114	32.12			

was limited to 3 factors using the Maximum Likelihood and Direct Oblimin rotation methods. It was considered that the factor eigenvalue of EFA was at least 1, the factor load was at least .40, and that there was a difference of at least .10 between the factor loads of the expressions that were under the two factors. As a result of the analysis, it was seen that the expressions related to market orientation in the hotel businesses were grouped under three factors explaining 65.484% of the total variance. These factors consisted of the customer orientation ($\alpha = .87$) explaining 47.084% of the total variance, the competitor orientation ($\alpha = .86$), describing 12.91% of the total variance, and the inter-functional coordination ($\alpha = .84$) describing 3.309% of the total variance. The factor loadings of market orientation expressions in the dataset ranged from .575 to .871. The reliability levels of the factors that made up the market orientation were between .761 and .946.

As a result of EFA applied separately to the data related to customer performance and financial performance in hotel businesses, expressions related to customer performance were collected under a single dimension explaining 68.681% of the total variance. The expressions related to financial performance in the hotel businesses were grouped under one dimension explaining 65.903% of the total variance. The factor loadings of the expressions forming these two variables were between .754 and .855. The reliability level for the customer performance variable was α=.84, and for the financial performance, it was α=.82. The resulting values show that the levels of reliability of customer performance and financial performance variables were quite high.

Confirmatory Factor Analysis

Confirmatory Factor Analysis (CFA) was applied to the data organized according to the EFA results in order to validate the structure suggested in the EFA to test the relationship between market orientation, customer performance, and financial performance in the hotel businesses. CFA aims to examine the extent to which a predetermined or designed structure is validated with the present data. Accordingly, a single level confirmatory factor analysis was applied separately to the market orientation scale, customer performance scale, and financial performance scale in hotel enterprises. Tab. 3 shows the results of CFA applied to the data regarding market orientation, customer performance, and financial performance in the hotels.

A number of fit indices are used in CFA to demonstrate the fit of the tested model. In this study, the values considered in general for CFA model fit were the fit values of the chi-square fit test NFI, GFI, CFI, IFI, RFI, AGFI, and RMSEA. Tab. 4 shows the CFA goodness of fit criteria in terms of market orientation, customer performance, and financial performance in the hotel businesses.

As shown in Tab. 4, the fit indices ($\chi2$=150.04, sd=83, p=.000, $\chi2$/sd=1.80) for the market orientation measurement model in the hotel businesses were significant. During the model fit testing process, the modifications were made between P1-P2, P5-P6, P7-P8 expressions, which were determined to contribute to the $\chi2$. The fit values that emerged as a result of the CFA show that the model fit was good. The factor loadings for all of the expressions in the model ranged from 0.52 to 0.89. In addition to that, t values between the internal factors included in the model and the expressions forming the observed variables were examined. The t values in the model ranged from 9.87 to 20.84. Moreover, there were no variables indicated by the red arrow. The values that were obtained showed that all of the observed variables in the model were significant at the 0.05 level.

As a result of the single level CFA applied to the customer performance variable in the hotel businesses, the fit indices of the four expressions that constituted the variable were $\chi2$=3.95, sd=2, p=.13652, $\chi2$/sd=1.97. The other fit indices were RMSEA=0.053, NFI=.99, CFI=1.00, IFI=1.00, RFI=0.98, AGFI=.97 and GFI=.99. The four expressions that made up the financial performance latent variable of

Tab. 3: Confirmatory Factor Analysis Results on Market Orientation, Customer Performance, and Financial Performance

Variables, Codes, and Items		Standard solutions	t-value	Error var.	Mean
Market Orientation					
Customer Orientation (α = .887)					
P1	Customer commitment	.70	14.28	.27	4.29
P2	Create customer value	.79	16.92	.38	4.23
P3	Understand customer needs	.73	15.24	.46	4.26
P4	Customer satisfaction objectives	.75	15.75	.44	4.32
P5	Measure customer satisfaction	.69	14.02	.39	4.16
P6	After-sales service	.71	14.48	.37	4.32
Customer Orientation (α = .869)					
P7	Salespeople share competitor information	.67	13.61	.37	3.89
P8	Respond rapidly to competitor' actions	.71	14.59	.32	3.98
P9	Top managers discuss competitors' strategies	.83	18.10	.31	4.00
P10	Target opportunities for competitive advantage	.89	20.04	.21	4.11
Interfunctional Coordination (α = .842)					
P11	Interfunctional customer calls	.52	9.87	.50	4.04
P12	Information shared among functions	.76	16.27	.29	4.12
P13	Functional integration in strategy	.86	19.58	.26	4.14
P14	All functions contribute to customer value	.75	15.95	.44	4.19
P15	Share resources with other business units	.72	14.97	.49	3.95
Customer Performance (α = .847)					
MP1	Customer loyalty	.80	16.80	.36	3.69
MP2	Customer satisfaction	.82	17.42	.33	3.82
MP3	Customer lifetime value	.75	15.58	.43	3.67
MP4	Customer's willingness to maintain the relations	.68	13.64	.53	3.79
Financial Performance (α = .832)					
FP1	Market share	.82	16.50	.33	3.65
FP2	Sales growth	.81	16.24	.35	3.61
FP3	Margin	.57	10.46	.37	3.44
FP4	Financial turnaround of actions	.70	13.70	.30	3.58

Tab. 4: CFA Goodness of Fit Criteria for Market Orientation, Customer Performance, and Financial Performance

	χ^2	χ^2/df	RMSEA	NFI	CFI	IFI	RFI	GFI	AGFI
Market orientation scale (First level)	150.04	1.80	0.048	0.98	0.99	0.99	0.98	.95	.92
Customer performance scale (First level)	3.95	1.97	0.053	.99	1.00	1.00	.98	.99	.97
Financial performance scale (First level)	P = 1.00, The Model is Saturated, the Fit is Perfect!								

the hotel businesses were found to explain the financial performance latent variable, and it had a perfect model fit. In this context, the CFA results applied to the obtained data showed that the fit values were good for the variables included in the proposed model.

Testing the Proposed Model

A path diagram was set up between the measurement models confirmed in CFA for testing the proposed model for market orientation, customer performance, and financial performance in the hotels. The fit indices that emerged in the generated path diagram indicated that model fit was acceptable. Fig. 2 shows the standardized coefficients and t values regarding the results of the structural model between variables. The statistically insignificant interactions among the variables were shown in red.

The fit values of the proposed model indicated that the model fit was good. When the path analysis results shown in Fig. 2 were examined, it was determined that the customer orientation from the market orientation components in the hotel businesses had a significant effect on the customer performance (H1, $\beta = .34$, $t = 2.74$). On the other hand, there was no significant effect of customer orientation on financial performance (H2, β=-13, t=-1.12). In this context, hypothesis 2 was rejected while hypothesis 1 was accepted. As a result of the path analysis, it was determined that there was no significant effect of competitor orientation of the market orientation components in hotel businesses on customer performance (H3, β=.01, t=0.11) and financial performance (H4, $\beta = .10$, $t = 1.40$). Hence, hypothesis 3 and hypothesis 4 were rejected. In addition to that, it was determined that the inter-functional coordination variable had

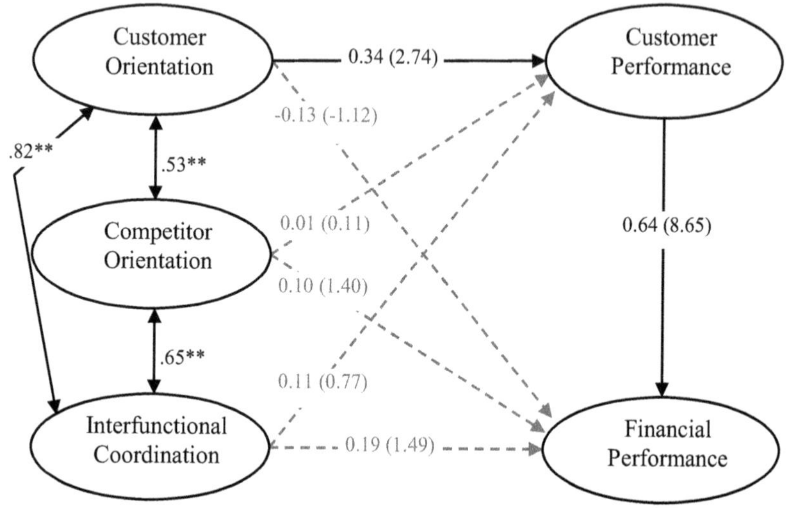

Fig. 2: Results of the Structural Model between Variables. Fit indices: $\chi 2$=335.62, sd=213, p<.001, Chi-square=1.57, GFI=0.92, CFI=0.98, RFI=0.99, IFI=0.99, GFI=.92, AGFI=0.90, RMSEA=0.040. 1. Values outside parentheses indicate standardized path coefficients, values inside parentheses, t values. 2. ---------- is not significant (p>.05). 3. ** indicates the covariance values between variables.

no significant effect on customer performance (H5, β=.11, t=.77) and financial performance (H6, β=.19, t=1.49) in the hotels. Based on the findings, hypothesis 5 and hypothesis 6 were rejected. Finally, the effect of customer performance on the financial performance in hotels was examined. As a result of the analysis, it was determined that the customer performance in the hotels had a significant effect on the financial performance (H7, β=.64, t=8.65). In this context, hypothesis 7 was accepted.

The findings of the path analysis showed that the only factor influencing customer performance in hotel business was customer orientation. Although competitor orientation and inter-functional coordination, which were the other dimensions of market orientation, did not have a direct effect on customer performance, the covariance values between these dimensions and the customer orientation dimension indicated that these dimensions indirectly supported customer performance. In the literature section of the study, it was stated that implementation oriented parts of the all three components of market orientation were customer-oriented applications. For example, there were customers at the center of the pricing decision that hotel management has given regarding the price reductions of its competitors. Alternatively, there was customer satisfaction at the target of a recreation organization that was held in the hotels. However, these practices relate to the reaction to competitor actions and the harmonious work between the departments of the business. In this respect, it can be seen as a regular case that there was a relationship between these variables, but that these two variables had no direct effect on customer orientation. However, the competitor orientation, a critical driver for decisions made against competitor actions, did not have a significant effect on the financial performance of the business, which can be regarded as an unusual finding.

Conclusion and Recommendations

Competition among hotels that want to meet customer needs and desires better than their competitors and to be attractive increases day by day in the hospitality industry. The main pillar of competitiveness in hotels is, rather than making decisions, the customers who turn these decisions into the financial output for the business. If customers prefer goods and services offered by a business to those offered by other businesses, this confirms that the decisions made for that business are correct, but otherwise it is considered to be the fallacy of the decisions taken. Having realized this fact, hotel businesses put customer desires and needs in the center of their strategic decisions. Taking customer desires and needs to the center of marketing efforts is the result of an understanding developing with the modern marketing philosophy. This understanding means that actions taken at every stage from the production of goods and services to after-sales services are customer-oriented. However, in today's communications age, where information and experience are shared very quickly, it is not easy for businesses to maintain their existence and profitability solely with customer orientation. The critical factor for businesses at this point is the level of customer value that competitor businesses offer their customers. Because, in parallel with the widespread use of information technology, customers often compare businesses in terms of price and other factors, and prefer the business that offers the best value for them.

This research builds on three components of market orientation, which includes inter-functional coordination actions of businesses to create customer, competitor, and superior customer value. Within the scope of the study, market orientation was specifically examined for five-star hotel businesses, and the effect of market orientation on customer performance and financial performance was examined. In addition to that, the impact of customer performance on the financial performance of hotels was analyzed. As a result of the analyses, it was concluded that in the hotels, only the customer orientation of the market orientation components significantly affected the customer performance; competitor orientation and inter-functional coordination did not significantly affect customer performance. The impact of customer orientation on customer performance is largely supported by findings in the literature (Grissemann et al. 2013; Ciric et al. 2014), while the effect of competitor orientation and inter-functional coordination on customer performance is in conflict with the findings in the literature (Agarwal et al. 2003; Wang et al. 2012).

In addition to this, the study showed that market orientation components had no significant effect on the financial performance of hotel businesses. This result supports research findings of Sin et al. (2005) and Ladipo et al. (2016) showing that competitor orientation has no impact on the financial performance in hotels. However, there are also studies that do not support these findings (Hilman and Kaliappen 2014). Beyond these, another finding in the study was that customer performance in five-star hotels had a significant effect on the financial performance of the business at a high level. This result shows that market orientation in hotels influences the financial performance of a business through customer performance. Considering that the market orientation component affecting customer performance in hotel businesses is customer orientation, the result that was obtained is in agreement with the finding of Sin et al. (2005) indicating that customer orientation is the dominant variable affecting financial performance.

In this direction, it is proposed that business managers should focus on long-term outcomes rather than short-term outcomes when assessing the financial outputs of actions targeting market orientation. After all, one of the principles of modern marketing is to focus on lifetime customer value instead of profitability in the short term. Although a significant portion of hotels could not go beyond the sales perspective towards profitability (Bilgin et al. 2016), hotels executives who want to maintain their profitability without focusing on lifetime customer value will not wait too long to test the fallacy of this approach in today's competitive markets.

The results of this study were obtained from twenty-five five-star hotels operating in Turkey. A significant portion of these hotels are hotels with private ownership status. In studies to be conducted on the topic, with a broader sample, different and generalizable results can be achieved by making a classification of hotel businesses in the form of ownership status or coastal and city hotels. In addition to that, the mediating role of customer performance can be examined in the relation between the variables of market orientation and financial performance.

Bibliography

Agarwal, Sanjeev / Erramilli, Krishna M. / Dev, Chekitan S.: "Market orientation and performance in service firms: role of innovation." *Journal of Services Marketing* 17 (1), 2003, pp. 68–82.

Bilgin, Yusuf / Çatı, Kahraman / Öncü, Mehmet Akif: "Otel işletmelerinin pazarlama anlayışları üzerine nitel bir araştırma." *Bartın Üniversitesi İktisadi ve İdari Bilimler Fakültesi Dergisi* 7 (14), 2016, pp. 241–285.

Carev, Danijel: "Guest satisfaction and guest loyalty study for hotel industry." Unpublished Master Thesis, Department of Hospitality-Tourism Management, Rochester Institute of Technology, New York. 2008.

Chand, Mohinder: "The impact of HRM practices on service quality, customer satisfaction and performance in the Indian hotel industry." *The International Journal of Human Resource Management* 21 (4), 2010, pp. 551–566.

Chow, Irene Hau-siu / Lau, Victor P. / Lo, Thamis Wing-Chun / Sha, Zhenquan / Yun, He: "Service quality in restaurant operations in China: decision- and experiential-oriented perspectives." *Hospitality Management* 26, 2007, pp. 698–710.

Ciric, Maja / Pocuca, Milan / Raicevic, Vuk: "Level of customer orientation and customer protectıon in hotels in Serbia." *Economics of Agriculture* 61 (1), 2014, pp. 25–39.

Civelek, Ayşen: "Konaklama işletmelerinde müşteri ilişkileri yönetiminin işletme performansına etkisi: 5 yıldızlı oteller üzerine bir uygulama." *Sosyal Bilimler Meslek Yüksekokulu Dergisi* 19 (2), 2016, ss. 233–252.

Conant, Jeffery S. / White, J. Chris: "Marketing program planning, process benefits, and store performance: an ınitial study among small retail firms." *Journal of Retailing* 75 (4), 1999, pp. 525–541.

Crosby, Lawrence A. / Evans Kenneth R. / Cowles, Deborah: "Relationship quality in services selling: an interpersonal influence perspective." *Journal of Marketing* 54 (3), 1990, pp. 68–81.

Çakıcı, A. Celil / Eren, Duygu: "Otel işletmeciliğinde pazar yönlülük ve pazar yönlülük- performans ilişkisi üzerine bir araştırma ve sonuçları." *H.Ü. İktisadi ve İdari Bilimler Fakültesi Dergisi* 23 (1), 2005, pp. 157–178.

Deng, Shengliang / Dart, Jack: "Measuring market orientation: a multi-factor, multi-item approach." *Journal of Marketing Management* 10 (8), 1994, pp. 725–742.

Deshpandé, Rohit / Farley, John U. / Webster, Frederick E.: "Corparate culture, customer orientation and innovativeness in Japanese firms: a guadrad analysis." *Journal of Marketing* 57, 1993, pp. 23–27.

Dev, Chekitan S. / Agarwal, Sanjee / Erramilli, M. Krishna: "Market-driven hotel brands: linking market orientation, innovation, and performance." *Hospitality Review* 26 (1), 2008, pp. 1–9.

Egeren, Marsha Van / O'Connor, Stephen: "Drivers of market orientation and performance in service firms." *Journal of Services Marketing* 12 (1), 1998, pp. 39–58.

Esteban, Águeda / Millan, Angel / Molina, Arturo / Consuegra, David Martín: "Market orientation in service: a review and analysis." *European Journal of Marketing* 36 (9-10), 2002, pp. 1003–1021.

Ghanavati, Mehdi: "The effect of corporate culture and market orientation on Iranian industrial SMEs' performance." *Iranian Journal of Management Studies* 7 (2), 2014, pp. 413–436.

Gray, Brendan / Matear, Sheelagh / Boshoff, Christo / Matheson, Phil: "Developing a better measure of market orientation." *European Journal of Marketing* 32 (9/10), 1998, pp. 884–903.

Grissemann, Ursula / Plank, Andreas / Sperdin, Alexandra Brunner: "Enhancing business performance of hotels: the role of innovation and customer orientation." *International Journal of Hospitality Management* 33, 2013, pp. 347–356.

Ha, Jooyeon / Jang, SooCheong: "Effects of service quality and food quality: the moderating role of atmospherics in an ethnic restaurant segment." *International Journal of Hospitality Management* 29, 2010, pp. 520–529.

Harris, Lloyd C.: "The organizational barriers to developing market orientation." *European Journal of Marketing* 34 (5/6), 2000, pp. 598–624.

Hilman, Haim / Kaliappen, Narentheren: "Market orientation practices and effects on organizational performance: empirical insight from Malaysian hotel industry." *SAGE Open*, 1–18,2014. DOI: 10.1177/2158244014553590.

Jaworski, Bernard J. / Kohli, Ajay K.: "Market orientation: antecedents and consequences." *Journal of Marketing* 57 (3), 1993, pp. 53–70.

Kalaycı, Şeref: *SPSS Uygulamalı Çok Değişkenli İstatistik Teknikleri*. 8. Baskı. Dinamik Akademi: Ankara. 2016.

Khan, Shahzad: "Determinants of customer retention in hotel industry." *Journal of Applied Economics and Business* 1 (3), 2013, pp. 42–64.

Kohli Ajay K. / Jaworski Bernard J.: "Market orientation: the construct, research proposition and managerial implication." *Journal of Marketing* 54 (2), 1990, pp. 1–18.

Kohli Ajay K. / Jaworski Bernard J. / Ajith Kumar: "MARKOR: a measure of market orientation." *Journal of Marketing Research* 30 (4), 1993, pp. 467–477.

Kotler, Philip / Armstrong, Gary / Saunders, John / Wong, Veronica: *Principles of Marketing*. Prentice Hall Europe: Milan. 1999.

Ladipo, P. K. A. / Rahim, A. Ganiyu / Oguntoyibo, C. Abayomi / Okikiola, I. Olatunji: "Market orientation and business performance: a study of interrelationships and effects in a small sized hotel within Lagos State Metropolis." *Academic Journal of Economic Studies* 4 (2), 2016, pp. 98–119.

Lafferty, Barbata A. / Hult, G. Tomas M: "A synthesis of contemporary market orientation perspectives." *European Journal of Marketing* 35 (1/2), 2001, pp. 92–109.

Matsuno, Ken / Mentzer, John T. / Rentz, Jozeph O.: "A refinement and validation of the MARKOR scale." *Journal of the Academy of Marketing Science* 28 (4), 2000, pp. 527–539.

McCullough, James / Heng, Lim Ser / Khem, Gan See: "Measuring the marketing orientation of retail operations of ınternational banks." *International Journal of Bank Marketing* 4 (3), 1986, pp. 9–18.

Narver, John C. / Slater, Stanley F.: "The effect of a market orientation on business profitability." *Journal of Marketing* 64, 1990, pp. 21–35.

Pitt, Leyland / Caruana, Albert / Berthon, Pierre R.: "Market orientation and business performance: some european evidence." *International Marketing Review* 13 (1), 1996, pp. 5–18.

Pulendran, Sue / Speed, Richard / Widing, Robert E.: "Marketing planning, market orientation and business performance." *European Journal of Marketing* 37 (3/4), 2003, pp. 476–497.

Qin, Hon G. / Prybutok, Victor R.: "Determinants of customer perceived service quality in fast food restaurants and their relationship to customer satisfaction and behavioral ıntentions." *Quality Management Journal* 15 (2), 2008, pp. 35–50.

Ranaweera, Chatura / Prabhu, Jaideep: "The influence of satisfaction, trust and switching barriers on customer retention in a continuous purchasing setting." *International Journal of Service Industry Management* 14 (4), 2003, pp. 374–395.

Raposo, Mario / Estevão, Cristina / Mainardes, Emerson / Domingues, Maria José: "Market orientation for the hotel segment: the Portuguese case." *China-USA Business Review* 9 (5), 2010, pp. 29–45.

Roxana, Stegerean / Anamaria, Petre / Corina, Gavrea: "Effects of customer orientation, learning orientation and ınnovativeness on hotel performance-evidence from Cluj County." *Annals of Faculty of Economics* 1 (1), 2013, pp. 807–814.

Ruekert, Robert W.: "Developing a market orientation: an organizational strategy perspective." *International Journal of Research Marketing* 9, 1992, pp. 225–245.

Schulz, Rina N. / Omweri, Josephat N.: "The effects of business ımage on customer retention in hotels in Eldoret, Kenya." *European Journal of Business and Management* 4 (18), 2012, pp. 185–193.

Shapiro, Benson P.: "What the hell is 'market oriented'?." *Harvard Business Review* 66, 1988, pp. 119–125.

Shoham, Aviv / Rose, Gregory M. / Kropp, Fredric: "Market orientation and performance: a meta-analysis." *Marketing Intelligence & Planning* 23 (5), 2005, pp. 435–454.

Sin, Leo Y. M. / Tse, Alan C. B. / Chan, Haksin / Heung, Vincent C. S. / Yim, Frederick H. K.: "The effects of relationship marketing orientatıon on business performance in the hotel ındustry." *Journal of Hospitality & Tourism Research* 30 (4), 2006, pp. 407–426.

Sin, Leo Y. M. / Tse, Alan C. B. / Heung, Vincent C. S. / Yim, Frederick H. K.: "An analysis of the relationship between market orientation and business performance in the hotel industry." *Hospitality Management* 24, 2005, pp. 555–577.

Slater, Stanley F. / Narver, John C.: "Market orientation, customer value, and superior performance." *Business Horizons* 37 (2), 1994, pp. 22–28.

Tajeddini, Kayhan / Detlev Remy / Phillip Pardo: "Market orientation and business performance: evidence from the hotel industry in Germany." *International Journal of Leisure and Tourism Marketing* 2 (3), 2011, pp. 232–247.

Wang, Cheng-Hua / Chen, Kuan Yu / Chen, Shiu-Chun: "Total quality management, market orientation and hotel performance: the moderating effects of external environmental factors." *International Journal of Hospitality Management* 31, 2012, pp. 119–129.

Wrenn, Bruce: "The Market Orientation Construct: Measurement and Scaling Issues." *Journal of Marketing* 5 (3), 1997, pp. 31–54.

Zafar, Hina / Hafeez, Muhammad Haroon / Shariff, Mohd Noor Mohd: "Relationship between market orientation, organızational learning, organizational culture and organizational performance: mediating impact of ınnovation." *South East Asia Journal of Contemporary Business, Economics and Law* 9 (2), 2016, pp. 40–56.

Zhou, Kevin Zheng / Brown, James R. / Dev, Chekitan S.: "Market orientation, competitive advantage, and performance: a demand-based perspective." *Journal of Business Research* 62, 2009, pp. 1063–1070.

İlkut Elif Kandil Göker

Effectiveness Analysis of Outward Foreign Direct Investment of Turkey in Banking Sector

Abstract: Outward foreign direct investment of Turkey, which has been increasing since 2001, has let her be home country in addition to the host country. Turkey's outward foreign direct investment in the banking sector, which began with the disintegration of the Soviet Union in the 1990s, has now spread to many European countries. Having laid the foundations of a strong banking structure after the financial crisis of 2001, Turkey has started to set up subsidiaries in many countries with its knowledge and experience. In this study, it is aimed to investigate the effectiveness of foreign subsidiaries of Turkish commercial banks abroad. Data Envelopment Analysis is conducted to assess the effectiveness scores of subsidiaries for the period of 2012–2016. The empirical results indicate that there aren't any banks that are efficient for all the given years. However, although none of the banks has the efficiency score equal to 1 for all the given years, there is an increasing trend of efficiency for most of the subsidiaries.

Keywords: Foreign direct investment, Effectiveness analysis, Banking sector

Introduction

IMF defines foreign direct investment as "*an investment made to acquire lasting interest in enterprises operating outside of the economy of the investor. Further, in cases of foreign direct investment, the investor's purpose is to gain an effective voice in the management of the enterprise. The foreign entity or group of associated entities that makes the investment is termed the 'direct investor'. The unincorporated or incorporated enterprise - a branch or subsidiary, respectively, in which direct investment is made - is referred to as a 'direct investment enterprise'*" (Hattari and Rajan 2010, p.500). In addition to branches and subsidiaries, foreign direct investment can enter the country in many different ways such as merger and acquisitions, investments through privatization, joint ventures, strategic alliances, licensing, fixed capital investments, expansion of existing operations. As the home country's degree of openness and internationalization is higher, emerging market economies benefit more from efficient flows of production factors within their globally coordinated networks. Thus, they can better arrange global value chains through vertical or horizontal integration (Luo et al. 2010, p.69). Since the 1980s, there has been a rapid increase in the growth of foreign direct investment. Especially in the 1990s, the form of foreign direct investment has undergone substantial changes in emerging economies. Until the 1990s developed countries had remained the leading hometown of outward foreign direct investment. Thereafter, the developing countries have also started to show up in outward foreign direct investment. According to UNCTAD statistics of 2016, foreign direct investment outflow from developed countries remained weak mainly due to a slump in investment from European multinational enterprises. It declined by 11% to $1 trillion. The flow of outward investment from developing economies registered a 1% decline to $383 billion, despite a surge of outflows from China, now the second largest investing country in the world (UNCTAD, 2017). When we look at the foreign direct investment outward stocks, we can see that it has been increased to $ 26.160 billion at the end of 2016 while it was $ 2.254 billion in 1990.

Outward Foreign Direct Investment of Turkey

Many studies were conducted to answer the question that why a business goes abroad. An empirical study about Turkey asserts that the major determinants of outward foreign direct investment for developing countries are the desire to be the first business in the market and get easy access to low-cost inputs. Whereas, reaching strategic assets and protecting export markets are the main motives of developed countries (Onder and Karal 2013, p.247). Turkish foreign direct investment outflows peaked up towards the end of the 1990s. Then the amount of foreign direct investment outflow fell dramatically as a result of the economic crisis of 2001. The decrease in outflow amounted to approximately 44% of 2000, which was followed by a further 65% in 2002. The overall decline in those two years was 80% of 2000, and it was not until 2005 the outflows reached their pre-crisis level. Outward foreign direct investment of Turkey has increased in line with the increase in world foreign direct investment flows after 2003 (Kayam and Hisarciklilar 2009). Currently, Turkey's outward foreign direct investment has increased by 12.05 % to 31.006 billion USD in 2016. Furthermore, as Çergibozan and Demir (2017) mentioned in their study, except for the 2001 national economic crisis, the outward foreign direct investment flows of Turkey demonstrate two distinguished and separated stages which are the pre- and post-2000 periods and after a three-year post-crisis recovery stage, the propensity for investing in abroad of Turkish investors has noticeably increased since 2004.

The regional and sectoral distribution of Turkey's outward foreign direct investment is displayed in Tab. 1, Fig. 1 and Tab. 2, Fig. 2, respectively.

According to Tab. 1 and Fig. 1, it is seen that Turkey has been making its investments mostly in Europe. Europe was followed by Asia, America, and

Tab. 1: Turkey's Outward Foreign Direct Investment in Regions 2001–2016 (Billion USD)

	EUROPE	AFRICA	AMERICA	ASIA	OCEANIA AND POLARS
2001	3.131	22	267	1.161	0
2002	4.164	60	281	1.342	0
2003	4.392	67	267	1.412	0
2004	4.702	72	278	2.008	0
2005	5.093	86	283	2.853	0
2006	5.407	90	293	3.076	0
2007	8.042	171	298	3.699	0
2008	11.210	381	1.476	4.778	1
2009	12.409	362	1.729	5.408	15
2010	12.894	530	1.942	5.355	40
2011	14.229	504	2.756	6.355	53
2012	17.300	412	2.271	7.286	244
2013	19.602	589	2.480	7.024	223
2014	20.653	581	2.845	9.564	295
2015	21.071	235	1.969	4.133	263
2016	24.457	631	2.090	3.643	185

Africa. The outward foreign direct investment to Europe has been increasing in acceleration since 2001. Central Asian Countries have a big share of Turkey's foreign direct investment outflows to Asia. Europe and Asia are also Turkey's major trade partners. The least amount of outward foreign direct investment was made in Oceania and Polars. However, it is definite that a decrease in the amount of outward foreign direct investment did not occur in any region.

It is observed from the Tab. 2 and Fig. 2 that outward foreign direct investment from Turkey has increased significantly over 15 years. Especially investment in services has had the largest share of total outward foreign direct investment, and it has been increasing year by year. Industry outward foreign direct investment has decreased last two years. Turkey started to make outward foreign direct investment in the agriculture sector in 2008. The agriculture sector outward investment has relatively low values.

Besides the advantages such as the transfer of know-how, the integration into the processes of the parent organization and the global market for corporate control, transfer of ownership and managerial control, foreign direct investment in financial sector provides many advantages for both host country and home country. Especially in emerging market economies, transfer of human capital

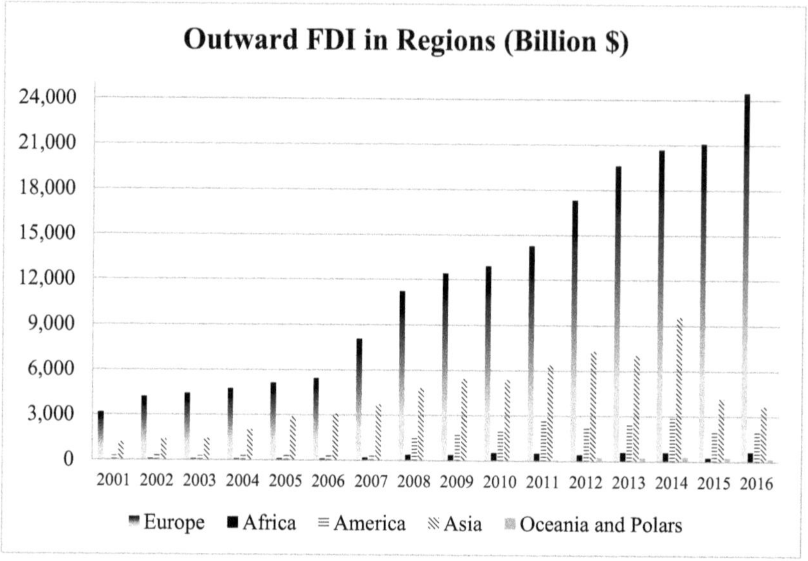

Fig. 1: Turkey's Outward Foreign Direct Investment Distribution in Regions 2001–2016 (Billion USD).

Tab. 2: Turkey's Outward Foreign Direct Investment in Sectors 2001–016 (Billion USD)

	AGRICULTURE	INDUSTRY	SERVICES	TOTAL
2001	0	2.170	2.411	**4.581**
2002	0	2.431	3.182	**5.613**
2003	0	2.507	3.401	**5.908**
2004	0	3.105	3.806	**6.911**
2005	0	4.135	4.101	**8.236**
2006	0	4.334	4.400	**8.734**
2007	0	4.822	7.182	**12.004**
2008	20	5.773	12.053	**17.846**
2009	5	6.563	13.356	**19.924**
2010	8	7.261	13.492	**20.761**
2011	9	7.459	16.429	**23.897**
2012	15	7.247	20.251	**27.513**
2013	8	7.890	22.020	**29.918**
2014	12	11.080	22.846	**33.938**
2015	5	5.157	22.509	**27.671**
2016	9	4.724	26.273	**31.006**

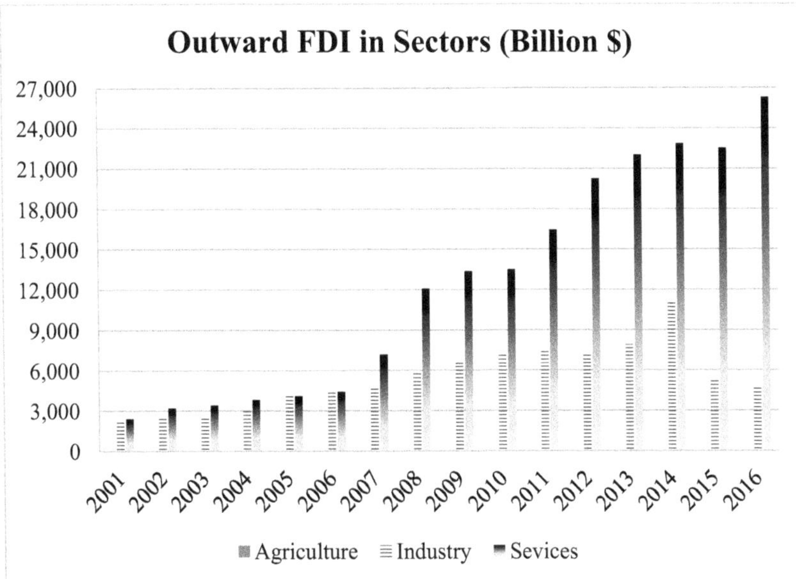

Fig. 2: Turkey's Outward Foreign Direct Investment Distribution in Sectors 2001–2016 (Billion USD).

on both managerial and operational level, transfer of reputation, the integration of decision-making and risk management of the local operation into that of the parent are important benefits of financial sector foreign direct investments (BIS 2004, p.10). Foreign direct investment in financial sector brings substantial benefits to host countries' financial system in terms of efficiency and stability. Turkey has been a home country for financial sector foreign direct investment, especially after 1980 liberalization activities. However, at the beginning of the 2000s, Turkey implemented the going out policy. As a result of this, the amount of foreign direct investment outflows has been increasing since 2001 financial crisis. Turkey's Outward foreign direct investment in Banking Sector is shown in Tab. 3 and Fig. 3.

Internationalization of Turkish Banking Sector

In the first stage of internationalization, banks executed their international operations from the local country where they are based. At this stage, also called arm's length banking, the international activities of the banks are mostly carried

Tab. 3: Turkey's Outward Foreign Direct Investment in Banking Sector 2001–2016 (Billion USD)

	Outward FOREIGN DIRECT INVESTMENT in Banking Sector
2001	1.169
2002	1.021
2003	1.178
2004	1.345
2005	1.396
2006	1.523
2007	2.157
2008	3.755
2009	4.545
2010	3.901
2011	4.843
2012	6.164
2013	5.897
2014	6.100
2015	5.529
2016	6.528

out within the framework of correspondent relations. The main activities are towards the financing foreign trade and transactions are made by the bank's international department. The most common transactions were making international payments, intermediating imports/exports, and providing funds for foreign trade. In the 1950s, the rapid growth of world trade was found to have an impact on the development of such activities. At the second stage, with the emergence of new customers and diverse needs in the 1960s, the banks have started to expand abroad, following multinational clients. For many banks, the first exit experience abroad has been defensive. In other words, when a domestic company invests abroad, banks needed to open a branch in the foreign country where the company entered with the aim of keeping customer. In the last stage of internationalization of banking sector, national banks offered banking services in competition with foreign local banks through their branches and subsidiaries in foreign countries. In this case, deposits are accepted using domestic money like domestic banks, credits are opened for local fund demanders, and other banking services are offered (Seyidoğlu 2003, pp.477–478). This last stage of internationalization of banking sector has brought out multinational banks that

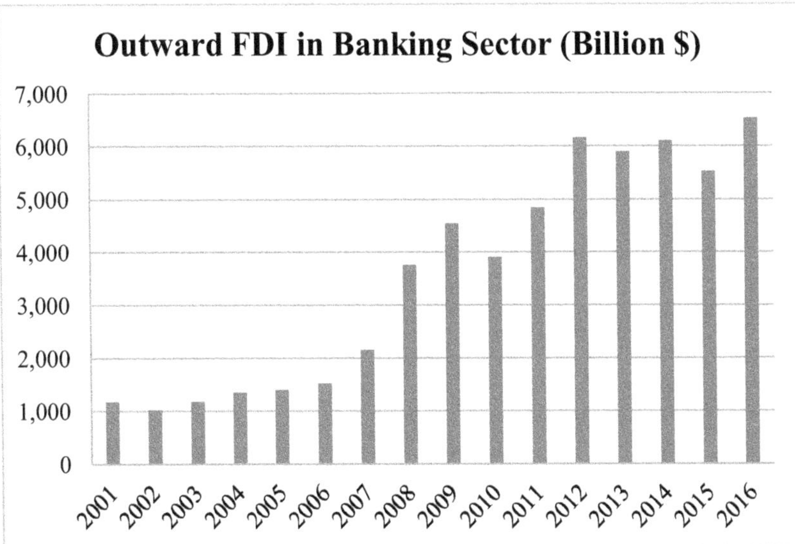

Fig. 3: Turkey's Outward Foreign Direct Investment in Banking Sector 2001–2016 (Billion USD).

have branches and subsidiaries abroad. Foreign direct investment outflows in the financial sector are the best way to be a multinational bank.

The Bank-ı Dersaadet, the first bank of Ottoman Empire, was established by the bankers J. Alleon and Th. Baltazzi with the support of the government in 1847. This bank was a foreign bank that operated until 1863, with the authority to issue banknotes and create emissions. In 1863, Bank-ı Osmani Şahane was established. Until the declaration of the Republic in 1923, many foreign banks were established in the Ottoman Empire. Most of the foreign banks operating in the first period of the Republic of Turkey were the banks established in the last days of the Ottoman Empire. In the Republican period, private sector banking was encouraged in order to eliminate the dependency on the banking system which is in the hands of foreign capital. The adoption of liberal economic policies in the country has led to the establishment of private banks. With the establishment of the Central Bank of the Republic of Turkey (CBRT) in 1930, the Ottoman Bank's emission authority was transferred to the central bank (Sümer 2016, p.489). The decisions of January 24, 1980, are of great importance for the development of Turkish banking. Decisions of January 24 led to radical changes in Turkey in every field. Turkish economy underwent a substantial liberalization, and an export-based growth policy was adopted. In this period, it was allowed the interest rates to be fluctuated and determined in the market. Besides, it was aimed to increase the competition by allowing the establishment of new domestic and foreign banks.

Turkey's first outward foreign direct investment was in the banking sector. In 1932 İşbank opened two branches abroad, one in Germany and the other in Egypt, to facilitate the foreign trade of the country. Although the mentioned branches were terminated in 1940 and 1959, İş Bank opened branches in Cyprus, London, and Frankfurt as other internationalization initiatives, opening the way for the internationalization of the Turkish banking sector (Kocabaşoğlu 2001). Another important milestone for Turkish outward foreign direct investment was experienced in 1961. As a result of increasing the number of Turkish immigrants to Western European countries commercial relations between Turkey and them increased. Also, as a result of increasing number of Turkish citizens, the increasing need for banking services in those countries has led Turkish banks to invest abroad. Ziraat Bank internationalized in Cyprus by opening agencies in Nicosia, Girne, Famagusta, Guzelyurt in 1975; by opening branches in Frankfurt in 1964 and Hamburg in 1975. Besides, Halkbank made its first foreign investment by opening agencies in 1978 in Lefkoşa, Yapı Kredi Bank made its first foreign investment by opening agencies in London in 1976, and New York, Munich, and Cologne in 1977. Similarly, Osmanlı Bank, Emlak Bank, Şekerbank, Akbank, Halkbank, Vakıfbank and Garanti Bank invested abroad by opening agencies in London in 1969, in Berlin in 1972, in Cologne in 1972, in London in 1973, in Cologne in 1974, in Frankfurt in 1974, in Geneva in 1975, respectively (Yavan, 2012). Outward foreign direct investment, mostly carried out in Europe, was directed towards the Commonwealth of Independent States (CIS), especially the Central Asian Turkish Republics through the support of Turkish Eximbank and various incentive legislation.

In recent years, many economic factors have played a role in outward foreign direct investment of Turkish banking sector. Current account deficits have become chronic in the Turkish economy. As a result, national banks have sought to raise funds in international markets by developing their overseas organizations since paying foreign debts requires foreign funds. The other factor is high inflation rates. In the high inflationary environment, the operations and strategies of banks are different from the normal average. On the one hand, banks try to avoid the harmful effects of inflation, and on the other hand, they are reassessing the methods of getting over the uncertainties and risks. In the Turkish financial sector, because national savings are not often sufficient for economic development, there has been a need for foreign funds and capital. Foreign capital also needs bank guarantees and loans as well as economic incentives such as high-profit margins. The provision of foreign capital required for development necessitates internationalization of the banking system (Algan 2006, p.114). One of the most important factors affecting the foreign capital decision is "stability." Stability refers not only to economic, but also political and social stability. If the investor cannot find a safe environment for the investment to be made and considers the risk is high for the investment, he avoids investing in that country, even his own country. For instance, political instability in Turkey had an important share in capital export (Çapraz and Demircioğlu 2003, p.67).

According to the Banks Association of Turkey statistics, there are 31 subsidiaries and affiliates of Turkish Commercial Banks' abroad. Ziraat Bank is the bank with the highest number of nine subsidiaries. Yapı Kredi has 4, Halbank, İşbank, Vakıfbank have 3, Garanti, Şekerbank, Denizbank have 2 and Akbank, Anadolu Bank, ING Bank have one subsidiaries abroad. On the other hand, the countries where Turkish banks invested most are the Netherlands and Cyprus with four subsidiaries in each. Germany, Azerbaijan Rep., Russian Fed. have 3, Austria has 2 and Ireland, Kazakhstan, Turkmenistan, Uzbekistan, Bosnia and Herzegovina, Montenegro, Romania, Macedonia, Serbia, Georgia, Switzerland and Malta have 1 Turkish Bank Subsidiary. When we focus on the foundation and affiliation dates of bank subsidiaries, it is seen that the earliest outward foreign direct investment was predominantly made to the Central Asian countries and Russia. Furthermore, Turkish Commercial Banks have 80 branches abroad as of the date of 31.12.2016, 36 of which belong to state-owned banks.

Methodology

This study measures the efficiency level of Turkish Commercial Banks' Subsidiaries abroad during the five years from 2012 to 2016. The aim of this paper is to assess the efficiency scores by using Data Envelopment Analysis (DAE) and to reveal whether Turkish outward foreign direct investments in the financial sector are efficient or not. There are 31 subsidiaries at the date of 31.12.2016 according to statistics of Bank Association of Turkey (Tab. 4). Due to the limitation of incomplete data, 20 banks constitute the sample. The data of financial statements of banks were obtained from banks' annual reports that announced on their websites. DEAP 2.1 program is used to assess efficiency scores.

DEA is defined as a nonparametric, linear programming-based technique aimed at measuring the activities of similar decision-making units (DMUs) in the presence of a large number of inputs and outputs. DEA was developed by Charnes, Cooper, and Rhodes as a CCR model in 1978 to measure the activities

Tab. 4: Turkish Bank's Subsidiaries and Affiliates Abroad, 31.12.2016. Source: The Banks Association of Turkey, Banks in Turkey 2016.

	Bank Name	Foundation Date	Affiliation Date	Country
1	Akbank AG	2006	2006	Germany
2	Anadolubank Nederland B.V.	2006	2006	Netherlands
3	Denizbank AG	1996	2002	Austria
4	Euro Deniz International Banking Unit Ltd.	1996	2002	Cyprus
5	ING European Financial Services Plc.	1994	1994	Ireland
6	Şekerbank International Banking Unit Ltd.	1994	1994	Cyprus
7	Şekerbank Kıbrıs Ltd.	1996	1996	Cyprus
8	Azer Türk Bank ASC	1995	1995	Azerbaijan
9	Kazakhstan Ziraat International Bank	1993	1993	Kazakhstan
10	Turkmen Turkish J. S. Commercial Bank	1993	1993	Turkmenistan
11	Uzbekistan Turkish Bank (UTBANK) JSC	1993	1993	Uzbekistan
12	Ziraat Bank BH D.D.	1996	1996	BosniaHerze.
13	Ziraat Bank Azerbaijan ASC	2014	2014	Azerbaijan
14	Ziraat Bank International AG	2001	2001	Germany
15	Ziraat Bank Montenegro AD	2015	2015	Montenegro
16	Ziraat Bank Moscow JSC	1993	1993	Russian Fed.
17	Garanti Bank International N.V.	1990	1990	Netherlands
18	Garanti Bank SA	2009	2010	Romania
19	Demir-Halk Bank (Nederland) N.V.	1992	1992	Netherlands
20	Halkbank A.D. Skopje	1993	2011	Macedonia
21	Halkbank A.D. Beograd	1956	2015	Serbia
22	Isbank AG	1992	1992	Germany
23	JSC Isbank	1994	2011	Russian Fed.
24	JSC Isbank Georgia	2015	2015	Georgia
25	Kıbrıs Vakıflar Bankası Ltd.	1982	1989	Cyprus
26	Vakıfbank International A.G.	1999	1999	Austria
27	Banque De Commerce Et De Placements S.A.	1963	1996	Switzerland
28	Yapı Kredi Bank Azerbaycan CJS Company	1998	1998	Azerbaijan
29	Yapı Kredi Bank Malta Ltd.	2014	2014	Malta
30	Yapı Kredi Bank Moscow	1994	1994	Russian Fed.
31	Yapı Kredi Bank Nederland N.V.	2001	2001	Netherlands

of similar decision-making units. In addition to the CCR model based on the assumption of a fixed return on a scale, other data envelopment analysis was developed in 1984, taking into account the assumption of a variable return on the scale, called the BBC model by Banker, Charnes, and Cooper (Cooper et al. 2011). Since the efficiency limits of the CCR model covers a larger area than the efficiency limits of the BCC model, the effectiveness of the CCR model of any bank is more difficult than that of the BCC model (Cooper et al. 2007). For this reason, the efficiency levels of the banks in this study are determined by taking the CCR model into consideration. DEA models can be examined in two groups as "input-oriented" and "output-oriented". While input-oriented DEA models investigate the most appropriate input composition to be used in order to produce a specific output composition most efficiently; output-oriented DEA models investigate how much output component can be obtained with a given input component. The input-oriented and constant returns to scale DEA model is conducted in this study as a result of related literature discussion and expert comments.

Since the most important function that banks undertake in the financial system is considered as intermediary service, the intermediation approach is employed to measure bank efficiency. According to intermediation approach, banks are qualified as mainly intermediator of funds between savers and investors. Because of this, in this study deposits, interest expenses, and non-interest expenses are used as input variables; loans, interest revenue, and non-interest revenue are used as output variables. Fig. 4 presents the inputs and outputs used in the analysis.

According to DEA analysis results, if the DMU's efficiency score is equal to 1, it means that it is an efficient DMU. If a DMU's efficiency score is smaller than 1, it indicates that such DMU appears inefficient and its efficiency can be improved by means of various management measures (Lin et al. 2009, p.8889). Tab. 5 presents the efficiency scores of Turkish Commercial Banks' Subsidiaries abroad.

Some banks did not declare their annual reports or their financial statements of 2012, 2013, and 2014. Because of that, such kind of banks' efficiency scores could not be assessed. The empirical results indicate that Anadolu Netherland, Denizbank AG, Halkbank AD Skopje have not been efficient at all for the period of 2012–2016. Besides, there aren't any banks that are efficient for all the given years. Halkbank Belgrade, JSC İşbank Georgia, JSC İşbank, Ziraat ASC Azerbaijan, Ziraat Moscow, and Ziraat Uzbekistan are relatively more efficient than the other banks for the period of 2012–2016. Although none of the banks has the efficiency score of 1 for all the given periods, there is an increasing trend of efficiency for most of the banks. It is shown in Tab. 5. There are twelve efficient banks in 2012, four efficient banks in 2013, six efficient banks in 2014, 11

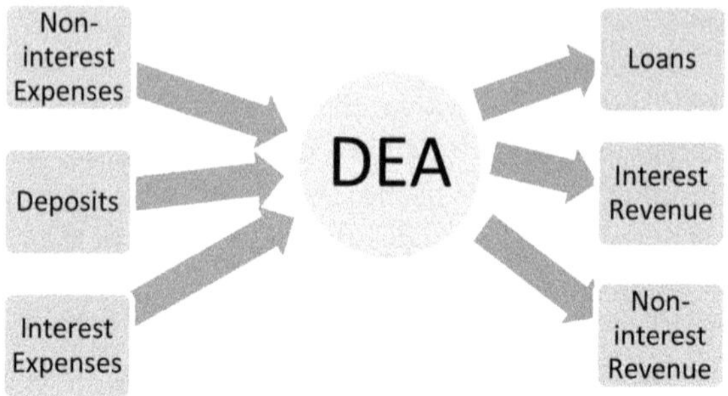

Fig. 4: Inputs and Outputs of DEA.

efficient banks in 2015, and ten efficient banks in 2016. According to the results, the most efficient Turkish Commercial Bank Subsidiaries belong to İşBank.

Conclusion

This study is undertaken to determine whether bank subsidiaries, which Turkey set up through foreign direct investment abroad, are efficient in the host countries. The growing number of branches and subsidiaries of Turkish banks abroad in recent years has transformed her into a home country. Outward foreign direct investment in banking sector provides many advantages both to the country of destination and to Turkey. When the dates of establishment of subsidiaries are examined, it is observed that the majority of the subsidiaries in the 1990s was established in the Central Asian Turkish Republics. The vast majority of this subsidiaries are the first foreign banks to be established in the countries concerned. The years of establishment, however, correspond to the beginning of the process of restructuring the financial system following their declaration of independence. Since the very beginning of the restructuring process in the banking sector, Turkish banks have supported these countries in terms of financing, knowledge, and experience as they exist in the relevant countries.

Competition in the banking sector forces banks to use their resources most effectively. To ensure this, banks assess their performance within the sector they compete in. On the other hand, the banks will decide whether or not to invest more abroad according to the efficiency levels of the banks there. To this end, the efficiency analysis in which inputs are used to obtain the desired outputs of the banks is a very important management tool. DEA is conducted to calculate the efficiency scores of Turkish commercial banks' subsidiaries abroad for the period

Tab. 5: DEA Efficiency Scores of Turkish Commercial Banks' Subsidiaries Abroad

		2012	2013	2014	2015	2016
1	Akbank Ag	***1.000***	0.716	***1.000***	***1.000***	0.780
2	Anadolu Nederland	0.785	0.613	0.496	0.821	0.824
3	Azer Turk Bank	***1.000***	0.557	***1.000***	0.743	***1.000***
4	Demirhalkbank	***1.000***	0.590	0.713	***1.000***	***1.000***
5	Denizbank AG	0.991	0.586	0.624	0.706	0.563
6	Garantibank Int.	***1.000***	0.515	0.594	0.882	0.575
7	Halkbank Belgrade	***1.000***	0.525	***1.000***	***1.000***	***1.000***
8	Halkbank Ad Skopje	0.730	0.515	0.619	0.722	0.638
9	Isbank Ag	***1.000***	0.772	0.868	***1.000***	1.000
10	Jsc Isbank Georgia	***1.000***	***1.000***	***1.000***	***1.000***	0.964
11	Jsc Isbank	***1.000***	0.726	***1.000***	***1.000***	***1.000***
12	Sekerbank Cyprus			0.551	***1.000***	***1.000***
13	Yapıkredi Azerbaijan	0.831	***1.000***	0.583	0.792	***1.000***
14	Vakıfbank Int.Ag	***1.000***	0.630	0.455	0.846	***1.000***
15	Ziraat Ag	***1.000***	0.776	***1.000***	***1.000***	0.773
16	Ziraat Asc Azerbaijan				***1.000***	0.947
17	Ziraat Bh D.D	***1.000***	***1.000***		0.957	0.692
18	Ziraat Montenegro				***1.000***	0.399
19	Ziraat Moscow				***1.000***	***1.000***
20	Ziraat Uzbekistan	***1.000***	***1.000***	0.714	0.984	***1.000***

of 2012–2016. According to the results, although none of the banks' subsidiaries has the efficiency score of 1 for the given period, there is an increasing trend of efficiency for most of the banks.

Bibliography

Algan A.: *Bankacılık Sektöründe Uluslararasılaşma Süreci ve Koçbank Örneği.* Ankara Üniversitesi Sosyal Bilimler Enstitüsü, Yayınlanmamış Yüksek Lisans Tezi. 2006.

Bank for International Settlements: *Foreign Direct Investment in The Financial Sector of Emerging Market Economies.* Bank for International Settlements Press & Communications: Basel. 2004.

Cooper W./ Lawrance M. / Kaoru T.: *Data Envelopment Analysis a Comprehensive Text with Models, Applications, References and DEA- Solwer Software,* Second Edition. Springer: USA. 2007.

Cooper W. / Lawrance M. / Zhu J.: *Handbook on Data Envelopment Analysis*, Second Edition. Springer: New York. 2011.

Çapraz İ. / Demircioğlu İ.: *Türkiye'den Yurtdışına Doğrudan Sermaye Yatırımları ve Türk Yatırımcıları*, İstanbul Ticaret Odası Yayınları: İstanbul. 2003.

Çergibozan R. / Demir C.: "Türkiye'den Yurt Dışına Yapılan Doğrudan Yatırımlar: Rejim Değişim Modeli Yaklaşımı", *Finans Politik & Ekonomik Yorumlar* 54 (625), 2017, pp. 53–63.

Hattari R. / Rajan R. S.: "India as a Source of Outward Foreign Direct Investment", *Oxford Development Studies* 38(4), 2010, pp.497–518.

Kayam, S. / Hisarciklilar, M.: "Determinants of Turkish Foreign direct investment Abroad", *Topics in Middle Eastern and North African Economies* 11, 2009.

Kocabaşoğlu, U.: *Türkiye İş Bankası Tarihi*, İş Bankası Kültür Yayınları: İstanbul. 2001.

Lin T.T. / Lee C.C. / Chiu T. F.: "Application of DEA in Analyzing a Bank's Operating Performance", *Expert Systems with Applications* 36, 2009, pp.8883–8891.

Luo Y. / Xue Q. / Han B.: "How Emerging Market Governments Promote Outward Foreign Direct Investment: Experience from China", *Journal of World Business* 45, 2010, pp.68–79.

Onder G. / Karal Z.: "Determinants of Foreign Direct Investments Outflow from A Developing Country: The Case of Turkey", *Business, Management and Education* 11(2), 2013, pp.241–255.

Seyidoğlu H.: *Uluslararası Finans*. 4. Edition. Güzem Can Yayınları: İstanbul. 2003.

Sümer G.: "Türk Bankacılık Sektörünün Tarihsel Gelişimi ve AB Bankacılık Sektörü İle Karşılaştırılması", *Gazi Üniversitesi İktisadi ve İdari Bilimler Fakültesi Dergisi* 18(2), 2016, pp.485–508.

UNCTAD: *World Investment Report Investment and The Digital Economy*, United Nations Publication: Geneva. 2017.

Yavan N.: "Türkiye'nin Yurt Dışındaki Doğrudan Yatırımları: Tarihsel ve Mekânsal Perspektif", *Bilig* 63, 2012, pp.237–270.

Part II Institutions and Socio-economic Performance

Hüsnü Bilir

The Roles of Habits and Instincts in Formation of Institutions in Veblen's Analysis[1]

Abstract: The institutional economics emphasizes that both social, historical, cultural factors and habits, instinct, norms, and institutions have important roles in formation and shaping of human behavior. This point is especially apparent in Veblen's analysis which approaches culture in the context of institution and defines the institution as "generally accepted habits of thought and behavior"; and considers habit and instinct as a starting point of institutions and culture. This paper aims to underline the role of habit and instinct in the process of formation of institutions and to demonstrate the evolutionary perspective in Veblen's integrated analysis with anthropological, sociological, and economic aspects.

Keywords: Institutional economics, Thorstein Bunde Veblen, Institution, Habit, Instinct

Introduction

Institutions are crucial elements in economic as well as sociological, cultural, and political aspects. Because they affect both individuals' and societies' habits of life and shape individual's (and groups of people as community or nation) behaviors and habits of thought. In this direction, they are one of the basic determinants of countries' socio-economic environment and performance. On the other hand, the term of "institution" implies not only financial or economic organizations as IMF, World Bank, or Central Bank but also social, political, religious associations as a family, church, habits, habits of thought, instincts, conventions, traditions, etc.

Moreover, within this framework, institutional economics emphasizes the importance of social, historical, cultural factors and argues that habits, instincts, conventions, norms, and institutions have substantial roles in formation and shaping of human behavior. Hence, as Hamilton (1919, pp. 309–311) pointed out, it could be said that institutional economics unifies economic science by indicating how parts of the economic system related to the whole. This point is especially apparent in Veblen's analysis. Drawing upon not only socio-economic but also biological elements such as evolution, instinct, and habit, Veblen discussed

1 The draft of this study was presented at *International Congress on Management, Economics and Business* in Zonguldak at 7-9 of September, 2017.

culture in the context of institution and defined the institution as "prevalent habits of thought" (Veblen 1899c, p. 88); and considered habit and instinct as a starting point of institutions and culture. In this regard, Veblen saw economics as a part of the social world and argued that social world is an evolutionary and institutional process. Therefore, concepts like institutions, habits, and instincts come into prominence in Veblen's analysis.

This chapter aims to underline the role of habit and instinct in the process of formation of institutions and to demonstrate the evolutionary perspective in Veblen's integrated analysis with anthropological, sociological, and economic aspects. For this purpose, firstly Veblen's conception of economics will be summarized, and then such basic concepts as institutions, habit, and instinct in Veblen's system of thought will be evaluated.

Veblen's Conception of Economics

Veblen is one of the most exceptional figures in the history of economic thought. Because, firstly he emphasized the role of habits, instincts, and institutions in individual's action and behavior, and secondly, he argued that economic science is evolutionary science. In this context, according to Hodgson (1998b, pp. 166–167), Veblen was the first social scientist to attempt to develop an economic theory in the light of institutional setting and evolutionary process.

Thus Veblen's analysis was linked to his evolutionary perspective. Veblen (1898b, pp. 373–376), in this regard, characterized the classical or neoclassical economics as pre-Darwinian and said that "economics is helplessly behind the times, and unable to handle its subject-matter in a way to entitle it to standing as a modern science" so economics was in need of rehabilitation. Moreover, any evolutionary science was a theory of process, of an unfolding sequence and in this regard economics was not evolutionary science.

There were two reasons for Veblen to consider that classical and neoclassical economics were not evolutionary sciences. Firstly, these schools conceived developmental process in terms of equilibrium, and secondly, these schools had a hedonistic conception of human being (Kologlugil 2016, p. 641). In Veblen's own terms: "Economic science, when it analyzes a sequence of events, a 'developmental process', conceives of this process 'in terms of a consistent propensity tending to some legitimate end.'" (Veblen 1898b, p. 378). In other words, for Veblen, in these pre-evolutionary sciences:

> "The process is rated in terms of the equilibrium to which it tends or should tend, not conversely. The outcome of the process, taken in its relation of equivalence within the system, is the point at which the inquiry comes to rest. It is not primarily the point of

departure for an inquiry into what may follow (…) In this lies its characteristic difference from the later evolutionary sciences." (Veblen 1900, p. 256)

In addition, these sciences conceived man's nature as static and embraced the utilitarian psychology and approached the man as *homo economicus* for Veblen (Murphree 1959, p. 314). However, as a consequence of his evolutionary approach, Veblen rejected utilitarian and hedonistic conceptions of human being, because they didn't include evolutionary explanation of the origin of the assumed behavioral characteristics (Hodgson 1998a, p. 419) and ignored the institutional features of human beings in a social setting (O'Hara 2002, pp. 86–87):

> "The economists have accepted the hedonistic preconceptions concerning human nature and human action, and the conception of the economic interest which a hedonistic psychology gives does not afford material for a theory of the development of human nature. Under hedonism, the economic interest is not conceived in terms of action. It is therefore not readily apprehended or appreciated in terms of a cumulative growth of habits of thought, and does not provoke, even if it did lend itself to, treatment by the evolutionary method." (Veblen 1898b, p. 394)

So Veblen proposed that economics had to include evolutionary aspects and conceive man as a social being, not fixed or given entity which governs by only pleasure and pain calculation. In this regard, Veblen criticized hedonistic conception of individual of neoclassical economics in his famous passage:

> "In all received formulations of economic theory, whether at the hands of English economists or those of the Continent, the human material with which the inquiry is concerned is conceived in hedonistic terms; that is to say, *in terms of a passive and substantially inert and immutably given human nature.* The psychological and anthropological preconceptions of the economists have been those which were accepted by the psychological and social sciences some generations ago. The hedonistic conception of man is that of a *lightning calculator of pleasures and pains*, who oscillates like a homogeneous globule of desire of happiness under the impulse of stimuli diat shift him about the area, but leave him intact. He has neither antecedent nor consequent. *He is an isolated, definitive human datum*, in stable equilibrium except for the buffets of the impinging forces that displace him in one direction or another. Self-imposed in elemental space, he spins symmetrically about his own spiritual axis until the parallelogram of forces bears down upon him, whereupon he follows the line of the resultant. When the force of the impact is spent, he comes to rest, a self-contained globule of desire as before. Spiritually, the hedonistic man is not a prime mover. He is not the seat of a process of living, except in the sense that he is subject to a series of permutations enforced upon him by circumstances external and alien to him" (ibid., pp. 389–390, emphasis added).

In other words, in hedonistic conception "human conduct is conceived of and interpreted as a rational response to the exigencies of the situation in which mankind is placed; as regards economic conduct it is such a rational and unprejudiced response to the stimulus of anticipated pleasure and pain" and "*such a theory can take account of conduct only in so far as it is rational conduct, guided by deliberate and exhaustively intelligent choice*" (Veblen 1909, p. 623, emphasis added). Besides that "in hedonistic theory the substantial end of life is individual gain (…) Moreover, *society*, in the utilitarian *is the algebraic sum of the individuals*; of the society is the sum of the interests individuals" (Veblen 1899b, p. 419, emphasis added). In this regard, neoclassical economics conceived man as a pain-pleasure calculator and had an atomistic conception of society, and therefore ignored the evolutionary and institutional process:

> "It is characteristic of the school that wherever an element of the cultural fabric, an institution or any institutional phenomenon, is involved in the facts with which the theory is occupied, such institutional facts are taken for granted, denied, or explained away." (Veblen 1909, pp. 621–622)

Moreover, for Veblen, in order to become an evolutionary science, economics must break with its Newtonian preconceptions that make it no more than a "taxonomic science" (Dulbecco and Dutraive 2007, p. 166). Because neoclassical economics makes statical analysis and this is not sufficient to take account institutional setting of individual conduct:

> "On the other hand, an adequate theory of economic conduct, even for statical purposes, cannot be drawn in terms of the individual simply-as is the case with the marginal-utility economics-because it cannot be drawn in terms of the underlying traits of human nature simply; since the response that goes to make up human conduct takes place under institutional norms and only under stimuli that have an institutional bearing." (Veblen 1909, pp. 628–629)

So economics has to change its static and inert conception because as later researches show, this conception is unadequate and focuses only one aspect of human being. However, man comprises of propensities and habits:

> "The later psychology, re-enforced by modern anthropological research, gives a different conception of human nature. According to this conception, it is the characteristic of man to do something, *not simply to suffer pleasures and pains* through the impact of suitable forces. He is not simply a bundle of desires that are to be saturated by being placed in the path of the forces of the environment, but rather *a coherent structure of propensities and habits* which seeks realization and expression in an unfolding activity. According to this view, human activity, and economic activity among the rest, is not apprehended as something incidental to the process of saturating given desires. *The activity is itself the substantial fact of the process*, and the desires under whose guidance the action takes place are circumstances of temperament which determine the specific direction in which the activity will unfold itself in the given case. These circumstances

> of temperament are ultimate and definitive for the individual who acts under them, so far as regards his attitude as agent in the particular action in which he is engaged. But, in the view of the science, *they are elements of the existing frame of mind of the agent, and are the outcome of his antecedents and his life up to the point at which he stands.* They are the products of his hereditary traits and his past experience, cumulatively wrought out under a given body of traditions, conventionalities, and material circumstances; and they afford the point of departure for the next step in the process. *The economic life history of the individual is a cumulative process of adaptation of means to ends that cumulatively change as the process goes on,* both the agent and his environment being at any point the outcome of the past process. His methods of life today are enforced upon him by his habits of life carried over from yesterday and by the circumstances left as the mechanical residue of the life of yesterday." (Veblen 1898b, pp. 390–391, emphasis added).

Consequently, man is not an isolated, fixed or given; he/she is a dynamic human being who adapts to changing and concrete conditions. Therefore, contrary to the equilibrium analysis of neoclassical economics, Veblen saw the economic system not as a "self-balancing mechanism" but as a "cumulatively unfolding process" (Hodgson 2002, p. 217) and argued that economics should be an evolutionary science, by which he meant that economic action should be its subject matter, rather than the material objects that were the principal concern of other economists (Walker 1977, p. 215):

> "*An evolutionary economics* must be the theory of a process of cultural growth as determined by the economic interest, *a theory of a cumulative sequence of economic institutions stated in terms of the process itself.*" (Veblen 1898b, p. 393, emphasis added)

So Veblen (1909, p. 627) argued that, for modern science examined the phenomena of life, it was occupied about questions of genesis and cumulative change. And the main postulate of evolutionary science for Veblen (1900, p. 266) is "the notion of a cumulative causal sequence". In this respect, Veblen conceives economics in terms of evolutionary process and "the concrete subject-matter of the science is, of course, the process of economic life" (Veblen 1900, p. 255). So "proper concern of economics" for Veblen (1909, pp. 627–628) was "the conduct of man in his dealings with the material means of life".

Thereby Veblen rejected both methodological individualism and methodological collectivism by embracing an evolutionary perspective. He, accordingly, admitted that there was an interference between individual and society or in other terms institutions. So Veblen saw both agency and structure as a result of an evolutionary process (Hodgson 1998a, p. 423) and acknowledged that human is a social being, or in his own terms, "(man) is a social animal" (Veblen 1898a, p. 193). But on the other hand, Veblen emphasized that human is also an individual. While he criticized the materialistic theory in his critical review of Max Lorenz's book entitled "Die Marxistische Socialdemokratie", Veblen (1897, p. 137) emphasized this point by saying that this approach "conceives of man as exclusively a social being, who counts in the process solely as a medium for the transmission and expression of social laws and changes; whereas he is, in fact, also an *individual, acting out his own life as such*" (emphasis added). Hence economics has to be interested in individual conduct:

> "*Scientific inquiry in this field, therefore, must deal with individual conduct and must formulate its theoretical results in terms of individual conduct.* But such an inquiry can serve the purposes of a genetic theory only if and in so far as this individual conduct is attended to in those respects in which it counts toward habituation, and so toward change (or stability) of the institutional fabric, on the one hand, and in those respects in which it is prompted and guided by the received institutional conceptions and ideals on the other hand" (Veblen 1909, pp. 629–630, emphasis added).

Veblen (1899a, pp. 121–123), in this respect, described the economics of a past generation as a taxonomic science and stated that later writers of all schools diverged from the taxonomic line of "pre-evolutionary" days; so modern sciences could be characterized as "evolutionary." And evolutionary economics has to deal with men in the context of time and space because man's action and behaviors depend on the institutional setting for Veblen. So as institutional setting changes, man's action, and behaviors change too. And the most important factors in this change are habits and instincts.

Institutions, Habits, and Instincts in Veblen's Analysis

As it's seen already, Veblen embraced an evolutionary perspective for economics and criticized the static and hedonistic conception of human being in neoclassical economics. So the agent was a subject of an evolutionary process, and he/she could not be taken as fixed or given (Hodgson 1998a, p. 424):

> "The economic life of the individual is a cumulative process of adaptation of means to ends that cumulatively change as the process goes on, both the agent and his environment being at any point the outcome of the past process." (Veblen 1898b, p. 391)

According to Veblen (1914, p. 1) humanity is guided in large part by habits and tropisms, rather than by rational pleasure and pain calculations:

> "It is characteristic of man to do something, *not simply to suffer pleasures and pains* through the impact of suitable forces (…) but rather *a coherent structure of propensities and habits* which seeks realization and expression in an unfolding activity." (Veblen 1898b, p. 390, emphasis added).

Veblen, according to Cordes (2014, p. 6), from this point of view, suggested a psychology based on instincts and habits that was crucially inspired by McDougall's work[2] and integrated it into his model of institutional change. He saw the determinants of human behavior as driving forces of institutional change. So that there are two determinants of behavior: the basic drive of instinctive factors and the drive to conform to habits.

Thus institutions, habits, and instincts are key elements of change in Veblen's analysis. And the base unit of change process was the notion of "cumulative causation" for Veblen: "The base of action -the point of departure- at any step in the process is the entire organic complex of habits of thought that have been shaped by the past process" (Veblen 1898b, pp. 392–393).

Hence Veblen's economic theory was of evolutionary nature. Man shapes and re-shapes along with this evolutionary process, which is also a social process (Kırmızıaltın 2017, p. 164) and there are three basic notions in this system[3] (Anderson 1933, p. 605): First, instincts basically govern human behavior which give rise to action of a dynamic sort; second, institutions immediately guide human behavior; third, institutions change continually over time. Within this framework, social, cultural, political and economic events and institutions are determined at any one time by group characteristics formed by the historical sum of instinctual, tropistic, and habitually determined human behavior for Veblen (Ault and Ekelund Jr. 1988, p. 433). In other words, institutions are never wholly unique, they have been grafted on what had gone before (Murphree 1959, pp. 311–312):

> "*Institutions must change with changing circumstances* since they are of the nature of a habitual method of responding to the stimuli which these changing circumstances afford. *The development of these institutions is the development of society. The institutions are, in substance, prevalent habits of thought* with respect to particular relations and particular functions of the individual and of the community; and the scheme of life, which is made up of the aggregate of institutions in force at a given time or at a given point in the development of any society, may, on the psychological side, be broadly characterized as a prevalent spiritual attitude or a prevalent theory of life. As regards its generic features, this spiritual attitude or theory of life is in the last analysis reducible to terms of a prevalent type of character. *The situation of today shapes the institutions of tomorrow through a selective, coercive process, by acting upon men's habitual view of things, and so*

2 Veblen's psychological insights are based on the American Pragmatist School (Almeida 2014, p. 112). In this regard, William James, Charles Sanders Peirce, and William McDougall influenced Veblen's system of thought (Hodgson 1998a, pp. 417-418).

3 According to Poirot Jr. (2008, p. 410), Veblen's theory of evolution includes the concepts of cumulative causation, gradualism, and non-teleological change.

> *altering or fortifying a point of view or a mental attitude banded down from the past.* The institutions -that is to say the habits of thought- under the guidance of which men live are in this way received from an earlier time; more or less remotely earlier, but in any event they have been elaborated in and received from the past. Institutions are products of the past process, are adapted to past circumstances, and are therefore never in full accord with the requirements of the present. In the nature of the case, this process of selective adaptation can never catch up with the progressively changing situation in which the community finds itself at any given time; for the environment, the situation, the exigencies of life which enforce the adaptation and exercise the selection, change from day to day; and each successive situation of the community in its turn tends to obsolescence as soon as it has been established." (Veblen 1899c, p. 88, emphasis added)

As it's seen from this passage, Veblen defined institutions as "prevalent habits of thought"[4] and these (prevalent) forms of thinking are habitual because they are settled and automatically triggered in appropriate conditions (Lawson 2014, p. 12). So behaviors are "routinized", habits of thought are supervised by institutions (Garrouste 2008, p. 18). In this regard, "each individual is but a single complex of habits of thought" (Veblen 1899a, p. 143) and habit is an acquired proclivity or capacity (Hodgson 2006, p. 6) or a propensity or disposition (Hodgson 2004a, p. 652) for Veblen. And when habitual thoughts and actions become established and patterned over time, Veblen refers to them as institutions (Edgell 1975, p. 272):

> "Like all human culture, this material civilization is a scheme of institutions -institutional fabric and institutional growth. But *institutions are an outgrowth of habit. The growth of culture is a cumulative sequence of habituation*, and the ways and means of it are the habitual response of human nature to exigencies that vary incontinently, cumulatively, but with something of a consistent sequence in the cumulative variations that so go forward --incontinently, because each new move creates a new situation which induces a further new variation in the habitual manner of response; cumulatively, because each new situation is a variation of what has gone before it and embodies as causal factors all that has been effected by what went before; consistently, because the underlying traits of human nature (propensities, aptitudes, and what not) by force of which the response takes place, and on the ground of which the habituation takes effect, remain substantially unchanged." (Veblen 1909, p. 628, emphasis added)

Thus Veblen apprehended culture in the context of institution, and the institution as habits – habits of thought. And the habits of thought depend on the

4 Veblen defined institutions in that way in his another study: "That is what is meant by calling them institutions; they are settled habits of thought common to the generality of men" (Veblen 1909, p. 626).

industrial life and also the efficiency of industry determines the stage of culture in Veblen:

> "This habit of thought is a selectively necessary consequence of industrial life, and, indeed, of all human experience in making use of the material means of life. It should, therefore, follow that, in a general way, the higher the culture, the greater the share of the mechanical preconception in shaping human thought and knowledge, since, in a general way, the stage of culture attained depends on the efficiency of industry." (Veblen 1899a, pp. 141–142)

And the dynamic bases of human action and behavior are instincts and habits for Veblen in this respect (Walker 1977, p. 235). Thereby he evaluated instincts and habits as the prime movers and explicable in terms of both biological and socio-economic processes of evolution (Hodgson 1998a, p. 425). So human conduct is largely influenced by habits and instincts: "Like other animals, man is an agent that acts in response to stimuli afforded by the environment in which he lives. Like other species, *he is a creature of habit and propensity*" (Veblen 1898a, p. 188, emphasis added). So "the inquiry into institutions will address itself to the growth of habits and conventions, as conditioned by the material environment and by the innate and persistent propensities of human nature" (Veblen 1914, p. 2).

To this end, Veblen traced the growth of economic institutions from primitive beginnings and thought that nothing was permanent for a long time. Because institutions are the part of the social world for Veblen (Papageorgiou et al. 2013, pp. 1234–1235). So that Veblen conceived institutions in terms of social evolution because institutions are cumulative causal processes. In this regard, Veblen does not necessarily mean improvement by evolution, but rather cumulative modification (Almeida 2016, p. 350):

> "The life of man in society, just like the life of other species, is a struggle for existence, and therefore it is a process of selective adaptation. *The evolution of social structure has been a process of natural selection of institutions.* The progress which has been and is being made in human institutions and in human character may be set down, broadly, to a natural selection of the fittest habits of thought and to a process of enforced adaptation of individuals to an environment which has progressively changed with the growth of the community and with the changing institutions under which men have lived. *Institutions are not only themselves the result of a selective and adaptive process which shapes the prevailing or dominant types of spiritual attitude and aptitudes; they are at the same time special methods of life and human relations, and are therefore in their turn efficient factors of selection.* So that the changing institutions in their turn make for a further selection of individuals endowed with the fittest temperament, and a further adaptation of individual temperament and habits to the changing environment through the formation of new institutions." (Veblen 1899c, p. 87, emphasis added)

So it could be said that there is both upward and downward causation in Veblen's analysis; that is to say on one hand individuals create and change institutions, but on the other hand institutions mold and constrain individuals (Hodgson 2000, p. 326). Namely, conduct always occurs in an institutional context and on the other hand, the institutional scheme depends upon the practices of individuals that are members of groups and/or communities in the end (Lawson 2014, p. 21):

> "*Not only is the individual's conduct hedged about and directed by his habitual relations to his fellows in the group, but these relations, being of an institutional character, vary as the institutional scene varies. The wants and desires, the end and the aim, the ways and the means, the amplitude and drift of the individual's conduct are functions of an institutional variable that is of a highly complex and wholly unstable character* (…) The growth and mutations of the institutional fabric are an outcome of the conduct of the individual members of the group, since it is out of the experience of the individuals, through the habituation of individuals, that institutions arise; and it is in this same experience that these institutions act to direct and define the aims and end of conduct. It is, of course, on individuals that the system of institutions imposes those conventional standards, ideals, and canons of conduct that make up the community's scheme of life." (Veblen 1909, p. 629, emphasis added)

Besides that, habits may be long- or short-termed, and this depends upon the scheme of life in any community or race. For being habits long-termed, these habits need to promote by culture and be passed from generation to generation. So repeated behavior is important in establishing a habit. For example, the habits of thought that are the fittest tend to survive and evolve while those which are obsolete tend over time to decay (O'Hara 2002, p. 88):

> "The habituation is not simply individual and sporadic but is enforced upon the group or the race by a selective elimination of those individuals and lines of descent that do not conform to the required canon of knowledge and conduct. Where this takes place, the acquired proclivity passes from the status of habit to that of aptitude or propensity. It becomes a transmissible trait, and action under its guidance becomes right and good, and the longer and more consistent the selective adaptation through which the aptitude arises, the more firmly is the resulting aptitude settled upon the race, and the more unquestioned becomes the sanction of the resulting canon of conduct." (Veblen 1898a, p. 195)

Another crucial factor besides habit in Veblen's institutional scheme is instinct. Because, for Veblen, human beings are driven by instincts that give rise to specific habits selected in an institutional context. Veblen (1914, p. 1) admitted that every human being has instinct and that instincts are the hereditary characteristics and main forces in human behavior. According to Ault and Ekelund Jr. (1988, p. 441), the role of habits and institutions is to help individuals survive by achieving instinctually determined goals for Veblen. Similarly, Camic and Hodgson (2011, p. 409) argued that instincts are translated into behavior through the medium of habits, which are prompted by instincts but modified by contingent cultural and institutional circumstances in Veblen.

In this context, instinct has important role in Veblen's analysis. Because Veblen (1914, pp. 3–4) believed that mankind is always engaged in purposeful behavior and this purposeful behavior arises from instincts:

> "*In his economic life man is an agent, not an absorbent; he is an agent seeking in every act the accomplishment of some concrete, objective, impersonal end* (…) (And) within the purview of economic theory, the last analysis of any given phenomenon must run back to this ubiquitous human impulse to do the next thing." (Veblen 1898a, p. 189, emphasis added)

Accordingly, Veblen argued that purposeful behavior was the result of both inherited instinct and the material and cultural environment within which the individual is situated (Hodgson 1998a, pp. 423–424). In addition, Veblen (1914, p. 6) identified instincts with human spirit: "Men take thought, but the human spirit, that is to say the racial endowment of instinctive proclivities, decides what they shall take thought of, and how and what effect". And these instinctive proclivities are basically simple, and the ends are sought to be reached, and the ways and means by which they may be sought are diverse and various (ibid., p. 7).

Thereby Veblen examined instincts that are the product of the interaction of biological, psychological, and cultural factors. Instinctual potentiality is ensured by the biological and psychological foundations, while for enabling certain instincts to be realized at the social level the cultural environment is a so crucial element. Besides that, for individuals, instincts provide for the activation of certain aims or objectives (O'Hara 2002, p. 80).

Veblen, in turn, identified three basic instincts that shape and govern human behavior[5]: "the instinct of workmanship", "parental bent", and "idle curiosity". Firstly, the instinct of workmanship or the impulse to work is defined as a proclivity for doing things efficiently which is of service in the achievement of whatever ends the other instincts might appoint. Or in other words, the instinct of workmanship is the desire to perform efficiently the activities that fulfill the goals set by the other instincts. Secondly, the parental bent is defined so as to include all sentiments of an unselfish sort, relating not just to the family but to

5 According to O'Hara (1997, p. 81) the instincts of workmanship, parental care, and idle curiosity were dominant instincts, while the instincts underlying pecuniary gain, emulation, and exploitation were secondary instincts in Veblen's analysis.

the whole social group, so it is the urge to care for the welfare of others. And thirdly, the instinct of idle curiosity is simply a desire for knowledge and refer to the propensity to understand and explain the external world through the use of imagination (Anderson 1933, p. 603; Walker 1977, p. 220).

Men have such instincts but on the other hand this does not mean that these instincts are unchanged or fixed. Because Veblen distinguished instinct from instinctive behavior. And accordingly, as Hodgson (2004b, p. 165) emphasized, the instincts of an individual cannot be changed; but 'instinctive behavior' can. Behavior promoted by instincts can be modified or repressed, through constraints or countervailing habits or reflection. Parental bent, for example, is biologically inherited and innate but can be changed by cultural and environmental factors.

As it's seen, Veblen distinguished instinct which is an innate and persistent propensity from the habit which is a propensity that is molded by environmental circumstances (Hodgson 2004b, p. 164). But Veblen admitted that there was an interaction between instinctive behavior and habit. For example, on the one hand, "all instinctive behavior is subject to development and hence to modification by habit" (Veblen 1914, p. 38), while on the other hand social habits can be stronger if they are reinforced by instincts (Veblen 1899c, pp. 83–84). So modificatory power of instincts was so important, and habits were additional and necessary means for instinctive proclivities to be pursued in a changing environment (Hodgson 2004a, pp. 654–655). Because instinct is the departure point for both habit and institution; but the instinctive behavior itself is modified by habit (Kırmızıaltın 2017, p. 173).

Concluding Remarks

Veblen, one of the founders of the institutional economics, embraced an evolutionary perspectives, approached culture in the context of institution and defined institution as "generally accepted habits of thought and behavior"; and considered habit and instinct as a starting point of institutions and culture. Within this framework, there is an interrelation between institutions, individual behavior, habits, and instincts.

In this respect, men are "a creature of habit and propensity" and neoclassical economics which conceives human being as given and in terms of hedonistic or utilitarian psychology is inadequate for Veblen. Veblen, consequently, criticized the hedonistic conception of man on the ground that this approach did not include evolutionary and institutional factors and it conceived man as an outcome of mysterious social forces. Likewise, he asserted that a psychology of this kind ignored the influences of habit and convention and that it can explain conduct only in so far as it is thoroughly rational and intelligent conduct (Anderson 1933, p. 601).

On the other hand, in line with his evolutionary perspectives, Veblen saw human agency as a subject of an evolutionary process, and so he or she could not be taken as fixed or given (Hodgson 2004b, pp. 155–158). Moreover, economics must have an evolutionary perspective, consequently "the concrete subject-matter of the science is, of course, the process of economic life". So "proper concern of economics" is "the conduct of man in his dealings with the material means of life." In men's ordinary life, the basic factor that shapes and governs human behavior is a habit of thought. And also traditional habits of thought arise from instinctive behavior (Walker 1977, p. 217). According to O'Hara (2002, p. 83), instincts provide the potentiality for human beings to engage in social action; social habits structure the thinking and behavior of individuals; and institutions are those social patterns of regularity that establish a set of clustered norms and more often within an organizational setting such as a firm or a family or the community in Veblen's analysis.

So there is an interaction between individuals and culture in Veblen's analysis. Besides, that behavioral habit and institutional structure are mutually entwined and mutually reinforcing (Hodgson 2006, p. 8). That is to say, the man could be conceived only in terms of evolutionary socio-economic process, because institutional and cultural structure determines man's action and behaviors. However, on the other hand, man is not only a social being, but also an individual. So individual's decisions and actions may change the institutional setting, while institutional and cultural setting shapes individual's actions and behaviors.

Bibliography

Almeida, Felipe: "Thorstein Veblen and Albert Bandura: A modern psychological reading of the conspicuous consumer". *Journal of Economic Issues* 48(1), 2014, pp. 109–122.

Almeida, Felipe: "Society and brain: A complementary approach to Thorstein Veblen's conspicuous consumer based on Tibor Scitovsky's neuropsychology". *Nova Economia* 26(2), 2016, pp. 347–367.

Anderson, Karl. L.: "The unity of Veblen's theoretical system". *The Quarterly Journal of Economics* 47(4), 1933, pp. 598–626.

Ault, Richard W. / Ekelund Jr., Robert B.: "Habits in economic analysis: Veblen and the neoclassicals". *History of Political Economy* 20(3), 1988, pp. 431–445.

Camic, Charles / Hodgson, Geoffrey M.: “Introduction to Part IV”. In: Charles Camic/Geoffrey M. Hodgson (Eds.): *Essential Writings of Thorstein Veblen*. Routledge: London and New York. 2011. pp. 401–409.

Cordes, Christian: “The application of evolutionary concepts in evolutionary economics”. *Papers on Economics and Evolution*, Working Paper No. 1402. 2014, retrieved 14.10.2017, from ftp://ftp.repec.org/opt/ReDIF/RePEc/esi/discussionpapers/2014-02.pdf.

Dulbecco, Philippe / Dutraive, Veronique: “The meaning of the market: Comparing Austrian and institutional economics”. In: Geoffrey M. Hodgson(Ed.): *The Evolution of Economic Institutions: A Critical Reader*. Edward Elgar: Cheltenham. 2007. pp. 160–180.

Edgell, Stephen: “Thorstein Veblen's theory of evolutionary change”. *The American Journal of Economics and Sociology* 34(3), 1975, pp. 267–280.

Garrouste, Pierre: “The emergence and evolution of institutions: The complementary approaches of Carl Menger and Thorstein Veblen”. *ICER Working Paper Series*, No: 17. 2008, retrieved 11.09.2017, from http://www.biblioecon.unito.it/biblioservizi/RePEc/icr/wp2008/ICERwp17-08.pdf.

Hamilton, Walton H.: “The institutional approach to economic theory”. *The American Economic Review* 9(1), 1919, pp. 309–318.

Hodgson, Geoffrey M.: “On the evolution of Thorstein Veblen's evolutionary economics”. *Cambridge Journal of Economics* 22, 1998a, pp. 415–431.

Hodgson, Geoffrey M.: “The approach of institutional economics”. *Journal of Economic Literature* 36, 1998b, pp. 166–192.

Hodgson, Geoffrey M.: “What is the essence of institutional economics?”. *Journal of Economic Issues* 34(2), 2000, pp. 317–329.

Hodgson, Geoffrey M.: “Varieties of capitalism and varieties of economic theory”. In: Geoffrey M. Hodgson (Ed.): *A Modern Reader in Institutional and Evolutionary Economics: Key Concepts*. Cheltenham: Edward Elgar. 2002, pp. 201–229.

Hodgson, Geoffrey M.: “Reclaiming habit for institutional economics”. *Journal of Economic Psychology* 25, 2004a, pp. 651–660.

Hodgson, Geoffrey M.: *The Evolution of Institutional Economics: Agency, Structure and Darwinism in American Institutionalism*. Routledge: London and New York. 2004b.

Hodgson, Geoffrey M.: “What are institutions?”. *Journal of Economic Issues* 40(1), 2006, pp. 1–25.

Kırmızıaltın, Eren: *İktisat ve Rasyonalite: K. Marx, W. S. Jevons ve T. B. Veblen'de Rasyonalite, İnsan, Teori*. Heretik Yayıncılık: Ankara. 2017.

Kologlugil, Serhat: "Thorstein Veblen, Darwinism, and genre-culture coevolution theory". *The European Journal of the History of Economic Thought* 23(4), 2016, pp. 641–672.

Lawson, Tony: "Process, order and stability in Veblen". *Cambridge Journal of Economics* 39(4), 2014, pp. 1–38.

Murphree, Idus: "Darwinism in Thorstein Veblen's economics". *Social Research* 26(3), 1959, pp. 311–324.

O'Hara, Phillip A.: "Veblen's critique of Marx's philosophical preconceptions of political economy". *The European Journal of the History of Economic Thought* 4(1), 1997, pp. 65–91.

O'Hara, Phillip A.: "The contemporary relevance of Thorstein Veblen's institutional-evolutionary political economy". *History of Economics Review* 35(1), 2002, pp. 78–103.

Papageorgiou, Theofanis / Katselidis, Ioannis / Michaelides, Panayotis G.: "Schumpeter, Commons, and Veblen on institutions". *American Journal of Economics and Sociology* 72(5), 2013, pp. 1232–1254.

Poirot Jr., Clifford S.: "Eat grubs and live: The habir-instinct problem in institutional evolutionary economics". *Journal of Economic Issues* 42(2), 2008, pp. 407–413.

Veblen, Thorstein B.: "Review of 'Die Marxistische Socialdemokratie by Max Lorenz'". *Journal of Political Economy* 6(1), 1897, pp. 136–137.

Veblen, Thorstein B.: "The instinct of workmanship and the irksomeness of labor". *American Journal of Sociology* 4(2), 1898a, pp. 187–201.

Veblen, Thorstein B.: "Why is economics not an evolutionary science?". *The Quarterly Journal of Economics* 12(4), 1898b, pp. 373–397.

Veblen, Thorstein B.: "The preconceptions of economic science I". *The Quarterly Journal of Economics* 13(2), 1899a, pp. 121–150.

Veblen, Thorstein B.: "The preconceptions of economic science II". *The Quarterly Journal of Economics* 13(4), 1899b, pp. 396–426.

Veblen, Thorstein B.: *The theory of leisure class: An economic study of institutions*. New York: B. W. Huebsch, 1899c.

Veblen, Thorstein B.: "The preconceptions of economic science III". *The Quarterly Journal of Economics* 14(2), 1900, pp. 240–269.

Veblen, Thorstein B.: "The limitations of marginal utility". *Journal of Political Economy* 17(9), 1909, pp. 620–636.

Veblen, Thorstein B.: *The Instinct of Workmanship, and the State of the Industrial Arts*. Augustus Kelley: New York. 1914.

Walker, Donald A.: "Thorstein Veblen's economic system". *Economic Inquiry* 15, 1977, pp. 213–237.

Öznur Bozkurt[1], İrfan Yurt[2] and Sağbetullah Meriç[3]

An Evaluation of the Organizational Culture and Its Relationship to Performance in Public Institutions

Abstract: Culture as a distinctive element in all sectors constitutes all of the values shared and transmitted between individuals. Cultural features are the driving and supporting power of the differentiation process and performance in business. Organizational culture, which directs and coordinates the behavior of individuals within an organization, is discussed and examined in this study as regards performance. Public institutions are the entities which are most often mentioned, since they often have bulky, bureaucratic structures. Reflecting on the steps taken within public reform in recent years, however, it appears that this view has begun to change. In light of this data, the cultural values that exist in public institutions and how those values reflect on employees' performance has become a valid topic to examine through research. The research focused on the officers working in a public institution affiliated with the Düzce Governorship. The data, collected by the questionnaire method in quantitative research, were analyzed with the SPSS program. According to the results, there was found a positive and significant relationship between organizational culture and employee performance. In addition, it was concluded that involvement, a dimension of organizational culture, has a significant effect on employee performance.

Keywords: Culture, Organizational Culture, Performance, Public Institution, Civil Servant

Introduction

There are many factors that affect performance either organizationally or individually. Performance enhancement is the decisive factor in achieving the goals established in the organizations. Organizational performance increases or decreases depending on the performance of the individuals in the organization. Cultural values of the institutions are the most important factors affecting the performance of their employees. The cultural structure that guides the behavior of the people

1 Corresponding Author Düzce University, Faculty of Management, oznurbozkurt@duzce.edu.tr
2 Karabük University, Safranbolu Vocational School, irfanyurt@karabük.edu.tr
3 Van Centennial University, School of Tourism and Hotel Management, smeric@yyu.edu.tr

and the elements that form this structure differs from institution to institution. It is easier to undertake joint efforts and maximize performance in organizations with cultural values that are adopted and then shared by their members. It is believed that public institutions are underperforming due to the bureaucratic structures and policies that restrict or protect the employees who work within this structure. These policies, according to this belief, provide a guaranteed job for the institutions' employees regardless of performance. Thus, the policies lead to a low performance by many of the employees at these organizations. The lack of a reward system, especially for those who perform well, and the institutions' seniority-based approach instead of a performance system may have a negative impact on employees' performance. With the advent of reforms in public policies, however, some of these institutions may abandon these old habits and accept new values that lead to higher employee performance. This study is designed to determine the effect of organizational culture on the performance of civil servants in public institutions. The basic assumption of this research is that overall, public institutions' employees underperform, an old perception which needs to change. Furthermore, the study examines the possibility that the road to change in public employees' performance will come from within the organizational culture itself.

Culture and Organizational Culture

Culture is the totality of the unofficial rules that shape people's attitudes within a group (Çetin 2004, p. 5–6), apart from persons' intuitions, reactions, and stereotyped modes of thought conveyed symbolically with the exceptional successes of the individuals in the social environment in which they exist. Culture is seen as one of the most dominant and regular powers shown in an institution (Schein 1996). Culture affects the attitudes of people in an institution and is influential on their organizational and individual achievement (Sezgin 2009, p. 10). As for Hofste, culture is defined as mental programming that distinguishes individuals from others. Geertz's definition of culture is a meaningful formation that explains the experiences of individuals and what guides their behavior (Köse and Ünal 2003, pp. 1–3). Organizational culture is defined as the whole of values, opinions, and principles that constitute the movements, actions, and the general framework of the organization's personnel at every level (Doğan 2007, p. 104). The institution's employees absorb the cultural character of the institution and form permanent traditions within the institution (Çatıkoğlu 2006, p. 2). Schein defines organizational culture as the guiding values for the new members of a group, values which solve its problems of external adaptation and internal integration (Schein 2004, p. 17). The common denominator among the definitions of organizational culture is that it is a fulcrum that integrates and encompasses the institution as a whole, in addition to its originality. As each institution has its own unique culture, it harbors changes according to its own norms, values, vision, and mission (Eker Akgöz 2013, p. 15).

The Elements of Organizational Culture

The components of organizational culture are key elements in bringing, keeping, and differentiating the culture. Information about an institution's culture can be obtained through these elements. The institution benefits from these basic elements in the process of accepting and transferring the culture to beginners and future generations (Yaman 2009, p. 22). These elements consist of material as well as spiritual elements throughout its structure. The constituent elements of the institution's culture are a group of thoughts which help the institution to reach from the past to the present and are accepted by the employees of the institution, taught to the new members, and which constitute "we" consciousness in the institution (Eker Akgöz 2013, pp. 12–15).

The elements of organizational culture can be examined in two forms: as culture carriers (symbols, symbolic movements, rituals, ceremonies, traditions, habits, legends, stories, tale, language, and rumors) and a system of thoughts (values, norms, and faiths). Each of these elements plays an effective role in organizing the organizational culture (Keskin 2014, p. 4). Values reveal which attitudes are good, right, and desirable (Ataman 2009, pp. 627–628). Other elements in a system of organizational culture are its norms and beliefs. In a society, values are more comprehensive than beliefs, but beliefs are stronger and less elastic than values. Beliefs derive from the individual's knowledge of what truth is and what truth will be in the future. Norms, which are strictly required to comply with, provide information about what types of behavior are approved (Doğan 2007, pp. 50–51).

Some norms and values in society can be expressed more concretely with certain symbols. These symbols can be a sign, a mimic, a word, or a person. Material symbols like furniture, decoration, use of space, costume, logos, etc., can be descriptive of the cultural values within the organization (Keskin 2014, p. 6).

Myths, ceremonies, stories, language, and rituals, which are shaped in different patterns in institutions, are the results of systems of different values, beliefs, and norms. The prominent characteristics of the institution through stories, rituals, and ceremonies formed in the organization should dominate its culture. The language used by the individuals in the institution will also enable the institution itself to be defined. The "norms" and "values" that make up the institution's culture are understood through the "language." "Stories" and "tales" are the events that are important for the institution and are mostly related to past events important to the institution and its heroes and leaders, sometimes with a little exaggeration. Tales and stories about the institution are important because they serve as a bridge between the institution's past and present situations and direct the attitudes of the institution's members. Thus, the members of the institution are informed about how they should act in any case (Ataman 2009, p. 629).

Organizational Culture Models

From the past to the present day, the concept of organizational culture has been explained according to different models. Each organizational culture model examined different perspectives to understand the corporate culture (Eker Akgöz 2013, p. 41–42). Some of the most prominent models among the models of institutional culture: Handy's Organizational Culture Model, Kilmann's Organizational Culture Model, Quinn and Cameron's Models, and Denisson's Organizational Culture Model are examined in this research. The topic and the related institution within this study were analyzed according to the Denisson's Culture Model.

Handy's Approach: One of the first studies on organizational culture model was made by Handy. Handy examines organizational culture as a system of norms that constitutes the attitudes, ideas, and values of employees in the organization. Handy addresses the different cultures that institutions have: power culture, role culture, task culture, and person culture (Ataman 2009, p. 634).

Quinn and Cameron's Model: Cameron and Quinn(1999) express the cultural structure of institutions in four different cultural structures. Cameron and Quinn(1999) point out that the cultural structure of each institution will be inclined to fall under one of the following classifications: clan, adhocracy, market, and hierarchy; they also point to different cultural approaches in institutional dilemmas (Erdem et al. 2010, p. 77). Cameron and Quinn(1999) examined the cultural influences on institutional successes and activities in their model. In addition to the financial success of the institution, the strategy was found to have wage as a motivating factor for members and as an effect of proper personnel management. Cameron and Quinn developed a "**Competing Values**" model that examines the relationship between corporate culture and corporate success. On the basis of this model lies the empirical analysis of value judgments that people have for their organizational activity (Kalkan 2013, p. 55).

Kilmann's Model: Organizational culture also affects employees' desire to work and their efficiency. This is because the culture of an organization is a reflection of the beliefs dominating the institution and its climate as it concerns attitudes.

In this regard, organizational culture, which has two distinctive functions under good or bad culture typology, can be referred to as bureaucratic and innovative culture (Kalkan 2013, p. 54). Kilmann etc, (1985), described the organizational culture as a power to run an institution and direct individuals.
Denison Organizational Culture Model: Corporate culture is defined as norms, values, and unspoken assumptions that are seen in daily occupational behavior and embedded in organizational processes (Denison and Mishra 1995, pp. 213–216). Denison and Mishra (1995) emphasize the four core areas of culture and evaluate the strengths of "involvement, consistency, adaptability, and mission" (Büyük 2010, p. 229).

Characteristics and Importance of Organizational Culture

An institution is composed of the cultural characteristics it carries from its establishment to the present day. These characteristics are the factors that distinguish an institution from other institutions. They have their own rules and reveal the personality of the institution (Eker Akgöz 2013, p. 18). The most basic characteristic of organizational culture is that it is as determinative of organizational identity as fingerprints are of a person. Other features of the institution's culture are the holistic, common values, behaviors, and beliefs that can be shared among the employees of the institution, which are usually not written texts. Individuals who are new to the institution observe, adapt, and implement these behaviors learned or acquired later in the organization (Terzi 2000, p. 9). Apart from that, organizational culture has features that are difficult to change, constitute the control mechanism, organize the social relations in the institutions, regulate work, and empower the feeling of membership among the employees.

Organizational culture increases the harmony in employees' behaviors by creating an audit mechanism hidden within the organization, showing individuals in the organization how to behave (Şimşek and Fidan 2005, p. 25). Culture has an important role in the formation of policies, goals, decisions, methods, and fulfillment of the organizational objectives, leading the way for success and connecting the employees (Akıncı Vural and Gül 2007, p. 21). Today, organizational culture has an important feature in providing institutions with a competitive advantage over similar institutions (Çatıkoğlu 2006, p. 8). In the strong institutional cultures, regulations such as promotion, punishment, and reward are clearly and equally applied to all individuals. In individuals who believe that the institution is honest in its approach, it is expected that they will have increased commitment and motivation to the institution (Eker Akgöz 2013, p. 26).

The Concept of Performance and Its Importance

Nowadays, public institutions, like every business venture, are also in a competitive environment with different economic conditions and priorities of the individuals within these institutions. The increasingly competitive environment and the fact that consumers are more conscious than ever before are also pushing public institutions as much as the ones in the private sector. These constraints require more communication with the individuals whom they serve on both sides (Yerli 2006, p. 4). Performance, which is a qualitative or quantitative expression of what the individual or the worker can reach and what he or she has achieved (Karakaş and Ak 2003, p.338), varies depending on the dialogue established with the environment (Canman 1993, p. 164). Although the concept of performance has been thought far away from the public domain, this has changed in public institutions as well, due to the influence of customers, anticipation of politicians, new management techniques, and a developing environment, and it has increased its importance day by day. The overall performance of an institution will increase when the employees have fulfilled their duties and responsibilities related to the business (Yerli 2006, p. 7). Since it is the responsibility of a manager to increase the individual performance of the employees in the institution, the management of the organization tends to provide the organization's regular functioning with high performance (Çalık 2003, p. 8). Organizational culture, at this stage, should be guiding the administrators in the institution.

Factors Affecting Performance

Today, performance is at the forefront of what both public and private sector management have to deal with. High or low-performance levels are the factors that increase or reduce an institution's productivity.

Studies show that members of the same organization showed great differences in their performance, and that the success of the same employees also changed visibly over time. These differences and changes are known to be caused by various factors (Timur 1983, pp.4–6). Five factors are mentioned in performance measurement, reward, and management: personal factors, system factors, leadership factors, team factors, and situational factors (Mwita 2000, p. 21). *Leadership Factors*: Leadership factors affecting performance can be listed as motivational qualities, being a pioneer, reward, and support given by managers and organizational leaders. Employees tend to exhibit behaviors based on the characteristics of the manager. For this reason, it is necessary to give importance to the presence of these characteristics in administrators who are to be appointed to public institutions (Eren and Durna 2007, p. 113). *Team Factors*: Achieving productive work can happen through teams of individuals with different backgrounds and abilities. Performance targets set in institutions will increase team effectiveness. These targets should be clear, appropriate for examination, understandable, and measurable (Zehir and Özşahin 2008, p. 269). *System Factors*: Shortcomings that may have a negative impact on performance should be removed by examining existing business processes in the public sector. Regulations should be made to facilitate the performance of employees (Eren and Durna 2007, p. 113). *Situational Factors*: Public institutions, like private sector organizations, have to face internal and external pressures. Due to their position in the process of decision-making and activities, public institutions must consider the needs of different groups of social interest. These processes are necessary factors to be considered while assessing public administration performance (Eren and Durna 2007, p. 113). In addition, the factors affecting performance in the study conducted by Yerli in 2006, "Performance Management and Performance Evaluation in Public Administration," are considered as personal, organizational, and environmental factors. *Personal Factors*: These consist of personal talent, speech, writing, perception, experience, physical strength, intelligence, psychological structure, tendencies, values, approaches, sense of trust, and obedience (Canman 1993, p. 163). *Organizational Factors*: These are the factors that affect organizational structure, objectives, responsibilities, management policies, sharing of duties and powers, working environment conditions, and the performance of personnel (Yerli 2006, p. 10). *Environmental Factors*: Institutions that are part of the social system interact with the social environment. Institutions must establish relationships with the community, obtain some input from their environment, and present their output to their environment (Timur 1983, p. 5). The technology used by the institution, the population, the importance it attaches to the individual, as well as the economic, cultural, psychological, and ideological structure of the environment influence the institution's performance (Canman 1993, p. 164).

Organizational Culture and Performance Relationship

Organizational culture started to emerge in the 1940s, and at that time, it was considered as a management technique based on regular function and control. Over the years, this perspective has begun to change with an understanding that increases loyalty and cooperation within the organization (Dedehayır 2014, p. 4). A strong, positive link between corporate culture and business performance has been found through research. In the long run, organizational culture has been considered to be an effective factor in maintaining the continuity of institutions. One of the best-known studies on this topic was undertaken by Peters and Waterman (1984). According to Peters and Waterman, the high performance of companies such as Procter and Gamble and McDonald's is a reflection of their corporate culture. Morley and Heraty (1995) examined high-performing organizations and found that the hierarchical levels of these companies were minimized and that their strengthened human resource practices were supported (Çatıkoğlu 2006, p. 9).

Organizational culture is an important factor in achieving a strong performance. In order to obtain successful results with talented employees, it is necessary for these employees to accept the organizational culture based on effective performance. Culture affects the attitude of the individual towards the business; the job satisfaction of the individual provides the satisfaction of the customer. A satisfied customer, in turn, increases the value of the institution (Özgür 2010, p. 59–60). A culture that is given importance increases the quality of work, reduces labor costs, and contributes to the establishment of an effective and satisfactory working system (Çatıkoğlu 2006, p. 10).

Organizational culture has a significant influence on the long-term performance of institutions. Culture directs the institution's performance by guiding how colleagues should act with each other and how they should act on issues such as decision-making, quality, consumers, teamwork, and innovation that directly affect the institution's performance (Yılmaz and Karahan, 2010, p. 275). Because organizational culture has explanatory justifications, organizations now consider it as a performance factor to be strengthened. This is evident with the increase in income, profits, stock values, and the number of qualified employees, which are achieved by a culture that supports high performance (Kotter and Heskett, 1992).

A strong performance culture plays an active role in ensuring that institutions have a loyal and empowered workforce. Together with a high-performance culture, an institution can more effectively determine institutional targets and produce more accurate results (Yılmaz and Karahan, 2010, p. 279).

Evaluation of Organizational Culture and Its Relationship to Performance in a Public Institution

The Purpose and Importance of Research

This study evaluated the relationship between organizational culture and performance in the context of public organizations. This work has been carried out with the assumption that each public organization has its own cultural values and it is not right to approach organizations to evaluate them in the context of a single culture (bureaucratic culture). Studies on organizational culture and performance are seen to be predominantly done in the private sector. This study examined the relationship between organizational culture and performance within the framework of public employee evaluations and assessed organizational culture in the public organization, which is thought to be dominated by bureaucratic structures and entrenched values, in the framework of Denison's model. In this study, researchers aimed to determine how the cultural characteristics included in this model appear in the selected institution, whether these characteristics are related to performance, and whether there are significant differences in cultural perception and performance according to demographic characteristics.

Method

In the study, a theoretical basis has been established upon a review of relevant literature. The questionnaire, one of the quantitative research methods, was used to collect data from the sample. In order to measure the organizational culture, Denison's Organizational Culture Survey, a questionnaire of 36 questions adapted and validated by Yahyagil (2004) into Turkish, was used. This scale examines culture under four dimensions: "involvement, consistency, harmony, and vision." Also, in order to measure performance, Erdoğan (2011)'s six-item performance scale, developed from Kirkman and Rosen (1999); Fuentes, Saez, and Montes (2004), and Rahman and Bullock (2004)'s scales were used in this study. In the study, all the individuals working in the selected public institution were included in the universe of the study and the "complete counting method" was used. Questionnaires filled out by 140 people out of a total of 162, were analyzed with the SPSS program.

Findings

In the survey, the data were collected from 140 people. When the demographic characteristics of the survey participants were examined, 55.0% (77 persons) were females. 70.0% (98 people) of the participants were married. 39.3% (55 people) of the participants were between the ages of 20 and 30. When the participants' working time is examined, it is seen that 41.4% (58 people) have worked in the existing institution for 17 years or more. 62.9% (88 people) of the survey participants have a bachelor's degree.

Within the scope of the research, employee performance is addressed in one dimension, while organizational culture is addressed in four dimensions. The averages evaluated out of a total of five points are as follows:

The average of the employees' performance was calculated at 3.92. The average of all organizational culture was calculated at 3.00. The involvement dimension (from the four organizational culture dimension) is 3.00; consistency is 3.01; harmony is 2.95; and vision has an average of 3.02. It is observed that the performances of the participants in the survey are high and that the perceptions of organizational culture are moderate and close to each other. It has been seen that Denison(1996) 's model of organizational culture assessed by the sample and the cultural perceptions in this frame are moderate.

As a result of the correlation analysis to determine the relationship between the variables, it has been found that the dimensions of organizational culture have a strong positive correlation with each other. Employee performance is positively related to involvement, consistency, adaptability, and mission from the subdimensions of organizational culture. All of the existing relationships are significant at the 0.01 significance level. The cultural dimension with the highest correlation for performance was found to be "involvement." As involvement increases, it can be said that performance will increase in the same direction. This result shows that the employee involvement factor, which is often emphasized for private sector enterprises, also applies to public organizations. Regression analysis was performed upon the correlation analysis to determine the effect of independent variables: specifically, involvement, consistency, adaptability, and mission on performance, which is a dependent variable. According to the regression analysis, there is a significant effect only on the performance of the involvement dimension from organizational culture. In other words, the involvement rate in the organizational culture affects the performance of the employees by 13% (R^2: .135). Regression analysis shows that involvement as a cultural value influences employee performance.

Lastly, it was examined whether the perceptions of employees differ according to demographic characteristics within the scope of organizational culture and performance. From the gender and marital status perspective, it was determined that employee performance did not display any significant difference in terms of organizational culture. In terms of age, significant differences within the scope of involvement and vision were determined. Involvement perceptions of employees 25 years of age and under are significantly higher than those of employees in other age groups. It has been seen that the employees in this group place more importance on the decision-making process than others. Vision perception is lower for new employees compared to the old ones, and their perceptions of commitment are low as well because the tendency always to evaluate alternatives outside their organization is high.

When the variable of the employees' duration of work in the institution is considered, the performance, cultural consistency, and the vision dimension become significantly different. Long-time employees' performance perceptions were high, since they have been working for a long time for the organization, and the perception of vision is accordingly higher. Determinacy and consistency perceptions of those in the middle of their working years are higher than those of the other groups. There is a desire to see things clearly and anticipation on how the business processes in the organization will be shaped in the future.

Regarding educational status, significant differences were determined within the scope of involvement, consistency, harmony, and vision. Postgraduates' perceptions of organizational culture were significantly lower than those of associate degree, undergraduate, and high school graduates. Employees with the highest level of education have lesser perceptions of the organizational culture's dimensions than other groups. It can be said that the increase in the level of education increases expectations.

Result

In this study, the relationship between the performance and organizational culture was examined in terms of public personnel. The data obtained in the study were first grouped according to their frequencies and then assessed in terms of whether they were fit for the intended research questions. When the demographic characteristics of the persons within the scope of the research are examined, it is seen that there are not many differences among the groups. Most of the participants are female. The majority of the persons in the study are married. The vast majority of those surveyed are aged between 20 and 30. Most of the participants are found to have worked in the current institution for 17 years and more. More than half of the participants are graduates from universities.

Average points were provided to determine participants' perceptions towards the variables. The performance average of employees is the highest one. The averages of organizational culture dimensions are seen to be very close to each other. These averages indicate that the employees have an unstable attitude in terms of organizational culture dimensions. Employees in the researched institution have high evaluations of their performance. Perceptions of the organizational culture at the institution are found to be not high, but rather moderate.

As a result of the correlation analysis conducted to reveal the relationship between organizational culture and employee performance, it is seen that the dimensions of organizational culture are strongly related to each other. In addition, a moderate positive correlation was found between the dimensions of organizational culture and the performance of the institution. As a result of the regression analysis made, only the involvement dimension of the organizational culture has a significant effect on the employees' performance. The employees at the institutions have the expectation of asking and presenting their own ideas; their performances increase as long as these are met. Involvement creates a driving force in revealing the potential of employees. Managers must never ignore this fact.

Independent sample T-Test and ANOVA analyses were conducted to determine whether employees' perceptions of organizational culture and performance differed in terms of research demographics. As a result of the analysis, it was determined that the employees showed significant differences according to the variables of age, duration of employment, and graduation. If these analyses are interpreted in general, it is possible to say that older participants are ahead of younger ones in terms of vision. The employment period in the institution can be concluded to affect employees' perceptions of the organizational, those with more experience in the institution have higher organizational perceptions than those of less experienced or newer persons. In terms of the education variable, perceptions of postgraduates were found to be lower than other employees within the scope of the dimensions of organizational culture. This means that as the level of education increases, the perception of organizational culture declines.

As young employees' vision perceptions are low in the selected organization, it may be suggested that the organization should make a comprehensive review of the issue. Management should make an effort to create a shared vision. In addition, it is necessary to explore the reasons for the low-level perception of organizational culture among the postgraduates and to seek ways to utilize these employees to contribute to the institution. This research was conducted using the survey technique with the participation of employees of a public institution operating in Düzce. In the future, it could be advised for those who will conduct research in this area to collect in-depth information on this topic by using qualitative methods and to conduct studies that will enable comparisons among managers and employees. It may be advisable to use different models in cultural evaluations or to use the same model to determine the differences between the public and private sectors.

Bibliography

Akıncı Vural, Beril / Coşkun, Gül: *Organizational Culture*. Nobel Publication: Ankara. 2007.

Ataman, Göksel: *Business Management: Basic Concepts and Approaches*. Türkmen Publication: İstanbul. 2009.

Büyük, Köksal: "A Study on measurement of organizational culture as an element of strategic performance management". *Eskişehir Osmangazi University Journal of Economics and Administrative Sciences* 5(2), 2010, pp. 219–235.

Çalık, Temel: *Performance Management*. Daytime Education and Publishing: Ankara. 2003.

Cameron, Kim. S. / Quinn, Robert. E.: *Diagnosing and Changing Organizational Culture*. Jossey-Bass Publication: San Francisco. 1999.

Canman, Doğan: "New approaches in evaluation of personnel and implementation in public sector in turkey". *Journal of Amme Administrative* 26(1), 1993, pp. 159–184.

Çatıkoğlu, Mehmet. E.: *Comparative Analysis of Factors Affecting Organizational Culture, Motivation and Job Satisfaction*. (T.C. Adnan Menderes University Institute of Social Sciences). (Master Thesis). Aydın. 2006.

Çetin Ölçüm, M.: *Organizational Culture and Organizational Commitment*. Nobel Publication: Ankara. 2004.

Dedehayır, Handan.: *Sürdürülebilir Kültür Turizmi*, http://cekulvakfi.org.tr/makale/surdurulebilir-kultur-turizmi, 2014

Denison, Daniel R. / Mishra, Aneil K.: Toward A Theory Of Organizational Culture And Effectiveness. *Organization Science* 6(2), 1995, pp. 204–223.

Denison, Daniel. R.: "What is the difference between organization culture and organizational climate, a native's point of view on a decade of paradigm wars". *The Academy of Management Review* 21(3), 1996, pp. 619–654.

Doğan, Binali: *Organization Culture*. Beta Publication: İstanbul. 2007.

Eker A., Burcu: The Effect of Communication Satisfaction to Organizational Commitment in The Context of Denison's Corporate Culture Model. (T.C. Marmara University Institute of Social Sciences Public Relations and Publicity Department, Public Relations Science Department). (Doctoral Thesis) İstanbul. 2013.

Erdem, Ramazan / Adıgüzel, Orhan. / Kaya, Aslı: Organizational culture types that the academicians perceive and prefer in relevant with their institutions". *Erciyes University Journal of Economics and Administrative Sciences* (36), 2010, pp. 73–88.

Erdoğan, Ebru.: *Örgütsel Sessizlik ve Performans İlişkisi* Yayınlanmamış Yüksek Lisans Tezi, Gebze İleri teknoloji Enstitüsü Sosyal Bilimler Enstitüsü. Kocaeli. 2011

Eren Veysel / Durna, Ufuk: (2007). "Understanding and Developing Performance in The Public Sector". *Journal of Amme Administrative* 40(1), 2007, pp. 107–134.

Fuentes, M. Mar, Carlos A. Albacete-Saez-F/Javier Llorens-Montes: *The Impact Of Environmental Characteristics On TQM Principles and Organizational Performance*, The International Journal Of Management Science, 32, pp. 425–442. 2004

Kalkan, Abdullah: *The Effect of Percieved Organizational Culture on Organizational Citizenship Behavior: A Theoretical and Empirical Study*. (T.C. Selçuk University, Graduate School of Social Sciences Department of Business Administration, Department of Administration Organization). (Doctoral Thesis) Konya. 2013.

Karakaş, Bülent / Ak, Rengin: "Is Performance Management In Public Administration Important? Quality In Public Administration. 3. National Congress Reports, TODAİE Publications: Ankara. 2003. pp. 337–351.

Keskin, Burak: *A Research About the Relationship Between Organizational Culture and Job Satisfaction Depending On the Model of Kilmann and Quinn & Cameron*. (T.C. Marmara University Graduate School of Social Sciences Department of Business Administration). (Master Thesis) İstanbul. 2014.

Kilman Ralph H, Saxton, Mary.J./Sepra, Roy: *Five Key Issues in Understanding and Changing Culture", Gaining Control of the Corporate Culture, Ralph H. Kilman (Ed.), Jossey-Bass., pp.*1–16. 1985

Kirkman, Bradley L./Rosen Benson: *Beyond Self-Management: Antecedents and Consequences of Team Empowerment*, Academy of Management Journal, 42(1), pp. 58–74. USA, 1999

Köse Sevinç / Ünal Aylin: *Different Social Cultures, Organizational Structures, Leadership Behaviors*. İmaj Publication: İzmir. 2003.

Kotter, John P. / Heskett, James L.: *Corporate Culture and Performance*. The Free Press: New York.1992.

Morley Michael / Heraty Noreen: *The High-Performance Organization: Developing Teamwork Where It Counts*, Management Decision, 33 (2), pp. 56–63. 1995

Mwita, Isaac J.: Performance management model: a systems-based approach to public service quality. *The International Journal of Public Sector Management* 13(1), 2000, pp. 19–37.

Özgür, Eylem D.: *Balanced Scorecard in Performance Management and an Application*. (T.C. İstanbul University Institute of Social Sciences Department of Labor Economics and Industry Relations). (Doctoral Thesis). İstanbul. 2010.

Peters Thomas J. / Waterman Robert H.: *In Search of Excellence: Lessons from America's Best-Run Companies*. Harper & Row Publication: New York. 1984.

Rahman, Shams-ur/Bullock Philip. *Soft TQM, Hard TQM, And Organizational Performance Relationships: An Empirical Investigation*, Omega, 33-1, pp. 73–83. 2005. Australia

Schein, Edgar H.: *Organizational Culture and Leadership*. The Jossey-Bass Business & Management Series: The United States of America. 2004.

Schein, Edgar. H: "Three cultures of management: The Key to Organizational Learning". *Sloan Management Review* 38 (1), 1996, pp. 9–20.

Sezgin, Orhan: *Exploring The Relationship Between the Concepts of Organization Culture, Organizational Justice and Organizational Citizenship Behavior*. (Yeditepe University Institute of Social Sciences). (Doctoral Thesis). İstanbul. 2009.

Şimşek Nevin / Fidan Mehmet: *Organizational Culture and Leadership*. Tablet Bookstore: Konya. 2005.

Terzi Ali R.: *Organizational Culture*. Nobel Publication: Ankara. 2000.

Timur, Hikmet: "Personnel achievement evaluation and Turkish judicial justice example." *Journal of Amme Administrative* 16(3), 1983, pp. 4–11.

Yahyagil, Mehmet. Y.: "The validity and reliability study of the Denison organizational culture measurement tool: an empirical application". *Istanbul University Graduate School of Business, Journal of Management* 47, 2004, pp. 53–76.

Yaman, Rabia: *The Effects of Corporate Culture On Job Satisfaction A Research*. (T.C. Marmara University Institute of Social Sciences Department of Labor Economics and Industrial Relations, Management and Labor Psychology). (Master Thesis). İstanbul. 2009.

Yerli, Esra: *Performance Management and Performance Evaluation in Public Administration*. (T.C. Selçuk University Institute of Social Sciences Department of Public Administration). (Master Thesis). Konya. 2006.

Yılmaz, Hüseyin / Karahan, Atilla: "Development of high performance culture and ıts effects to the firm success". *Selçuk University Journal of Institute of Social Sciences* 23, 2010, pp. 273–282.

Zehir, Cemal / Özşahin, Mehtap: "Team management and the determinants of team effectiveness: a field research on the team operating in research and development in defense industry". *Journal of Doğuş University* 2, 2008, pp. 266–279.

Işık Çiçek

Organizational Socialization with the Organizational Tenure Perspective

Abstract: The importance of human is becoming more important in today's competitive environment. Antecedents of employees' individual contribution to reach organizational efficiency have been studied for a long time in management literature. In this context, organizational socialization by an employee has gained significant value. Achievement of socialization process properly is paid attention by academicians and practitioners. Organizational tenure can be a critical factor due to organizational life planned by the institution and experienced by employees. The fact that socialization is experienced efficiently depending on organization and individual can result in a guide for desirable outcomes. Therefore, organizational tenure can be a critical factor for completing socialization in an institution by employees. Definition of "organizational socialization" expands beyond employees' diagnosing organizational values, learning and their congruence with their individual ones. Four hundred and twenty nine employees are selected from 16 organizations in convenient sampling technique. Demographic data contains organizational tenure measured via nominal scale with 6-category. Socialization dimension is gathered via questionnaire method. Correlation and Kruskal-Wallis tests are utilized hypothesized relationship after diagnosing normality. History, language, politics, people, aim, and values, employees' performance competencies constitute dimensions of organizational socialization. According to research findings, history-goal, politics-duty, and performance proficiency dimensions differentiate depending on tenure categories, whereas learning organizational language does not.

Keywords: Organizational socialization, Organizational tenure, Organizational efficiency

Introduction

Increasing interest in positive psychology cause tendency about positive variables to be measured in management literature mostly. The effects of existing positive variable are stronger than that of missing negative variable for the considered situation.

Starting from orientation term, socialization process has a critical role for new employees to form a high level of performance, trust, well-being, and so forth. Inefficient socialization process directly affects employees' subsequent work attitudes and performance in the institution. Therefore, the dimensions of organizational socialization are researched in management studies.

Employees' positive attitudes in the institution increase individuals' commitment to organization and motivation level (Dirks and Ferrin 2001), which in turn leads to the better fulfillment of psychological contracts (Robinson 1996). Given these positive outcomes, efficient organizational socialization process can be linked to the desired level of the individual, group, and organizational variables. Therefore, organizational socialization process should be managed efficiently depending on situational factors in the institution. From this perspective, can organizational tenure be a critical factor in executing and achieving organizational socialization process? What degree of tenure for employees to experience organizational life is sufficient in this process? Planned organizational socialization process and its content will be useful for long-term organization contract and employee commitment.

The aim of this research is to investigate the level and content of organizational socialization process depending on the degree of tenure starting from organization entry term.

Organizational Socialization

Socialization is that individual gains knowledge and experience about roles in social life by transferring societal value systems and ideal in sociology perspective. An individual can learn group norms and adopt them into his/her attitudes. In this circumstance, the societal system is provided to be in harmony. That is to say, socialization is a learning process (Dönmezer 1994; O'Sullisan 1997; Feldman 1980; Memduhoğlu 2008). In terms of business perspective, socialization is individual' internationalization of environmental perception, value and, a belief shared by a group (Weiner 1982). It is synchronization of individual's value, norm, and belief with that of organization (Balay 2000). Inasmuch as this process enables employees to consider organization priority and behave in light of these aims/targets, members of organization adopt similar values with the organization. ASA Theory proposes that employees are attracted to the organization, selected by the institution, and those who cannot match their values with organizational values leave the institution (Schneider 1987). Socialization process has a critical role after individuals are selected at the institution for ASA Theory (Chatman 1991). In this perspective, organizational tenure can have a critical role in achieving socialization phases.

Considering measurable dimensions, operational definitions for organizational socialization are seen in Tab. 1 (Özdemir, 2015).

Organizational socialization exists at any time an employee experiences a change of organization border (Van Maanen and Schein 1979, p. 215). The

Tab. 1: Operational Definitions of Organizational Socialization

Variable	Operational Definition	Source
Performance Proficiency	The degree to which an employee learns the tasks, skills, and abilities required for the job	Chao et. Al, 1994, p.731 Watchfogel, 2009, p.43
People	refers to an understanding of who the key players are in the organization that can help the employee adjust to organization and the job	Chao et. Al, 1994, p.731 Watchfogel, 2009, p.43
Politics	concerned with obtaining knowledge about formal and informal networks as well as an understanding of the power structures within the organization	Chao et. Al, 1994, p.731 Watchfogel, 2009, p.43
Language	includes the individual's understanding of the profession's technical language as well as the jargon, slogans, and acronyms particular to that organization	Chao et. Al, 1994, p.731 Watchfogel, 2009, p.43
Organizational goals and values	Focus on the individual's knowledge about the formal and informal goals and values of the organization	Chao et. Al, 1994, p.731 Watchfogel, 2009, p.43
History	Concerned with the individual understanding the organization traditions, myths, customs and rituals that foster particular work culture	Chao et. Al, 1994, p.731 Watchfogel, 2009, p.43

changes in individual attitudes, perceptions, behaviors, knowledge, skills, and sense making cognition system are influenced by organizational socialization (Cooper-Thomas and Anderson 2006; Wachtfogel 2009; Özdemir 2015).

The organizational socialization literature has two different types of the research field, naming as the process and the content of organizational socialization (Chao et al. 1994; Woo 2006).

Several researchers proposed various structures regarding dimensions of organizational socialization. Feldman (1989) defined four domains of the learning process: job-related tasks, work roles, the group process, and organizational attributes. Fisher (1986; as cited in Woo, 2006) described three similar fields while adding two more domains: (1) preliminary learning, whereby newcomers realize that learning is needed and identify what and from whom they need to learn; (2) learning about the organization; (3) learning to operate in a work-group; (4) how to do the job; and (5) personal learning and change, whereby newcomers learn more about.

Some organizational socialization tactics are described in the literature Van Maanen and Schein (1979). The tactics are classified into six types: (1) collective versus individual, which show whether employees are subjected to a common series of experiences, (2) formal versus informal, that used to describe the degree to which employees are apart from other workers during socialization period, (3) sequential versus random, contains the degree to which steps for postulating a role are created and identifiable, (4) fixed versus variable, demonstrates the degree to which a determined time for the stages included in order to propose a role is provided, (5) serial versus disjunctive, defined as whether or not, a role model is provided in order to help newcomer during transition, (6) investiture versus divestiture, which implies to the degree of an organization's evaluation of conformity or creativity and entrepreneurship (Wachtfogel 2009).

In this process, psychological contract and power of organizational culture, existing of sub-cultures are efficient factors. Especially, time for individual's socialization is affected by mentioned elements.

Organizational socialization causes newcomers to change attitude, values, and behaviors. Organizational socialization process has a continuous dynamic. The consequence of socialization is fit of an employee with a new job, co-worker, and organizational applications. One of the main elements of socialization is an interaction between employee and supervisor. Early period in socialization has critical importance for the employee. Learning job descriptions and duty necessities, getting in contact with individuals, diagnosing the people having organization power, learning the common organizational language, being aware of organizational aims and values, learning organization history.

Schein (1968) proposed a three-stage socialization model: "Entry, accept organizational reality, mutual acceptance". Feldman (1976) asserted another three stage socialization model: "Anticipatory socialization (getting in), accommodation (breaking in), and role management"

Organizational Demography

Organizational demography investigated social group composition of group members. Demography is considered as a feature of the group in these studies. Most research that aims to explain the results of differentiation focus on the demographic dissimilarities of the working group. Heterogeneity in terms of age, race, gender, tenure is mostly investigated in demography studies. This aim of this scope is easy measurement by the feature of researchers, observing these differentiations/similarities by group members, and the belief about some psychological effects stemming from these variables (Bantel and Jackson 1989; Jackson et al. 1993; Pfeffer, 1983; Tsui et al. 1992; Harrison et al. 1998).

Demographic variables such as age, organizational tenure, job tenure, education level, race, gender are linked to performance (Waldman and Avolio, 1986), recruitment and increment decisions (McIntyre et al. 1980) and turnover (Mobley et al. 1978) meaningfully (Tsui et al. 1992). Steffens et al. (2014) investigated the relationship between organizational tenure and employee performance. Positive incremental effects of employee organizational tenure, team leader organizational leader, and team organizational leader have been reported.

Pfeffer (1983) stated that demographic similarity with group affects organization related outputs such as creativity, performance, and managerial success. According to Pfeffer, to investigate synchronous demographic features such as age, gender, and education level have more valuable effects instead of individual effects (O'Reilly et al. 1989; Sürgevil 2008). Therefore, the term relational demography is introduced. Comparing demographic similarity among group members can explain attitude and behaviors of employees. That is to say, the demographic characteristics affecting work outputs appeared in groups, efficiently (Tsui and O'Reilly 1989).

Last studies in this field have focused on the distributional or compositional effects of demographic properties beyond solely demographic effects (Pfeffer 1983; Sürgevil 2008).

It is proposed that the individual level-effects of demographic properties be searched beside to department/group level (Tsui and O'Reilly 1989).

In the concept of organizational demography, the interpersonal relationships are not compulsory (Mannix and Neale 2005).

Joshi (2006) researched the effect of organizational demography on external communication in theoretical study adapted from Cox's organizational typology (1993). In this model, three stages are described depending on demographic and structural composition shown in Fig. 1.

How Does Organizational Socialization Differentiate with respect to Organizational Tenure?

Pfeffer (1981, 1983) suggested that the distribution of employees in an organization along with some demographic dimension such as tenure influences

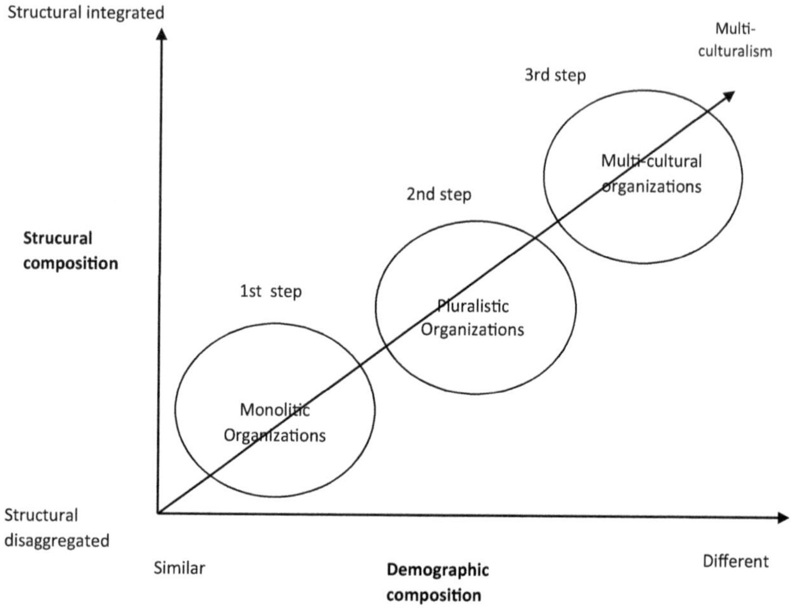

Fig. 1: 3 Stage-organizational Demography Model (Joshi, 2006)

communication frequency. Because communication between different tenure groups becomes more difficult, tenure time is a remarkable factor for obtaining culture and institution awareness from other employees. Organizational demography does influence the frequency of communication, higher tenure for employees result in higher level socialization for employees. According to Attraction-Selection-Attrition theory employees obtain knowledge about informal and formal sides of organization and working group after selection phase. This socialization process is influenced by several internal environment components, one of which is tenure (Zenger and Lawrence 1989). Within organizations, the development of a shared language between employees results from their similar backgrounds and experiences; tenure is one critical element enabling this shared cohesiveness.

Allen and Mayer (1990) reported that newcomer employees' organizational commitment level is significantly different from that of employees' after six months.

As tenure in an organization increases, employees gain a more efficient understanding of strategies, policies, and procedures. Thus, because of tenure functions as an indicator of organizational experience, it also means a sign of familiarity with the organizational language (March and Simon 1958; Zenger and Lawarence 1989). Since all employees are likely to seek communication with others whose tenure is at least as much as their own, communication among employees of similar tenure is interchangeable. Individuals having similar tenure develop unique interpretations, awareness, and understandings depending on shared experiences and organizational events.

Entrance to established communication networks in organization or group is difficult for new employees. This situation disrupts current networks (Roberts and O'Reilly 1979). Therefore; it damages the value of social investments in these networks for longer-tenured employees. Newcomers need to develop communication links; they find it easy to communicate with other new employees. Tenure similarity exerts a stronger influence on technical communication than age similarity (Zenger and Lawarence 1989).

There are other tenure types that can be investigated in organization research except for organizational tenure. They are job tenure (total experience), job tenure in that organization, tenure for supervisor-employee relation, group tenure with the same members/ with different individuals.

According to mentioned theoretical knowledge and previous research findings, the hypothesis below can be proposed.

H: Content of organizational socialization experienced by employees will be different in terms of organizational tenure for employees.

Research in Turkey

Sampling and Method

The research was carried out in several types of work field in sectors in Turkey. Sampling was selected from white-collar employee via convenience method. Four hundred and seventeen participants from 15 companies are included in this research. Sub-work fields consist of oil, screw production, consumer financing, medicine, chemistry, food, cleaning, jewelry, and tourism.

Tenure is measured as a categorical variable. Six categories are determined: Less than 6 months, between 6 months and 1 year, 1 and 5 years, 6 and 10 years, 11 and 15 years, and above 15 years. Questionnaire technique is utilized for gathering data of organizational socialization content and level. 6-degree Likert scale (ranging from definitely disagree to fully agree) is used for participants' evaluation. Data obtained from questionnaires is analyzed through the SPSS statistical packet program. The proposed relation is tested through Kruskal Wallis

H non-parametric test. Normality test for data is diagnosed through histogram with normal curve, skewness-kurtosis co-efficient, and Kolmogorov-Smirnov test. Reliability and validity of scales are investigated via Cronbach alpha internal consistency, and Varimax rotated factor analysis, respectively.

Measurement

In the first part demographic data is asked to the participant. This demographic information involves age, gender, marital status, organization tenure, job tenure, educational background, and position in the organization.

Organizational socialization: 34 out of 36 item-scale is used in the study (Turkish version from Özçelik 2008). The original scale is developed by Chao et al. (1994). Six dimensions of organizational socialization are history, language, and politics, aims, and values of the organization, people in the organization, employees' performance adequacy are measured. Thirteen items are reverse coded.

Findings

Demographic Information

Demographic information of participants is shown in Tab. 2.

Descriptive statistics values of organizational socialization are shown in Tab. 3.

Reliability and Validity of Scales

The items that have eigenvalue higher than 1 and loaded by the value of 0,45 or higher on the one factor are considered. The item loaded on more than one factor with the difference score of 0,1 or lower are removed from the analysis. That is to say, after factor analysis result, one iteration is carried out. Cronbach alpha internal consistency is calculated (above 0,7) for reliability analysis. Factor analysis results and reliability results are shown in Tab. 4.

Several iterations are carried step by step. Finally, seven factors are grouped, but the 28th item is grouped into one dimension (7th dimension), solely. So, it is not considered for analysis. Six factors are grouped as 1-history-goals, 2- politics-duty, 3-performance, proficiency, 4- people, 5-personal prestige, 6- language. The factors are named depending on involved items' meaningful content.

First, second, third, and sixth factors are utilized for correlation and regression analysis. Other factors do not have acceptable reliability value ($x < 0,65$)

Tab. 2: Demographic Data of Participants

Demography	Category	Frequency	Percent (%)
Age	20-30	205	49,3
	31-40	254	37
Gender	male	223	53,6
	female	191	45,9
Education level	Vocational college	78	18,6
	Under graduation	213	51,2
Organizational tenure	Less than 6 month	31	7,5
	6 month -1year	53	12,7
	1-5 year	185	44,5
	6-10 year	99	23,8
	10-15 year	39	9,4
	Above 15 year	9	2,2
Total job tenure	Less than 1 year	20	4,8
	1-5 year	117	28,1
	6-10 year	119	28,6
	11-15 year	80	19,2
	16-20 year	30	7,2
	Above 20 year	35	8,4

Tab. 3: Descriptive Statistics of Variables

Variable	Mean	Standard deviation	Skewness	Kurtosis
Organiz. socialization	4,87	0,552	-0,436	-0,160

Significant Effects

Correlation values among dimensions of organizational socialization are shown in Tab. 5.

Among variables, the relation between performance proficiency and language has the highest value (0,568). All socialization dimensions have significant correlation values with each other.

Even though organizational socialization variable has normal distribution as a whole, the data that is split into six categories for each dimension does not have normal distribution. For testing hypothesis, Kruskal Wallis H test is utilized.

Tab. 4: Validity and Reliability of Organizational Socialization Scale

Factor	Items	Factor Loads	Eigenvalue	Explained variance (%)	Sub-dimension reliability
1	1. I have learned how things "really work" on the inside of this organization	0.698	4.934	11.122	0.686
	3. I would be a good a good representative of my organization	0.690			
	2. I know very little about the history of my workgroup/department (R)	0.687			
	21. I would be a good resource for describing the background of my workgroup/department	0.539			
	9. I am not familiar with the organization's customs, rituals, ceremonies, and celebration (R)	0.458			
2	20. I understand the goals of my organization.	0.826	1.793	11.094	0.710
	19. I have mastered the required tasks of my job	0.812			
	7. I know who the most influential people are in my organization	0.557			
	30. I understand what most of the acronyms and abbreviations of my trade/profession mean	0.491			
3	22. I have not fully developed the appropriate skills and abilities to successfully perform my job (R)	0.796	1.495	9.062	0.646
	26. I am not always sure what needs to be done in order to get the most desirable work assignments in my area (R).	0.710			
	5. I have not yet learned "the ropes" of my job (R)	0.559			

Tab. 4: (continued)

Factor	Items	Factor Loads	Eigenvalue	Explained variance (%)	Sub-dimension reliability
4	10. I am usually excluded in social get together given by other people in the organization (R)	0.667	1.373	8.72	0.524
	17. I do not always believe in the values set by my organization (R)	0.666			
	27. I am usually excluded in informal networks or gatherings of people within the organization (R)	0.663			
5	33. I believe most of my co-workers like me	0.796	1.317	8.670	0.602
	34. I support the goals that are set by my organization	0.646			
	31. I am pretty popular in the organization	0.586			
6	12. I have not mastered this organization's slang and special jargon (R)	0.852	1.796	7.462	0.655
	6. I have not mastered the specialized terminology and vocabulary of my trade/profession (R)	0.843			
Total				62.357	0,792
Kaiser-Meyer-Olkin			0,792		
Bartlett's Test of Sphericity	Approx. Chi-square		1969.741		
	d.f.		210		
	Sig.		0.00		

Four socialization dimensions emerged after factor analysis with acceptable reliability value are tested depending on 6 tenure categories, separately.

1st dimension (history-goals), 2nd dimension (politics-duty), and 3rd dimension (performance proficiency) of organizational socialization are differentiated among employees according to 6 tenure categories (p=0,000), whereas 6th dimension (language) has similar levels for all employees (p=0,275). There are no significant differentiations among employees' tenure categories in terms of organizational language. Means and standard deviation values of socialization dimensions depending on tenure category are shown in Tab. 6.

Result and Discussion

According to research findings, proposed hypothesis is supported except for language dimension of organizational socialization. Levels of history-goals, politics-duty, and performance proficiency dimensions are different for the employees having different tenure time. Since non-parametric statistics is utilized for diagnosing comparing sub-groups, tenure categories are not separated as homogenous or heterogeneous groups. Considering means and standard deviation values of sub-groups, higher level of differences among variables can be inferred.

At history-goal dimension, the highest value is for 15-year tenure group. The relatively lowest value is 4,207 for six months-one-year tenure. Politics-duty of the organization is being learned in 10-15-year tenure at most by employees. The lowest level of that is in 15 years above tenure. The employees in this time interval have an older age. It is likely that these individuals have not anymore played an active role in organizational aims. Performance proficiency dimension has the lowest value for just after newcomer term (6 month-1 year), whereas the highest value corresponds to 6 years-10 years term. The employees expect an increment in this term at their institutions. From beginning the tenure 6 month-1 year to 10 year-15 years, performance proficiency level is increasingly in progress. Occupying new position in an institution for an employee causes necessity of performance proficiency level to diminish. Similarly, Saruhan (2007) reported the significant differences among job tenure groups and organizational tenure groups for the understanding organization as a dimension of socialization in his study. 1-5 year-group is significantly different from 6-10 year-group and 11-15 year-group, whereas other two groups do not. This finding corresponds to the dimensions of history-goals and politics-duty in our research. Nartgün and Demirer (2016) found both similar and different findings among socialization dimensions depending on job tenure categories in their study. The dimensions of performance proficiency, organizational history, congruence with aims and values, and organizational politics among job tenure year have differentiated. Means of socialization dimension for tenure have increased depending on tenure year in a positive direction sequentially that is different from this research finding. In our research findings, means for socialization dimension do not increase with the increment in tenure category years. The authors reported that performance proficiency level is significantly different

Tab. 5: Correlation Values between Variables

	History-goals	Politic- duty	Performance proficiency	language
History-goals	1			
Politic-duty	0.507**	1		
Perform. Proficiency	0.369**	0.323**	1	
language	0.116*	0.030	0.568**	1

** Correlation is significant 0.01 at level
* Correlation is significant at 0.05 level

Tab. 6: Means and Standard Deviation Values of Socialization Dimensions

Dimension of socialization	Tenure category	Mean	Standard deviation
History-goals	1	4.475	0.71
	2	4.407	0.934
	3	4.859	0.734
	4	5.045	0.804
	5	5.312	0.670
	6	5.475	0.861
Politics-duty	1	5.327	0.518
	2	4.879	0.890
	3	5.305	0.645
	4	5.452	0.554
	5	5.679	0.405
	6	4.875	1.445
Performance proficiency	1	3.903	1.196
	2	3.620	1.126
	3	4.397	1.125
	4	4.563	1.031
	5	4.517	0.879
	6	4.500	0.666
Language	1	3.689	1.263
	2	3.539	1.420
	3	3.955	1.473
	4	3.831	1.704
	5	3.315	1.868
	6	4.062	1.741

for 0-5 year category from other subgroup tenures. Besides, 6-10 year group is different from 20 year-above tenure group. In our research, 0-6 month group and 6 months-1 year group have lower mean value than those of other tenure groups. It is inferred that socialization process for 0-1 year is remarkable so as to be aware of organization life. For the organizational history, 0-5 year-group is significantly different from 11 year-above group. In our research, 0-6 month and 6 month-1 year have relatively lower mean value than other tenure groups. Completing 1 year to learn organizational history results in awareness for employees. Socialization of goals and values differentiated between 0-5 year-group and 16-year above-group that is similar to our research findings. The dimension of organizational politics differs between 1-5 year-group and 21-year above-group, but 15-year above-group has relatively the lowest mean value in our research. Similarly, Çalışkan (2009), Çapar (2007), Elci (2008), Özkan (2005) have reported differences among tenure groups for socialization dimensions, but Mutlu (2008) and Kartal (2003) did not reveal different socialization dimension values depending on tenure.

Considering Tab. 6, language dimension of socialization is approximately the same for all employees having different tenure. Standard deviation values of this dimension are the highest among all socialization dimensions. Like this finding, Zenger and Lawarence (1989) reported that tenure similarity of employees who are not members of the same project group has a significant effect on the frequency of technical communication outside project groups in their research.

The effect of tenure similarity on the frequency of communication in organizations decreases over time. Because individuals enter organizations in relatively uninformed manner, they have strong incentives to develop the language skills that get easier effective communication. Therefore, employees make their most quick gains in organizational language skills during an initial socialization period. However, after employees obtain basic language skills, further gains in language development make increasingly less remarkable differences in their ability to understand organizational language efficiently. Thus, differences in the understanding organizational language associated with differences in tenure are likely to diminish over time. For instance, when two employees have been in a company, one and five years, respectively, the difference of four years of organizational experience between them may block communication and interpersonal relations. However, ten years later, significant language differences between these individuals may not exist. The four-year difference in organizational experience may not affect their ease of communication (Zenger and Lawarence, 1989).

Bibliography

Allen, Natalie. J. / Meyer, John P.: "The measurement and antecedents of affective, continuance, and normative commitment to the organization". *Journal of Occupational Psychology* 63, 1990, pp.1–18.

Balay, Refik: *School Managers' and Teachers' Organizational Commitment.* Nobel Publishing: Ankara. 2000.

Bantel, Karen. A. / Jackson, Susan. E.: "Top management and innovations in banking: Does the composition of the top team make a difference?". *Strategic Management Journal* 10, 1989, pp.107–124.

Chao, Georgia. T. / O'Leary-Kelly, A. M. / Wolfe, S. / Klein, H. J. / Gardner, P. D.: "Organizational socialization: Its content and consequences". *Journal of Applied Psychology* 779(5), 1994, pp.730–743.

Chatman, Jennifer A.: "Matching people and organizations: Selection and socialization in public accounting firms". *Administrative Sciences Quarterly* 36, 1991, pp.459–484.

Cooper-Thomas, Helena D. / Anderson, Neil Robert: "Organizational socialization: A new theoretical model and recommendations for future research and HRM practices in organizations". *Journal of Managerial Psychology* 21(5), 2006, pp.492–516.

Cox, Taylor. (Jr.). 1993. *Cultural diversity in organizations, theory, research and practice*. Berrett-Koehler Publishing, San Fransisco.1993

Çalışkan, İ. Güniz: "Organizational leadership style of teachers regarding their perception of social according to school administrators review: Special education teachers sample". unpublished master thesis Maltepe University. İstanbul. 2009.

Çapar, Dilek: "The perception level of the organizational socialisation of the primary and junior high school teachers". unpublished master thesis Akdeniz University. Antalya. 2007.

Dirks, Kurt / Ferrin, Donald. "The role of trust in organizational settings". *Organization Science,* 12, 2001. 450–467.

Dönmezer, Sulhi: *Toplumbilim*. Beta Yayınları: İstanbul. 1994.

Elci, Devrim: "The study of the organizational socializational levels of the primary school teachers". unpublished master thesis Selçuk University. Konya. 2008.

Feldman, Dainel Charles: "A Contingency Theory of Socialization". Ph.D. Dissertation. Yale University. New Hawen, CT. 1976.

Feldman, Daniel Charles: "A Socialization process that help new recruits succeed". In J. R. Hackman / E. E. Lawler / L. W. Porter (Eds.) *Perspectives on*

Behaviour in Organization. Mc Graw-Hill Book Company: NewYork. 1980. pp.170–178.

Feldman, Daniels Charles: "Socialization, resocialization, and retraining: Refraining the research agenda". In Goldstein, Irwin. L (Ed.) *Training and Development in Organizations* Jossey Bass San Francisco, CA. 1989. pp.376–416.

Harrison, David. A. / Price, Kenneth. H. / Bell, Myrtele: "Beyond relational demography: Time and the effects of surface-and deep diversity on work group cohesion". *Academy of Management Journal* 41(1), 1998, pp.96–107.

Jackson, Paul. R. / Wall, Tobby. D. / Martin, Robin / Davids, Keith: "New measures of job control, cognitive demand, and production responsibility". *Journal of Applied Psychology* 78, 1993, pp.753–762.

Joshi, Aparna: "The influence of organizational demography on the external networking behavior of teams." *Academy of Management Review* 31(3), 2006, pp.583–595.

Kartal, Sadık: "Organizational socialization levels of primary school principals and teachers". unpublished master thesis Ankara University. 2003.

March James G / Simon Herbert A. *Organizations*. Wiley: New York. 1958.

Mannix, Elizabeth / Neale, Margaret. A.: "What differences make a difference: the promise and reality of diverse teams in organization". *Psychological Science in the Public Interest* 6(2), 2005, pp.31–55.

McIntyre, Shelby. J. / Moberg, Dennis. J. / Posner, Barr. Z.: "Discrimination in recruitment: An empirical analysis (comment)". *Industrial and Labor Relations Review 33*(4), 1980, pp.543–547.

Memduhoğlu, Hasan Basri: "Organizational Socialization and the process of Organizational Socialization in the Turkish Educational System". *Yüzüncü Yıl University Journal of Educational Faculty* V(II), 2008, pp.137–153.

Mobley, William. H./ Horner, Stanley. O / Hollingsworth, A. T. "An evaluation of precursors of hospital employee turnover". *Journal of Applied Psychology*, 1978, 63, 408-414.

Mutlu, Bakile: "School culture at secondary school of İstanbul and teachers? organizational socialization". unpublished master thesis Beykent Üniversity. İstanbul. 2008.

O'Reilly, Charles. A. / Caldwell, Davis. F. / Barnett, William. P.: "Work group demography, social integration, and turnover". *Administrative Science Quarterly* 34, 1989, pp.21–37.

O'Sullisan, Fergus: "Learning organizations-reenginering schools for life long learning". *School Leadership and Management* 17(2), 1997, pp.217–229.

Özçelik, Firuzhan: "The effect of organizational socialization on organizational commitment: A research". unpublished master thesis Marmara University. İstanbul. 2008.

Özdemir, Yasin: "The relationship between organizational socialisation and organizational citizenship behavior: The role of person-environment fit". unpublished master thesis Marmara University. İstanbul. 2015.

Özkan, Y.: "The effect of teachers organizational commitment in organizational socialization process". unpublished master thesis Gazi University. Ankara. 2005.

Pfeffer, Jeffrey. *Power in Organisations*, Pitman, Boston.1981.

Pfeffer, Jeffery: "Organizational demography". In Larry L. Cummings / Barry M. Staw (Eds.) *Research in Organizational Behavior*. JAI Press: Greenwich CT. 1983. pp: 299–357.

Roberts, D. H. / O'Reilly Charles A.: "Some correlates of communication roles in organizations". *Academy of Management Journal* 22, 1979, pp.42–57.

Robinson, Sandra L.: "Trust and breach of the psychological contract". *Administrative Science Quarterly 41*(4), 1996, pp.574–599.

Saruhan, Sümeyra: "The impact of organizational socialization on organizational identification". unpublished master thesis. Kırıkkale University. 2007.

Schein, Edgar H.: "Organizational socialization and the profession of management". *Industrial Management Review* 9, 1968, pp.1–16.

Schneider, Benjamin: "The people make the place". *Personnel Psychology* 40, 1987, pp.437–453.

Sezgin Nartgün, Şenay / Demirer, Sibel: "Effects of Teachers' Collective Efficacy with Organizational Socialization and Identification Level". *Mersin University Journal of the Faculty of Education* 12(1), 2016, pp.474–503.

Steffens, Niklas / Shemla, Meir / Wegge, J. / Diestel, Stefan:. "Organizational Tenure and Employee Performance: A Multilevel Analysis". *Group and Organization Management* 39(6). 2014, pp. 664-690.

Sürgevil, Olca: "The Socio-Psychological Theories and Approaches that forms the Base of Diversity and Diversity Management". *Balıkesir University Journal of Social Sciences* 20, 2008, pp.111–124.

Tsui, Anne. S./O' Reilly III, Charles. A. "Beyond simple demographic effects: The importance of relational demography in superior-subordinate dyads". *Academy of Management Journal*, 32 (2). 1989. pp. 402–423.

Tsui, Anne. S. / Egan, Terri D. / O'Reilly, Charles A.: "Being different: Relational demography and organizational attachment". *Administrative Science Quarterly* 37(4), 1992, pp.549–579.

Van Maanen, John / Schein, Edgar H.: "Toward a theory of organizational socialization". In Barry. M. Staw (Ed.) *Research in Organizational Behavior*, JAI Press: Greenwich, CT. 1979, pp. 209–264.

Wachtfogel, Marc: "Organizational Socialization, Person–Environment Fit and Commitment of Recent College Graduates". Unpublished Ph.D. Thesis. New York University Steinhardt School of Culture, Education, and Human Development. 2009.

Waldman, David. A. / Avolio, Bruce: "A meta analysis of age differences in job performance". *Journal of Applied Psychology* 71, 1986, pp.33–38.

Wiener, Yoash. 1982. "Commitment in Organizations: A normative view". *Academy of Management Review,* 7(3).1982. pp. 418-428.

Woo, Ha-Young: "Identification and Validation of New Employees' Organizational Socialization Dimensions within a Large Bank in Korea". Ph.D. Thesis University of Minnesota. 2006.

Zenger, Todd / Lawrence Barbara: "Organizational Demography: The Differential Effects of Age and Tenure Distributions and Technical Communication". *Academy of Management Journal* 32(2), 1989, pp.353–376.

Yusuf Esmer[1] and Muhammet Yüksel

Relationship between Entrepreneurship and Organization of Akhism

Abstract: Entrepreneurship is seen as one of the main building blocks of the economy in the promotion of economic growth, expansion, employment and development and social welfare. Entrepreneurship is one of the production factors, as well as the organization of other production factors such as labor, capital, nature, and technology. Therefore, entrepreneurship is constantly encouraged by various institutions, organizations and professional organizations in order to increase production, revive the economy, establish new business areas and increase employment. In the 13th century, Ahi Evan aimed to educate moral entrepreneur by encouraging entrepreneurship of the Organization of Akhism which was founded in Anatolia. The Organization of Akhism has paved the way for entrepreneurs who are sensitive to moral values such as integrity, honesty, altruism, fraternity, sharing, kindness, cooperation, generosity and solidarity, as well as economic entrepreneurship. It has also caused the development of profit-free social entrepreneurship. Thus, it has provided the realization of the provision of quality goods and services and has tried to produce social benefit by solving social and economic problems such as poverty, unemployment, and ignorance. In this context, the aim of the study is to contribute to the literature by establishing the relationship between entrepreneurship and the Organization of Akhism. For this purpose, the connection between entrepreneurship and the Organization of Akhism is examined after providing basic information about entrepreneurship and the Organization of Akhism. As a result, the researches show that there is a very close relationship between the Organization of Akhism and entrepreneurship and both the economic entrepreneurship and social entrepreneurship movements are seen in the Organization of Akhism.

Keywords: Entrepreneurship, Social Entrepreneurship, Moral Entrepreneurship, Organization of Akhism, Social Benefit

Introduction

Entrepreneurship, which has developed significantly in recent years, attracts both academicians and the business world because it creates individual and social prosperity (Onay and Cavusoglu, 2010, p.47). Entrepreneurship is one of the factors of production, and at the same time, it refers to the organization

1 Corresponding author

of other production factors such as labor, capital, nature, and technology. Entrepreneurship is recognized as a fundamental factor in reducing unemployment, sustaining and accelerating economic growth, and initiating a transformative or innovative process in the social structure. For this reason, individuals with the spirit of entrepreneurship need to be discovered. Socio-economic and cultural structure, family, social behavior, educational quality and level, general economic conditions and the incentive applications of the state and various institutions, organizations, civil and professional organizations are needed to reveal these individuals and develop the entrepreneurship (Cetinkaya-Bozkurt et al., 2012, p.230). Entrepreneurship is not only an economic activity; it is also a social and cultural activity. There is always an interaction between economic values and cultural values (Tutar and Altinkaynak, 2014, p.1). The belief, culture, morality, and all values that a society has are influencing entrepreneurship. Therefore, value-focused entrepreneurship must be encouraged. When the history of Anatolia is examined, it is seen that entrepreneurship is supported and constantly encouraged by some professional organizations. Organization of Akhism is at the head of these professional organizations. The Organization of Akhism was founded in the 13th century by Ahi Evran in Anatolia. The Organization of Akhism is a professional organization that is formed by tradesman and craftsmen and influences socio-economic structure with its activities and principles (Soysal, 2013, p.10). The basis of the Organization of Akhism lies in developing solutions to socio-economic and cultural problems of the society and creating social value. Some of the basic features of the Organization of Akhism are cooperativeness, altruism, and benevolence (Durak, 2016, p.101). From this point of view, the Organization of Akhism seems to open the way for profit-free social entrepreneurship as well as the development of economic entrepreneurship by providing moral entrepreneurs who are sensitive to moral values such as integrity, honesty, altruism, brotherhood, sharing, benevolence, cooperation, generosity, solidarity and cooperation.

This study aims to provide a contribution to the literature by establishing the relationship between Entrepreneurship and Organization of Akhism. In this respect, the connection between entrepreneurship and the Organization of Akhism is examined after giving basic information about entrepreneurship and Organization of Akhism. Researches show that there is a very close relationship between the Organization of Akhism and entrepreneurship, and both the economic and social entrepreneurship movements are seen in the Organization of Akhism.

Entrepreneurship

In this section, the concepts of entrepreneurship and entrepreneurs are defined first, then the characteristics of entrepreneurs, types of entrepreneurship, factors affecting and determining entrepreneurship are explained respectively.

Entrepreneurship and Entrepreneurs

Entrepreneurship, which has been the subject of much research in recent years, is seen as one of the main factors of the economy in raising social welfare with development, economic growth, development, employment. "Entrepreneurship is defined as a set of activities, such as the establishment and execution of a business, the execution of managerial processes, and the undertaking of all the risks that arise from the basic functions of the business such as production, and marketing" (Kucuk, 2014, p.28). Entrepreneurship refers to the organization of production factors. The person who realizes this organization is "entrepreneur". According to J.B. Say, an entrepreneur is a person who brings together all the factors of production, produces goods or services, and endures the risk of profit-loss (Tutar and Altinkaynak, 2014, p.4). An entrepreneur is the fourth and most important factor of production after, labor, capital, and natural resources. At the same time, an entrepreneur is a manager who establishes the business.

Entrepreneurship is defined in different ways by many researchers in the literature. Hisrich and Peters (1992) try to summarize the researchers and definitions that try to define entrepreneurship in Tab. 1 (Korkmaz 2012, p.210-211).

Characteristics of Entrepreneurs

It appears that there are various opinions in the literature on the characteristics of entrepreneurs. In Tab. 2, the characteristics of entrepreneurs are indicated by different researchers (Cetinkaya-Bozkurt et al. 2012, p.232-233).

On the other hand, Marangoz (2012, pp.7-11) lists the characteristics that must be found in a successful entrepreneur. These are loyalty, stability and resolution, success requirement, opportunity tendency, tolerance to uncertainty, internal locus of control, risk-taking, innovation and productivity, optimism, leadership, and self-direction. The success of an entrepreneur depends on the degree to which he has these characteristics.

Types of Entrepreneurship

Entrepreneurship is classified in various forms, and it can be seen that different types of entrepreneurship exist in the literature. Some of these have briefly explained below.

Tab. 1: Definitions of Entrepreneurship. **Source:** Korkmaz, 2012b: 210–211.

Year	Researcher	Definition
1725	Richard Cantillon	Entrepreneurship is the process of accumulating capital by bearing certain risks.
1797	Beaudeau	Entrepreneurship is the process of bearing risks, planning, managing, and organizing.
1803	Jean Baptiste Say	Entrepreneurship is the separation of earnings from capital gains.
1876	Francis Walker	The distinction is made between the person who provides the capital and the person who receives the interest and the person who makes a profit by using his managerial skills.
1934/ 1950	Joseph Schumpeter	Entrepreneurship is innovation. Entrepreneurship is a revolution in the product model by reorganizing the industry, using new products and new energy sources, using an invention, or more generally using new and untested technological possibilities and using the old in a new way.
1961	David McClelland	Entrepreneurship is the process of moving in an energetic and risky environment.
1964	Peter Drucker	Entrepreneurship is the maximization of opportunities.
1975	Albert Shapero	Entrepreneurship is to put up with failure by taking the initiative and organizing some socio-economic mechanisms.
1980	Karl Vesper	Entrepreneurship is a phenomenon that involves economists, psychologists, businessmen, and politicians.
1983	Gifford Pinchot	Entrepreneurship is to establish a new organization.
1985	Robert Hisrich	Entrepreneurship is the process of creating goods and services that take the necessary time and effort by taking financial, psychological and social risks in order to obtain monetary and personal satisfaction.

Opportunity entrepreneurship: To present a good or service to the marketplace by watching for potential and existing opportunities in the market (Kucuk, 2014, p.49).

Innovative entrepreneurship: To present new products to the market by making changes in existing products or designing new products (Tutar and Altinkaynak, 2014, p.43).

Follower entrepreneurship: It is the type of entrepreneurship that follows only developments in the market and entrepreneurs who make innovation (Kucuk, 2014, p.50).

Tab. 2: Characteristics of Entrepreneurs. **Source**: Cetinkaya-Bozkurt et al., 2012c: 232–233.

Characteristics	Researchers
Innovation	Herron (1992), Geisler (1993), Drucker (1998), Daft (2005), Hisrich et al.(2005), Hitt et al. (2005), Kucuk (2005)
Risk	Geisler (1993), Johnson and Hayes (1996), Drucker (1998) Hisrich et al.(2005), Hitt et al.(2005),Kucuk (2005), Zhao et al. (2005), Hewison and Badger (2006)
Change orientation	Luchsinger and Bagby (1987), Herron (1992), Hisrich et al. (2005), Hitt et al.(2005)
Focus on opportunities	Corbett and Hmieleski, (2005), Hitt et al.(2005)
Productivity	Daft (2005), Hitt et al. (2005), Hewison and Badger (2006)
Advanced communication skills	Hitt et al. (2005)
Proactivity	Hisrich et al. (2005)
Conscience and high achievement motivation	Daft, (2005)
Insistence on decisions	Hitt et al. (2005)
Internal control mood, tolerance to uncertainty, self-confidence	Koh (1996)

Internal entrepreneurship: Entrepreneurship is carried out in the current and operational business, or it is defined as the behavior of a manager as an entrepreneur (Agca and Yoruk, 2006, p.155).

Social entrepreneurship: it is to determine the ideas of the producers by using the interventional features, to create new structures and processes and to operate them in order to meet the social needs without regard to profit (Marangoz, 2012, p.84).

Opportunity entrepreneurship, innovative entrepreneurship, internal entrepreneurship, and follower entrepreneurship have economic benefits such as cost and profit. Therefore, these types of entrepreneurship can be described as "economic entrepreneurship". Social entrepreneurship is separated from other types of entrepreneurship because it is not considered profit-oriented. Social entrepreneurship aims to provide solutions to social problems and create social value.

Factors Influencing and Determining Entrepreneurship

Since entrepreneurship is a socio-economic phenomenon, it is influenced by many factors. It is argued that personality is one of the most important factors influencing and determining entrepreneurship. A person's need for success, risk-taking, and focus of the audit is the personal characteristics of an entrepreneur. However, entrepreneurship is a process of interaction and composition of many factors together with personality (Uckun and Girginer, 2012, p.99):

Kucuk (2014, p.67-68) collects factors that influence and determine entrepreneurship in four groups mainly as genetic, individual, demographic and environmental factors.

Genetic factors: These are innate factors such as communication skills in family, risk-taking and perseverance.
Individual factors: They include knowledge and positive or negative experiences.
Demographic factors: They are factors such as age, gender, level of education and income.
Environmental factors: They include the family and the immediate surroundings.

Marangoz (2012, p. 20) examines the factors that influence entrepreneurship in six groups: culture and education, family structure and social environment, psychological factors, legal, political and administrative factors, financial environment and religion:

Culture and education: While entrepreneurship is supported in some cultures, it is not supported in some cultures. It is called "entrepreneurship culture" that sets the stage for the development of entrepreneurship. On the other hand, education has a very important role in the development of entrepreneurship. For this reason, entrepreneurship-promoting training is needed.
Family structure and social environment: Family structure and social environment can have an encouraging or restrictive effect on entrepreneurship. While the presence of entrepreneurs in the family and social environment entail entrepreneurship, the absence of financial possibilities in the family limits entrepreneurship.
Psychological factors: Psychological factors such as having a responsibility, taking risks, having a sense of independence, having a high energy level, a tendency to think and forethought, behaving professionally, willingness to work, using brain power are influencing entrepreneurship.
Legal, political and administrative factors: Legal, political, and administrative arrangements in a country can be restrictive as well as encouraging entrepreneurship.
Financial environment: Governments are seriously influencing entrepreneurship with their fiscal policies. There is a need for appropriate fiscal policy and stable financial environment for entrepreneurship.

Religion: Religious values also affect entrepreneurship. In all religions, it can be seen that the activities are supporting entrepreneurship. Islamic religion shows support for entrepreneurship with verses and hadiths. Hz. Muhammad (SAV) himself traded and said that nine times out of ten of earnings is in trade and courage namely in entrepreneurship.

Morality: On the other hand, it can be said that moral values influence entrepreneurship. Only entrepreneurs who are actively seeking to earn money cannot succeed, but in order to succeed, they are necessary to consider moral values, that is, they must be moral entrepreneurs.

Organization of Akhism

Akhism means Arabic "brother, sister" or Turkish "generous, open-handed" (Ceylan, 2013, p.12). All the institutions or organizations founded by this name, on the meaning of the Akhism word also have a social purpose in it. Organization of Akhism, which reflects the concepts of Tradesmen and Craftsmen as of the foundation, is a social organization thought to have been founded in the 13th century by Ahi Evran-i Veli who is Seyh Nasiruddin Ebul-Hakayik Mahmut Bin Ahmad el Hoyri (Karagul, 2012, p.3). Akhism, together with a name given to tradesmen and craftsmen associations in Anatolia from the 13th century to the beginning of the 19th century (Bayram, 2012, p.83), it is a systematic structure that is very well regulated according to the era and established to provide "social justice" by making good and strong relations between the rich and the poor, the producer and the consumer, the labor and capital, the people and the state (Ozturk, 2015, p.1).

The Organization of Akhism, which has been recognized as an important institution in history since it leads the Turks to gain by halal way in Anatolia, to win with great effort, to give importance to merit and to respect the labor, stipulate not only among the craftsmen and tradesman but also with the social, political, and economic relations between all people and it is based on mutual respect and honesty; professional ethics and honesty, generosity and a debonairness foundation (Bakir, 2014, p.407). When the structure of the organization of Akhisim is examined, we encounter with a comprehensive structure. The Organization of Akhism is managed from a center, and the appointment and abdication of the Ahi presidents in all other centers connected to this center were accomplished with the approval of the president of Ahi Organization called Seyh'ul-Mesayih in Kırsehir (Koksal, 2007, p.110). It was not easy to become a member of the Organization of Akhism, which was very systematically developed, but it could be entitled to membership only after a rigorous education and discipline. The young person who wishes to join the Organization of Akhism has started the process by applying to a member who is a member of the Organization of Akhism. The young apprentice who applied organization subject to a long period of examination, training, and follow-up by the parent before the admission and the young apprentice was not accepted as a member even in the slightest discipline (Bayram, 2012, pp.85-87). In addition, moral and nurture researches are made about the young apprentice who wishes the membership, if the researches made are positive, the situation is discussed in the upper board meetings and if the candidate is suitable as a result of the interview, the apprentice is accepted to the membership with a ceremony (Ekinci, 1990, p.25). There were two types of memberships in the Organization of Akhism, both internally and externally. Those were apprentices, chiefs, and masters who actively worked were internal members of the organization and those who were unable to work for any reason were external members while members of the organization (Kilinc, 2010, p.11). Education in the Organization of Akhism was carried out mostly in the frame of Islamic rules and the aim of the organization was to train a good person to be happy in both worlds. In addition to moral education, there is a vocational education in the Organization of Akhism as well as moral and vocational training by starting from the moment of entering into the alliance of young Ahi. In these trainings, which based on the basis of obeying his ahi's, his acceptance of every word of his Ahi's, absence in any work without permission, and keep Ahi's promise, young apprentice was trained in shops and workshops and took vocational education by participating to workshop practices. (Kayadibi, 2000, p.179). These aspirants who get moral and vocational training fulfill the work that they done deservedly when they were Ahi. The basic values that the Akhism system reveals and the need for mankind today are briefly as follows (Ceylan, 2013, pp.79-82):

- Human is the most superior creature in the world.
- The world is a place of study and examination.
- Every man should be a profession and produce.
- Morality carry both earthly and aethereal value.
- It is important in Akhism is to educate the person and win the pleasure of Allah.
- Akhism is model to the whole humanity by bringing the measure to art, trade, and business ethics.
- There is a significant place for women in Akhism.
- Arrangements are made on the basis of "competency and merit".
- The "Mediation" implemented by the Ahi people nowadays it is called the "Ombudsman" system has been modeled on many countries in Europe.

- The Akhism system is the foundation of today's "syndicate" system as it protects the rights of producers and employees.
- The Akhism System, unlike the capitalist and socialist approach, has revealed an economic understanding based on human. The Akhisim System has trained entrepreneurs who value to humanity and take into account moral values.
- According to the Organization of Akhism, it is necessary to educate the ideal human type that takes care of human rights so that all these can be realized.
- The Organization of Akhism is the basis of both private and public institutions and organizations such as current Turkish Chambers of Tradesmen and Craftsmen, Employer Associations, Chambers of Commerce, Chambers of Industry, Chambers of Turkish Chambers and Commodity Exchanges (TOBB), Independent Industrialists and Businessmen Association (MUSIAD) Institution (SGK), Turkish Standards Institute (TSE), cooperatives and municipality (Demir, 1993, p.45; Ceylan, 2013, p.83).

Entrepreneurship in the Organization of Akhism

Enterprise and entrepreneurship are the main factors of economic development in our rapidly changing, developing, and the globalizing world in the recent period. The more the free economy and competition-based entrepreneurship expressed with free enterprise develop in a country the more the level of economic prosperity increases in that country. Therefore, entrepreneurship and economic development are directly proportional (Ozcan, 2013, p.1).

Entrepreneurship is not only dealt with in terms of materiality, but it also appears that many different areas entrepreneurial activities have been undertaken. No matter how the concepts of enterprise and entrepreneurship are taken into account, enterprise and entrepreneurship have both the aims of profit making and the provide services to the society services (Kucuk, 2011, p.15). Enterprise or entrepreneurship is one of the most important factors for production or an output to occur. Entrepreneurship is a process of creating value by undertaking financial, psychological and social risks while the entrepreneur has a vision, can look at events from different angles, desires to grow, and has a conceptual and innovative perspective (Karadal, 2016, pp.1-13). Sabuncuoglu and Tokol (2016, p.5) identify some of the functions of the entrepreneur and list them as follows:

- To produce goods or services by combining production factors,
- To determine the policies that the enterprise will follow,

- To increase the quality of the products to be produced and to find new customers,
- Find new products, new production methods, new distribution channels, new raw material channels,
- Taking risks, making profits or putting up with a loss.

Economic, social, cultural and political reasons are driving people to become entrepreneurs. In addition, reasons such as achieving social status, making a career, proving oneself, serving the community, contributing to employment, working freely, carrying out ideas and projects, obtaining economic power, using financial power and lacking other possibilities also push people to become entrepreneurs (Karadal, 2016, pp.5-17). Though concepts of entrepreneur or entrepreneurship bring material conclusions to mind, it is understood that in recent scientific studies entrepreneur or entrepreneurship concepts exist in many fields. These include corporate entrepreneurship, social entrepreneurship, internal entrepreneurship, social capital and entrepreneurship, ethical values, social responsibility and entrepreneurship, women entrepreneurship, immigrant entrepreneurship, global entrepreneurship. At the same time, in all these areas, entrepreneurship activities are supported both by private institutions and by state institutions. These institutions or organizations and their support are listed as follows (Karadal, 2016, p.323):

- KOSGEB New Entrepreneur Support and Applied Entrepreneurship Training
- Technical-Enterprise Capital Support
- TUBITAK Entrepreneur Programs
- TOBB Executive Committee
- Technoparks / Tech Parks
- Angel Investors
- Risk Capital
- Leasing
- Factoring- Forfaiting
- ISGEMs
- Business Development Centers
- TEKMERs
- Credit Guarantee Fund Inc. (KGF)
- Turkish Union of Tradesmen and Artisans Credit Cooperatives Unions (TESKOMB))

All these institutions or organizations that support enterprise or entrepreneurship contribute to the welfare of their communities. Entrepreneurship is at the heart of mankind and always shows itself in every field. If there are no entrepreneurs which is the most important factor of production factors, production cannot be realized even if other factors of production are brought together. Beyond being an economic value production, entrepreneurship is closely linked to social, cultural, and political dynamics. For this reason, the concept of entrepreneurship in researches comes to the forefront together with social and cultural concepts, and entrepreneurship seems to gain increasingly sociological content (Aytac, 2006, p.140). In this context, the Organization of Akhism, which is one of the most important social and moral organizations in the history of Turkish economy, has given importance to social and cultural assets as well as vocational and technical education and the organization was systematically found in services in order to raise the level of social welfare, to increase happiness, to reduce unemployment. In the understanding of Ottoman-Islamic society and state, it has been taken as basis that social interests come before personal interests. It is seen that this understanding starts from the closest units of responsibility understanding and encompasses the whole society and forms a type of social solidarity. The idea of service has emerged as an important element of morality and to serve the community is one of the most important tasks of each institution or organization (Solak, 2010 p.8). As these aims take place in the substructure of the Organization of Akhism, it may be said that the Organization of Akhism is a combination of Islamic beliefs and Turkish mores and customs, In addition, Akhism is not a sect, but in terms of its structure, stand working system it shows various similarities with a Sufi structure (Erdem, 2008, p.14). As a union that takes care of spiritual and moral aspects, the Organization of Akhism has always observed the benefit of both its members and society.

In the Organization of Akhism, which is an example of systematic study and structure, every trades group was collectively located at a certain market. Thus, the buyer could easily select the goods that he desired, as well as the tradesmans could easily control each other. Working together is also important for the quality control, but traders are prevented from selling the goods under the standards by this method which has possibilities to control each other and if the people who produce and sell goods below standards do not ignore the warnings and continue these trades, their workplace could close up and they could be removed from membership (Solak, 2010, p.12-13).

The Organization of Akhism has thought the benefits of its members, tradesmen, and craftsmen as much as the community. The Akhism organizations have worked in full solidarity with each other, and the most important features of these organizations were to have a mutual aid and social security fund called Middle Box, Tradesman Foundation, Tradesman Sector, or Tradesman

Box. Thanks to these aid boxes, the organization provided social security to its members, protected them from the lenders and provided raw materials (Bayram, 2012, p.88). From the old, mutual aid and social security fund that known as "Tradesmen Foundation", "Tradesman Box" and "Tradesman Pouch" was available in places where Turks lived in Anatolia. These boxes were called the Middle Box and the "Middle Box" was established separately for each occupational group in a city and town. Union members would donate to the box a certain portion of the income derived from trade. On the other hand, a certain amount was paid in the promotion of the slave, the apprentices, and the chiefs. In addition, the property income of box and the various donations made to the fund would constitute the other incomes of box. In order to open a shop for the new master, help would provide from the middlebox which constitute for the purpose of helping and solidarity among the tradesmen, and his master also would contribute to the capital (Durak, 2016, p.112). The expenses of the middlebox was constituting expenses of social trades meetings, expenses related to the purchase of raw materials which are distributed to the members of the union, expenses related to repair of union properties, taxes, dues, salaries, money spent on charitable works, aids for fares, illnesses, funeral burials and aids for tradesman who has bad economic situation and who expand to their works (Durak, 2016, p.112). At the same time, thanks to these boxes and cooperation, the doors to new business opportunities for the members of the organization were opened by facilitating their activities for entrepreneurship. It was believed that the human has solidaristic soul in structure in the Organization of Akhism and Organization of Akhism philosophy based on to the logic of walking together to great goals in unity and togetherness (Durak and Yucel, 2010, p.152). With this sentence of Ahi Evran, the founder of the union, "Being generous enough to give to others while you are in need", with this sentences the hope has been given to youth in apprenticeship and cruciferous periods. Thus, the future worries of the young people would be removed, and they were prevented from staying in the gap and was provided to work for a purpose (Irmis, 1998, pp.37-40). In this direction, the purposes of the Organization of Akhism can be summarized in general as follows:

- To provide solidarity among tradesmen,
- To increase the knowledge of the members' religion, moral, and other fields,
- To provide diplomas by training apprentices and masters as a result of vocational education,
- To increase the production quality and to adjust the prices,
- Help those who want to start a new business and those who want to grow their business.

According to the Ulgener, the Organization of Akhism has become an economic organization, as well as a professional organization that provides a warm and sincere community spirit among individuals (Ceylan, 2013, p.15). Support for those who want to establish a new business or want to expand their business, which is included in the main purposes of the Organization of Akhism, can be considered as the most important proof of the support given to the entrepreneurs by the organization. The concept of entrepreneurship, which should not only be restricted to the west or a certain turn, has been virtually brought in to action by supporting the entrepreneurs for almost six centuries when the Organization of Akhism was in existence. The ahi concept which means "my brother" has meanings like "generous, open-handed, high-minded" in old Turkish works such as "Divan-i Lugat`it Turk" and "Kutadgu Bilig" (Ozerkmen, 2004, p.59).The members of the Organization of Akhism are constantly help and support each other. Labor power, consumer, briefly human and nature are not exploited in the Organization of Akhism, justice is ensured between them, and individual and social prosperity and tranquility is provided. It is believed that in the Organization of Akhism, people have a solidarity spiritual structure and that people will walk to big targets in unity and togetherness (Soysal, 2013, p.9). This organization, which constantly support of being virtuous, moral, honest and not only serving each other but also serving to the society itself, has increased incomes of society and its members during the periods of existence and organization also has make an offer to the young people for establishment of self-business, and has materially and morally support the people who set up the business and who want to expand their business.

Conclusion and Discussion

Entrepreneurship is not only economic activity; it is also a social phenomenon. Entrepreneurs have social aims such as offering services and providing prosperity, social responsibility and fighting poverty as well as economic purposes such as being in production and making profits. In this context, entrepreneurship is constantly supported by various private and public institutions. In the thirteenth century, Organization of Akhism established in Anatolia with the suggestion of Haci Bektasi Veli to Ahi Evran and Organization of Akhism encouraged and supported the entrepreneurship. The Organization of Akhism can be regarded as one of the first entrepreneurship movements known before the Renaissance and Industrial Revolution in history. Unlike the entrepreneurial activities that started with the Renaissance and Industrial Revolution, Akhism is based on moral values such as brotherhood, unity, solidarity, cooperation, generosity, truthfulness and honesty and combines entrepreneurship with ethics. The Organization of Akhism attaches importance to ethical elements in entrepreneurship and adopts a human-focused working system that is not focused on economic interest

When the entrepreneurial activities of the Organization of Akhism are examined, it is seen that the concept of entrepreneurship which adopts human-focused, liberal and halal gains is different from capitalist and socialist economic understanding. Therefore, the Organization of Akhism attaches more importance to social entrepreneurship than economic entrepreneurship, and goes even further and leads the development of the concept of "moral entrepreneurship" by raising "moral entrepreneurs". The Organization of Akhism is a role model for future generations with its moral entrepreneurial activities.

As a result, it is revealed that there is a very close relationship between entrepreneurship and Organization of Akhism in this study by using related researches. Research shows that both economic entrepreneurship and social entrepreneurship movements are seen in the Organization of Akhism. It is understood that the Organization of Akhism has raised entrepreneurs (moral entrepreneurs) who consider the interests of others rather than their own interests, who are in prosocial (positive social) behaviors and who observe business ethics but do not ignore moral values.

Bibliography

Agca, V. / Yoruk, D.: "Bagimsiz Girisimcilik ve Ic Girisimcilik Arasindaki Farklar: Kavramsal Bir Cerceve". *Afyon Kocatepe Universitesi IIBF Dergisi VIII* (2), 2006, pp.155–173.

Aytac, O.: "Girisimcilik: Sosyo-Kulturel Bir Perspektif". *Dumlupinar Universitesi Sosyal Bilimler Dergisi 15*, 2006, pp.139–160.

Bakir, S.: "Bir Egitim Kurumu Olarak Ahilik ve Hulya Tas'in "*Gunumuz Bursa Esnafinda Ahilik Kulturunden Izler*"Adli Eseri". *Uluslararasi Turkce Edebiyat Kultur Egitim Dergisi 3*(1), 2014, pp.406–415.

Bayram, S.: "Osmanli Devleti'nde Ekonomik Hayatin Yerel Unsurlari: Ahilik Teskilâti ve Esnaf Loncalari". *Istanbul Universitesi Ilahiyat Fakultesi Dergisi 21*, 2012, pp.81–115.

Cetinkaya-Bozkurt, O. / Kalkan, A. / Koyuncu, O. / Alparslan, A. M. "Turkiye'de Girisimciligin Gelisimi: Girisimciler Uzerinde Nitel Bir Arastirma". *Suleyman Demirel Universitesi Sosyal Bilimler Enstitusu Dergisi 1*(15), 2012, pp.229–247.

Ceylan, K.: *Ahilik, Turk-Islam Medeniyetinde Dunyevi ve Uhrevi Sistem*. T.C. Gumruk ve Ticaret Bakanligi Kultur Yayinlari: Ankara. 2013.

Demir, G.: "Ahilik = Calisma, Bilim, Akil, Ahlak". *Perpa Dergisi 3*(22). 1993.

Durak, I.: "Sosyal Girisimcilik ve Ahilik Teskilati: Teorik Cerceve". *Erciyes Universitesi Iktisadi ve Idari Bilimler Fakultesi Dergisi 47*, 2016, pp.101–120.

Durak, I. / Yucel, A.: "Ahiligin Sosyo-Ekonomik Etkileri ve Gunumuze Yansimalari". *Suleyman Demirel Universitesi Iktisadi ve Idari Bilimler Fakultesi Dergisi 15*(2), 2010, pp.151–168.

Ekinci, Y.: *Ahilik ve Meslek Egitimi*. MEB Yayınları: Istanbul. 1990.

Erdem, E.: *Ahilik: Ahlakla Kalitenin Bulustugu Bir Esnaf Teskilatlanma Modeli*. Detay Yayincilik: Ankara. 2008.

Irmis, A.: "Bir Orgut Kulturu Ornegi Olarak Turk Milli Kulturunde Ahilik". *Turk Yurdu 18*(126), 1998, pp.35–42.

Karadal, H.: *Girisimcilik* (Gelistirilmis 4. ed.). Beta Yayincilik:Istanbul. 2016.

Karagul, M.: "Ahilik ve Sosyal Sermaye Baglaminda Is Ahlaki ve Uretim Iliskisi". *Akademik Bakis Dergisi Uluslararasi Hakemli Sosyal Bilimler Dergisi 32*, 2012, pp.1–16.

Kayadibi, F.: "Anadolu Selcuklular Doneminde Ahi Teskilatinda Egitim". *Istanbul Universitesi Sosyoloji Konferanslari Dergisi 26*, 2000, pp.177–188.

Kilinc, M.: "Ahiler ve Ahilik Kültürü". *EBA*, 2010, *pp.*1–16.

Koksal, M.: *Ahilik Kulturunun Dunu ve Bugunu*. Kirsehir Belediyesi Egitim Kultur Daire Baskanligi Yayinlari: Anakara. 2007.

Korkmaz, O.: "Universite Ogrencilerinin Girisimcilik Egilimlerini Belirlemeye Yonelik Bir Arastirma: Bulent Ecevit Universitesi Ornegi". *Afyon Kocatepe Universitesi IIBF Dergisi XIV*(II), 2012, pp.209–226.

Kucuk, O.: *Stratejik Isletme Bilgisi ve Yonetimi* (Gozden Gecirilmis 2. ed.). Seckin Yayincilik: Ankara. 2011.

Kucuk, O.: *Girisimcilik ve Kucuk Isletme Yonetimi* (Gozden Gecirilmis 7. ed.). Seckin Yayincilik: Ankara. 2014.

Marangoz, M.: *Girisimcilik* (1. ed.). Beta Yayincilik: Istanbul. 2012.

Onay, M. / Cavusoglu, S.: "Isletmelerde Girisimcilik Ozelligini Etkileyen Faktorler: Ic Girisimcilik". *Yonetim ve Ekonomi 17*(1), 2010, pp.47–67.

Ozcan, B.: *Anadoludaki Girisimcilik Faaliyetlerimiz*. 2013. (Retrieved 08, 22, 2017, from http://www.yildiraycicek.com/makale/4400/anadoludaki_girisimcilik_faaliyetlerimiz.html#.WZwWjj5JaM8).

Ozerkmen, N.: "Ahiligin Tarihsel-Toplumsal Temelleri ve Temel Toplumsal Fonksiyonlari-Sosyolojik Yaklasim". *Ankara Universitesi Dil ve Tarih-Cografya Fakultesi Dergisi 44*(2), 2004, pp.57–78.

Ozturk, N.: "Ahilik Teskilati ve Gunumuz Ekonomisi, Calisma Hayati ve Is Ahlaki Acisindan Degerlendirilmesi". *Dumlupinar Universitesi Sosyal Bilimler Dergisi 7*, 2002, pp.43–56.

Sabuncuoglu, Z. / Tokol, T.: *Isletme* (10. ed.). Alfa Aktuel Yayinlari: Bursa. 2016.

Serinkan, C. / Cabar, H.: Ahilikte Yonetim Kulturu. In: *Turk Kultur Tarihinde Ahilik ve Denizli Ahiligi*. Denizli Belediyesi Kultur Yayinlari: Denizli. 2012. pp. 42–51.

Solak, F.: *Ahilik Kurulusu, Ilkeleri ve Fonksiyonlari*. Istanbul Ticaret Odası: Istanbul. 2010.

Soysal, A.: "Isletmelerin Basarisinda Ahilik Ilke ve Uygulamalarinin Onemi: Bir Degerlendirme". *Cimento Endustrisi Isverenleri Sendikasi 27*(2), 2013, pp. 6–19.

Tutar, H., / Altinkaynak, F.: *Girisimcilik (Temel Girisimcilik ve Is Kurma Sureci)* (2. ed.). Detay Yayincilik: Ankara. 2014.

Uckun, N., / Girginer, N.: "Girisimciligi Etkileyen Faktorler: Eskisehir Organize Sanayi Bolgesindeki Metal Sektoru Girisimcilerine Yonelik Bir Uygulama". *Girisimcilik ve Inovasyon Yonetimi Dergisi 1*(1), 2012, pp.97–112.

Hamza Çeştepe[1] and Gizem Mukiyen Avcı

Globalization, Institutional Quality and Foreign Direct Investment: Panel Data Analysis for Developing Countries

Abstract: Foreign direct investment, as an important instrument of economic development for developing countries, provides employment, technology transfer and productivity improvement by eliminating the capital deficiency in these countries. In recent years, foreign direct investments have increased considerably in developing countries. This increase makes it necessary to investigate the determinants of foreign direct investment. This paper focuses particularly on globalization and institutional quality variables that determine foreign direct investment using panel data of 48 developing countries from 1996 to 2015. The results suggest that globalization and institutional quality have a positive effect on foreign direct investment.

Keywords: Foreign Direct Investment, Globalization, Institutional Quality, Developing Countries, Panel Data Analysis

Introduction

Foreign direct investment which represents an investment that has been carried out by people or organizations, in foreign countries outside their national borders, is considered as one of the main factors that affect long-term economic growth. Therefore, the study of the relationship between foreign direct investment and the economic growth and the factors which affect foreign direct investment are among the subjects which draw attention in the economics literature.

The foreign direct investment brings various economic benefits to the host country. First of all, foreign direct investment directly contributes to the capital stock and the production capacity of the host country. At the same time, it affects the production process positively by bringing along the knowledge of technology and industry to the country it has gone. In other words, foreign direct investment indirectly contributes to the economic growth of the host country by providing both direct capital stock and technology transfer (Okada 2013, p. 132). Foreign currency that enters the country via foreign direct investment increases the export in long-term and creates positive progress on the balance of

1 Corresponding author

payments as a result. Through all these contributions, foreign direct investment has an increasing effect on domestic competition and in the number of new firms entering the market and has a decreasing effect on the unemployment problem.

Aside from these positive impacts, foreign direct investment has certain negative impacts on the countries it has gone to. In this regard, countries have various policies in accordance with their own structure and objectives. When the country experience is studied, it can be seen that some countries have promotive and some have restrictive policies regarding foreign capital mobility.

The development of foreign direct investment dates back to the 1950s. In the first years of this period, most of the foreign direct investment was directed to Latin American countries, due to Japan's limiting policies toward investment and due to the fact that the countries such as England, France and Germany were mostly interested in portfolio investment rather than foreign investment. As a result of oil crisis which took place in the 1970s, there was a deceleration in the pace of increase in the foreign direct investment, even though it continued to rise. In this period, the investment of Western Europe – and Japan-based multinational corporations were on the rise along with American-based multinational corporations, but the underdeveloped countries had some decrease in their investment as a result of their negative policies. The instabilities in Latin American countries and the liberal and supportive policies in line with the international expansion policies of underdeveloped countries after the debt crisis which took place in the 1980s resulted in foreign direct investments orienting to Eastern Asia countries (Seyidoğlu 2009, p. 610).

With the financial liberalization and the globalization process which occurred in the 1980s, many countries carried out various policies in line with programs which were introduced by international organizations such as IMF and the World Bank, in order to encourage foreign direct investment (Gammoudi et al. 2016, p. 3). Liberal policies which were applied to encourage economic growth increase, to reduce poverty, and to provide of foreign direct investment entry, resulted in a worldwide increase in foreign direct investment. According to the World Investment Report which was published by the United Nations Conference on Trade and Development (UNCTAD) in 2017, world foreign direct investment flow reached 1.9 trillion in 2007. The foreign direct investment entry which was directed to developing countries doubled between 1980–1985 and 1985–1990. It can be seen that by the year of 2014, the developing countries had reached a higher point than developed countries with a 703-billion-dollar worth of foreign direct investment (UNCTAD, 2017). These developments require a detailed study of the factors which caused the foreign direct investment increase in developing countries.

There are various studies available in the literature on the factors which determine foreign direct investment, although the number of studies that analyze the subject within the context of globalization and institutive quality is rather limited. The impact of the factors in question to the foreign direct investment has been analyzed in the example of developing countries in this study. The foreign direct investment determinants for the period of 1996–2015 have been studied with the panel data analysis in 48 developing countries.

The study consists of three chapters apart from the introduction and conclusion. The theories on foreign direct investment have been addressed in the second part of the study, and the empirical studies on the area in question were given in the following chapter. In the fourth chapter on which the empirical analysis was applied, the model and the data set were introduced, and after that, the method and the results of the analysis were given. Lastly, a general evaluation regarding the study has been carried out in the conclusion.

Theoretical Framework

There are various theories which address the subject of foreign direct investment. Regarding the scope of this study, The Neoclassical Trade Theory, The Internalization Theory and The OLI Theory brought forward by Dunning which includes both of these aforementioned theories were given in this chapter.

The Neoclassical Trade Theory, which has been brought forward in the 1960s, is based on the main argument of Hechsher-Ohlin Trade Model. The theory suggests the idea which the foreign companies were motivated to transfer their abundant production factor to the places where the gainings on the factor are higher. With the motivations in question, foreign companies will continue to be located in different countries until the factor prices are even. In other words, The Neoclassical Trade Theory tries to explain the motivation which supports the investors who manage an abroad production chain, but export the products back to their own countries, with the Hechsher-Ohlin Trade Model (Phung 2016, p. 3).

Another theory is The Internalization Theory which was brought forward by Buckley and Casson in 1976. The internalization theory is grounded on the companies internalizing their markets and making foreign direct investments regarding their own production processes in order to avoid the negative effects of market uncertainties under imperfect market conditions. The internalization of the production process causes certain advantages and disadvantages. The advantages of internalization can be classified as minimizing the governmental intervention in the forms of avoidance of bargain and buyer uncertainty, prevention of time delays, enabling transfer and discriminatory pricing. Management and communication expenses can be presented as internalization costs. Locating the imperfections in the main areas such as the human capital, information, marketing and management expertise causes crucial time lapse and transaction costs in the imperfect market conditions. The internalization process which has been preferred in order to avoid these factors will continue to the point where the advantages of internalization is even with the costs (Agarwal 1980, p. 753).

The last theory in hand regarding foreign direct investment is Dunning's eclectic theory OLI. The origin of eclectic theory dates back to the mid-1950s. In the doctoral thesis written by Dunning (1958) and afterward turned into a book, British Manufacturing Industry's foreign direct investments directed to the USA are addressed. The activities of companies outside their national borders have been explained in the general sense, through three sub-paradigms called Ownership-O, Location-L and Internalization-I.

According to the OLI paradigm, there are three conditions for companies to meet in order to make foreign direct investment abroad. First of these conditions is related to the extent of a national firm's *competitive advantages* to another national firm on supplying their products to a certain market or staple. These advantages which are defined as ownership-specific effects can arise from the firm's privileged possession, possessing a series of income-generating assets, or the ability to coordinate these assets along with other assets within national borders. Another condition is about to what extent the firms see it fit to do these added-value increasing activities abroad. The transportation and shipment costs are influential on the investment decision. The last condition is that to what extent the firms consider the usage of assets and/or the internalization of the markets for production in the best/most profitable way. Factors such as the market uncertainties originating from imperfect market conditions, transaction costs, trade barriers, etc., influence the firm's decision of making a production on its own country or making foreign direct investment in the process in question (Dunning 2001, pp. 174–176). In the broad sense, it is stated that for a firm to make foreign direct investment outside its national borders, it is required to have certain advantages on possession, location and internalization.

On the basis of OLI paradigm, Dunning (1980) classified foreign direct investment as four groups called *market-seeking, resource-seeking, efficiency-seeking* and *strategic asset-seeking* investments. Market-seeking investments aim to reach local and/or sectional markets, resource-seeking investments aim to reach physical and human resources, efficiency-seeking investments aim to provide production rationalisation by benefiting from scale economies and strategic asset-seeking investments aim to connect the assets such as technology, organizational economy and markets with foreign nets and to develop sectional and global strategies (Faeth 2009, pp. 171–172).

On the basis of the theories regarding foreign direct investment and especially Dunning's eclectic theory, the studies which examine the factors affecting the decision on foreign direct investment demonstrate that the differences in the gainings of the host country's cost structure, the market size and the institutional structure of the country are of crucial importance. In other words, it is expected that for countries to have a proper trade and investment regime, a good substructure, property rights, political consistency, macroeconomic consistency and a well-educated labor force would be an influence on countries which want to make investment abroad/overseas (Thirlwall 2006, p. 491).

Empirical Literature

Studies regarding the determinants of foreign direct investments are on the rise since the 2000s. It can be seen from the studies which mainly use panel data analysis method that the variables such as capital controls and financial openness are mostly used as the indicators of globalization. The findings of the studies present vary (Okada 2013, Asiedu and Lien 2004, Lane and Milesi-Ferretti 2007, Montiel and Reinhart 1999). Some studies have shown that globalization has a positive effect on direct foreign investments, while in some studies it has a negative effect.

In the recent years, studies which accept institutional quality as a crucial factor to foreign direct investment have come into prominence. In the relevant studies, there is an agreement on the idea that the improvement in the countries' institutional quality would have a direct positive impact on foreign direct investment. It is stated that with the disappearance of uncertainties and building an environment of trust in the countries without corruption, political inconsistencies and bribe, where the freedom of speech, intellectual property rights, democracy, fundamental rights, and freedoms are protected, foreign direct investment will increase (Stein and Daude 2001, Globerman and Shapiro 2002, Li and Resnick 2003, Busse and Hefeker 2007, Bénassy-Quéré et al. 2007, Masron and Nor 2013).

Okada (2013), who discusses the effect of institutional quality on the international capital movements, has studied 112 countries in 1985–2008 in his study. The result of this study is that the financial openness and institutional quality do not have a meaningful effect on international capital movements, but the interactions between variables have a meaningful effect. In other words, the partial effect of financial openness has shown an increase based on institutional quality level.

Anyanwu (2012) who studied the foreign direct investment movements in 53 African countries in 1996–2008 used OLS, FGLS, and GMM analysis techniques. The study approached foreign direct investment as a function of market size, financial openness, financial development, macroeconomic consistency, exchange rates, human capital, growth rate, institutional quality and natural resources equipment. As a result of the analysis, it has been concluded that the financial growth has a negative effect on foreign direct investment, although the rest of the variables in the model have a meaningful and positive effect.

Mottaleb and Kalirajan (2010) intended to determine the factors which affect foreign direct investment in developing countries, on the basis of panel data which belong to 68 low-income and lower-middle income countries in 2005–2007. After the analysis, it was concluded that in terms of countries' level of income, lower-middle income countries and Asian countries are very successful on attracting foreign direct investment compared to low-income African and Latin American countries. It is stated that lower-middle income countries and Asian countries possess more connections with the global markets via the trade route and they provide more work-friendly environment compared to other countries is influential.

In Leitao (2012)'s work which discusses the relationship between foreign direct investment and globalization, the market size, trade openness, globalization index, human capital and rural population variables have been included into the model as foreign direct investment determinants. As a result of the analysis which was performed on the basis of the dataset gathered from 33 countries in 1990–2008, it can be seen that market size, trade openness, human capital and globalization have a statistically meaningful effect on foreign direct investment.

Wadhwa and Reddy (2011) have studied the effects of the certain market, resource, efficiency-seeking factors to foreign direct investment in 10 Asian countries in 1991–2008. In the study, level of income, population and export have been included in the model to represent the market-seeking investments; inflation has been included in the model to represent the efficiency-seeking investment and export, internet users, mobile subscribers and roads paved have been included in the model to represent the resource-seeking investments. It was concluded that all the factors in hand have a meaningful effect on foreign direct investment.

In her work which she studied the foreign direct investment determinants, Phung (2016) classified the foreign direct investment determinants as financial development, market size, macroeconomic consistency, trade, substructure, natural resources and labor force on the basis of Dunning's OLI paradigm. Three datasets have been used in the study which are 1990–2014 (45 countries),

1980–2014 (30 countries) and Barro and Lee dataset 1980–2014 (34 countries). According to the results of the analysis, it was concluded that trade and infrastructure quality is important for developing countries, and countries which do more trade and have better infrastructure can attract more foreign direct investment. It has been found that natural resources and labor force have a meaningful effect on foreign direct investment but human capital, macroeconomic consistency, market size and financial development do not have a meaningful effect.

Kar and Tatlısöz (2008), who studied the factors which determine the foreign direct investment movements which came to Turkey between 1980 and 2003, have concluded that net international reserves, GNP, external openness, electric energy production index and investment encouragements have a positive effect on foreign direct investment but real exchange rates and labor force costs have a negative impact.

Artan and Hayaloğlu (2015) have analyzed the economic and institutional determinants of foreign direct investment. According to the results of the analysis of 29 OECD countries in 1990–2012, it has been concluded that the improvement in institutional structure has a positive effect on foreign direct investment.

Özşahin (2016) studied the effect of Turkey's institutional quality level on the foreign direct investment level. According to the results of the analysis regarding the years between 1998 and 2014 and conducted on the basis of three different models, it was concluded that the low economic risk level has an increasing effect on the foreign direct investment towards Turkey, and at the same time has a reducing effect on foreign direct investment volatility.

Empirical Analysis

The factors which determine foreign direct investment have been examined in the study with panel data analysis for 48 developing countries[2] with lower- and higher-middle income for the years 1996–2015. Firstly, cross-sectional dependency has been examined by using CDLM test which was developed by Pesaran (2007), and because of the existence of cross-sectional dependency, the

2 Related countries are Albania, Algeria, Angola, Argentina, Bangladesh, Bolivia, Botswana, Brazil, Bulgaria, Cameroon, China, Colombia, Republic of Congo, Cote d'Ivoire, Dominican Republic, Ecuador, Egypt, El Salvador, Gabon, Ghana, Guatemala, Guyana, Honduras, India, Indonesia, Iran, Jordan, Kenya, Malaysia, Mexico, Mongolia, Morocco, Nicaragua, Nigeria, Pakistan, Panama, Paraguay, Peru, Philippines, Romania, South Africa, Sudan, Surinam, Thailand, Tunisia, Turkey, Vietnam, Zambia.

stationary of the series has been examined with Cross-sectionally Augmented Dickey-Fuller (CADF) unit root test from the second generation of unit root tests which are used under the cross-sectional dependency. At the same time, the necessary tests regarding the efficiency of random and fixed effects estimator, and unit and/or time effects in panel data model have been applied. In this context, it was concluded that the one-way unit effect is valid and the random effects estimators are effective. Lastly, it was checked if there are deviations from the assumptions, and finally the model was predicted via Parks-Kmenta robust estimator for the removal of variance, autocorrelation and cross-sectional dependences.

The model used in the study is as follows:

$$FDI_{it} = \propto_{0it} + \propto_{1it} KOF_{it} + \propto_{2it} INS_{it} + \propto_{3it} TRADE_{it} + \propto_{4it} INF_{it} + \propto_{5it} GDPpc_{it} + \propto_{6it} LABOR_{it} + \propto_{7it} MOBILE_{it} + \mu_i + \lambda_t + \varepsilon_{it}$$

$$(i=1\ldots n;\ t=1\ldots.t)$$

where FDI denotes foreign direct investment entry's share within GDP, KOF is globalization index, INS is institutional quality index, TRADE is foreign trade's share in GDP, INF is annual inflation GDP deflator, GDPpc is per capita income growth, LABOR is the labor force participation level for above the age of 15 and MOBILE is cellular mobile subscription. Additionally, i and t, respectively, identify country and time, α is prediction index, μ is country constant, λ is time constant and ε represents error term.

On the basis of studies about the potential determinants of foreign direct investment, the determinants of foreign direct investment can be narrowed down to market size, macroeconomic consistency, trade, financial development, substructure, natural resources, labor force and skilled labor force. In this regard, market size, labor force and macroeconomic consistency are considered essential for market-seeking, natural resource–seeking and trade openness–seeking investors, and financial development, substructure and skilled labor force are considered essential for efficiency-seeking investors (Phung 2016, p. 4). However, the fact that the variables which have been supported theoretically have not been proved empirically in a clear way necessitate a research on different country samples with different explanatory variables.

In this context, especially the globalization and the institutional quality variables on focus have been included in the model, along with the foreign trade, inflation, domestic income level, labor force and cellular subscriptions. The globalization data was obtained from KOF Globalization Index, which was prepared by Swiss Economic Institute, and institutional quality data was obtained from Political Risk Components dataset, which was prepared by The

International Country Risk Guide (ICRG). The other variables in the model were obtained from World Development Indicators (WDI) dataset. The inflation, domestic income level and labor force have been included in the model as market-seeking, foreign trade as resource-seeking and cellular mobile subscriptions as efficiency-seeking. All the variables in the model except inflation are expected to have a positive effect on foreign direct investment. As a sign of macroeconomic instability, the increase in the inflation rate is expected to have a negative effect on foreign direct investment. The information regarding variables is included in Tab. 1.

KOF Globalization Index surveys the general globalization level of countries by using five sub-indexes called actual economic flows, economic restrictions, data on information flows, data on personal contact and data on cultural proximity data in addition with three sub-indexes called economic, social and political. The index in question values between 1 and 100. The fact that the globalization index values high demonstrates that the globalization level of the country is high.

Institutional quality data obtained from the Political Risk Rating which consists of 12 subcomponents is presented by ICRG. The subcomponents in question are Government Stability, Socioeconomic Conditions, Investment Profile, Internal

Tab. 1: Information Regarding Variables

Abbreviation	Definition	Data Sources	Representing	Expected Signs
FDI	Net Foreign Direct Investment inflows (%of GDP)	WDI	–	
KOF	KOF Globalization Index	ETH, Zurich	Globalization	+
INS	Institutional Quality Index	ICRG-PRS Group	Institutions	+
TRADE	Trade (%of GDP)	WDI	Trade Openness	+
INF	Inflation GDP Deflator (Annual)	WDI	Macroeconomic Stability	+
GDPpc	GDP Per Capita Growth (Annual %)	WDI	Market Size	+
LABOR	Total Labor Force Participation Rate (%of total population ages 15+)	WDI	Employment	+
MOBILE	Mobile Cellular Subscriptions	WDI	Infrastructure	+

Tab. 2: Descriptive Statistics

Variable	Obs.	Mean	Standard Deviation	Minimum	Maximum
FDI	960	3.543	4.596	-16.589	43.912
KOF	960	53.151	10.038	22.560	79.120
INS	960	61.870	8.528	27.167	79.417
TRADE	960	76.808	38.996	15.636	220.407
INF	960	17.297	178.591	-29.691	5399.507
GDPpc	960	2.759	3.599	-14.347	30.357
LABOR	960	61.668	9.557	39.904	79.479
MOBILE	960	50.036	47.589	0.00	180.699

Conflict, External Conflict, Corruption, Military in Politics, Religious Tensions, Law and Order, Ethnic Tensions, Democratic Accountability and Bureaucracy Quality. The index which consists of the total of all the subcomponents is 100 points to the maximum. The fact that the index is of high value implies that the country has low political risk regarding institutional quality and its institutional quality is high. The descriptive statistics regarding variables are included in Tab. 2.

When Tab. 2 is examined, it can be seen that the foreign direct investment's share within GDP occurred approximately in the level of 3.54 for 48 developing countries in the years between 1996 and 2015. In the research period, the most foreign direct investment attracting country is Mongolia in 2011, and the lowest investment level belongs to Surinam in 2000. The country with the lowest globalization and institutional quality levels is Sudan with 22.56 and 27.17, respectively, and the country with the highest levels is Malaysia with 79.12 and 79.42.

Before applying the unit root tests for the stationary of the series, the presence of cross-sectional dependence should be investigated in the series and the model. The detection of cross-sectional dependence has importance for the selection of unit root tests which will be applied. In the case of the existence of cross-sectional dependence, unit root tests which take cross-sectional dependence into account should be used. For this reason, cross-sectional dependence analysis was performed with the CD_{LM1} test in the study, and the findings of the test are included in Tab. 3.

In Tab. 3, "The cross-sectional dependence is absent" hypothesis, which is the null hypothesis for both the whole series and CD_{LM1} test, was rejected. Hence, the existence of cross-sectional dependence is decided.

Tab. 3: Results of the Cross-Sectional Dependence Test (CD_{LM1} Test)

Variables	T-value	P-value
FDI	10.33	0.000
KOF	101.06	0.000
INS	23.34	0.000
TRADE	27.29	0.000
INF	22.87	0.000
GDPpc	29.02	0.000
LABOR	−1.78	0.000
MOBILE	143.66	0.000
MODEL	−3.294	0.000

Tab. 4: CADF Unit Root Test Results

Variables	CIPS Test (Levels)	CIPS Test (First Differences)	
	Constant+Trend	Constant	Constant
FDI	-2.804*	-2.381*	
KOF	-2.888*	-2.434*	
INS	-2.898*	-2.389*	
TRADE	-2.045	-1.624	-2.609*
INF	-3.124*	-3.039*	
GDPpc	-2.845*	-2.319*	
LABOR	-2.096	-1.827	-2.263*
MOBILE	-3.213*	-2.703*	
Critical Values:			
1 %	-2.760	-2.250	-2.250
5 %	-2.620	-2.110	-2.110
10 %	-2.540	-2.030	-2.030

* indicates significance in 1 %.

In the presence of cross-sectional dependence, second-generation unit root tests which take the cross-sectional dependence into account must be used, in order to analyze the stationary of the series. In this context, the findings obtained from Cross-sectionally Augmented Dickey-Fuller (CADF) unit root test which has been brought forward by Pesaran (2007) are included in Tab. 4.

TRADE and LABOR variables are stationary for *I(1)*. In the estimation of panel data models, there are alternative models such as classical model, primary

Tab. 5: Test Results Regarding the Presence of Individual and/or Time Effects

Test	Statistic	P-value	Null Hypothesis	Decision
Presence of Individual and Time Effects				
LR Test	291.38	0.00	H_0: At least one of standard deviation of individual and time effects is equal to 0.	H_0 Reject
Presence of Individual Effects				
F Test	12.33	0.00	H_0: Individual effects are equal to 0.	H_0 Reject
LR Test	95.71	0.00	H_0: Standard deviation of individual effects is equal to 0.	H_0 Reject
Breush-Pagan LM Test	977.65	0.00	H_0: Variance of individual effects is equal to 0.	H_0 Reject
Presence of Time Effects				
LR Test	0.00	1.00	H_0: Standard deviation of time effects is equal to 0.	H_0 Not Reject
Hausman Test				
Hausman Test	12.89	0.075	H_0: No correlation between explanatory variables and individual effect	H_0 Not Reject

differences model, fixed effects model and random effects model. Hence, it is necessary to apply certain tests in order to determine the proper model among the models. In a situation with no individual or time effects, in other words, in a situation that all the observations on the model are homogeneous, using the fixed effects model or random effects model is suitable. Therefore, the first thing to decide after the establishment of one-way or two-way units and/or the time effects' presence is to decide if these effects are fixed or random (Tatoğlu 2012, pp. 161–180). In this sense, the test results regarding the presence of individual and/or the time effects and if these effects are fixed or random are included in Tab. 5.

When the test results regarding the presence of individual and time effects are studied, LR test H_0 hypothesis which examines the presence of individual and time effects is rejected. Thus, it is concluded that the two-way model is not valid. Afterward, the presence of individual and time effects has been tested one by one. According to the results of these tests, it is concluded that there is a one-way individual effect, therefore the classic model is not suitable. At the same time, by applying the Hausman test, "There is no correlation between explanatory variables and individual effect" hypothesis has been tested. Since H_0 hypothesis

Tab. 6: Deviations from the Basic Assumptions

Test	Statistic	P-value	Null Hypothesis	Decision
Heteroscedasticity				
Levene, Brown and Forsythe Test	W0: 16.172 W50: 11.302 W10: 14.498	0.000 0.000 0.000	H_0: No Heteroscedasticity	H_0 Reject
Autocorrelation				
Bhargava et al. Durbin-Watson	0.949		H_0: No Autocorrelation	H_0 Reject
Baltagi-Wu LBI	1.034			
Cross-Sectional Dependence				
Pesaran Test	12.330	0.000	H_0: No Cross-Sectional Dependence	H_0 reject

could not be rejected, it is concluded that the random effect estimators are more efficient.

The last condition that should be checked is if there is any deviation from the basic assumptions. It is supposed that there is no heteroscedasticity, autocorrelation or cross-sectional dependence in panel data models. Heteroscedasticity can be tested with Levene, Brown and Forsthe test, autocorrelation can be tested with Franzi and Narendranathan's Durbin Watson test and Baltagi-Wu's Locally Best Invariant tests (LBI), and cross-sectional dependence can be tested with the Pesaran test in the random effects model (Tatoğlu 2012, p. 232). The information regarding the test results in question is included in Tab. 6.

When Tab. 6 is reviewed, Levene, Brown and Forsythe test statistics and Pesaran test statistics have demonstrated that there are heteroscedasticity and cross-sectional dependence, respectively. At the same time, it is concluded there is an autocorrelation since critical value of DW and LBI statistics was lower than two.

When at least one of heteroscedasticity, autocorrelation and cross-sectional dependence is present, the efficiency of standard errors is affected. In such a case, robust estimations must be made by acquiring robust standard errors. By taking deviations from the assumption into account, random effects model has been estimated with Parks-Kmenta robust estimator in the study. The information regarding random effects regression results and robust random estimator results were concluded in Tab. 7.

According to the results of robust estimation, globalization and institutional quality have an increasing effect on foreign direct investment as expected.

Tab. 7: Regression Results

	Random Effect Regression Results		Robust Regression Results (Parks-Kmenta)	
Variables	**Coefficient**	**P-value**	**Coefficient**	**P-value**
KOF	0.129	(0.000)***	0.074	(0.000)***
INS	0.071	(0.009)***	0.036	(0.053)*
ΔTRADE	0.047	(0.001)***	0.037	(0.000)***
INF	0.017	(0.000)***	0.006	(0.024)**
GDPpc	0.093	(0.011)**	0.035	(0.006)***
ΔLABOR	0.336	(0.032)**	0.123	(0.029)**
MOBILE	0.008	(0.027)**	0.009	(0.002)***
Constant	-8.533	(0.000)***	-3.246	(0.047)**

***, **, * indicates significance at 1 %, 5 % and 10 %, respectively.

A one-unit increase in the country's globalization level increases the foreign direct investment level by 0.07. Similarly, a one-unit increase in the country's institutional quality increases the foreign direct investment level approximately by 0.03. Globalizaiton and institutional quality have a positive impact on investment and economic growth in the countries with strong institutional structure such as protection of the entrepreneur's rights, the absence of expropriation and corruption, protection of property rights, an environment of trust which ensures the practice of contracts. In countries with strong institutional structures; protection of entrepreneurs' rights, lack of risk of expropriation and corruption, protection of property rights, and an environment of trust which ensures the applicability of contracts play a role as a factor promoting investment and economic growth.

On the other hand, results for control variables show that trade's share in GDP, per capita income variable, labor-force participation rate and cellular mobile subscriptions series are significant and have a positive effect on foreign direct investment as expected. Apart from other control variables, the labor force has a relatively stronger effect on foreign direct investment. These findings can be explained by developing countries having a relatively cheaper and more labor force. Cheap labor force as a production cost reducing factor may cause foreign countries to direct their investments towards developing countries. Even though the inflation variable is expected to have a negative effect on foreign direct investment, since it represents macroeconomic instability in a country, the results of the analysis showed that it has a positive and significant effect. However, it can be seen that it has a much lower efficiency when compared to the other explanatory variables in the model. Countries having a low infrastructure quality would increase production and transportation costs, resulting in a reduction in productivity, production and investments. The results of the analysis which indicated that foreign direct investment would increase in a country with better infrastructure have met the expectations.

Conclusion

What are the factors that affect the foreign direct investment which is one of the main factors of economic growth? Which factors are crucial for countries to attract foreign direct investment? There are many studies that address these questions and investigate the determinants of foreign direct investment. The studies in question differ by country, year and variables they examined. In the recent years, it can be seen that the studies which analyze the effect of the countries' institutional structures on the foreign direct investment level within the frame of institutional economics point of view have come into prominence.

Foreign direct investment determinants have been analyzed with panel data analysis in 48 developing countries for the period of 1996–2015 in this study. The findings of the analysis demonstrate that the improvement on the country's globalization and institutional quality levels has an increasing effect on foreign direct investment. Countries' liberal policies in the financial liberation and globalization process have an important part on the increase in foreign direct investment. The institutional quality levels of countries along with their globalization levels are efficient in the elimination of market uncertainties, in the providing of a trustworthy investment environment and the increase of foreign direct investment. The findings of the analysis have met the expectations in this regard.

The findings of the study demonstrate to the policymakers that since the further progress of countries' globalization levels is inevitable, it is important to enhance the institutional quality levels in order to ensure the necessary capital entry, particularly in the developing countries.

References

Agarwal, Jamuna P.: "Determinants of foreign direct investment: A survey". *Review of World Economics* 116(4), 1980, pp. 739–773.

Anyanwu, John C.: "Why does foreign direct investment go where it goes?: New evidence from African countries". *Annals of Economics & Finance* 13(2), 2012, pp. 425–462.

Artan, Seyfettin / Hayaloğlu, Pınar: "Dogrudan yabancı sermaye yatırımlarının kurumsal belirleyicileri: OECD ülkeleri örneği". *Ege Akademik Bakış* 15(4), 2015, pp. 551–564.

Asiedu, Elizabeth / Lien, Donald: "Capital controls and foreign direct investment". *World Development* 32(3), 2004, pp. 479–490.

Bénassy-Quéré, Agnès / Coupet, Maylis / Mayer, Thierry: "Institutional determinants of foreign direct investment". *The World Economy* 30(5), 2007, pp. 764–782.

Buckley, Peter J. / Casson, Mark: The Future of the Multinational Enterprise. The Macmillan Press: London. 1976.

Busse, Matthias / Hefeker, Carsten: "Political risk, institutions and foreign direct investment". *European Journal of Political Economy* 23(2), 2007, pp. 397–415.

Dunning, John H.: "American investment in British manufacturing industry". *London: Allen & Unwin*. 1958.

Dunning, John H.: "Toward an eclectic theory of international production: Some empirical tests". *Journal of International Business Studies* 11(1), 1980, pp. 9–31.

Dunning, John H.: "The eclectic (OLI) paradigm of international production: Past, present and future". *International Journal of the Economics of Business* 8(2), 2001, pp. 173–190.

Faeth, Isabel: "Determinants of foreign direct investment – A tale of nine theoretical models". *Journal of Economic Surveys* 23(1), 2009, pp. 165–196.

Gammoudi, Mouna / Cherif, Mondher / Asongu, Simplice A.: "FDI and growth in the MENA countries: Are the GCC countries different?" *African Governance and Development Institute AGDI Working Paper 16/015*, 2016, pp. 1–42.

Globerman, Steven / Shapiro, Daniel: "Global foreign direct investment flows: The role of governance infrastructure". *World Development* 30(11), 2002, pp. 1899–1919.

Kar, Muhsin / Tatlısöz, Fatma: "Türkiye'de doğrudan yabancı sermaye hareketlerini belirleyen faktörlerin ekonometrik analizi". *KMU İİBF Dergisi* 10(14), 2008, pp. 436-458.

Lane, Philip. R. / Milesi-Ferretti, Gian Maria: "The external wealth of nations mark II: Revised and extended estimates of foreign assets and liabilities, 1970–2004". *Journal of International Economics* 73(2), 2007, pp. 223–250.

Leitao, Nuno C.: "Foreign direct investment and globalization". *Actual Problems of Economics* 4, 2012, pp. 398–405.

Li, Quan / Resnick Adam: "Reversal of fortunes: Democratic institutions and foreign direct investment inflows to developing countries". *International Organization* 57 (1), 2003, pp. 175–211.

Masron, Tajul A. / Nor, Eliza: "FDI in ASEAN-8: Does institutional quality matter?" *Applied Economics Letters* 20(2), 2013, pp. 186–189.

Montiel, Peter / Reinhart, Carmen M.: "Do capital controls and macroeconomic policies influence the volume and composition of capital flows? Evidence from the 1990s". *Journal of International Money and Finance* 18(4), 1999, pp. 619–635.

Mottaleb, Khondoker A. / Kalirajan, Kaliappa: "Determinants of foreign direct investment in developing countries: A comparative analysis". *Australia South Asia Research Centre Working Paper* 13, 2010, pp. 1–27.

Okada, Keisuke: "The interaction effects of financial openness and institutions on international capital flows". *Journal of Macroeconomics* 35, 2013, pp. 131–143.

Özşahin, Şerife: "Kurumsal kalite doğrudan yabancı yatırımlar için ne kadar önemli? Türkiye üzerine ekonometrik bir analiz". *Journal of Yasar University* 11(44), 2016, pp. 251–262.

Pesaran, M. Hashem: "A simple panel unit root test in the presence of cross-section dependence". *Journal of Applied Econometrics* 22, 2007, pp. 265–312.

Phung, Hang Bich: "Determinants of FDI into developing countries". *Mark A. Israel '91 Endowed Summer Research Fund in Economics* 4, 2016.

Seyidoğlu, Halil: *Uluslararası İktisat Teori Politika ve Uygulama*. Güzem Can Yayınları 17. Baskı: İstanbul. 2009.

Stein, Ernesto / Daude, Christian: "Institutions, integration and the location of foreign direct investment", OECD Global Forum on International Investment New Horizons and Policy Challenges for Foreign Direct Investment in the 21st Century, 2001, pp. 1–37.

Tatoğlu Yerdelen, Ferda: *İleri Panel Veri Analizi*. Beta Basım Yayım Dağıtım 1. Baskı: İstanbul. 2012.

Thirlwall, Anthony P.: *Growth and Development with Special Reference to Developing Economies*. Palgrave Macmillan 8th Edition: London. 2006.

United Nations Conference on Trade and Development (UNCTAD): *World Investment Report Investment and the Digital Economy*. UNCTAD: Geneva. 2017.

Wadhwa, Kavita / Reddy S., Sudhakara: "Foreign direct investment into developing Asian countries: The role of market seeking, resource seeking and efficiency seeking factors". *International Journal of Business and Management* 6 (11), 2011, pp. 219–226.

Şenay Saraç and Aykut Yağlıkara

Relationship Between Economic Freedom and Innovation: Panel Data Analysis

Abstract: The concept of economic freedom implies the individual's freedom to engage in the financial activity and the liberty to utilize, without hindrance, its income and all the factors it claims ownership of. This situation implies that governments place no limitations regarding the production, distribution and consumption of goods and services. The concept of Innovation means the emergence of a new or improved form of good, service, means of production or type of organization. The goal of this study is to investigate the effects of the components of economic freedom which ensures the security of those under one's rightful ownership and allows one to decide what to produce, how to produce goods and services and to whom to sell (freedom of trade, size of government, monetary liberty, fiscal liberty, intellectual property rights and others) to the innovation capacity of countries. In the literature, the studies conducted on the subject of economic freedom were often linked to the growth, and there has been no prior study we come upon that linked the concept to innovation. Low income and patent data for developed countries were taken from World Development Indicators (WDI). Other data were obtained from Heritage Foundation database. The variables between country groups for the period 1996–2014 were researched with panel data method.

Keywords: Economic Freedom, Innovation, Panel Data

Introduction

The concept of freedom is an important building block that determines the institutional structure. A good institutional structure is one of the factors that increase production and lead to growth in countries. Freedom and institutional structure, which differ between countries, are at the top among the most significant factors that determine the prosperity level of countries and their quantities of output. Additionally, while there are studies which reported that growth leads to freedom, the relationship between freedom and economic growth has started to appear more frequently in the literature (Tunçsiper and Biçen 2014, p.26).

It has been agreed upon that, since the late 20th century, the concept of freedom is one of the most important factors that globally affect the economic parameters of countries. In this context, the concept of freedom has started to be included more in the economics literature in terms of its economic, political and civil aspects. Considering the concept of freedom in general, the concept would remain hollow as long as one of the three pillars it is defined upon is missing. With the increasing interest in the concept of freedom, the issue of measurement of economic freedoms has become important, and several organizations have started to measure economic freedoms with the criteria they determined.

The word innovation refers to novelty and reform. Innovation is needed for growth to be sustainable, as well as for achieving increased prosperity. While it is seen that the levels of prosperity in countries where innovation and technological advancement were adopted earlier are high, the environment of competition emerging as a result of globalization urges other countries also to innovate. Therefore, after the value of innovation was understood after the 1980s, investments in the R&D work in this field also increased continuously. Increased competition along with the process of globalization forced countries to differentiate the goods and services they release into the market in comparison to other countries. Moreover, countries have become more willing to increase their R&D investments, decrease their costs and diversify the goods and services they produce. It was possible only this way for them to adapt to the international market and get a significant slice from it (Özbek and Atik 2013, p.194).

The purpose of this study is to contribute to the economics literature which contains various studies that discussed freedom-growth and innovation-growth relationships, with an empirical study which discusses the effects of economic freedoms on innovation. The study used that data from the period of 1996–2014 and involved developed countries using the panel data method and examined the relationship between economic freedoms and innovation. The reason why the study involved developed countries was that it was easier to reach the data on economic freedoms and innovation in these countries, and the results to be obtained from countries with a more solid institutional structure would be more reliable. Following the introduction section, the study discusses economic freedom and innovation. The third section reviews the literature on economic freedoms-growth and innovation-growth. The fourth section describes the methodology and the data. The fifth section presents the findings. The conclusion section provides a summary of the analyses and provides policy recommendations.

Economic Freedom and Innovation

Economic freedom covers the ability of individuals to make their own decisions, security of individuals and their property, freedom of individuals and institutions in competition and voluntary transformation of individuals. If there is economic freedom in a society, individuals determine which goods and services will be produced, and how they will be produced. Due to the property they own, individuals are free in the way they use their skills and time, and they do not have the right to use the skills, time and resources of others. Laws that are designed by policies and institutions to prevent people from resorting to violence or other means to confiscate the property owned by other people comply with economic freedom. Therefore, if the policies in practice are effective in protection of property rights, economic freedoms will also be improved. Moreover, steps taken by governments to stabilize their own currency, that is, to establish a solid monetary environment, will contribute to the improvement of economic freedoms (Gwartney and Lawson 2003, pp. 406–407).

Economic freedoms facilitate protection of the private property of the individual through taxing, publicly owned property and regulations within a limited, pre-determined framework. Furthermore, it is aimed that the confidence of the society in the rule of law is achieved through establishing its confidence in contracts, and market economy is made stronger in this context. For economic growth to be sustainable, it should be based on theoretical foundations in terms of economic freedom. Efficient or inefficient usage of incentives provided by governments by entrepreneurs, investors or other economic actors is dependent on institutions. Institutions' priorities in production will determine the course of economic growth. Promotion of economic growth may only be achieved by taking economic freedoms under complete guarantee by institutions. Protection of individuals' private property and achievement of low-level taxing in the economy will promote growth. Additionally, an economy where institutions establish market competition and restrict interventions with the economy will also encourage capital investment and increase growth (Berggren 2003, pp. 194–197).

Economic freedom is seen as a right of individuals to be free in turning their production, consumption, work and savings into investment, use their property in a way they want to and utilize their labor in any form they like. Governments, through their policies, need to prevent actors in the market to encounter restrictions in their relationships with each other and ensure free movement of goods, labor and capital. Economic freedoms have a positive interaction with various economic and social factors. These include per capita income, democracy and humanitarian development. Economic freedoms also play a significant role in increasing the prosperity levels of the society (Heritage Foundation 2017).

While there are multiple studies on measurement of economic freedoms, this study used the economic freedoms index values reported by the organization named Heritage Foundation. Heritage Foundation (2017) discusses economic freedoms under four main categories, which has three sub-categories each. A total of 12 economic parameters are a score in the range of 0–100 index points, and the results are averaged by weighting the parameters equally. The 12 economic variables defining economic freedom are the following:

I) *Rule of Law*
   a) Property Rights: This measures the protection of the right of individuals to own private property by the state, the extent to which laws protect property rights, and how much economic and political actors respect these laws. The index value for property rights is affected by physical property rights, quality of land management, how much the investor is protected, intellectual property rights and risk of nationalization.
   b) Judicial Effectiveness: This measures the extent to which the judicial system works in a just and effective way, and all individuals are equal before the laws. Quality of the judicial process, independent judiciary and positive processing of judicial decisions are sub-factors for judicial effectiveness.
   c) Government Integrity: While corruptions in governments decrease the trust in economic activities, they also increase the costs of economic activities and obstruct economic mobility. Measurement of government integrity considers confidence of the public in politicians, regular payments, transparency of policy-makers, whether there is corruption or not, how the public perceives corruption and transparency of the government and civil services.

II) *Government Size*
   a) Tax Burden: Marginal tax rates on the incomes of organizations and individuals and the ratio of taxes in GDP determine how the tax burden is socially effective for individuals and organizations. The sub-factors in measuring tax burden are a top marginal tax rate of organizational income, a top marginal tax rate of individual income, the ratio of taxes in GDP.
   b) Government Spending: This refers to the burden created on the economy by the spending of the government. Excessive government spending, which is one of the most significant factors effective on economic liveliness, leads to a reduction of economic efficiency. There may be differences among countries in determining the levels of government spending.
   c) Fiscal Health: When there is a deficit in the budget managed by the government, this is an indicator that the fiscal structure is not operated healthily, and it has destabilizing effects on especially macroeconomic factors. Calculation of this index involves consideration of the ratio of average deficits in the last 3 years in GDP and the ratio of debts in GDP.

III) *Regulatory Efficiency*

a) Business Freedom: A set of infrastructure investments, regulations and easiness of opening and closing firms in the market are important factors that influence the efficiency of businesses. Cost of starting a business, cost of closing a business and the duration required to close a business are among factors used in measuring business freedom.

b) Labor Freedom: This includes measurement of how much legislation is effective in regulating the labor market by considering the minimum wage, working hours and regulations that make firing employees difficult. Additionally, severance payments, difficulties in working hours and rate of involvement in the workforce are also among factors used in determining labor freedom.

c) Monetary Freedom: Government intervention in the free market disrupts price stability. Therefore, price control and inflation factors are used to measure monetary freedom.

IV) *Open Markets*

a) Trade Freedom: The obstacles encountered by goods and services subject to foreign trade due to customs and agreements are important in measuring trade freedom. Non-tariff barriers and tariff rates are two factors used in measuring trade freedom.

b) Investment Freedom: In economically free countries, individuals and organizations are free to make both domestic and international investments, but investment freedom was defined over certain activities.

c) Financial Freedom: State intervention in banking and other capital market institutions reduce the competition in the market and credit rates, which are important for banking. A banking and finance system which is inspected by an independent central bank and minimally affected by government intervention will provide the optimum utility (Heritage Foundation, 2017).

In the innovation process, the ideas presented by individuals form the creative aspect of innovation, and the idea of animating this by turning it into goods and services is a novelty. Considering the innovation as a catalyst for growth, innovation may be understood as providing the customers who buy goods and services with more than expected. The essence of innovation is the acceptance of new offers by the customers in terms of goods and services. That is, an innovator should create the perception of a new value for the customer. When the customer sees the formation of new value for the good or service to purchase, they will purchase the good or service anyway (Tucker 2008, pp. 16–18).

Schumpeter had a significant influence on the emergence of the concept of innovation in the literature on economics. The main point of the Schumpeterian approach is that the top factor in economic growth is innovation. According to Schumpeter, innovation is defined by creating a new production function, while in more detail, innovation may be defined as proposing a new method of organization or production, creating a new market or inventing a new product. Although this much importance is paid to innovation in the Schumpeterian approach, the Classical and Neo-classical economic approaches kept innovation in the background. The concept of technology was included in the model exogenously in Neo-classical economics, and the inclusion of technology in the model was carried out by Romer, Lucas, Howitt and Aghion, who proposed the endogenous growth theory (Işık and Kılınç 2016, pp. 14–15).

There are three types of innovation necessary for economic growth: product innovation, process innovation and strategy innovation.

Product Innovation: A product covers a car, a computer, an airplane or anything similar produced around us. Additionally, services are also products and goods and services carry the same value in the innovation process. At this point, product innovation may be considered to increase the customer's utility and be a consequence of attempts at solving a problem that the customer has.

Process Innovation: Process innovation provides the customer with higher utility and increases profitability by raising efficiency and reducing costs. The customer is not able to notice that the emerging novelty is caused by process innovation. Process innovation increases quality by including new technologies and methods of production in the process of production.

Strategy Innovation: Strategy innovation is a process that usually affects the preferences of the end user. In this type of innovation, the customer is able to feel the novelty directly. Examples of strategy innovation include making goods and services more preferable in the market by advertising, presenting new techniques in selling goods and services, and proposing different methods in services provided to the customer (Tucker 2008, pp. 18–20).

Literature Review

There are several studies in the literature on the relationship between economic freedoms and growth. Some of such studies are discussed below:

Hann and Sturm (2000) compared various indicators for economic freedom. While their results were occasionally diverse in terms of the countries they studied, in general, they concluded that economic freedoms affected economic growth positively.

Heckelman (2000) investigated whether economic freedoms led to economic growth or economic growth led to economic freedoms. According to the results of their analysis based on the sub-indicators of economic freedoms obtained from the Heritage Foundation, the public intervention was effective on growth, but taxing and trade policy were not.

Carlsson and Lundström (2002) found that economic freedoms had a significant effect on economic growth. Despite this, they stated that it could not be argued as a generalization that increased economic freedoms will have positive effects on economic growth. They concluded that some sub-categories of economic freedoms had adverse effects on growth.

Dawson (2003) investigated the long-term relationship between political and economic freedoms and economic growth. According to empirical results, while there was a correlation between the variables, no causality was present. The results revealed which economic freedom affected growth the most.

Stroup (2006) discussed the interaction between economic freedom and democracy and variables that closely concern the public such as education and health. According to their findings, while increased economic freedoms increased economic prosperity, they also had a positive effect on education and health. Moreover, it was reported that democracy had a weaker effect in comparison to economic freedoms.

Sufian and Habibullah (2010), in their study on Malaysia for the period of 1999–2007, investigated the effects of economic freedoms on bank performances. They observed that economic freedom and business freedom increased the profitability of banks. They also found that corruption and monetary freedom had a detrimental effect on the profitability of Malaysian banks.

Compton et al. (2011) investigated the effects of economic freedoms on economic growth in 50 states in the USA from 1981 to 2004. While they found a positive and significant relationship between the two variables, they concluded that not all components of economic freedom affected economic growth in the same way.

Williamson and Mathers (2011) discussed the effects of economic freedoms and culture on economic growth. They reached the conclusion that economic freedoms were more effective on growth in comparison to culture. They also stated that economic freedoms and culture might be substituted.

Akıncı et al. (2015) investigated the relationship between economic freedoms and corruption in Turkey for the period of 1995–2013. As a result of their analyses, they presented the economic freedoms that reduced corruption as: trade freedom, property rights, financial freedom, monetary freedom and fiscal freedom. The economic freedoms that increased corruption were reported as investment freedom, independence from the state and professional freedoms.

In addition to these, the studies in the literature by Dawson (1998), Gwartney et al. (1999), Leschke (2000), Weede and Kämpf (2002) and Ashby and Sobel (2008) reported a positive relationship between economic freedoms and economic growth.

Coe and Helpman (1995), in their study on the period of 1971–1990, discussed technological advancement in a way that considered it as a product of innovation activities in the market. Domestic R&D investments and foreign R&D capital were included in the analysis in the context of their model. According to the findings, foreign R&D capital had a positive effect on domestic efficiency.

Zachariadis (2003), in their study on manufacturing industry data in the USA, showed that promoting R&D investments increased the number of patents. According to the Schumpeter growth model, increases in number of patents increase technical advancement and facilitate economic growth.

Falk (2007) investigated the long-term relationship between R&D spending and economic growth in a study on OECD countries for the period of 1970–2004. According to the results, the ratio of R&D spending in GDP and the ratio of the high-technology sector in R&D investments had an effect on per capita GDP in the long run.

Zang et al. (2012) investigated the relationship between scientific innovation and economic growth in Beijing as a dynamic relationship using the VAR model. According to their findings, there was a mutually incentivizing relationship between economic growth and scientific innovation.

Gülmez and Akpolat (2014) analyzed the relationship among innovation, R&D spending and economic growth for Turkey and 15 selected European Union countries in a long-term. According to the findings of the study, increases in the number of patents and R&D spending increased economic growth.

Bujari and Martinez (2016) investigated the relationship of technological innovation with economic growth in Latin American countries for the period of 1996–2008. According to the results of the analyses carried out using the dynamic panel method, there was a positive relationship between innovation and economic growth. As a result of the study, it was concluded that promoting technological innovation in Latin American countries would increase economic growth.

Özkul and Ürün (2016), in their study where panel data analysis was used for 9 OECD countries for the period of 2002–2013, found that intensity of technological innovation had a positive effect on economic growth.

In addition to these, the studies in the literature by Freire-Serén (1999), Wang (2007) and Hasan and Tucci (2010) reported positive relationships between R&D spending and economic growth.

Methodology and Data

This study used annual panel data from 31 developed countries for the period of 1996–2014 to investigate the effects of economic freedom on the process of innovation in the context of number of patents. In addition to this main variable, variables such as per capita income and the ratio of R&D spending in GDP were included in the model as control variables. The data on per capita GDP and number of patents were obtained from the World Development Indicator (WDI) database. The shares of R&D spending in GDP were, again, taken from this database. Finally, the data on economic freedom indices were collected from the Heritage Foundation (2016) database. While investigating the effects of economic freedoms on innovation, the study used the index values for business freedom, trade freedom, fiscal freedom, monetary freedom, investment freedom, financial freedom, property rights, corruption and government spending. The variables in the study, their abbreviations and units are provided in Tab. 1.

We selected the countries used in the study from among the countries in the high-income group in the income classification list by the World Bank. We selected the countries from among those with a per capita GDP of $12736 or higher because these are similar to each other in terms of economic interactions

Tab. 1: Variables Used in the Analysis

Name	Abbreviation	Unit
Number of Patents	PATENT	Number of Units
Per capita GDP	GDP	Dollars
R&D spending	RD	%GDP
Business freedom	BUF	Index
Trade freedom	TRF	Index
Fiscal freedom	FISF	Index
Monetary freedom	MOF	Index
Investment freedom	INF	Index
Financial freedom	FIF	Index
Property rights	PRR	Index
Corruption	FRC	Index
Government spending	GOS	Index

Tab. 2: Countries Examined in the Study

Argentina	France	Latvia	Slovenia
Australia	Germany	Lithuania	South Korea
Belgium	Greece	Norway	Spain
Canada	Hong Kong	Poland	Sweden
Czech Republic	Hungary	Portugal	The Netherlands
Denmark	Ireland	Russia	The United Kingdom
Estonia	Israel	Singapore	The United States
Finland	Japan	Slovakia	

and institutional structures. Tab. 2 shows the countries examined in the scope of the study.

In the model where the dependent variable was the number of patents, the dependent variables of the model include the sub-indices of economic freedom, business freedom (BUF), trade freedom (TRF), fiscal freedom (FISF), monetary freedom (MOF), investment freedom (INF), financial freedom (FIF), property rights (PRR), corruption (FRC), government spending (GOF). Additionally, per capita GDP and ratio of R&D spending in GDP were added to the model as control variables. In scope of the established model, the effects of both sub-indices of economic freedom and per capita GDP and R&D activities on the innovation process were investigated in the context of number of patents using panel data analysis. The advantages of panel data analysis over time series or cross-section analysis are the following:

(1) Individuals, firms and countries are considered as heterogeneous in panel data. As time series and cross-section analyses cannot control for heterogeneity, these analyses may provide biased results. (2) While time series analyses have multilinearity problems, panel data analyses provide lower collinearity among variables, more variability and more data. (3) Panel data analysis provides more reliable information in dynamic studies because cross-sectional distributions hide various changes. This is why examining the effects of economic policy changes on variables via panel data analysis is more reliable in terms of results. (4) Effects that cannot be determined simply by cross-section and times series analysis can be measured using the method of panel data analysis. (5) Additionally, with panel data analysis, we have the chance to analyze more complex behavioral models in comparison to the case in times series or cross-section analyses (Baltagi, 2005).

The model where the number of patents was taken as the dependent variable for the method of panel data analysis was as the following:

$$PATENT = \beta_0 + \beta_1 GDP + \beta_2 RD + \beta_3 PRR + \beta_4 FRC + \beta_5 FISF + \beta_6 GOS + \beta_7 BUF + \beta_8 MOF + \beta_9 TRF + \beta_{10} INF + \beta_{11} FIF + ec$$

Findings

Achievement of stationarity in variables is an important factor in the reliability of the model's estimation. The unit root results for the variables in the model concerning developed countries are given in Tab. 3. The analysis findings showed that some of the variables in the unit root tests were stationary at level, while others were stationary at the first difference values.

In the literature, there are two different groups of unit root tests for testing stationarity: While the first group includes the Levin, Lin & Chu, Breitung and Hadri tests, the second group includes the Im-Pesaran-Shin, Fisher ADF and Fisher PP tests. For acceptable results of stationarity for variables, the same result should be obtained by conducting at least one test from each group. Levin-Lin-Chu (LLC), Breitung Im-Pesaran-Shin, Fisher ADF and Fisher PP unit root analyses test the hypothesis that there is a unit root. In order to see whether there is a unit root as a result of unit root tests, probability values are checked. If the probability values in the test results are lower than 0.05, the hypothesis is rejected, and it is concluded that there is no unit root. The results of the unit root tests which tested the stationarity of the variables used in the study are given in Tab. 3.

As a result of the unit tests, the hypothesis was rejected for the variables number of patents, per capita GDP, fiscal freedom, monetary freedom, corruption, government spending and trade freedom, and it was determined that the variables are stationary at level: I (0). The hypothesis was rejected for the variables R&D spending, property rights, business freedom, investment freedom and financial freedom as a result of the unit root tests, and it was seen that these were not stationary. Their first differences were taken, they were made stationary and included in the model: I (1). After testing the stationarity of the variables in the study, the redundant fixed effect test was used to determine the approach to be used for panel data analysis. The results of the test are given in Tab. 4.

This test was used to decide on which of the ordinary least squares (OLS) random effects and fixed effects models would be used. Test results are interpreted by their probability values. The probability value in our results was lower than 0.05. This suggests that we should use one of the random effects and fixed effects approach instead of the OLS approach.

Tab. 3: Unit Root Test

	With Intercept			
	Number of Patents (LPATENT)			
	T-stat I (0)	**Prob. I (0)**	**T-stat I (1)**	**Prob. I (1)**
Levin, Lin and Chu	−4.089	0.000*		
Im, Peseran and Shin	−2.145	0.016**		
ADF Fisher Chi Square	104.73	0.000*		
PP Fisher Chi Square	83.001	0.038**		
	Per Capita Income (LGDP)			
	t statistic I (0)	Prob. I (0)	t statistic I (1)	Prob. I (1)
Levin, Lin and Chu	−10.450	0.000*		
Im, Peseran and Shin	−4.034	0.000*		
ADF Fisher Chi Square	124.746	0.000*		
PP Fisher Chi Square	198.641	0.000*		
	R&D Spending (LRD)			
	t statistic I (0)	Prob. I (0)	t statistic I (1)	Prob. I (1)
Levin, Lin and Chu	−2.383	0.008*	−12.525	0.000*
Im, Peseran and Shin	0.813	0.792	−10.669	0.000*
ADF Fisher Chi Square	64.765	0.380	225.567	0.000*
PP Fisher Chi Square	70.041	0.225	247.362	0.000*
	Property Rights (PRR)			
	t statistic I (0)	Prob. I (0)	t statistic I (1)	Prob. I (1)
Levin, Lin and Chu	−0.348	0.363	−4.395	0.000*
Im, Peseran and Shin	0.346	0.635	−6.219	0.000*
ADF Fisher Chi Square	16.884	0.769	50.973	0.000*
PP Fisher Chi Square	18.064	0.702	48.089	0.000*
	Fiscal Freedom (FISF)			
	t statistic I (0)	Prob. I (0)	t statistic I (1)	Prob. I (1)
Levin, Lin and Chu	−3.959	0.000*		
Im, Peseran and Shin	−2.886	0.001*		
ADF Fisher Chi Square	98.011	0.002*		
PP Fisher Chi Square	121.445	0.000*		
	Business Freedom (BUF)			
	t statistic I (0)	Prob. I (0)	t statistic I (1)	Prob. I (1)
Levin, Lin and Chu	−1.331	0.091***	−19.690	0.000*
Im, Peseran and Shin	1.212	0.887	−15.159	0.000*
ADF Fisher Chi Square	47.143	0.918	320.698	0.000*
PP Fisher Chi Square	58.583	0.599	507.138	0.000*

Tab. 3: (continued)

	With Intercept			
	Number of Patents (LPATENT)			
	T-stat I (0)	**Prob. I (0)**	**T-stat I (1)**	**Prob. I (1)**
	Monetary Freedom (MOF)			
	t statistic I (0)	Prob. I (0)	t statistic I (1)	Prob. I (1)
Levin, Lin and Chu	−6.677	0.000*		
Im, Peseran and Shin	−3.826	0.000*		
ADF Fisher Chi Square	124.013	0.000*		
PP Fisher Chi Square	143.784	0.000*		
	Investment Freedom (INF)			
	t statistic I (0)	Prob. I (0)	t statistic I (1)	Prob. I (1)
Levin, Lin and Chu	−1.453	0.073***	−12.168	0.000*
Im, Peseran and Shin	−0.322	0.373	−10.978	0.000*
ADF Fisher Chi Square	51.915	0.399	170.644	0.000*
PP Fisher Chi Square	56.207	0.253	242.378	0.000*
	Financial Freedom (FIF)			
	t statistic I (0)	Prob. I (0)	t statistic I (1)	Prob. I (1)
Levin, Lin and Chu	−1.554	0.060***	−10.563	0.000*
Im, Peseran and Shin	−0.189	0.424	−9.675	0.000*
ADF Fisher Chi Square	48.212	0.545	146.072	0.000*
PP Fisher Chi Square	42.113	0.778	170.532	0.000*
	Corruption (FRC)			
	t statistic I (0)	Prob. I (0)	t statistic I (1)	Prob. I (1)
Levin, Lin and Chu	−7.945	0.000*		
Im, Peseran and Shin	−9.393	0.000*		
ADF Fisher Chi Square	207.827	0.000*		
PP Fisher Chi Square	251.340	0.000*		
	Government Spending (GOS)			
	t statistic I (0)	Prob. I (0)	t statistic I (1)	Prob. I (1)
Levin, Lin and Chu	−5.156	0.000*		
Im, Peseran and Shin	−4.397	0.000*		
ADF Fisher Chi Square	133.288	0.000*		
PP Fisher Chi Square	98.112	0.002*		
	Trade Freedom (TRF)			
	t statistic I (0)	Prob. I (0)	t statistic I (1)	Prob. I (1)
Levin, Lin and Chu	−9.027	0.000*		
Im, Peseran and Shin	−5.930	0.000*		
ADF Fisher Chi Square	135.967	0.000*		
PP Fisher Chi Square	121.039	0.000*		

Tab. 4: Redundant Fixed Effect Test

Redundant Fixed Effects Tests			
Test Cross-Section Fixed Effects			
Effects Test	**Statistic**	**d.f.**	**Prob.**
Cross-section F	228.242187	(30,484)	0.0000
Cross-section Chi square	1429.572550	30	0.0000

Tab. 5: Hausman Test

Correlated Random Effects - Hausman Test			
Test Cross-Section Random Effects			
Test Summary	**Chi-Sq. Statistic**	**Chi-Sq. d.f.**	**Prob.**
Cross-section random	72.491451	11	0.0000

The fixed effects and random effects approaches are usually employed in panel data studies with a static model. The fixed effects approach is a model constructed by adding different constants to each country to fix the differences among the countries. The random effects approach does not take into account the difference among the countries, and the effects are revealed only in the error terms part of the model. The Hausman test is used to choose between the fixed effects and random effect approaches. If the Chi-squared value obtained as a result of the test is lower than 1 %, the hypothesis is rejected, and it is seen that it will be better to use the fixed effects model (Baltagi, 2005). The results of the Hausman test are given in Tab. 5.

The Hausman test assesses the hypothesis that using the random effects approach is right. The results are evaluated on a 0.05 significance level. If the probability of random distribution of cross-section error terms is lower than 0.05, the hypothesis is rejected, and the right model is the fixed effects approach. The results of the fixed effects model are given in Tab. 6.

According to the results of the analysis where the fixed effects model was used, statistically significant results were obtained for some economic freedom indices in terms of the relationship between economic freedom and number of patents in developed countries. There was a statistically significant and positive relationship between per capita income, which was included in the model as a control variable, and number of patents. There was also a significant and positive relationship between R&D spending and number of patents. This result supports the finding in the literature that increased R&D spending results in the

Tab. 6: Fixed Effects Model Findings

Fixed Effects Model			
Variable	**Coefficient**	**t-statistic**	**Prob.**
LGDP	0.750176	-4.848328	0.0000
DLRD	0.409274	-1.599325	0.0104
DPRR	-0.001809	-0.493645	0.6218
FISF	-0.006885	-3.527961	0.0005
DBUF	0.003401	0.885630	0.3763
MOF	0.000423	0.205015	0.8376
DINF	0.000102	0.051606	0.9589
DFIF	0.007942	2.530458	0.0117
FRC	0.008441	2.681287	0.0076
GOF	-0.006888	-2.907176	0.0038
TRF	0.002570	0.689568	0.0908
C	15.78443	10.36736	0.0000
Descriptive Statistics			
R2=0.968 F:363.950 F(p):0.000 DW:1.864			

number of patents. That is, increases in the per capita income and R&D spending in the countries evaluated here affected the numbers of patents in these countries positively.

There were both positive and negative, statistically significant relationships in the economic freedom indices that we investigated in the scope of the model. However, the relationships were generally positive. While the relationship between property rights and number of patents was not statistically significant, it was negative. The relationship regarding the variable fiscal freedom was statistically significant and negative. This suggests that decreasing fiscal freedoms in developed countries, based on the power of the state in taxing, may increase the number of patents. The relationship regarding the variable business freedom was significant by a 10 % level of significance and positive. The relationships regarding the variables monetary freedom and investment freedom were insignificant and positive.

Again, in the scope of the analyses, it was found that increased financial freedoms and reduced corruption affected the number of patents positively and significantly. Lifting the obstacles and restrictions in financial markets and preventing corruptions make the process of innovation more operable in developed countries by increasing the number of patents. Government spending and number of patents had a significant and negative relationship. This result suggests that decreased levels of government spending in developed countries would accelerate the increase of the number of patents. Finally, the relationship regarding the variable trade freedom was significant at a 10 % level of significance, and it had a positive effect on the dependent variable.

Conclusion

Our study investigated the effects of economic freedoms on number of patents in 30 developed countries for the period of 1996–2014 using panel data analysis. In the scope of the panel data analysis, firstly, various unit tests were conducted to collect information on the stationarity of the variables. It was seen that some variables contained unit roots, and the first difference values of such variables were taken to rid them of unit roots. For determining the magnitude of the effects of economic freedoms on number of patents, the Hausman test was used to realize that the optimum results would be provided by the fixed effects model. As a result of the fixed effects model used in the study:

It was observed that increases in most of the economic freedom sub-indices provided positive outcomes in terms of number of patents. This means, as the institutional structure in countries gets stronger, economic freedoms will get better, and as the R&D expenditures increase, number of patents will increase. The process of innovation, which is one of the greatest driving forces in achieving sustainable and healthy economic growth, will take part in stimulating growth in terms of number of patents, and more prosperous countries will emerge.

High levels of achievement of liberalization in domestic and international trade, a stable money and finance system where state intervention is minimal, the private sector is dominant in the market, property rights of the individual and companies are guaranteed by laws and strong currency is dominant in the market, achievement of low tax rates and an effective market mechanism, and finally, ensuring that investors can freely make investments in the market mechanism, increase economic freedoms in developed countries. Increased economic liberalization increases economic freedom while reinforcing the innovation processes of countries.

References

Akıncı, M. / Erkal, G. / Yılmaz, Ö: "Ekonomik özgürlükler ve yolsuzluk ilişkisi: Türkiye için bir zaman serisi analizi". *HAK-İŞ Uluslararası Emek ve Toplum Dergisi*, 4(8), 2015, pp. 144–165.

Ashby, N. J. / Sobel, R. S.: "Income inequality and economic freedom in the U.S. States". *Public Choice* 134, 2008, pp. 329–346.

Baltagi, B. H.: *Econometric analysis of panel data*. 3rd Edition, Jonh Wiley & Sons Inc.: New York. 2005.

Berggren, N.: "The benefits of economic freedom: A survey". *The Independent Review* 8(2), 2003, pp. 193–211.

Bujari, A. A. / Martinez, F. V.: "Technological innovation and economic growth in Latin America". *Revista Mexicana de Economia y Finanzas* 11(2), 2016, pp. 77–89.

Carlsson, F. / Lundström, S.: "Economic freedom and growth: Decomposing the effects". *Public Choice* 112, 2002, 335–344.

Coe, D. T. / Helpman, E.: "International R&D spillovers". *European Economic Review* 39(5), 1995, pp. 859–887.

Compton, R. A. / Giedeman, D. C. / Hoover, G. A.: "Panel evidence on economic freedom and growth in the United States". *European Journal of Political Economy* 27, 2011, pp. 423–435.

Dawson, J. W.: "Institutions, investment, and growth: New cross-country and panel data evidence". *Economic Inquiry* 36, 1998, pp. 603–619.

Dawson, J. W.: "Causality in the freedom-growth relationship". *European Journal of Political Economy* 19, 2003, pp. 479–495.

Falk, M.: "R&D spending in the high-tech sector and economic growth". *Research in Economics* 61, 2007, pp. 140–147.

Freire-Serén, M. J.: Aggregate R&D Expenditure and Endogenous Economic Growth. UFAE and IAE Working Papers, No.WP 436.99, 1999.

Gülmez, A. / Akpolat, A. G.: "Ar-Ge, inovasyon ve ekonomik büyüme: Türkiye ve AB örneği için dinamik panel veri analizi". *AİBÜ Sosyal Bilimler Enstitüsü Dergisi* 14(2), 2014, pp. 1–17.

Gwartney, J. / Lawson, R.: "The concept and measurement of economic freedom". *European Journal of Political Economy* 19, 2003, pp. 405–430.

Gwartney, J. / Lawson, R. / Holcombe R.G. : "Economic freedom and the environment for economic growth". Journal of Institutional and Theoretical Economics 155, 1999, pp. 643-663.

Hann, J. / Sturm, J. E.: "On the relationship between economic freedom and economic growth". *European Journal of Political Economy* 16, 2000, pp. 215–241.

Hasan, I. / Tucci, C. L.: "The innovation-economic growth nexus: Global evidence". *Research Policy* 39, 2010, pp. 1264–1276.

Heckelman, J.C.: "Economic freedom and economic growth: A short-run causal investigation", *Journal of Applied Economics* 3(1), 2000, pp. 71–91.

Heritage Foundation: *The Economic Freedom Index 2016*. https://www.heritage.org/index/

Heritage Foundation: *The Economic Freedom Index* 2017. https://www.heritage.org/about/

Işık, N. / Kılınç, E. C.: "İnovasyon-temelli ekonomi: Seçilmiş ülkeler üzerine bir uygulama". *Anadolu Üniversitesi Sosyal Bilimler Dergisi* 16(1), 2016, pp. 13–28.

Leschke, M.: "Constitutional choice and prosperity: A factor analysis". *Constitutional Political Economy* 11(3), 2000, pp. 265–279.

Özbek, H. / Atik, H.: "İnovasyon göstergeleri bakımından Türkiye'nin Avrupa Birliği ülkeleri arasındaki yeri: İstatiksel bir analiz". *Erciyes Üniversitesi İktisadi ve İdari Bilimler Fakültesi Dergisi* 42, 2013, pp. 193–210.

Özkul, G. / Örün, E.: "Girişimcilik ve inovasyonun ekonomik büyüme üzerindeki etkisi: Ampirik bir araştırma". *Girişimcilik ve İnovasyon Yönetimi Dergisi* 5(2), 2016, pp. 17–51.

Stroup, M.D.: "Economic freedom, democracy and the quality of life". *World Development* 35(1), 2006, pp. 52–66.

Sufian, F. / Habibullah, M. S.: "Does economic freedom fosters banks' performance? Panel evidence from Malaysia". *Journal of Contemporary Accounting and Economics* 6, 2010, pp. 77–91.

Tucker, R. B.: *Driving growth through innovation*. Berrett Koehler Publishers, Inc.: San Francisco. 2008.

Tunçsiper, B. / Biçen, Ö. F.: "Ekonomik özgürlükler ve ekonomik büyüme arasındaki ilişkinin panel regresyon yöntemiyle incelenmesi". *Eskişehir Osmangazi Üniversitesi İİBF Dergisi* 9(2), 2014, pp. 25–45

Wang, E. C.: "R&D efficiency and economic performance: A cross-country analysis using the stochastic frontier approach". *Journal of Policy Modeling* 29(2), 2007, pp. 345–360.

Weede, E. / Kämpf S.: "The impact of intelligence and institutional improvements on economic growth". *Kyklos* 55(3), 2002, pp. 361–380.

Williamson, C.R. / Mathers, R.L.: "Economic freedom, culture and growth". *Public Choice* 148, 2011, pp. 313–335.

Zachariadis, M.: "R&D, innovation and technological progress: A test of the Schumpeterian framework without scale effects". *Canadian Journal of Economics* 36(3), 2003, pp. 566–586.

Zang, L. / Song, W. / He, J.: "Empirical research on the relationship between scientific innovation and economic growth in Beijing". *Technology and Investment* 3, 2012, pp. 168–173.

Şenay Saraç

The Role of Technoparks in Socio-Economic Development: Analysis of Current Situation in Turkey

Abstract: The economic and social development of the countries is closely related to their technological development. Implemented for the production and transfer of technology in the world and Turkey, technoparks are one of the most tangible aspects of university-industry-government cooperation. It has emerged as an effective concept supported by research institutes where academic, economic, and social structures come together. Technoparks are applications that support tech entrepreneurs in the financial, academic, and managerial direction for the production of new and advanced technologies and contribute to the commercialization of new products and technologies. This study examines the technoparks in Turkey, which have developed quantitatively and qualitatively in recent years. In this context, the current status of technoparks in Turkey was discussed, and technoparks were evaluated based on empirical studies.

Keywords: Technology, Socio-Economic Development, Technopark, Turkey

Introduction

Today, the main objective of countries is economic and social development. For economic development to take place, sustainable growth, structural changes in production and consumption patterns, technological progress, social and institutional modernization, and widespread improvement in living standards have to occur (Küçük 2010, p.10). Recent economic developments emphasize that special attention needs to be given to technological development and innovation. This is because the main driving forces of high growth/development are provided by technology and innovation (Ünlükaplan 2009, p.236). Technology transfer and/or technology production are the two ways that a country can possess technology (Jeremy, 1991). Policy makers aware of this situation have developed various tools to be able to become competent in technology and innovation. The ability of countries to produce their own technologies and succeed by transforming them into innovations depends on their ability to manage their own national-regional innovation systems. One of the main actors of this system is technoparks.

Technopark, which refers to science and technology parks, entered the literature as the Turkish version of "technopark" which is a combination of the words "technology" and "park" in English (Babacan 1995, p. 3). When we look at the developed countries in the world, similar formations are named differently in different countries. The terms Science Park in the United Kingdom, Research Park in the USA, Technopole in France, Technopolis in Japan, and Grunderzentrum in Germany have been adopted. Furthermore, "Enterprise Center", "Innovation Center", "Excellence Center", and "Industrial Park" are also used (Babacan 1995). Although there are slight nuances between them, science park, research park, technopark, technopolis, technocity, etc., concepts are used in the same sense. In Turkey, *"Technology Development Zones (TDZ)"* concept is used for technoparks in the Technology Development Zones Law No. 4691 that has been issued on this subject.

Since technoparks are a strategic issue for our country, it is thought that more academic studies to be done in this respect will be beneficial in terms of more detailed examination of technoparks, and the results will have a positive effect in eliminating deficiencies. In this context, the theoretical framework of the technopark concept is outlined in the second and third sections of this study, and then the benefits and success measures of technoparks are mentioned. In the fourth section, the history of technoparks and the major technoparks in the world are discussed. In the fifth section technoparks in Turkey are analyzed in terms of investment, employment, intellectual property rights, and relations with industry. Studies on technoparks in Turkey are mentioned in section six, and the current state of technoparks in Turkey is evaluated in the last section based on the results obtained in these studies.

Technopark Concept and Its Purpose

According to Harmancı and Önen (1999), technoparks are places where industry and university cooperation is concretized. They are places where entrepreneurs who want to produce goods, with usually new or advanced technologies, are able to conduct their industrial and commercial activities near or in the vicinity of universities and to benefit from universities. Castells and Hall (1995, p.89) have identified the technopark as a new type of industrial zone that brings together high-tech firms that will provide employment and job skills within a specific area, enabling them to survive in new conditions brought by international competition and knowledge-based production. Kılıç (2009) also stated that technoparks are organizations where technological production takes place, which have a positive impact on the efforts of the country, firms, and universities in order to compete in the global market. The International Association of Science Parks (IASP) describes technopark as an organization managed by a professional executive, whose main objective is to provide value of its members by developing their competitiveness and innovation culture (T.C. Presidential Supervisory Board, 2009: 30). According to Bülbül and Özbay (2011, p.20), "technoparks are enterprises that aim to create suitable environments for the establishment and development of technology-based companies by bringing together research institutes, public and private companies". The concept of technopark, which can be found in various definitions, generally includes the following three characteristics in all definitions (Bülbül and Özbay 2011, p.20).

- Obtaining a suitable location for the park,
- Organizational program of activities for transfer of technology,
- Establishing a partnership between academic institutions, public and private sector.

The main purpose of technoparks is to conduct scientific research, to transform information into technological products, and to ensure their dissemination. T. Development Bank (1999) stated that the purpose of technoparks is to strengthen technology-intensive industries in the places where they are located, to support industrial development in new regions, to carry out innovative studies, to increase productivity with more effective conditions as well as education, and to increase international competitiveness. The United Nations Science and Technology Development Fund has emphasized the importance of technoparks with the statement that "Although Technoparks are organizations associated with universities, technology development and application for achieving higher quality and cheaper production processes are more important and have a higher priority here to increase international competition" (Arslantekin 2002, p.2). Çetin (1997) argues that the purpose of technoparks is to enable young and talented people who have a business idea and preliminary design for a new industrial enterprise but who cannot find enough starting capital to establish their businesses – preferably within universities – by providing them affordable renting spaces with the required infrastructure and to support them in their initial efforts.

In their studies, Babacan (1995, p.25) and Özbay (2000, p.1111) compiled the purposes of technoparks. These are:

- ✓ To revitalize the region, to increase the number and diversity of economic activities in the region,
- ✓ To transform R&D activities into investment, to encourage the revitalization and modernization of the local industry by providing a suitable environment for product innovation,

- ✓ To provide infrastructure for regional innovation efforts,
- ✓ To establish more efficient and active relations between the regional resources and the research capacity of the region and higher education institutions,
- ✓ To commercialize creativity and knowledge in universities,
- ✓ To ensure long-term increase in employment and the emergence of technology-based small businesses and partnerships as a source of innovation,
- ✓ To create job opportunities for university graduates in the region,
- ✓ To bring high-tech companies to the region,
- ✓ To contribute to R&D efforts in restructuring the regional and local economies.

Benefits of Technoparks and Success Criteria

In addition to contributing to the economy of the country, technoparks also have various benefits to entrepreneurs, university, and the region. These contributions have been addressed in the following headings (Polat 2007; Tepe and Zaim 2016).

Benefits to Entrepreneurs

Technoparks create synergy between firms, academic institutions, and other companies. Therefore, technoparks provide an important resource network to the firm. Companies that need to cover a lot of ground in a short amount of time gain new perspectives by communicating with other companies, spending time together, making projects, and participating in conferences. In technoparks, a tax concession is provided for the companies, and companies also receive assistance in finance, marketing, and management from technoparks. Universities transmit scientific knowledge and expertise to the companies. Thus, the mutual exchange of information, data, and even technology between stakeholders is stimulated and developed. Companies learn and develop the project-based working culture by receiving counseling from universities. Qualified staff capacity increases, and companies find ways to produce new products with a high customer focus and high added value.

Benefits to University

Thanks to technoparks, universities obtain additional financial resources from the state. In addition, technopark is a positive stimulus for the University, which has the opportunity to commercialize its works, for developing and updating research agendas. Making joint projects with companies in technoparks in order to observe the sector needs and keeping up-to-date information about the sector give the universities a dynamic structure. They can include outputs of interactions with stakeholders in education programs. Thus, universities offer learning opportunities to their students. With the advantage of being in close contact with the industry, laboratories in universities have the opportunity of keeping the test and measurement devices, hardware and equipment constantly up-to-date and in a way that meets the needs of the industry. In fact, technoparks serve as the gate that opens universities to the market.

Benefits to the Region

By providing communication between universities and industry, technoparks strengthen the reputation of the country, increases its productivity, contributes to its competitiveness, reduces the unemployment rate, and becomes an instrument for the country to have a say in the international scene. Technoparks have a positive effect on the income level of people living in the vicinity. The education level of the region increases. As a result, regional socio-economic development takes place where there are technoparks.

The success of technoparks can be examined under two headings: operational and business success. The criteria that should be considered in measuring the operational success of technoparks are as follows (Sarıçiçek 2005 pp. 2–3 cited by Görkemli, 2011):

- ✓ Domestic and foreign companies, which are included in the technopark,
- ✓ Technopark's occupancy rate,
- ✓ Compliance with the activities carried out in the region by technoparks to attract focused technological fields with the regional targets,
- ✓ Total number of personnel employed in the technopark,
- ✓ The ratio of R&D personnel in the technopark to the total number of personnel,
- ✓ The created superstructure (office space, industrial space, warehouse space) and its quality,
- ✓ The created infrastructure (such as high-speed internet) and its quality,
- ✓ Access to the financial resources required for the establishment of technopark,
- ✓ The amount of foreign investment attracted to technopark,
- ✓ Sustainability and profitability of the activities,
- ✓ The return rate of investments made to technopark,
- ✓ The amount of additional income created for founding universities and organizations,
- ✓ Quality support services and financial resources provided in technopark,
- ✓ High-quality common spaces that are created,

- ✓ The rate of utilization of services, common areas, and other facilities offered in the region,
- ✓ Formal and informal cooperation mechanisms established with national and international universities, technoparks, and other related institutions,
- ✓ The national and international recognition of the region and its prestige,
- ✓ The quality of the work and living area offered,
- ✓ Prices consistent with the quality of the infrastructure and services offered,
- ✓ The satisfaction of the companies regarding the services provided by the technopark and the facilities provided.

We can list the success criteria regarding the activities of the businesses within the technopark as follows (Sarıçiçek 2005, p.4 cited by Görkemli, 2011):

- ✓ New products and production technologies produced in the region,
- ✓ Patents and other intellectual property rights resulting from the studies in the region,
- ✓ Prototypes produced in the region,
- ✓ Products that have passed into production phase and commercialized,
- ✓ Technology transfers realized in the region,
- ✓ Research publications made as a result of activities in the region,
- ✓ New products or production technologies sold in domestic and international markets,
- ✓ Establishment of new companies working in R&D and software,
- ✓ Diversification of the technological activities carried out in the companies in the region, and increased work on new fields,
- ✓ Additional employment created through newly established companies,
- ✓ Additional employment created as a result of the increase in the activities of existing firms, and company growth,
- ✓ Value added created in the region (revenue/total cost of sales),
- ✓ Exports based on R&D and software in the region,
- ✓ The import substitution as a result of products and services produced in the region,
- ✓ Number of academicians and researchers employed in the region,
- ✓ Number of students (internship and part-time) employed in the region,
- ✓ The ratio of R&D expenditures to total sales,
- ✓ The return rate of R&D expenditures,
- ✓ Number of partnerships established with foreign companies,
- ✓ Number of joint projects carried out by universities and research institutions and technopark companies,

- ✓ The number of scientific studies that have been put into commercial practice as a result of the activities in the region,
- ✓ Number of joint projects and cooperation developed between technopark firms,
- ✓ The connection between technopark firms and R&D centers in the firms and other technology regions outside the technology zone,
- ✓ The increase in the use of university resources,
- ✓ The number of employees outside the technopark,
- ✓ Number of start-ups (newly established companies),
- ✓ Number of spin-offs (companies that the university or institutional research teams establish to commercialize knowledge and skills).

Besides these, the number of successful firms that produce high-added-value technological products in industrial zones outside the technopark, and the positive impact they have on the regional and national economies are influential in the success of technoparks (Görkemli 2011). Public sector support and legal regulations have taken the first two spots in a study aimed at determining the importance of the factors that directly or indirectly affect the development of technoparks. Socio-political, economic crises, etc., took third place, because these external influences can cause change (T.C. Presidency State Supervision Board 2009). In order to measure the successes of technoparks, it is preferable that a certain period of time should pass first, and the technopark evaluated later (Keleş 2007, p.128). Technoparks begin to produce their intended results 5–10 years after they are established.

History of Technoparks and Technoparks in the World

The concept of "technopark", which refers to science and technology parks, appeared in the USA in the 1950s and became increasingly popular throughout the world, especially in European countries. The first technopark applications in the world began in the 1950s in the USA in the form of "Science Parks" established around universities in order to develop university-industry collaboration, especially in industrialized areas, but no significant success was achieved until the 1970s. The emergence of technoparks especially in European countries occurred in the 1980s (Keleş 2007, p.96).

The Stanford University Technopark, also known as Silicon Valley in the United States, has an important place today in the development of computer, electronic information, and communication technologies. Companies in Silicon Valley, which contained about 8,000 high-tech companies in 1983, owned 60 % of the Nobel Science Awards at different times. The Route 128 technopark, another example of a leading technopark in the United States, was established in 1952 in Boston. Route 128, established near the Massachusetts Institute of Technology (MIT), one of the world's foremost research institutes, had about 800 companies mostly operating in electronics in the 1970s (Görkemli 2011).

After the United States, technoparks have also become common in Europe. Edinburgh Heriot-Watt and Cambridge Trinity College technoparks were established in England in 1972. After the success of these first technoparks, there have been significant increases in the number of technoparks in the 1980s, and Merseyside (1982), Aston et al. (1983), Oxford (1990), and Emmerson and Cranfield (1992) technoparks were established. The Cambridge technopark at Trinity College is now the largest technopark in the UK, and R&D studies and quality testing rather than production is performed in this technopark, where multinational companies operate (Keleş 2007, p.103). The first technopark in France was established in 1969 by a non-profit company in the vicinity of Nice in southern France. The objective of this technopark, named Sophia Antipolis, was to accelerate regional economic development (Görkemli 2011).

Another pioneer country in terms of technoparks is China (Tepe and Zaim 2016, p.24). The most important step taken by the Chinese government in the technological field is the technopark established in the Zhongguancun region. The entire Zhongguancun region, which was established in the 1980s, has been declared a Technology and Science Zone. Today, Zhongguancun is in the way of becoming one of the world's top technology bases. Zhongguancun, located in the western Beijing region of the Chinese government, is China's "Silicon Valley", inspired by the Silicon Valley in the United States. The largest state-of-the-art technology park of the country, Zhongguancun hosts local companies such as Lenovo, Baidu, and Sohu.com, as well as international companies such as the famous Google, Microsoft, and Intel (Eren 2011, p.54).

Technoparks also started to be established in the Far East especially in Japan and Taiwan. In Japan, the first technopark was established in 1970 under the name Tsukoba technopark after the decisions made in 1963 (Keleş 2007, p.104; Polat 2007, p.17). Technoparks, which developed rapidly in the following years, are financially supported by the Japanese government. In Japan, technoparks are also being used as a tool to create new techno-cities and promote regional development by spreading industrial technology centers concentrated in the Pacific Ocean to other regions (Görkemli 2011). In Taiwan, technoparks began to be established in the late 1980s to create a favorable environment to support the manufacturing industry and especially export companies. In 2001, the country had four technoparks, Hsinchu (1980), Tainan (1995), Chunan (1998), and Taichung (2001), the number of patents held in Taiwan increased, and companies built closer relationships with each other with the advantage of being located in the same technopark, thereby significantly contributing in regional economic development (Hu et al., 2005, pp. 370–372).

With the liberalization of the economy in India in the 1990s, a new era began in the field of technology development. University-industry cooperation in the country started to gain traction, and important steps were taken in the field of technological development with the collaborations established. Undoubtedly, the most important of these steps has been the establishment of technoparks in international standards. International Technology Park (ITPL) was founded in 1997 and is the most important and the biggest of the technoparks established in India (Tepe and Zaim 2016, p.24; Eren 2011, p.57). Software Technology Parks-India, which was established to increase software exports in India, has been making great strides in the field of computer software (Jussawala 2003, p.23).

Since the 1940s, Israel has been working to develop in the field of technology. In 1946, the first technopark was established in Israel with private sector initiative. The five technoparks established by Stef Wertheimer in Israel are still the few technoparks that produce competitive products around the world. The roots of Israel's success in the software and R&D sector are based on policies and state support to increase the level of technology after the country gained its independence (Eren 2011, pp. 60–61).

Eastern Europe did not show the same pace of development as Western Europe on technoparks. The political structure of these countries not supporting entrepreneurship for years played an important role in this (Görkemli 2011). In Russia, the significance of science parks was conceived after China, and in 1990, the first science park in Tomsk was established. Among the technoparks in Russia, St. Petersburg Technopark is the most significant one. The number of technoparks that are now spreading rapidly in Russia has reached 62 in 1998 (Polat 2007).

Technoparks in Turkey

In Turkey, the topic of technoparks was first discussed in the University-Industry Relations Development Project report, conducted by the State Planning Organization (DPT), and supported by UNDP (United Nations Development Programme) and UNIDO (United Nations Industrial Development Organization) (DPT 1989, p.66, cited by Keleş 2007).

At the invitation of DPT, UNFSTD (United Nations Fund for Scientific and Technological Development) came to Turkey in 1990, and the experts appointed by UNFSTD made examinations in Ankara, Istanbul, Izmir, Gebze, and Eskisehir, and gave seminars to industry chambers. In line with the efforts pioneered by DPT, TUBITAK MAM Research Center was established on its own, and ITU, METU, Ege University and Anadolu University established their first research centers jointly with KOSGEB. Afterwards, METU and TUBITAK MAM, which reached the sufficient number of firms, passed the second phase of their investments by initiating their technopark projects in 1996 (Sarıhan 1998, pp. 152–153, cited by Keleş 2007).

With the "Technology Development Zones Law" numbered 4691 issued on June 26, 2001, and "Technology Development Zones Implementation Regulations" dated June 19, 2002, many universities rapidly started to build technoparks. In the "Technology Development Zones Law" numbered 4691, technoparks are defined as; "*A site in which firms using high/advanced technology or aiming to develop new technologies produce/develop new technologies or software, perform activities to transform a technological innovation into a commercial product, method or service, and thereby contributing to the development of the region, by making use of the facilities and opportunities provided by a certain university, advanced technology institute or R&D center or institute, located in or near the same university, advanced technology institute or R&D center or institute, where academic, economic, and social structures integrate; or a technopark with these characteristics.*"

Again, according to Law No. 4691, the purposes of technoparks established in Turkey are listed as: the development of technological knowledge, the commercialization of the produced knowledge, the improvement of product quality and standards in products and production methods, the development of innovations that will increase productivity and reduce production costs, the adaptation of small- and medium-sized enterprises to new and advanced technologies, the provision of employment opportunities for researchers, and increasing the competitive power of the industry by accelerating high-tech investment of foreign capital in the country.

With this law, since 2001, a total of 69 Technology Development Zones (8 in Ankara, 7 in Istanbul, 4 in Kocaeli, 4 in Izmir, 2 in Konya, Antalya, Kayseri, Trabzon, Adana, Erzurum, Mersin, Isparta, Gaziantep, and 1 in Eskişehir, Bursa, Denizli, Edirne, Elazığ, Sivas, Diyarbakır, Tokat, Sakarya, Bolu, Kütahya, Samsun, Malatya, Urfa, Düzce, Çanakkale, Kahramanmaraş, Tekirdağ, Van, Çorum, Manisa, Niğde, Burdur, Yozgat, Kırıkkale, Balıkesir, Hatay, Karaman, Muğla, Afyon-Uşak, Aydın, Batman, Osmaniye, Zonguldak, and Karabük) have been established (as of December 2017). Technology Development Zones are located in 48 cities in total.

Of the 69 Technology Development Zones, 56 are in operation (Tab. 1) and 15 have not yet been operational (Tab. 2), as infrastructure works continue. According to Tab. 1, among the operational TDZs, 6 are in Ankara, 6 are in Istanbul, 4 are in Kocaeli, 4 are in Izmir, 2 are in Konya, and the remaining TDZs are located in Gaziantep, Antalya, Kayseri, Trabzon, Adana, Erzurum, Mersin, Isparta, Eskişehir, Bursa, Denizli, Edirne, Elazığ, Sivas, Diyarbakır, Tokat, Sakarya, Bolu, Kütahya, Samsun, Malatya, Şanlıurfa, Düzce, Çanakkale, Kahramanmaraş, Tekirdağ, Çorum, Van, Kırıkkale, Yozgat, Afyon, Niğde, Manisa, and Aydın with 1 TDZ in each city. According to Tab. 2, there are 2 TDZs in Ankara, and 1 TDZ each in İstanbul, Burdur, Balıkesir, Hatay, Karaman, Muğla, Batman, Osmaniye, Zonguldak, Karabük, Gaziantep, Antalya, and Nevşehir that are not yet operational.

As can be seen from Graph 1, the number of TDZs, which was only 1 in 2001, reached 69 by the end of 2017.

The number of firms operating in the Technology Development Zones reached 4,624 as of December 2017 (Graph 2). In terms of foreign capital, there are 73 foreign companies and 177 companies with foreign partners in Technology Development Zones (Ministry of Science and Industry, 2018).

Tab. 3 shows the sectoral distribution of firms in the TDZs as of the end of January 2018. Approximately 55 % of the companies are in software (37 %) and computer and communication technologies (17 %) sectors.

In Technology Development Zones, a total of 45,274 people were employed as of December 2017 (Graph 3). While approximately 37,500 of this number were R&D personnel, the remaining personnel were employed in support and out-of-scope units.

Innovative companies in Technology Development Zones are mostly concentrated in *Software, Informatics, Electronics, Advanced Material Technologies*, in particular, as well as *Design, Nanotechnology, Biotechnology, Automotive, Medical Technologies and Renewable Energy*, and the number of R&D projects implemented in TDZs are *7,843 as of December 2017* (Graph 4). The number of completed projects is 26,377 as of January 2018 (Ministry of Science and Industry, 2018).

Technology exports made by companies in the operational Technology Development Zones have reached *2.9 Billion US Dollars* as of December 2017, with exports to the most developed countries in the world such as the *United States, as well as Japan, Israel, United Kingdom, and Germany.*

In today's world, one of the most important factors determining the competitive power and social well-being of a country is the Science and Technology studies in that country being turned into a commercial product or production method and resulting in a patent.

Tab. 1: Technology Development Zones in Operation. Source: T.C. Ministry of Science and Industry (2018). *Statistics*, Access date: 05.02.2018, https://teknopark.sanayi.gov.tr/.

	TECHNOLOGY DEVELOPMENT ZONE	UNIVERSITY	CITY	ESTABLISHED IN
1	METU Technopolis Technology Development Zone	Middle East Technical University	ANKARA	2001
2	TUBITAK Marmara Research Center Technopark	TUBİTAK-TTGV	KOCAELİ	2001
3	Ankara Technology Development Zone	Bilkent University	ANKARA	2002
4	İzmir Technology Development Zone	İzmir Advanced Technology University	İZMİR	2002
5	GOSB Technopark Technology Development Zone	Sabancı University	KOCAELİ	2002
6	Hacettepe University Technology Development Zone	Hacettepe University	ANKARA	2003
7	İTÜ Arı Technopolis Technology Development Zone	İstanbul Technical University	İSTANBUL	2003
8	Eskişehir Technology Development Zone	Anadolu University	ESKİŞEHİR	2003
9	Selçuk University Technology Development Zone	Selçuk University	KONYA	2003
10	Kocaeli University Technology Development Zone	Kocaeli University	KOCAELİ	2003
11	Western Mediterranean Technopolis Technology Development Zone	Batı Akdeniz University	ANTALYA	2004
12	Erciyes University Technology Development Zone	Erciyes University	KAYSERİ	2004
13	Trabzon Technology Development Zone	Karadeniz Technical University	TRABZON	2004
14	Çukurova Technology Development Zone	Çukurova University	ADANA	2004

Tab. 1: (continued)

	TECHNOLOGY DEVELOPMENT ZONE	UNIVERSITY	CITY	ESTABLISHED IN
15	Mersin Technology Development Zone	Mersin University	MERSİN	2005
16	Lakes Region Technology Development Zone	Süleyman Demirel University	ISPARTA	2005
17	Ulutek Technology Development Zone	Uludağ University	BURSA	2005
18	Gaziantep University Technology Development Zone	Gaziantep University	GAZİANTEP	2006
19	Gazi Technopark Technology Development Zone	Gazi University	ANKARA	2007
20	Trakya University Edirne Technology Development Zone	Trakya University	EDİRNE	2008
21	Fırat Technology Development Zone	Fırat University	ELAZIĞ	2007
22	Erzurum Ata Technopolis Technology Development Zone	Atatürk University	ERZURUM	2005
23	Pamukkale University Technology Development Zone	Pamukkale University	DENİZLİ	2007
24	Yıldız Technical University Technology Development Zone	Yıldız Teknik University	İSTANBUL	2003
25	Ankara University Technology Development Zone	Ankara University	ANKARA	2006
26	İstanbul University Technology Development Zone	İstanbul University	İSTANBUL	2003
27	Sakarya University Technology Development Zone	Sakarya University	SAKARYA	2008
28	Boğaziçi University Technology Development Zone	Boğaziçi University	İSTANBUL	2009

(continued on next page)

Tab. 1: (continued)

	TECHNOLOGY DEVELOPMENT ZONE	UNIVERSITY	CITY	ESTABLISHED IN
29	Cumhuriyet Technology Development Zone	Cumhuriyet University	SİVAS	2007
30	Dicle University Technology Development Zone	Dicle University	DİYARBAKIR	2007
31	Bolu Technology Development Zone	İzzet Baysal University	BOLU	2009
32	Düzce Technopark Technology Development Zone	Düzce University	DÜZCE	2010
33	Malatya Technology Development Zone	İnönü University	MALATYA	2009
34	Kahramanmaraş Technology Development Zone	Sütçü İmam University	K.MARAŞ	2011
35	Dokuz Eylül Technology Development Zone	Dokuz Eylül University	İZMİR	2013
36	Namık Kemal University Technology Development Zone	Namık Kemal University	TEKİRDAĞ	2011
37	Kütahya Dumlupınar Design Technology Development Zone	Dumlupınar University	KÜTAHYA	2009
38	Tokat Technology Development Zone	Gaziosmanpaşa University	TOKAT	2008
39	İstanbul Technology Development Zone	İstanbul Commerce University	İSTANBUL	2009
40	Çanakkale Technology Development Zone	18 Mart University	ÇANAKKALE	2011
41	Samsun Technology Development Zone	On Dokuz Mayıs University	SAMSUN	2009
42	Marmara University Technology Development Zone	Marmara University	İSTANBUL	2014
43	Ege Technopark Technology Development Zone	Ege University	İZMİR	2014
44	Harran University Technology Development Zone	Harran University	URFA	2010

Tab. 1: (continued)

	TECHNOLOGY DEVELOPMENT ZONE	UNIVERSITY	CITY	ESTABLISHED IN
45	Bozok Technology Development Zone Bozok University	Bozok University	YOZGAT	2013
46	Kırıkkale University Technology Development Zone	Kırıkkale University	KIRIKKALE	2013
47	İzmir Science and Technology Park Technology Development Zone	İzmir Economy University	İZMİR	2012
48	Yüzüncü Yıl University Technology Development Zone	Yüzüncü Yıl University	VAN	2012
49	Çorum Technology Development Zone	Hitit University	ÇORUM	2012
50	Konya Technology Development Zone	Selçuk -Necmettin Erbakan - Aksaray Karamanoğlu Mehmet Bey - KTO Karatay Universities	KONYA	2015
51	Afyon-Uşak Zafer Technology Development Zone	Afyon Kocatepe and Uşak University	AFYON	2016
52	Niğde University Technology Development Zone	Niğde University	NİĞDE	2013
53	Celal Bayar University Technology Development Zone	Celal Bayar University	MANİSA	2012
54	Ankara Teknopark Technology Development Zone	Yıldırım Beyazıt University	ANKARA	2014
55	Muallimköy Technology Development Zone	Gebze Advanced Technology Institute	KOCAELİ	2011
56	Adnan Menderes University Technology Development Zone	Adnan Menderes University	AYDIN	2016

Tab. 2: Technology Development Zones That Are Not Yet Operational (Ongoing Infrastructure Works)*. Source: T.C. Ministry of Science and Industry (2018). *Statistics*, Access date: 05.02.2018, https://teknopark.sanayi.gov.tr/.

	TECHNOLOGY DEVELOPMENT ZONE	UNIVERSITY	CITY	ESTABLISHED IN
1	ASO Technopark Technology Development Zone	TOBB University	ANKARA	2008
2	MAKÜ-Baka Technology Development Zone	Mehmet Akif Ersoy University	BURDUR	2013
3	Balıkesir University Technology Development Zone	Balıkesir University	BALIKESİR	2014
4	OSTİM Ecopark Technology Development Zone	Ankara- Hacettepe- Atılım-Çankaya Başkent- TOBB Universities	ANKARA	2014
5	Hatay Technology Development Zone	Mustafa Kemal University	HATAY	2014
6	Finans Technopark Technology Development Zone	Boğaziçi University	İSTANBUL	2014
7	Karaman Technology Development Zone	Karamanoğlu Mehmet Bey University	KARAMAN	2015
8	Muğla Technology Development Zone	Sıtkı Koçman University	MUĞLA	2015
9	Batman University Technology Development Zone	Batman University	BATMAN	2017
10	Osmaniye Technology Development Zone	Osmaniye Korkut Ata University - Adana Science and Technology University	OSMANİYE	2017
11	Zonguldak Technology Development Zone	Bülent Ecevit University	ZONGULDAK	2017
12	Karabük University Technology Development Zone	Karabük University	KARABÜK	2017
13	Gaziantep OSB Technology Development Zone	Hasan Kalyoncu University	GAZİANTEP	2017
14	Antalya OSB Technology Development Zone	Akdeniz University Antalya Science University	ANTALYA	2018
15	Kapadokya Technology Development Zone	Nevşehir Hacı Bektaş Veli University	NEVŞEHİR	2018

* Statistical information as of January 2018.

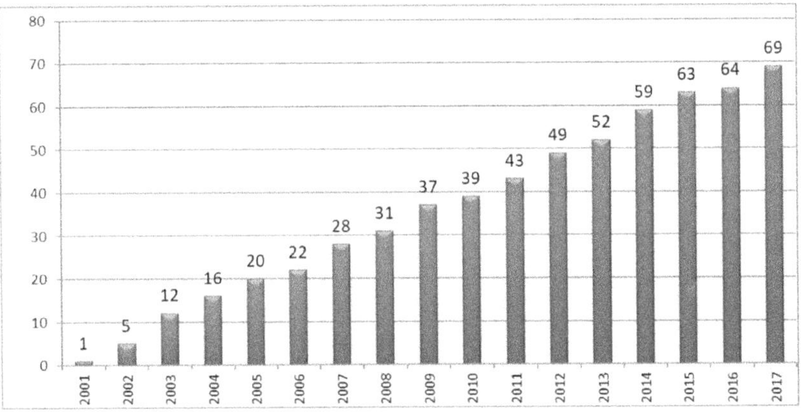

Graph 1: Number of Technology Development Zones by Years

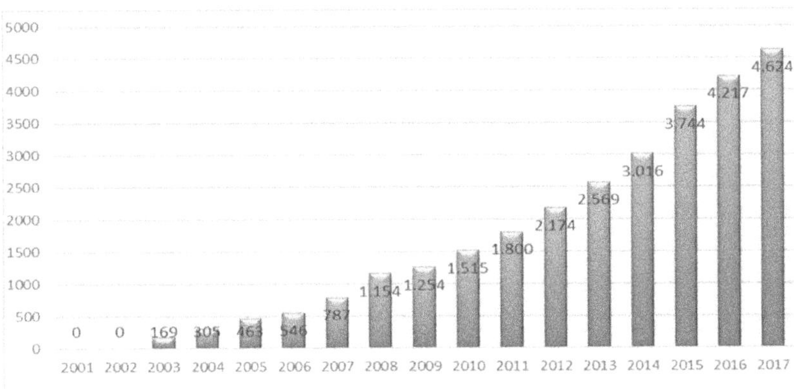

Graph 2: Total Number of Companies in Technology Development Zones

The Intellectual Property status of the companies operating in Technology Development Zones as of January 2018 is given in Tab. 4 below.

In conclusion, the current status of Technology Development Zones in Turkey as of December 2017 is summarized in Tab. 5 below.

When we look at the rankings of Technology Development Zone performance index in 2016, we see that ODTU Technopolis is ranked one, followed by ITU, Cyberpark, Mersin and Erciyes TDZs.

Tab. 3: Sectoral Breakdown of Firms in Technology Development Zones. Source: T.C. Ministry of Science and Industry (2018). *Statistics*, Access date: 05.02.2018 https://teknopark.sanayi.gov.tr/.

SECTOR	%	SECTOR	%
Software	37	**Construction**	1
Computer and Communication Technologies	17	**Telecommunication**	1
Electronics	8	**Automotive**	1
Manufacture of Machinery and Equipment	6	**Aviation**	1
Energy	4	**Medicine**	1
Medical	3	**Animal Husbandry**	1
Health Care	3	**Maritime**	1
Defense industry	3	**Manufacturing Industry**	1
Chemistry	3	**Recycling**	1
Food industry	2	**Automotive Design Engineering**	1
Agriculture	2	**Other**	2

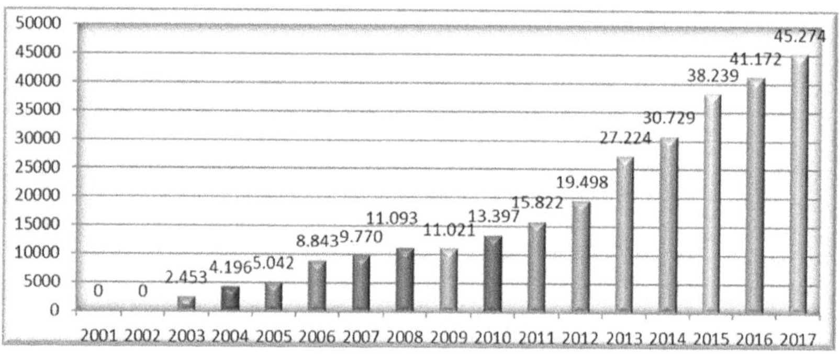

Graph 3: Number of Personnel Employed in Technology Development Zones

Studies on Technoparks in Turkey: Literature Research

In his study, Keleş (2007) applied a questionnaire to technopark managers and administrators to investigate and obtain information on issues such as the physical status of technoparks since their establishment, personnel, problems, companies, organizational structure, development status, etc., and take a look at the current status.

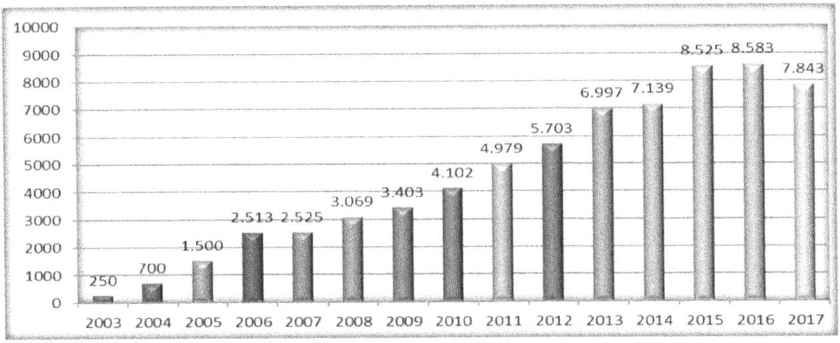

Graph 4: Number of Projects Implemented in Technology Development Zones by Years

Tab. 4: Intellectual Property Status of Companies in Technology Development Zones. Source: T.C. Ministry of Science and Industry (2018). *Statistics*, Access date: 05.02.2018, https://teknopark.sanayi.gov.tr/.

INTELLECTUAL AND INDUSTRIAL PROPERTY	NUMBER
Number of Patent Registrations (National/International)	940
Number of Patent Applications (Ongoing)	1,853
Number of Utility Model Registrations	461
Number of Utility Model Applications (Ongoing)	146
Number of Industrial Design Registrations	85
Number of Industrial Design Applications (Ongoing)	20
Software Copyright (Taken)	94

Some of the analysis results of the questionnaire applied to the technopark managers are as follows (Keleş 2007):

- Technopark administrators are mostly young, graduate and Ph.D. degree holders, have management experience, and know the university that the technopark is located in (most of them are also university personnel). In technoparks where innovative R&D companies operate, having managers with these characteristics is an advantage.
- To be able to realize university-industry cooperation efficiently, technopark management should know well the university it is in, the areas in which it conducts projects and researches, and the opportunities that it can provide to the companies. In particular, they should be able to communicate these to industrialists in the region to attract them to the technopark.

Tab. 5: Current Status of TDZs in Turkey (December 2017). Source: T.C. Ministry of Science and Industry (2018). *Statistics*, Access date: 05.02.2018, https://teknopark.sanayi.gov.tr/.

Number of Announced Technology Development Zones	**69**
Number of Operational Technology Development Zones	**56**
Number of Companies	**4,624**
Number of Foreign Companies	**73**
Number of Companies with Foreign Partners	**177**
Number of Companies with Academician Partners	**909**
Number of Employed Personnel	**45, 274 people**
R&D Personnel	**37,201 people**
Support Personnel	**2,786 people**
Out-of-Scope Personnel	**5,287 people**
Number of Completed Projects	**26,052**
Number of Ongoing Projects	**7,843**
Total Sales	**55,440,099,738.41 TL**
Exports	**2.9 Billion US Dollars**

- Universities and the industry, which have been two separate entities until now, are getting the chance to get to know each other more closely thanks to technoparks. The doors of the university are opened to industrialists through technoparks. Both sides have profits from this cooperation. The university benefits from the work experience and practical knowledge of the industry, and the students get the opportunity to make internships and work part-time. By doing so, they get a better chance of finding a job when they graduate. Students get the chance of self-improvement and will be successful in their professional careers after graduation.
- Industrialists often have the problem of inefficiency when they hire university graduates due to lack of practice in university education. Therefore, there is a lot of personnel circulation in companies, salaries are low, and university graduates have to wait for a long time in order to reach desired working conditions. This situation also has negative reflections on the society. Therefore, in universities, the practice should be given importance, and current practices in the market should be taught.
- According to the analysis results, it is seen that there is no connection of teaching staff in more than half of technopark firms operating in Turkey. The

Tab. 6: Performance Index Ranking of Technology Development Zone in Turkey (2016). Source: T.C. Ministry of Science and Industry (2018). *Statistics*, Access date: 05.02.2018, https://teknopark.sanayi.gov.tr/.

Rank No.	Technology Development Zone
1	ODTÜ Technopolis Technology Development Zone
2	İTÜ Arı Technopolis Technology Development Zone
3	Ankara Technology Development Zone (CYBERPARK)
4	Mersin Technology Development Zone
5	Erciyes University Technology Development Zone
6	İzmir Technology Development Zone
7	Yıldız Technical University Technology Development Zone
8	İstanbul Technology Development Zone
9	İstanbul University Technology Development Zone
10	Ankara University Technology Development Zone
11	Sakarya University Technology Development Zone
12	Selçuk University Technology Development Zone
13	Ulutek Technology Development Zone
14	Gazi Technopark Technology Development Zone
15	GOSB Technopark Technology Development Zone
16	TÜBİTAK Marmara Research Center Technopark
17	Dokuz Eylül Technology Development Zone
18	Hacettepe University Technology Development Zone
19	Namık Kemal University Technology Development Zone
20	Boğaziçi University Technology Development Zone
21	Trabzon Technology Development Zone
22	Ege Teknopark Technology Development Zone
23	Pamukkale University Technology Development Zone
24	Çukurova Technology Development Zone
25	Kocaeli University Technology Development Zone
26	Fırat Technology Development Zone
27	Düzce Technopark Technology Development Zone
28	Trakya University Edirne Technology Development Zone
29	Tokat Technology Development Zone
30	Samsun Technology Development Zone
31	Erzurum Ata Technopolis Technology Development Zone
32	Kahramanmaraş Technology Development Zone
33	Eskişehir Technology Development Zone
34	Bolu Technology Development Zone

(*continued on next page*)

Tab. 6: (continued)

Rank No.	Technology Development Zone
35	Western Mediterranean Technopolis Technology Development Zone
36	Bozok Technology Development Zone Bozok University
37	Cumhuriyet Technology Development Zone
38	Çanakkale Technology Development Zone
39	Gaziantep University Technology Development Zone
40	Harran University Technology Development Zone
41	Lakes Region Technology Development Zone
42	Dicle University Technology Development Zone
43	Malatya Technology Development Zone
44	Kırıkkale University Technology Development Zone
45	Kütahya Dumlupınar Design Technology Development Zone

ratio of firms established by teaching staff was 13 %, and the ratio of companies where teaching staff was working as consultants was 35 %.

- R&D companies established in the form of start-ups without large capital accumulations are obliged to meet conditions that are difficult for new companies to meet in the first place such as a bank letter of guarantee when they apply to supply side (KOSGEB, etc.) institutions in order to get resources, finance and project support in order to realize their projects; thus, they are not able to benefit from the credit or grant support needed.
- The rate of providing services such as quality assurance, marketing, export-import, legal advice, etc., required for both newly established and previously established businesses by technoparks was found to be low. Efforts to increase the provision of such services and supports to technology companies need to be accelerated. These services are especially important for start-up companies. Such companies need the above-mentioned management information to be able to survive and produce new projects.
- The success of a technopark will be determined by the number of R&D projects, the number of patents registered, number of registered utility models, number of registered trademarks, amount of exports, number of qualified personnel employed, increase in number of start-up and spin-off companies established by teaching staff, and the economic contribution to the region and the country, etc. Technopark administrations should give incentive awards (plaque, rent for a certain period of time, etc.) to companies that have good performance (number of R&D projects, patents received, etc.).

- According to the results, the largest stakeholders in the technoparks in Turkey are universities. Universities are followed by industrial representatives such as chambers of commerce and industry, trade exchanges, private companies. One of the most important aims of technoparks is to establish university-industry cooperation. When we look at the capital distribution of technoparks, the two largest partners being universities and industry representatives are also reflected in the number of collaborations between these two entities. However, the efforts to be shown in terms of the efficient and purpose-driven operation of technoparks should not only be in capital partnership, but each party should try to perform its duties at the highest level regardless of the ratio of its share of capital.
- Considering the problems faced by the technopark administrations, the most significant problems were found to be an insufficiency of financing, the problems stemming from the TDZ Law No. 4691, and the excess of bureaucracy.
- Looking at the sectors of the companies operating in technoparks, it was observed that most of the companies were focusing on Information Technologies – Information – Software and Electrics – Electronics – Telecommunications. It is a great advantage that the widespread technologies of our age are concentrated in technoparks. However, incentives should also be provided for companies working in other fields where Turkey's infrastructure is strong (agriculture, environment, renewable energy sources, etc.). In addition, companies working towards the utilization of the infrastructure and resources in the region should also be employed in technoparks.

Erün (2012) investigated the effect of cooperation between technopark firms in Ankara on the technology transfer performance. Five technoparks operating in Ankara were analyzed. In addition, differentiation tests were conducted with the help of demographic data about the technological cooperation levels and technology transfer performances of the companies operating in the technopark, and some syntheses were conducted. Based on the research and the obtained results, recommendations were made to increase cooperation practices, which were determined to have positive effects on technology transfer performance of firms operating in technoparks.

In her study, Görkemli (2011) reveals the role of technoparks in regional development from the Konya Technopolis example. In the field survey conducted on all three groups, it was found that Konya Technopolis had positive effects on the growth of turnover, exports, employment, investment, and a market cap of the companies. The biggest problem mentioned by companies operating in Konya

Technopolis during their R&D activities was finding financial support and qualified R&D personnel. It is proposed to increase the R&D support programs and encourage cooperation of companies with universities, other companies in the technoparks, and public institutions. The other findings obtained in the study are as follows (Görkemli 2011):

- It was found that Konya Technopolis was effective in the growth of turnover, exports, employment, investment, and market capitalization of companies.
- High satisfaction rate of companies in Konya Technocity can be expressed as a sign of being at the right place for R&D projects. This is confirmed by the fact that the number of projects per firm increase by years.
- The registered intellectual and industrial property rights are also important values for Konya Technopolis and the city. R&D support is an important element in promoting and concluding the research of companies. Increasing R&D support will contribute to the innovation process. At this point, the public and private sector that provides R&D support have an important role. Increased R&D support will be able to mobilize even more innovation activities.
- The fact that the level of cooperation between the technopolis companies, and with universities and public institutions, was not at the desired level is another result of this study. Taking steps to increase these collaborations is of great importance for spreading knowledge and increasing value. Engaging in activities that promote cooperation, bringing public institutions, universities and industrial institution together on different platforms, and encouraging R&D activities, supporting the publishing and promotional activities of established innovation activities will further contribute to regional development.

In their study, Gül and Çakır (2014) examined the determinants of the innovation performance of firms in İzmir Technology Development Zone (İZTEKGEB). The results of the econometric estimations made on the data obtained by a questionnaire showed that international R&D cooperation, R&D supports, academic staff working at the firm, and cooperation with other firms in the technopark increased the possibility of firms to make patent and utility model applications.

Tepe and Zaim (2016) interviewed 110 companies in Technopark Istanbul and proposed a model of how technopark performance should be assessed. In his study, Sakarya (2012) evaluated the effect of collaborations aimed at increasing technology transfer within the technopark and technopark support activities on the assimilation capacities of firms and utilization levels of services provided with the help of questionnaires in Ankara. Kayalıdere (2014) has discussed tax benefits towards technoparks and emphasized the importance of technoparks in Turkey's technology policy.

Conclusion

Today, developed countries are leaders because they are countries that attach high importance to science and technology, have high R&D expenditures, and produce high-tech products. Therefore, developing countries like Turkey have to produce their own technology to compete in the international arena and not be dependent on the developed countries. In particular, as in developed countries, policies emphasizing topics such as the importance of R&D, allocating more resources to R&D, the need for effective implementation of university-industry cooperation, and the need for qualified personnel who can bring knowledge and production together, etc., should be produced and implemented.

The most concrete example of methods that enable countries to develop and increase their welfare implemented in Turkey is the "Technology Development Zone Law" enacted in 2001 which legalized the establishment of technoparks. When we consider that this establishment started to appear in the world since the 1950s, it is obvious that Turkey has been a latecomer in this race. As of the end of 2017, the findings obtained on technoparks in Turkey are as follows:

- In Turkey, the number of technoparks has increased considerably over the years. The number of technoparks, which was 1 in 2001, has reached 69 in 2017. While 56 of these 69 technoparks continue their activities, 13 are not yet operational since their infrastructure works continue. Technology Development Zones are located in a total of 48 provinces in Turkey.
- In parallel with the increasing number of technoparks, the number of firms in technoparks also increased. The number of firms, which was 169 in 2003, reached 4,624 as of December 2017. In terms of foreign capital, 73 of these firms are foreign, and 177 companies have foreign partners. The number of companies with academician partners is 909.
- When we look at the sectoral distribution of firms in technoparks, the software sector takes the first place with 37 %, followed by the computer and communication technology sector with 17 %. In other words, approximately 55 % of the 4,624 firms are in the software, computer, and communication technologies sectors.
- When we look at the number of personnel employed in technoparks, we can see that a total of 45,274 people were employed by December 2017. While there is continuity in employment growth over the years, the fastest increase

occurred between 2012 and 2015. According to the statistics obtained from the Ministry of Science and Industry, about 37,500 of this figure is R&D personnel while the remaining personnel is employed in support and out-of-scope departments.

- In Technology Development Zones, most innovative companies are concentrated in *Software, Informatics, Electronics, Advanced Material Technologies,* in particular, as well as *Design, Nanotechnology, Biotechnology, Automotive, Medical Technologies, and Renewable Energy*, and the total number of R&D projects being implemented in TDZs is *7,843 as of December 2017.* While the number of projects continuously increased over the years, a decrease was observed in 2016–2017. The number of projects fell from 8,583 in 2016 to 7,843 in 2017. The number of completed projects is 26,377 as of January 2018.
- Technology exports made by companies in the operational Technology Development Zones have reached 2.9 Billion US Dollars as of December 2017, including exports to the most developed countries in the world such as the United States, as well as Japan, Israel, United Kingdom, and Germany.
- When the Intellectual Property status of firms operating in technoparks was examined as of January 2018, the number of registered patents was 940, and the number of patent applications was 1,853. While the number of registered utility models is 461, the number of utility models applications is 146. In the same period, 85 industrial designs were registered, and 85 industrial design applications were made. In addition, the number of software copyrights acquired by the companies is 94.
- According to the evaluation results of Technology Development Zones based on the performance index rankings in 2016, METU Technopolis was in the first place, followed by ITU, CYBERPARK, Mersin, and Erciyes. In the last place was Kütahya Dumlupınar Design Technology Development Zone.

References

Arslantekin S.: *Teknokent ve Üniversitelerimiz*. Elektronik Gelişmeler Işığında Araştırma Kütüphaneleri Sempozyumu – Bolu, 2002, 24–26 Ekim, Ankara Üniversitesi: Ankara.

Babacan, M.: *Dünyada ve Türkiye'de Teknoparklar (Bilim ve Teknoloji Parkları)*. Dokuz Eylül Üniversitesi Yayınları: İzmir. 1995.

Bülbül, Y. / Özbay, R.D.: *Teknoparklar: Teknolojik Bilginin Ticarileşmesi*. İstanbul Ticaret Odası Yayınları: İstanbul. 2011.

Castells, M. / Hall, P.: *Technopoles of the World: The Making of Twenty-First-Century Industrial Complexes*. Routledge Pub.: London and New York. 1995.

Çetin, A.C.: "Teknolojide Yeni Bir Ufuk: Teknoparklar". *Süleyman Demirel Üniversitesi İİBF Dergisi* 2, 1997, pp. 209–217.

Eren, M.: *Türkiye'nin Teknolojik Gelişmesinde Teknoparklar ve Ar-Ge Desteği*. Yayımlanmamış Yüksek Lisans Tezi, Marmara Üniversitesi Sosyal Bilimler Enstitüsü, İstanbul, 2011.

Erün, T.: *Ankara'daki Teknopark Firmalarının Teknopark İçerisindeki İşbirliği Uygulamalarının Teknoloji Transfer Performansları Üzerine Etkisi*. Yayımlanmamış Yüksek Lisans Tezi, Kara Harp Okulu Savunma Bilimleri Enstitüsü: Ankara, 2012.

Görkemli, H. N.: *Bölgesel Kalkınmada Teknoparkların Önemi ve Konya Teknokent Örneği*, Yayımlanmamış Doktora Tezi, Selçuk Üniversitesi Sosyal Bilimler Enstitüsü: Konya, 2011.

Gül, T.G. / Çakır, S.: "Teknoparklar Ve Teknoloji Üretimi: İzmir Teknoloji Geliştirme Bölgesi Örneği". *Bilgi Ekonomisi ve Yönetimi Dergisi* IX(I), 2014, pp. 79–90.

Harmancı, M. / Önen M. O.: *Dünyada ve Türkiye'de Teknopark ve Teknokent Uygulamaları*. Türkiye Kalkınma Bankası Yayını: Ankara. 1999.

Hu, T. / Lin, C.-Y. / Chang S. L.: "Technology-based regional development strategies and the emergence of technological communities: a case study of HSIP, Taiwan". *Technovation* 25 (4), 2005, pp. 367–380.

Jeremy, D.J.: *International Technology Transfer: Europe, Japan and the USA, 1700–1914*. Edward Elgar: Aldershot. 1991.

Jussawala, M.: *Information Technology Parks of the Asia Pacific: Lessons for the Regional Digital Divide*. M.E. Sharpe Inc.: New York. 2003.

Kayalıdere, G.: "Türkiye'nin Teknoloji Politikalarında Teknoparkların Önemi ve Teknoparklara Yönelik Vergi Avantajları". *Gazi Üniversitesi Sosyal Bilimler Dergisi* 1(1), 2014, pp. 75–96.

Keleş, M. K.: *Türkiye'de Teknokentler: Bir Ampirik İnceleme*. Yayımlanmamış Yüksek Lisans Tezi, Süleyman Demirel Üniversitesi Sosyal Bilimler Enstitüsü: Isparta, 2007.

Kılıç, A.: *Ankara'daki Teknoparklarda Türk Savunma Sanayi Tarafından Sürdürülen Teknoloji Transfer Uygulamalarının Analizi: ODTÜ ve Bilkent Uygulamaları*. Yayımlanmamış Doktora Tezi, Kara Harp Okulu, Savunma Bilimleri Enstitüsü: Ankara, 2009.

Küçük, N.: *Yerel Ekonomik Kalkınmada Yeni Bir Açılım: Teknoparklar (Gaziantep Teknopark Örneği)*. Yayımlanmamış Yüksek Lisans Tezi, Niğde Üniversitesi Sosyal Bilimler Enstitüsü: Niğde, 2010.

Özbay, M.: "Bilime Dayalı Teknoloji Üretim Merkezleri veya Teknoparklar". *Gazi Üniversitesi Fen Bilimleri Enstitüsü Dergisi* 13(4), 2000, pp. 1109–1118.

Polat, Ç.: *Assessment of Technology Development Activities in Turkish Technoparks*. Yayımlanmamış Yüksek Lisans Tezi. Boğaziçi Üniversitesi, Fen Bilimleri Enstitüsü: İstanbul, 2007.

Sakarya, F.: *Teknopark İçerisindeki Teknoloji Transferini Artırmaya Dönük İşbirlikleri ve Teknopark Destek Faaliyetlerinin Firmaların Özümseme Kapasitesi Üzerine Etkisi*. Yayımlanmamış Yüksek Lisans Tezi, Kara Harp Okulu Savunma Bilimleri Enstitüsü: Ankara, 2012.

T.C. Ministry of Science and Industry: *Statistics*, 2018, retrieved 05.02.2018, from https://teknopark.sanayi.gov.tr/.

T.C. Presidential Supervisory Board: *Teknoloji Geliştirme Bölgeleri Kanunu Uygulamalarının Değerlendirilmesi ile Uygulamada Ortaya Çıkan Sorunların Çözümüne İlişkin Öneri Geliştirilmesi*, Research and Review Report: Ankara, 2009.

T. Development Bank: *Dünyada ve Türkiye'de Teknopark ve Teknokent Uygulamaları*. Türkiye Kalkınma Bankası Araştırma Müdürlüğü, Ankara, 1999.

Tepe, S. / Zaim, H.: "Türkiye ve Dünyada Teknopark Uygulamaları: Teknopark İstanbul Örneği". *İstanbul Ticaret Üniversitesi Sosyal Bilimler Dergisi* 15(29/1), 2016, pp. 19–43.

Ünlükaplan, İ.: "Avrupa Birliği Üyesi Ülkelerde İktisadi Kalkınma, Rekabetçilik ve İnovasyon İlişkilerinin Kanonik Korealasyon Analizi ile Belirlenmesi". *Maliye Dergisi* 157, 2009, pp. 235-250.

Osman Bayraktar[1] and Canan Ataç

The Effects of Industry 4.0 on Human Resources Management

Abstract: The opportunity of the internet in terms of eliminating the distance and the ability to instantly transfer large data influence many areas of life, and deeply affect industrial production and processes. High-tech manufacturing operations feel these changes earlier. It is inevitable for the enterprises operating with traditional technologies to be exposed to this effect in parallel with the change of environmental structure. In this study, the concept of Industry 4.0 is considered as a concept and secondly how human resources managers perceive this process from the viewpoint of human resources management of the four advanced technology companies operating in the Bursa region is investigated. An in-depth interview method was used to gather information in the study. As a result of the research, the expectation is that the Industrial 4.0 transformation of the industry will deeply affect human resources management processes due to its business environment. At each stage, it is foreseen that technology-integrated business processes will cause some of the unskilled employees to lose their jobs, while the higher qualified employees will be needed more, but it will be difficult to find these employees and keep them at work.

Keywords: Industry 4.0,Big Data, Internet of Objects, Smart Factories

Introduction

The greatest power of European economy is based on industry. Seventeen percent of the European Union GNP is of industrial origin. This industry power provides 32 million jobs. Despite this, in recent years industrialized European countries have been having difficulty competing with developing countries. The main reason for this is the aging population structure. According to the estimates of the Economic Policy Committee and the European Commission, by 2050 the population in the 24–60 age group will decline by 16 % to 48 million while the elderly population will increase to 58 million (Qina et al. 2016). Western countries, which anticipate that this change in population structure will force them to compete in the future, have attempted to redesign their industries in such a way as to require the least labor force. The most important factor behind the industry's 4th move is the incentive to stay behind.

1 Correspondent writer: Osman Bayraktar e-mail: obayraktar@ticaret.edu.tr

Industry 4.0 nomenclature belongs to Germans (ESO 2015). However, other industrial countries in the world are aware of this new wave in the industry, and every country develops a policy on its own within this area. China called its own industrial development plan "Made in China 2015" (Qina et al. 2016), which is similar to Industry 4.0 in 2015.

With this change, intelligent robots will be used more effectively in all business processes. When we look at the case from the perspective of human resource management, the change aimed at the Industry 4.0 initiative will require less manpower in production, and qualifications in the labor force will change. The human resources departments have to keep up with this transformation by renewing themselves. After all these changes, not only the enterprises but also the state policies should be updated in line with the formation of the Industry 4.0. It will be inevitable to lag behind the global economy by losing the competitive power for companies and states that cannot make this update (ESO 2015).

Overview of Industrial Revolutions

The Industrial Revolutions are seen as the basis of many innovations, modernity, and transformation in the world. The economic transformation that began in England in 1760 spread to other European countries. Prior to the Industrial Revolution, the economy was based on agriculture and animal husbandry, and tradesmen and craftsmen engaged in crafts such as weaving, blacksmithing, and handcrafted benches. With the invention of the steamer, economical structure based on economics, mechanization and serial production based on soil, agriculture, and muscle power has been passed. The amount of production and sales increased with the mechanization. The capital, which is in production, has made more production using machinery, and big companies have begun to be born. The population started to gather in the cities with new job opportunities, which resulted in a rapid population increase. The economy has recovered, and the standards of living have begun to improve (EKOIQ 2014). Below are the stages of three Industrial Revolution and production processes.

First Industrial Revolution

The First Industrial Revolution covers the period beginning in the 1760s and going through the 1830s. In this process, production has evolved from hand and muscle strength to machine use. By using coal and steam instead of wood, the power of the machines has been increased. This situation has caused mechanization and establishment of factories. Family companies and small enterprises have left their place in large factories. The use of steam, coal, and iron as energy sources and raw materials accelerated railway development. The first Industrial Revolution was defined as the machinery of production (Siemens 2016).

The First Industrial Revolution, which began in England, spread throughout Europe and America over time. This radical change in production has also affected social construction. The average lifespan was prolonged, and the population increased. Everyday life has become practical, and quality of life has increased.

With the increase in the number of products produced with the reason of mechanization, Europe has turned to the Middle, Near, and Far East where it can offer prizes and sources of raw materials. International relations have been affected by this situation (ESO 2015).

Second Industrial Revolution

The Second Industrial Revolution covers the period 1840–1870. After the first Industrial Revolution and the mechanization of production, the foundations of the new revolution have begun to emerge. The Second Industrial Revolution started with Henry Ford's mass production band design. The Second Industrial Revolution has emerged with changes in basic raw materials and energy sources. Steam, coal, and iron, as well as steel, electricity, petroleum, and chemical materials have been used in the production process (Alçın 2016).

The development of steel production has played a major role in the development of the production network, especially the railways. The facilitation of transportation made it easy for the products to reach new markets and supply raw materials. On the other hand, other new developments such as telephone, radio, typewriter, and cheap newspaper paper have also shaped communication and transmission.

In the Second Industrial Revolution, electric technology was developed and started to be used in production lines. This has allowed us to develop the machines, increase the amount of production, and meet the concept of mass production. The main actors of the Second Industrial Revolution were England, Germany, USA, and Japan. This revolution is defined as the massification of production.

Third Industrial Revolution

In the first half of the twentieth century, industrialization and technological progress slowed down due to the two great world wars. In addition, negative economic developments such as the 1929 global crisis were experienced. The

Third Industrial Revolution began to use programmable machines, which in 1970 caused mechanical and electronic technologies to leave their place in digital technology. In this period, technologies such as computers, microelectronics, fiber optics, lasers, telecommunication, nuclear, biotechnology have influenced the direction and form of development production. With the use of computer and communication technologies in production processes, mechanical and practical products have begun to enter our lives (ESO 2015).

In the Third Industrial Revolution, renewable energy sources such as the sun and the wind have become important with the irreparable sources and environmental concerns. Thus, the need for body power begins to grow.

Now we are in a period of a new industrial revolution. It started with a period in which interrelated processes were in communication, objects connected to each other via internet gathered data and completely changed the production process, and machines started to emphasize interaction with people.

New Revolution: Industry 4.0

The concept of the Industry 4.0 can be described as an increase in the amount of digitization throughout the entire value chain, and a possible structuring of data transfer between people, objects, and systems in real time. The Fourth Industrial Period emerged when the machines used in production started to manage themselves and production processes without the need for human power. This structure, which is referred to by the concept of "the Internet of objects", extends to the self-management of the manufacturing factory.

The Fourth Industrial Revolution was first spoken at the Hannover Fair in 2011. In October 2012, the Bosch Group and former SAP CEO Henning Kagermann created a working group and presented the Fourth Industrial Revolution proposal file to the German Federal Government. The German government began preparing its own Industry 4.0 transformation roadmap in 2013. Bosch took part in the Industry 4.0 working group and played a leading role (Siemens 2016).

Industry 4.0, which was adopted at the beginning of 2011, has become a market of billions of euros from a technical term within a period of 6 years. By 2020, it is expected that only 140 billion Euros will be invested in Industry 4.0 within Europe. Furthermore, it is anticipated that 14 billion devices will interact with each other through the Internet of objects (ESO 2015).

In 2013, the "Industry 4.0 Platform" (www.plattform-i40.de) was put into practice to prevent the Industry 4.0 from being just one theory and to take action. This platform is primarily aimed at supporting the development of new technologies, defining the basic standards for the Industry 4.0 vision, identifying new business models, and conducting community awareness activities (Siemens 2016).

Over time, the concept of Industry 4.0 has become the focus of all countries that have developed beyond Germany to design a new industrial system. With the support of the necessary legal regulations, this concept is intended to be more widespread and to create more effective opportunities for new products and processes. Industry 4.0 also presents various challenges and threats for businesses. The difficulties of this diversity can be summed up in four areas: economic, social, technical, and environmental (Hecklaua et al. 2016).

Distinctive Features of Industry 4.0

The distinguishing innovations this new era brings are as follows:

- Global interaction of storage systems and resources with machines.
- The development of unique intelligent products with location knowledge.
- The smart factories, adapting to product specifications.
- Realization of new business models.
- New social infrastructure in the workplace for the employees, business structure being sensitive to individual differences.
- Better work/life balance.
- Responding to individual consumer demands.
- Intelligent software developed for immediate response to engineering and problems.

Concepts Related to Industry 4.0

It is necessary to know its concepts in order to understand Industry 4.0. Knowing these concepts gives important clues about what might be happening today and in the future.

3D Printers

The 3D printer is a machine that transforms digital three-dimensional computer data into real objects that can be handled. All mechanical parts except engine and electronic parts are printed by 3D printers (Festo 2016).

3D printer technology addresses a wide area. The areas of usage of this technology have a range from information technologies, genetics, medicine, to industry, food, and jewelry. With 3D printers, a lot of things are produced, including human tissues and musical instruments. These devices drastically reduce production costs.

While the creation of the design in the virtual environment is achieved through various CAD programs, the CAD is scanned with an existing object and transferred to the virtual center by scanning. Prototypes that can move with unlimited color options are produced with 3D printers.

Internet of Objects

Objects must communicate with each other through the use of the Internet as an intermediary, and their work is their own management. It is really important in terms of facilitating our daily life. Smart home technologies are examples of this. This structure, also called "Internet of Industrial Objects", makes smart factories even smarter. Thus, products with many different and complex structures can be produced in shorter time and in quality (ESO 2015).

Virtual Reality

The virtual reality is the main feature of Industry 4.0. Virtual reality is the live, direct, and indirect imagery of the real-world objects enriched by computer-generated sound, image, graphics, and GPS data (ESO 2015). The concept of virtual reality is applied in many different areas such as video games, entertainment sector, military applications, health sector, education, tourism, architecture, and sales-marketing. In the industry, the virtual environment is used at every point such as production planning, design, production, service, maintenance, testing, and quality control (Bayraktar and Kaleli 2007).

Smart Factories

Digitalization has confronted humanity with the concept of intelligent life. In the past, the everyday work carried out by muscular power can now be realized by machines and internet networks. The application of cyber-physical systems in production systems is called Smart Factory. Fifty percent of German companies are planning industrial networks, while 20 % have already transitioned to the intelligent factory of Industry 4.0 (PWC 2016).

Features of smart factories include:

- Being successful in managing complex production processes smoothly and quickly.
- Its products being smooth and long-lasting.
- Inside them, machines, people, and production resources are in interaction.

Cyber-Physical Systems

The cyber world is based on the physical side of the world. The boundaries of the physical world expand with the cyber world. The cyber-physical systems that the cyber and physical world come together are made up of these two elements. These two worlds communicate with each other with a designated internet address on the Internet. It is called the virtual environment which is created by the simulations of the objects in the real world. Cyber-physical systems include monitoring, control, and coordination, as well as computation and communication.

The cyber-physical systems, which aim to raise the boundaries between real and virtual worlds, and to create a wide communication network with the Internet of objects, constitute one of the forces at the core of Industry 4.0. Cyber-physical systems are intelligent systems in which ever-changing data are simultaneously linked together in a virtual cloud system. The aim of this system is to realize "intelligent monitoring" and "intelligent control". The best example of this is the Smart Factories. For example, failures occurring at any stage of production can be eliminated immediately and on the spot, and the system can operate at full capacity and without any problems. This system can also make a difference in R&D, design, and marketing processes. For example, before a factory is physically installed, all feasibility studies can be done by simulation. A significant number of manufacturers have begun using radio frequency identification (RFID) production, which can be evaluated under "Smart environments" or "Wireless sensor networks". First, Volvo Trucks used RFID systems based on information systems in the production of Toyota automobile parts (Siemens 2016) to ensure continuity in production.

Big Data

The advancement of technology, the development of the Internet, and the social media revolution have facilitated access to information. The information that is easy to access also brings the problem of useless and wrong information with it. This mass of information has been described as information garbage. Extracting real and reliable information from this area, where so much information is involved, leads us to the concept of Big Data.

Big Data, social media sharing, Internet statistics, blogs, photos, videos, logs, etc., transform all collected data from sources such as textures into meaningful and workable forms. When this converted data is correctly interpreted, it makes a great contribution to companies taking strategic decisions and managing their risks. Accurate strategic decisions are made up of accurate information. That's why it's great Big Data for Industry 4.0 (Alçin 2016).

Firms have understood how important even the slightest information is. It is known that such valuable data are everywhere. Every click we make while using the Internet is a very important data source. RFID and sensor technologies are constantly accumulating data due to their environment. All of this, financial data, medical data, when they all come together, are giant data. All the information we need is in Big Data. For example, they record every move made by an information technology company's systems and find answers to questions such as "which faults are related to each other", "how much does your problem system affect its performance". A bank can identify fraud attempts from customer actions. A social sharing site can analyze the likes and dislikes of its users and show them the best ads. A store can analyze the customers' products and offer them the best products and increase their sales. Big Data shed light on the future (Big Data 2017).

Smart Robots

The robot is described as an electro-mechanical device that performs pre-programmed tasks. The biggest use of robots is industrial production. Robot technology is called "Robotics" and "Mechatronics" in the literature. When we say "automation", robots or robotic technologies come to mind. Robots are still widely used in production. Robot technologies are important to increase the effectiveness of Industry 4.0. For example, in smart factories, robots will manage production by recognizing each other, doing business, communicating, analyzing, and adapting more quickly to changes. In the automotive sector, in a variety of production processes such as paint, assembly, welding, quality control, a large number of robots are used. With Industry 4.0, robots are aimed at achieving a totally robotic approach to production. For example, the robot responsible for the welding process may be able to provide other points of service by updating its software if necessary in the installation area. Moreover, it will do so entirely on the basis of its own observations, analyses, and predictions (Festo 2016).

Simulation

Simulation is defined as the creation of an artificial environment or imitation of the order in a timely manner for the operation of any process or system in the technical sense. Imitating processes or systems in the real world very close to reality provides great advantages in many respects from saving time from human effort to avoiding gains from economic gain (EKOIQ 2014).

After the steam, electricity, and computing forces entering the factory in the first three industrial revolutions, the simulation technology is now used in factories and provides significant benefits.

Horizontal and Vertical Integrations

The continuous stream of data provided by interconnected structures underlying Industry 4.0 is a critical point of production. In order to achieve this flow, horizontal and vertical integration must take place not only at certain points but also at every point.

"Horizontal integration" means a continuous flow between each step in the production and planning process itself, as well as between the steps of production and planning processes of different enterprises from raw material procurement to design, to production, to marketing, and to recycling.

"Vertical integration" means providing uninterrupted communication and flow of technological infrastructure used in all processes. The integration of sensors such as sensors, valves, motors, control panels, production management systems, and ERP software in the production area is covered in this scope.

With vertical and horizontal integration, Industry 4.0 is able to respond quickly to changes and problems in the production process, facilitating private and personalized production, and optimizing the global supply chain. Businesses are becoming more flexible. The changes are provided by simple interface updates (www.innovarobotik.com 2016).

Cloud Computing Systems

Along with the advances in information technology, increasing data volumes and increasing use of the internet have begun to force existing hardware systems and software. With this need, the concept of cloud computing systems has emerged. Cloud computing is the general name given to services that provide information sharing between computing devices. It has been adopted by computer theorists that the future of the Internet passes through the cloud system. There is a sense that the cloud system will be used instead of future hard disks (www.innovarobotik.com 2016).

The industry benefits from 4.0 cloud computing. Features such as large storage areas and advanced computational power make it possible to collect, analyze, and store data in production. Communication between intelligent devices has also led to a new breakthrough in the industry by working together with Big Data, the Internet of Objects, and Cloud Computing.

Compliance of Companies to Industry 4.0

Up to this point, we have been given information about the reasons for the emergence of Industry 4.0, its development, and the point it is at today. This information makes it clear that Industry 4.0 is experiencing breakthrough developments, that technology continues to progress continuously, and that companies outside of this development will be destroyed.

With Industry 4.0, the following developments will be faced.

- Production process will be digitized.
- Production processes will manage themselves.
- Products will be able to carry information and provide this information to consumers.
- The Internet of objects will dominate the entire factory, the firm, and the business world.
- Production performance will be higher.
- All data and business principles will be analyzed in digital programs and intelligent systems.
- Resources will increase, costs will decrease.

Difficulties in adapting to Industry 4.0 will be discussed below.

- Standardization
- Process/work organization
- Eligible products
- New business models
- Security/know-how applications
- Qualified workforce
- Research
- Training/professional development
- Legal infrastructure

We can foresee that companies and countries should take the following steps in order to comply with Industry 4.0.

- Strengthen the technological infrastructure.
- Informatics technologies should create training programs to strengthen innovation and entrepreneurship.
- Identify new business models.
- New technologies should be developed.
- Provide new collaborations appropriate to the digital world.

- Identify the priorities of producers.
- Increase the quality of the changing workforce.

The Impact of Industry 4.0 and Human Resources Management

In the United Kingdom, in a research study, there are three technological bases (Rhisiart et al. 2014) that have radically influenced the future of the business: artificial intelligence and robots, shaky developments on the Internet, and time and space constraints for the acquisition of skills. "At present, at least 65 % of children who go to primary school will work in jobs that do not yet exist when they have completed school education," said WEF (2016), the World Economic Forum's "Future of Jobs" report. Nine of the 18 factors that are predicted to affect business structure in the future are the roots of technology: mobile internet and cloud technology, the increase of computing power, hence the processing capacity of Big Data, new energy providers and technologies, Internet of objects, mass information exchange via internet, sharing economy, peer-peer sharing platforms, highly developed robotic and independent transportation, artificial intelligence and learning of machines, advanced production and 3D printing systems, advanced materials, biotechnology and genomics.

We actually see some of these effects in our lives. The results of one part will be reflected in your life in the next few years. These developments will affect the technological, socio-economic, geopolitical, and population structure, but will also lead to the emergence of new business categories and new professions while also removing some of them. These developments will change the set of skills needed in both old and new jobs, redefine how and where people will work, require a new management understanding and new management regulations. According to estimates, these developments in technology will lead to the disappearance of 7.1 million people in the period between 2015 and 2020; three out of which will be from the office and management business partner, and one third from other smaller business families (WEF 2016, p.13).

In the future, the ability to manufacture will come from a more critical factor than capital. The increase in the level of your ability will result in lower wages in the lower skill, higher wages in the higher skill, which will increase social tension (Schwab 2015).

Industry 4.0 will change the daily lifestyles of communities and all the habits of business life. This change will have to keep pace with states, societies, companies, and employees. Those who cannot catch up with change will face the risk of economic disappearance.

This change, which takes place over states, societies, companies, and employees, will also affect human resource management in a fundamental way. Industry 4.0 will change all steps from production to distribution, from distribution to marketing, and will incorporate radical innovations within the organization. At the center of these innovations will be human resources. Agile companies with easy-to-change adapters will pass before the competition. In order for the agile process to spread throughout the company, human resources will need to

Tab. 1: Knowledge and Skills Required for Activities in Your Future Factory. Source: Lars Gehrke et al. (2015), "Industry 4.0., A Discussion of Qualifications and Skills in the Factory of the Future", www.vdi.de.x

	Must	Should	Could
Technical Qualifications and Skills	IT knowledge and abilities, Knowledge Management, Computer programming/ coding abilities	IT knowledge and abilities, Knowledge Management, Computer programming/coding abilities	IT knowledge and abilities, Knowledge Management, Computer programming/ coding abilities
	Data and information processing and analytics	Interdisciplinary/ generic knowledge about technologies and organizations	Specialized knowledge about technologies
	Statistical knowledge	Specialized knowledge of manufacturing activities and processes	Awareness of ergonomics
	Organizational and proccessual understanding	Awareness of IT security and data protection	Understanding of legal affairs
	Ability to interact with modern interfaces (human-machine/ human-robot)		
Personal Qualifications and Skills	Self and time management	Trust in new technologies	
	Adaptability and ability to change	Mind-set for continuous improvement and lifelong learning	
	Team working abilities		
	Social skills		
	Communication skills		

redefine its mission, job definition, and responsibilities (Alayoğlu 2010). Tab. 1 summarizes the qualifications that are expected to have occupations for future employees.

The impact of Industry 4.0 on human resources management processes is explained below.

Strategic Perspective

In order for human resources to be able to contribute to business results, business units need to be strategic partners. In order to achieve this, HR specialists who can understand and interpret financial data, have a good command of the dynamics in the sector in which the company operates and to the up-to-date developments, and who contribute to important projects carried out in the company and develop applications and projects parallel to these elements will be needed.

Employment

According to the researches, employment is aimed to grow by 6 % in the 2020s. This growth will increase consumption, and the economy will be affected. The presence of equipped elements in the installation and development of intelligent devices and systems will be crucial. With digital conversion, all processes and customer expectations will change.

With the spread of robots, technological unemployment will arise. Technological developments will change the structure of the workforce in the short run and partly cause unemployment. In the long run, the labor force will increase in quantity and quality. The muscular power in the past will leave its place to the mind. Intelligence will also increase the level and quality of education. In the long run, highly qualified individuals will be employed. Robots and people will act together and be managed together in harmony (EKOIQ 2014).

It will be very difficult to find these talents. The definition of the workforce will change. Consultants, home office workers, freelancers, brand awareness professionals, and suppliers will contribute to the activities of periodic and project-based companies. These people will never be deprived of their jobs due to their talents. Objective perspective lines will present different perspectives as an eye from outside with fresh information. This will make the companies rich.

Performance Management

Depending on changing corporate structures, new generation performance measurement tools will emerge in the coming years. The concept of performance consulting will take its place in business life. From a classical performance perspective that values seniority, it will shift to a performance management understanding that rewards young and hardworking employees. Today, employees want to work with managers who empower and inspire them, to give feedback to managers, to regularly talk about company goals, and to follow developments in this area (Alayoğlu 2010). Still, many companies continue to incorporate new performance measurement methods into their work systems. New network performance measurement methods are much more active than the old ones. To build an effective system, it is necessary to build a complex structure with components such as continuous monitoring, routine checks, performance coaching, staff development, performance reviews, and returnability infrastructure for leaders. These data must also be viewed on a digital system. Companies that provide human resources software services will have to move very fast and keep pace with change.

Reaching the Talent

Human resources will find it difficult to find human resources with the capabilities required by digital conversion and Industry 4.0. Human resource management, which focuses on closing open positions, will leave a proactive approach to talent-oriented, talent-driven proactive approach (LinkedIn 2015). Human resources will want to reach out to qualified personnel from all over the world in order to find and deploy the company's required skills, and new strategies will be developed in this direction. These employees will provide flexible working opportunities for working in the countries where they are located.

Although their competencies are high and the number of qualified staff is high, finding the right talents and positioning them will be one of the biggest challenges in the coming periods. In the coming years, it will become even harder to find people with talent, experience, and skill and to put them into the right jobs. Populations in developed countries are declining, and the baby boomer generation will begin to retire. This necessitates finding talented people from developing countries and joining them in the workforce.

With the digital era, Turkey's most beloved countries have their own abilities; countries with employees who think their skills are inadequate are Germany, Japan, USA, Romania, and Hungary (EKOIQ 2014).

There will be deficiencies in skills in fields that require technical skills such as information technology, mathematics, medicine, and engineering. In this case, companies will try to find and win people with critical skills. The only way to be successful in this competition is to set up your own talent management systems and integrate them into HR processes. Companies that set up their own talent systems and actively use their processes have a financial performance that is over 300 % higher than their competitors and twice as much as their labor force applicants on the market (EKOIQ 2014).

Almost all employees in enterprises will be in the status of "knowledge workers" who do business with technology help. It will not be easy to find next-generation digital capabilities such as Data Scientist, Artificial Intelligence Specialist, Application Developer, Cloud Architect, or Agile Project Specialist. An important part of these abilities is very far from the concepts such as CV, LinkedIn, and Assessment. In this case, standard resource hiring and recruitment methods will not work. Companies like Facebook, Google, Microsoft, and Amazon, which are advantageous in terms of culture and activity, will gain importance in order to find these profiles and gain them to companies. In today's business world, we are experiencing serious problems in terms of the ability of digital talents to come out and be protected even if they do. The value judgments, habits, and behavior of companies cause this.

Training

Training is one of the most important elements of Industry 4.0. Recruitment of the intelligent machines and the qualified workforce that can use these machines, training of the expert staff, the formation of a structure that will perceive the cyber-physical systems, and the updating of the education system from primary school to the university parallel to these developments gains importance in time.

Data-Based Management

The most important decisions taken by institution concern employees. It is necessary to take into consideration the data and vital information that is vital for the company. HR analytics will be on the agenda of more and more companies, and governance-based management will become very important. It will be beneficial to incorporate data that will support personal comments and decisions in the HR field.

Protection of Information

Human resources have a detailed database of employees' personal information. The protection of these data is very important for both the employees and the company. In the business world, the protection of confidential information has become a critical process. Risks in human resources are the protection of the data, wrong recruitment decisions, and loss of ability in a short period of time.

ERP software, preferred by many companies, will leave their place to analytical tools that enable better measurement and decision-making on human-induced issues that run through the cloud. Technological systems will be used to evaluate employees. The storage of information on the cloud and the use of mobile technologies will bring new privacy policies and risks. In addition, the HR will need to tackle problems with information security and intellectual property rights (www.turkishtimedergi.com 2016).

Working Environments

With Industry 4.0, the Y and Z generations will feel the power. In the offices where these generations work intensively, common working areas such as corners and cafes that will support the use of the latest technology and individual work will be preferred. It will increase the number of companies that use office designs to make office work attractive. To attract large companies, young entrepreneurs and equipped young people to their companies, they are developing office designs using new systems in business environments.

In a social sense, a completely different working routine will emerge. The 9am–5pm shift is going to be a working concept that is not constrained by space, and time will be very flexible working away from the understanding of work. Companies that prefer office design to work with flexible hours will multiply (www.turkishtimedergi.com 2016).

Social Media

With social media, everything will go through a more transparent structure. Social media channels will evolve into a democratic platform where information workers can participate at all levels, from complaints or pleasures of customers to employees' side rights, working hours, or interactions with each other. The democratization of work will take the institution away from the hierarchy to a more horizontal organization. Employees can be effective in communicating with each other, producing solutions. This interaction will make people more proactive in making observations and taking responsibility for their work. This new order will be organizational and will change job descriptions from the root (Laleli 2017).

Business and Life Balance

Human resources should identify ways to improve the health and interaction of employees as well as work and life balance. Are your employees healthy? Do they have the habits and knowledge to make them energetic? Are the managers

Tab. 2: Demographic Information Related to Interviewed Operations

Company	A	B	C	D
Respondent	HR Manager	HR Manager	HR Manager	HR Manager
Position seniority/ Workplace seniority	12/12	26/19	6/20	5/28
Sector	Industry automation	Textile	Textile	Machine production/ Industry automation
Capital Structure	Foreign	Foreign	Foreign	Domestic
Age of Business	42	50	65	60
Number of Employees	1000	900	1500	1100
White Collar	200	175	300	250
Blue Collar	800	725	1200	850

helping them focus? Do they have the skills to do their jobs? Can they spare time for their friends and family? Do you have time for the hobbies? They should ask their questions.

Without discrimination, whether large or small, human resources departments in all companies need to incorporate factors such as undertaking the role of "helping people improve their performance", recreation rooms, sports programs, and job quality enhancement programs (Laleli 2017). (Lalei 2017).

Status of Businesses Prepared for Industry 4.0

This research covers four industrial operations operating in Bursa. Three of the businesses are foreign capital. Two of the interviewed firms are textiles, both operating in the field of technology. The number of employees working in the company ranges from 900 to 1500. Negotiations were held in May 2017 with interviews with managers of the human resources and managers responsible for technology, and interviews were conducted in the factory. Demographic information on the interviewed enterprises is given in Tab. 2.

The following four questions were basically directed to business managers:

1. What are the general challenges businesses are facing in the environment that Industries 4.0 brings?
2. How do you anticipate how these challenges will affect current and future business and business processes?

3. What are the core competencies that employees must have to fulfill their position in the current or future business?
4. Do you have any initiatives that you have developed as a business in this area?

The answers given by the enterprises to the questions are shown in Tab. 3.

Results

In response to the question "What are the general challenges that businesses will face in the environment created by Industries 4.0?" the work structure will become technologically more complicated, which will increase the demand for high-qualified staff, but it will be difficult to find and retain these qualities, whereas some of the low-quality staff will lose their jobs. The need for existing selection methods to be inadequate in the future and the need to organize adaptation programs to support existing employees in their adaptation to the new situation are emphases on direct human resources processes.

The answers to the question "How do you anticipate how these challenges will affect your current and future jobs and business processes?" emphasized that the role of consulting firms will become more prominent when it comes to achieving talent. Management directors seem to have agreed on the need for the public to make significant innovations in education in the new period.

The answers to the question "What are the basic competencies that employees must have to fulfill their current or future business?" show that the areas of common emphasis are information technology, communication skills, problem solving, and process skills.

In response to our question, "Do you have any initiatives to develop this field as a business?" it seems that every business is prepared for this. Programs related to Industry 4.0 are carried out centrally in foreign capital enterprises. Responsible persons have been identified and appointed in each business.

Conclusion and Evaluation

This study focuses on the theoretical background, the field research, and the working environment that Industry 4.0 will emerge in industrial enterprises and the possible effects of this environment on the human resources processes. Although the development of industry and technology in a country is realized by the innovation capability and performance of the enterprises, the fact that it can be achieved by the ecosystem approach requires a very wide participation including the public sector. It is unthinkable for the public to be indifferent to

Tab. 3: Responses of Business Managers to Interview Questions

Question	Answer
What are the general challenges businesses are facing in the environment that Industries 4.0 brings?	**A. Company.** The rise of technology will lead to a decrease in the number of blue collar workers. Employment will shift to a staff that is competent and skilled. Those who cannot use the technology will be the problem of adaptation of the X generation, and those staff who cannot renew themselves will be exported from their workplaces. It will be difficult to resume the exported talent and adapt to the companies. Managing the workforce centrally increases costs. The cost of a staff member working in Istanbul at my company is 1.5 times higher than Bursa. With digitization, the built-in labor force will cost less. It is important for companies to conduct cost-benefit analyses. **B. Company.** I think we will have the problem of retaining the qualified workforce to find a qualified workforce. For this reason, our company has diversified its motivation tools. We have actively involved our diversity team in the HR processes to manage diversity. In this way, I think that we can reach many human resources and make a difference. **C. Company.** The competencies of human power in the existing structure will not be enough. The development and exchange programs need to be prepared and implemented on the blue and white sides. Global human resources will be needed. We have the risk of losing employees who are working hard with digitization. I think this could harm the economy of the country. It will be difficult to find highly qualified employees. The selection methods available will not suffice. **D. Company.** Employment will vary. While the highly skilled workforce will have a 5 %–10 % increase in employment, the collar workforce will be in the same blue reduction. In this case it will cause unemployment. Orientation programs will need to be prepared for the adaptation of the new workforce to the company. Diversification of motivational actions and new proposal and reward systems will have to be put into effect. Implementation of a structured training development process is required. The consolidation of your abilities and the retention of these abilities will become an essential necessity. It is necessary for the public administration to determine some laws and policies to pass the Industry 4.0 process. It should support this through training and incentive processes. Otherwise, it is not possible to capture the Industry 4.0. We cannot go beyond a system that we learn from global companies.
How do you anticipate how these challenges will affect current and future business and business processes?	**A. Company.** The state needs to change its policies. A successful path cannot be pursued if the state policy does not own the Industry 4.0. Education is something that needs improvement at the beginning. There is a need for reform from primary education. **B. Company.** Regrettably, the current education system (including vocational high schools) is not enough to train qualified labor force. It is very difficult for us to get rid of assemblage and labor-intensive work if there is no education reform starting from the vocational high school.

(*continued on next page*)

Tab. 3: (continued)

Question	Answer
	C. Company. Managing human resources processes will be very difficult. With digitization, it will be difficult to manage people and technology together. It will be difficult to keep the talent in the company. Standard practices will bring difficulties to employees. They will ask for flexibility during their stay. The state's rules and harmonization process will force companies. Concurrently companies will be forced. **D. Company.** The expected qualification from the workers will change with Industry 4.0. The jobs that are simple, self-repetitive standard tasks will be replaced with a structure that can decide in complex situations, take visualization and action, and attach importance to preventive care. It will be difficult to find and manage talent. Consultants and supplier companies will be serious players.
What are the core competencies that employees must have to fulfill their position in the current or future business?	**A. Company.** Information technologies; technical skills; communication skills **B. Company.** Technological skills; problem-solving competencies; process skills; analytical skills. **C. Company.** Technical skills; innovation; change; technological capabilities; strong communication skill. **D. Company**. Cognitive flexibility; problem-solving; creativity; coordination; emotional intelligence; to think right and to decide; service centrality; compromise; people management.
Do you have any initiatives that you have developed as a business in this area?	**A. Company.** Our company has accepted the "technology for life" approach. Currently, we run more than 50 projects. In a project in our factory in Germany, people live and learn how to work in high-tech equipment and how products interact with each other. The machines are told which product to produce next. More than one product can be produced on the same line. With the RFID (radio frequency identification system) system, the status of the products can be monitored at any time. Technicians can see the instruction manuals in their glasses and use their hands freely. In case of any malfunction, the robots give the knowledge of the service. The aim of this project is to optimize production transport networks by bringing together information technology and production automation through the internet. A similar model is applied to our Bursa plant. A person in charge of Industry 4.0 has been assigned. This person is collecting data and improving the process. Then the project will be spread to all our companies in Turkey. It is imperative that we all have this change ready. **B. Company.** We have just started outsourcing work on digitization. So what we will do in this area will be planned in the coming period and roadmap will be drawn. The very active use of HR analytics now is important. This process, which is carried out globally, is also about to settle in Turkey. Many data will be used to improve processes. This year's motto "digitization" is that we are all excited to keep up with this shift.

Tab. 3: (continued)

Question	Answer
	C. Company. We divided the IT department into two and turned it into a unit working with Industry 4.0. Pilot applications in production have already begun. **D. Company.** We want our company to become a factory of future technology. We want to adapt our current conditions to the future with energy, efficient production lines with high flexibility, an optimized workflow of information and materials, efficient energy network for building and production processes, and a practical and integrated training factory. We want to optimize logistics and material flow, optimize inventories, produce without bottlenecks, and incorporate suppliers into the production process. We want to monitor and restore corrective measures with production cameras, sensors, RFIDs, and barcodes, to minimize energy consumption. We are working on an Industry 4.0 team for this and a computer engineer responsible for operations.

this issue, as industrial production affects both the economy and employment. Germany and China are the most striking examples of this.

The aim of this research is to clarify the state of opinion, expectation, and preparedness about how the Industrial Industry transformation in the industry will affect the processes of human resources. The information we receive from business managers shows that every business is prepared for the new business environment that this process will bring, and that they have developed initiatives and measures. The common opinion of business managers is that some of the low-qualified employees will lose their jobs, so some people in this group will lose their jobs, while Industry 4.0 will affect employees based on expected skills and skill profiles, resulting in higher demand for high-qualified employees.

The most important condition of sustainable competitive power is investing in technology. Staying behind the global economy will make competition almost impossible. The country, the companies, the machines, and the employees have to increase their capabilities in line with Industry 4.0.

Industry 4.0 will change the daily lifestyles of communities and all the habits of business life. This change will have to keep pace with states, societies, companies, and employees. Those who cannot catch up with change will face the risk of economic disappearance.

The research was carried out in the Bursa region and only on four enterprises. It is not possible to generalize the results obtained in this direction. However, it can be said that three of the interviewed companies are multinational corporations and the results are considerable in terms of human resources when considering the number of people they work with. A research that will cover different geographical regions and larger numbers of businesses will undoubtedly reveal the expectations in this area more reliably.

References

Alayoğlu, Nihat: "İKY'de Yeni Dönem Yetenek Yönetimi". *Ticaret ve Turizm Eğitim Fakültesi Dergisi 1*. 2010, pp. 1–97.

Alçın, Sinan: "Üretim İçin Yeni Bir İzlek Sanayi 4.0". *Journal of Life Economics* 8. 2016, pp. 19–30.

Bayraktar, Erkan / Kaleli, Fatih: *Sanal Gerçeklik Uygulama Alanları*. Akademik Bilişim, 31 Ocak-2 Şubat: Afyon. 2007.

Big Data, retrieved 24.05.2017, from http://devveri.com/big-data.

EKOIQ: "Endüstri 4.0 Akıllı Yeni Dünya". *EKOIQ*, Değişim Özel Eki. 2014.

ESO: "Sanayi 4.0". İzmir: Ege Sanayi Odası. 2015.

Festo. *Endüstri 4.0 Sunumu*, retrieved 24.05.2017, from http://www.tiad.org/assets/admin/js/plugins/kcfinder/upload/files/Festo_FikretKemalAkyuz.pdf. 2016.

Gehrke, Lars / Kühn, Arno / Rule David / Moore, Paul / Bellmann, Cristoph/ Siemes, Sebastian/Dawood, Dania/ Singh, Lakshmi/ Kulik, Julie / Standley, Matthew: *A Discussion of Qualifications and Skills in the Factory of the Future: A German and American Perspective*, retrieved 10.2017, from http://www.vdi.eu/fileadmin/vdi_de/redakteur/karriere_bilder/VDI-ASME__2015__White_Paper_final.pdf. 2015.

Hecklaua, Fabian / Galeitzkea, Mila / Flachsa, Sebastian / Kohlb, Holger: "Holistic Approach for Human Resource Management in Industry 4.0". *Procedia CIRP* (54). 2016, pp. 1-6.

Laleli, Şule: *Mobil Yakalılar*, retrieved 27.06.2018, from http://www.fortuneturkey.com/mobil-yakalilar-42504. 2017.

LinkedIn: *2015 Yetenek Trendleri*, retrieved 24.05.2017, from https://business.linkedin.com/content/dam/business/talent-solutions/global/en_us/c/pdfs/2015-T%C3%BCrkiye-Yetenek-Trendleri.pdf. 2015.

Qina, Jian/ Liu, Ying / Grosvenora, Roger: "A Categorical Framework of Manufacturing for Industry 4.0 and Beyond". *Procedia CIRP* (52). 2016, pp. 173–178.

PWC: *Industry 4.0: Building the Digital Enterprise*, retrieved 27.06.2018, fromhttps://www.pwc.com/gx/en/industries/industries-4.0/landing-page/industry-4.0-building-your-digital-enterprise-april-2016.pdf. 2016.

Rhisiart, Martin/ Glover, Peter / Beck, Helen: *The Future of Work Jobs and Skills in 2030*, retrieved 23.05.2017, from www.ukces.org.uk/thefutureofwork. 2014.

Schwab, Klaus: *The Fourth Industrial Revolution What It Means and How to Respond*, retrieved 23.05.2017, from https://www.foreignaffairs.com: https://www.foreignaffairs.com/articles/2015-12-12/fourthindustrialrevolution. 2015.

Siemens: *Endüstri 4.0 Yolunda*, retrieved 24.05.2017, from http://cdn.endustri40.com/file/ab05aaa7695b45c5a6477b6fc06f3645/End%C3%BCstri_4.0_Yolunda.pdf. 2016.

WEF: *The Future of Jobs*. World Economic Forum. Geneva, 2016.

www.innovarobotik.com: *Yatay, dikey entegrasyon*, retrieved 05.24.2017, from https://www.innovarobotik.com/yatay-dikey-entegrasyon. 2016.

www.turkishtimedergi.com: *2017'de İK'ya Yön Verecek Trenler*, retrieved 05.24.2017, from http://www.turkishtimedergi.com/insan-kaynaklari/2017de-ikya-yon-verecek-3-trend/. 2016.

Gülsüm Şeyma Koca, Gülnur İlgün and Seda Sönmez

Investigation of the Relation Between Sustainable Development and Health by Canonical Correlation Analysis

Abstract: *"Sustainable development"* is one of the development models addressed after the second half of the twentieth century, including the economic and social development of countries, the management of environmental policies and some social dimensions. The concept of sustainable development can be examined by various indicators such as the increase in real incomes per capita of countries, improvement in health and nutritional status, educational achievements, access to resources and increase in basic freedoms. The basic requirements for sustainable development are the necessity to examine health, environment and sustainable development together. For this reason, the aim of the study is to examine the relationship between sustainable development and health. The universe of work is consisting of 133 countries, according to income classification of the World Bank (WB), the upper-middle and upper-income group. Research variables include annual population growth, GDP, school enrollment rates (primary and secondary), the percentage of access to improved water resources, added value (percentage of GDP) of agriculture, industry, services, etc., employment to population ratio and labor force participation rate. The health variables of the study are life expectancy at birth, health expenditures, fertility rate, crude death rate, crude birth rate and infant mortality rate. Canonical correlation method was used in the analysis of the data. As a result of the analysis, a strong and meaningful relationship ($r_c = 0.75$) was observed between sustainable development and health. It is believed that the results obtained are important in terms of a holistic assessment of the health and economic interaction of the economic and social structure that is important in the development of countries.

Keywords: Sustainable Development Health Canonical Correlation Analysis

Introduction

Even though sustainable development notion is a concept that is dealt with and frequently discussed since the twentieth century, it is seen that there are different views on its definition. The main reason of these differences is that the concept is in the extent of requiring the human being to be taken into consideration from both environmental and social and economic perspective (Lélé 1991, p.607). However, it is observed that the definition made in the report prepared by World Commission on Environment and Development (Brundtland Commission) in

1987 is the one used most frequently in the literature (Mebratu 1998, p.496). According to this sustainable development is defined as "meeting the needs of the current generation by not removing the ability of future generations to meet their own needs" (UNECE, 2017). Based upon this definition, it can be stated that sustainable development concept keeps gaining importance day by day with the awareness about the socio-economic subjects such as the occurrence of environmental problems, increase in poverty and inequality and worries on humanity having a healthy future (Hopwood et al. 2005, p39).

Following the World Commission On Environment and Development's report, principles of sustainable development was improved in the report known as the Rio Declaration prepared by the General Assembly of the United Nations (UN) in 1992, and suggestions have been submitted about the strategies, programs, projects and other activities that can be implemented by the countries (Ríos-Osorio et al. 2012, p.739). In this period, sustainability of economy was also discussed and thus not only problems about the use of vital resources but also problems related to the well-being of the person were taken into consideration (Akgül 2010, p.137).

In the report called Agenda 21 prepared by UN in the same period, as in the Rio Declaration report, it is clearly stated that sustainable development is a progress paving way to increase the human potential; however, in case of a conflict, human welfare should be determinant (Richards, 2002: 1). Following these works Millennium Declaration was issued by the UN in 2000 and in this report, the Millennium Development Goals (MDGs) were determined. The MDGs comprises of a set of eight development goals related to enhancing conditions for excess poverty reduction, protection of the environment and aidless societies in the world (IOM, 2014: 2). Within this set, there are three goals related to health: (1) reducing the death of children under five years of age, (2) reducing the death rate of mother and (3) reversing HIV/AIDS, tuberculosis and malaria spread. Nonetheless, in the Sustainable Development Goals (SDGs) set determined in the meeting held by interstate Open Working Group within UN, seventeen goals were determined, but only one of them was seen to be related with health (improving the well-being of every segment of the society from every age and providing a healthy life) (Chapman 2017, p.1098; Buse and Hawkes 2015, p.2). As understood from all these reports, the understanding of health within the framework of sustainable development is basically a phenomenon and plays a key role in the realization of development model goals (Ríos-Osorio 2012, p.745).

The relation between sustainable development and health was discussed many times, and it is thought that health is an important factor in the realization of sustainable development. Also, the realization of sustainable development it shall be beneficial to the formation of a healthy society (Pantyley 2017, p.477). In order for sustainable development to realize development in both economic and social and environmental dimensions such as reduction of social isolation and excess poverty, maintaining environmental development and a good management should be provided. However, even if each dimension contributes to the other's development, health sector takes place as a key input in the realization of all dimensions (Sustainable Development Solutions Network 2014, p.8). From this point of view, it is stated that healthy individuals shall contribute more to economy and society, and at the same time success of sustainable development shall develop health as well. It is stated that with accurate strategies about transportation, accommodation, energy, agriculture and poverty, risks related to health can be decreased and especially non-contagious diseases can be reduced (Pan American Health Organization 2013, p.92).

As a result, realization of sustainable development depends if and only on the situation when there is no disease, society is in a well-being state in physical, mental and social way, and it is believed that it is important for comprehensive, equalitarian, economically productive and healthy societies to activate health for both poor and every segment of society (Boyacıoğlu 2012, p.148). In this study, the relationship between sustainable development and health is examined, and the effect of indicators about health on the indicators of sustainable development are evaluated. Results obtained from the study are thought to submit information based on important evidence to health politicians and planners.

Method

In this section of the study, information about the aim and importance of the study, universe, and sample, research variables, and data analysis, the used method take place.

Aim and Importance of the Research

Even if the processes towards the development of countries are focused essentially on economic (income distribution, employment, etc.), social and environmental analyses, one of the global aims regarding sustainable development is health. Some requirements towards enhancing health services of countries and health status of individuals reveal the need to analyze health, environment and sustainable development altogether. Therefore, the aim of the study is the analysis of the relationship between sustainable development and health.

Universe and Sample of the Research

The universe of the study includes 133 countries from upper-middle income group and upper-income group according to World Bank (WB) income classification. Because of the lack of data on the basis of research variables, 84 countries were included in the study. Data used in the study were acquired from the World Bank's data set of 2014.

Research Variables

In the research, sustainable development variables are considered as dependent variables. These are annual population growth, GDP, school enrollment rates (primary school, secondary school), the percentage of access to improved water resources, the added value of agriculture, industry, services (GDP percentage), employment to population ratio and labor force participation rate. Health variables (life expectancy at birth, health expenditures, fertility rate, crude death rate, crude birth rate and infant death rate) are determined as the independent variable.

Analysis of the Data and the Method Used

In the analysis of data, canonical correlation method was used. Canonical correlation method is one of the statistical methods whose original dates back to Hotelling (1936), and which comprises of at least two variables and is applied with the aim of analyzing the relationship between two variable sets (Thompson 1984, p.10). This method is one of the powerful methods by which the relationship between data sets can be analyzed with multivariable analyses (Reinsel 2012, p.59). The number of variables in the two variable sets of canonical correlation does not have to be the same, and one of the data sets may be dependent variable set whereas the other data set may be independent variable set. In addition to this situation without this condition may be observed (Alpar 2013, p.819). There are various assumptions of canonical correlation analysis. According to that (Gittins 2012, p.22; Alpar 2013, p.822):

- Canonical correlation values change between -1 and +1. Also, canonical correlation coefficient is shown as $r_{c,}$ and the correlation between variants are stated as u_c and v_c.
- Because of aiming of most highering of the relation in the two variable sets, it is aimed for the relation between variables in canonical correlation method to be linear. In cases when the linearity is not provided, the canonical analysis may be insufficient.

Tab. 1: Descriptive Statistics About Variables

Variables	*Mean*	*Standard Deviation*
GDP	2.47	2.22
Annual Population Growth	0.96	1.36
Life Expectancy at Birth	76.73	4.84
Fertility Rate	1.89	0.51
Primary School Enrollment Rate	103.27	5.94
Secondary School Enrollment Rate	102.92	16.82
Access Improved Water Resources %	97.48	3.74
Added Value of the Agriculture	4.92	1.52
Added Value of the Industry	30.59	12.65
Added Value of Services	64.38	12.88
Health Expenditures	7.39	2.67
Employment to Population Ratio	55.14	10.72
Labor Force Participation Rate	61.20	7.63
Crude Birth Rate	14.15	4.85
Crude Death Rate	7.88	2.89
Infant Mortality Rate	9.84	8.69

- The use of information about correlation coefficients in descriptive purposes for canonical correlation analysis is not required to show normal distribution; it is desirable that the data are not normally distributed in other analyses of the coefficient. In this method, extreme values in the data set affect normal distribution and correlations. Thus, it is required to pay attention to the matters for analyzing the data set in terms of extreme values before the analysis.

In the analysis of canonical correlation, it is not desirable that the correlations of the variables within the clusters be very high, but it is not desirable that the correlations of the variables are very high among the clusters.

In the next section, findings obtained from the research are given.

Findings

In this section of the research, findings acquired as a result of the analyses performed take place. In Tab. 1 there are descriptive statistics about the variables used in this study. Accordingly, when the GDPs of the countries are considered, the average value is $ 2.4 billion (± 6.79), whereas average annual population growth rate of countries is 0.96 ±1.36 %. It is observed that the average of enrollment rates as such is as follows: primary school enrollment percentage is 103.27 ± 5.94 %; secondary school enrollment percentage is 102.92 ± 16.8 %, while percentage of access to improved water resources is 97.48 ± 3.74 %, added value percentage of agriculture is 4.92 ± 1.52 %, added value percentage of industry is 30.59 ± 12.65 %, added value percentage of services is 64.38 ± 12.88 %, average of employment-population ratio is 55.14 ± 10.72 % and average of labor force participation rate percentage is 61.20 ± 7.63 %. By examining in terms of health variables, it was found that average life expectancy at birth is 76.73 ± 4.84, whereas health expenditures is $ 7.39 (± 2.67) million, average fertility rate is 1.89 ± 0.51, average crude death rate is 7.88 ± 2.89, average crude birth rate is 14.15 ± 4.85 and average infant mortality rate is 9.84 ± 8.68.

At the analysis phase of the research, the descriptive statistics about variables was investigated and the variables were analyzed considering the linearity approach. In addition, it was observed that the added values (GDP percentage) of annual population growth, agriculture, services, employment to population rate variables did not provide the linearity approach. It was seen that even with the logarithmic transformations this linearity was not maintained. Therefore, as these variables may affect the canonical correlation analysis, they are not included in the analysis. In the next phase of the analysis, correlation values between variables within sets themselves and between the clusters were analyzed. Information about the analysis results regarding the correlation analysis is provided in Tab. 2.

High correlations between variables within the cluster influence canonical correlation analysis. According to this, considering Tab. 2, between the fertility rate and crude birth rate, which are variables within the health set, there is a very high relation (0.92). Similarly there is a high relation between infant mortality rate and life expectancy at birth (0.82). Also there is high relation between infant mortality rate and crude birth rate (0.81). For these reasons, the variables infant mortality rate and fertility rate were extracted from the analysis as they may affect the canonical correlation analysis. When correlation values in development set are examined, it is observed that there is no high correlation value. Thus, there was not any extraction of variables within the development set. Besides, when examined in terms of correlation values between sets, it can be stated that all values are below 0.50. It is observed that this is acceptable for canonical correlation. Accordingly, in Tab. 3, canonical correlation value and test results between development and health set are submitted.

According to Tab. 3 1st canonical correlation (r_{c1}=0.75) and 2nd canonical correlation values (r_{c2}=0.57) are significant. Moreover, other canonical correlation

Tab. 2: Correlation Values Regarding Health and Development Sets

Variables	Life Expectancy at Birth	Fertility Rate	Crude Birth Rate	Health Expenditures	Crude Death Rate	Infant Mortality Rate	Primary School Enrollment Rate	Secondary School Enrollment Rate	Improved Water Resources %	Added Value of the Industry	Labor Force Participation Rate	GDP
Life Expectancy at Birth	1,000											
Fertility Rate	0.588**	1.000										
Crude Birth Rate	0.706**	**0.922****	1.000									
Health Expenditures	0.481**	0.381**	0.471**	1.000								
Crude Death Rate	-0.083	-0.279**	-0.327**	0.477**	1.000							
Infant Mortality Rate	**-0.825****	0.679**	**0.810****	-0.474**	-0.166	1.000						
Primary School Enrollment Rate	0.025*	0.034**	0.286**	0.122**	-0.193**	-0.199	1.000					
Secondary School Enrollment Rate	0.330**	0.187	0.330**	0.405**	0.286*	-0.457**	0.228	1.000				
Access Improved Water Resources %	0.257*	0.534**	0.473**	0.258*	0.252*	0.559**	0.249**	0.258**	1.000			

(continued on next page)

Tab. 2: (continued)

Variables	Life Expectancy at Birth	Fertility Rate	Crude Birth Rate	Health Expenditures	Crude Death Rate	Infant Mortality Rate	Primary School Enrollment Rate	Secondary School Enrollment Rate	Improved Water Resources %	Added Value of the Industry	Labor Force Participation Rate	GDP
Added Value of the Industry	0.473**	0,309**	0.257*	0.411**	-0.376**	0.281**	0.169	-0.051	0.321**	1.000		
Labor Force Participation Rate	0.034	0.263*	0.211*	0.209*	-0.328**	0.232*	0.029*	0.072	0.018*	0.086	1.000	
GDP	0.189	0.243*	0.335**	-0.323**	-0.296**	0.259*	0.045*	0.125	-0.163*	0.259	0.034	1.000

*p<0,05; **p<0.01

Tab. 3: Canonical Correlation Value and Test Results Between Health and Development Sets

	Wilk's	Chi-SQ	DF	Sig.	r_c
1	***0.254***	***96.632***	***24.000***	***0.000****	***0.753***
2	*0.586*	*37.700*	*15.000*	*0.001**	*0.570*
3	0.868	10.018	8.000	0.264	0.325
4	0.970	2.158	3.000	0.540	0.174

Tab. 4: Standardized Canonical Coefficients for Health Set

	1	*2*	*3*	*4*
Life Expectancy at Birth	**0.404**	**0.540**	**0.884**	**1.643**
Crude Birth Rate	0.227	1.443	0.280	-1.304
Health Expenditures	0.180	0.605	0.090	-1.229
Crude Death Rate	-0.577	-0.657	-0.493	1.353

values (r_{c3}=0.32; r_{c4}=0.17) are not significant. Hereunder, interpretations after this shall be submitted by considering the 1st canonical correlation value that has a higher canonical correlation value.

Canonical coefficients regarding the health set are submitted in Tab. 4. Therefore, 1-unit increase in standard deviation in life expectancy at birth causes an increase of 0.40 in the 1st variant of health set, while 1-unit increase in crude birth rate causes an increase of 0.23 in the first variant of health set. All the same, 1-unit increase in health expenditures causes an increase of 0.18 in the first variant of health set. However, 1-unit of decrease in the crude death rate variable causes a decrease of 0.58 in the first variant of health set. Thus, analyzing Tab. 4, it is observed that the variable which contributes most to the 1st canonic is crude death rate, and it has a negative contribution to the first variant of health set. And then the most contribution was provided by life expectancy at birth. Crude birth rate and health expenditures are the variables that contribute significant contribution to the health set canonical variables after other variables. The variables, life expectancy at birth, crude birth rate and health expenditures, have a positive contribution to the first variant of health set.

Canonical coefficients regarding the development set are submitted in Tab. 5. Therefore, 1-unit increase in standard deviation in GDP causes an increase of 0.21 in the 1st variant of development set, while 1-unit increase in labor force rate causes an increase of 0.33 in the first variant of development set. Besides, when the variables are examined, respectively, it is observed that the variables,

Tab. 5: Standardized Canonical Coefficients for Development Set

	1	*2*	*3*	*4*
GDP	**0.212**	**0.062**	**0.241**	**0.838**
Labor Force Participation Rate	**0.330**	0.051	0.543	0.145
Primary School Enrollment Rate	**0.176**	0.489	0.713	-0.428
Secondary School Enrollment Rate	**0.479**	0.270	0.038	0.183
Added Value of the Industry	**0.341**	0.704	0.038	-0.525
Access Improved Water Resources %	**0.338**	0.680	0.726	-0.060

Tab. 6: Canonical Loadings and Cross Loadings for Health Set

	Canonical Loadings				*Cross Loadings*			
	1	*2*	*3*	*4*	*1*	*2*	*3*	*4*
Life Expectancy at Birth	**0.614**	0.129	0.775	0.083	**0.462**	0.074	0.252	0.014
Crude Birth Rate	**0.866**	0.481	0.090	-0.103	**0.652**	0.274	0.029	0.014
Health Expenditures	**0.715**	0.480	0.226	-0.455	**0.538**	-0.274	0.073	-0.079
Crude Death Rate	**-0.739**	-0.130	-0.649	0.125	**-0.556**	-0.074	-0.211	0.022

primary school enrollment rate, secondary school enrollment rate, added value of industry and access improved to water resources percentage provide a positive contribution by causing an increase of 0.176, 0.479, 0.341 and 0.338 in the 1st variant of development set. Thus, when Tab. 5 is analyzed, it is seen that while the variable secondary school enrollment rate provides the most important contribution, other variables take values close to each other. The most important contribution is made by added value of industry, access improved water resources percentage and labor force rate, respectively.

Canonical loadings and cross loadings regarding the variables in health set are submitted in Tab. 6. Accordingly, in the first variant of the health set all variables (life expectancy at birth, crude birth rate, health expenditures, crude death rate) are correlated with the first variant of health set. Here, it is seen that crude birth

Tab. 7: Canonical Loadings and Cross Loadings for Development Set

	Canonical Loadings				*Cross Loadings*			
	1	*2*	*3*	*4*	*1*	*2*	*3*	*4*
GDP	**0.508**	0.016	0.134	0.706	**0.382**	0.009	0.043	0.123
Labor Force Participation Rate	**0.384**	0.098	0.530	0.181	**0.289**	0.056	0.172	0.031
Primary School Enrollment Rate	**0.219**	-0.607	0.506	-0.468	**0.165**	-0.346	0.164	-0.081
Secondary School Enrollment Rate	**0.596**	-0.216	0.286	-0.059	**0.449**	-0.123	0.093	-0.010
Added Value of the Industry	**0.610**	0.414	-0.005	-0.376	**0.459**	0.236	-0.002	-0.065
Access Improved Water Resources %	**0.692**	0.514	0.455	0.079	**0.512**	0.293	0.148	0.014

rate is most correlated with first variant of health set. Followingly, crude death rate and health expenditures are other variables that are most correlated.

Canonical loadings and cross loadings regarding the variables in sustainable development set are submitted in Tab. 7. Accordingly, excluding the primary school enrollment rate in the first variant of development set, all variables (GDP, secondary school enrollment rate, labor force participation rate, added value of industry and access improved to water resources percentage) are significantly correlated with the first variant of development set. While access improved to water resources percentage and added value of industry are correlated the most with the first variant of development set, respectively, secondary school enrollment rate and GDP are other variables that are most correlated.

In Tab. 8 are the explained variance and redundancy measures of the variables. Accordingly, while the explained percentage of the health set is 55% in its own set and the explained percentage of the development set is 28% in its own set. Thus explained percentage of development set to health set is 16%.

Discussion and Conclusion

Sustainable development is defined as "meeting the needs of current generations by not making concessions from future generations' abilities to meet their own needs" by Brundtland Commission in 1987 (UNECE 2017). Societies giving priority to sustainable development have the advantage of gaining superiority basically in four fields such as reducing poverty and social isolation, good management and maintenance of environmental durability. A development in each

Tab. 8: Explained Variance and Redundancy Measures

	Health Set Variant Explained Within Own Set		*Development Set Variable Explained Within Own Set*		*Variance Explained by Health Set of Development Set*
CV 1-1	0.546	***CV 2-1***	0.277	***CV 1-1***	**0.157**
CV 1-2	0.124	***CV 2-2***	0.143	***CV 1-2***	0.047
CV 1-3	0.270	***CV 2-3***	0.140	***CV 1-3***	0.015
CV 1-4	0.060	***CV 2-4***	0.150	***CV 1-4***	0.005

field mentioned causes the others to develop as well, and the health level of the society has a critical importance in the development of these four fields. The fundamental reason of this is that sustainable development depends on production, and the realization of production is only based on a healthy society (Sustainable Development Solutions Network 2014). As sustainable development depends on health, it also requires a source to be transferred to future generations. Therefore, in societies where disease prevalence is high and health status is weak and the sources cannot probably be used most effectively, it will not be possible to reach sustainable development goals (Von Schirnding et al. 2002). As it is understood from all these statements, sustainable development concept is closely related to health. From this point of view, in this study, it is aimed to reveal the correlation between sustainable development and health.

As a result of the analysis performed within the research, examining the canonical loads of the variables in health set inside themselves, it was found that in general the effect of all variables on health state is high (between 0.614 and 0.866), and the most effective variable was crude birth rate (0.866). Accordingly, an increase in crude birth rate causes an increase in the health set. It is considered that the correlation between all variables, especially crude birth rate and health set being high, arises from the fact that variables such as crude death rate, crude birth rate are the most essential indicators used in order to be informed about the health status of any country.

Similarly, another finding presented is the interpretation percentages of variables that are used for sustainable development and health both within themselves and by each other. Accordingly, it was found that the interpretation percentage of health set within itself is 54.6%, interpretation percentage of health set by development set is 30.9% and interpretation percentage of development set by health set is 15.7%. In the research it was also found that the correlation between development that is determined as dependent variable and health that is independent variable is (rc= 0.753) high. Considering that health set is actually not a direct dimension of development, it is seen that this interpretation percentage (15.7%) can be assessed as quite high and the calculated correlation coefficient reveals the connection between these two concepts very well.

In conclusion, it is seen that there is a very close relation between development and health concepts, and that it has been seen that sustainable development targets cannot be achieved without increasing the health status in terms of countries. This study, because of data constraint, was done on 84 countries in high- and middle-income groups according to the classification made by World Bank by using only six variables each for health variable and development variable. From this point of view, new studies are required in which all countries in the world are included and much more variables are used. However, together with all these constraints this study is in a quality supporting the statements in direction of existence of the relation between sustainable development and health that takes place in the literature. Therefore, it is thought that this study in which the contribution of improvements in health on the development levels of the countries is assessed submits important hints to the literature.

References

Akgül, U.: "Sustainable Development: Action Field of Applied Anthropology". *Ankara University Faculty of Language and History Geography Anthropology Journal* 24, 2010, pp. 133–164.

Alpar, R.: *Applied Multivariate Statistical Methods*. Detay Publishing: Ankara. 2013.

Boyacıoğlu, E. Z.: "The Importance of Health Expenditures on Sustainable Development". *International Journal of Social Sciences and Humanity Studies* 4(2), 2012, pp. 147–158.

Buse, K. / Hawkes, S.: "Health in the Sustainable Development Goals: Ready for a Paradigm Shift?" *Globalization and Health* 11(1): 2015, pp. 1–13.

Chapman, A. R.: "Evaluating the Health-Related Targets in the Sustainable Development Goals from a Human Rights Perspective". *The International Journal of Human Rights* 21(8), 2017, pp. 1098–1113.

Gittins, R.: *Canonical Analysis: A Review with Applications in Ecology*. (16. Edition). Springer Science & Business Media: Berlin, Heidelberg, New York, Tokyo. 2012.

Hopwood, B. / Mellor, M. / O'Brien, G.: "Sustainable Development: Mapping Different Approaches". *Sustainable Development* 13(1), 2005, pp. 38–52.

Hotelling, H.: "Relations Between Two Sets of Variants". *Biometrika* 28, 1936, pp. 321-377.

IOM (Institute of Medicine): *Global Development Goals and Linkages to Health and Sustainability: Workshop Summary*. The National Academies Press: Washington, DC. 2014.

Lélé, S. M.: "Sustainable Development: A Critical Review". *World Development* 19(6), 1991, pp. 607–621.

Mebratu, D.: "Sustainability and Sustainable Development: Historical and Conceptual Review". *Environmental Impact Assessment Review* 18(6), 1998, pp. 493–520.

Pan American Health Organization: *Health, Environment and Sustainable Development: Towards the Future We Want*. World Health Organization Publications: Washington, DC. 2013.

Pantyley, V.: "Health Inequalities Among Rural and Urban Population of Eastern Poland in the Context of Sustainable Development". *Annals of Agricultural and Environmental Medicine*, 24(3), 2017, pp. 477–483.

Reinsel, G. C.: *Elements of the Multivariate Time Series Analysis*. (11. Edition). Springer Science & Business Media: New York, Berlin, Heidelberg, London, Paris, Tokyo, Hong Kong, Barcelona, Budapest. 2012.

Richards, E. P.: *The Role of Medical and Public Health Services in Sustainable Development*. 2002. retrieved 23.11.2017, from https://ebookcentral.proquest.com.

Ríos-Osorio, L. A. / Salas-Zapata, W. A. / Ortiz-Lobato, M.: "Concepts Associated with Health from the Perspective of Sustainable Development". *Saúde e Sociedade* 21(3), 2012, pp. 735–746.

Sustainable Development Solutions Network: *Health in the Framework of Sustainable Development Technical Report for the Post-2015 Development Agenda*. 2014.

Thompson, B.: *Canonical Correlations Analysis: Uses and Interpretation*. Sage Publications: Newbury Park, London, New Delhi. 1984.

UNECE: *Sustainable Development - Concept and Action*, 2017. Retrieved 13.11.2017, fromhttp://www.unece.org/oes/nutshell/2004-2005/focus_sustainable_development.html.

Von Schirnding, Y. E. / Mulholland, C. / World Health Organization: *Health and Sustainable Development: Key Health Trends*. World Health Organization Publications: Geneva. 2002.

www.ingramcontent.com/pod-product-compliance
Ingram Content Group UK Ltd.
Pitfield, Milton Keynes, MK11 3LW, UK
UKHW021847100926
8556IPUK00020B/1109

9 783631 768525